Dedication

This book is dedicated to the concept of pikuach nefesh.

Limits of Liability and Disclaimer of Warranty

While every reasonable attempt has been made to ensure the accuracy, completeness, and correctness of the information contained in this book at the time of writing, neither the author nor the publisher shall be responsible or liable in negligence or otherwise howsoever in respect to any inaccuracy or omission herein. The author and the publisher make no representation that this information is suitable for every application to which a reader may attempt to apply it; many of the techniques, approaches, and theories are still subject to academic debate. The author and the publisher make no warranty of any kind, expressed or implied, including warranties of fitness for a particular purpose with regard to the documentation or theories contained in this book, all of which are provided "as is." Without derogating from the generality of the foregoing neither the author nor the publisher shall be liable for any direct, indirect, incidental, or consequential damages or loss caused by or arising from any information or advice, inaccuracy, or omission herein. This work is published with understanding that the author and publisher are supplying information but are not attempting to render engineering judgement or other professional services. If such services are required, the assistance of an appropriate professional should be sought.

Software Safety and Reliability

Techniques, Approaches, and Standards of Key Industrial Sectors

Debra S. Herrmann

IEEE
COMPUTER
SOCIETY

Los Alamitos, California

Washington   •   Brussels   •   Tokyo

Library of Congress Cataloging-in-Publication Data

Herrmann, Debra S.
  Software safety and reliability: techniques, approaches, and standards of
  key industrial sectors / by Debra S. Herrmann.
       p.   cm.
  Includes bibliographical references and index.
  ISBN 0-7695-0299-7
  1. Computer software — Reliability. 2. System safety. I. Title.

QA76.76.R44 H39 1999
005 — dc21

                                                          99-059636
                                                            CIP

IEEE Computer Society Press Order Number BP00299
Library of Congress Number 99-059636
ISBN 0-7695-0299-7

Additional copies may be ordered from:

IEEE Computer Society Press	IEEE Service Center	IEEE Computer Society
Customer Service Center	445 Hoes Lane	Watanabe Building
10662 Los Vaqueros Circle	P.O. Box 1331	1-4-2 Minami-Aoyama
P.O. Box 3014	Piscataway, NJ 08855-1331	Minato-ku, Tokyo 107-0062
Los Alamitos, CA 90720-1314	Tel: +1-732-981-0060	JAPAN
Tel: +1-714-821-8380	Fax: +1-732-981-9667	Tel: +81-3-3408-3118
Fax: +1-714-821-4641	mis.custserv@computer.org	Fax: +81-3-3408-3553
cs.books@computer.org		tokyo.ofc@computer.org

Executive Director and Chief Executive Officer: T. Michael Elliott
Publisher: Angela Burgess
Manager of Production, CS Press: Deborah Plummer
Advertising/Promotions: Tom Fink
Production Editor: Denise Hurst
Printed in the United States of America

IEEE
COMPUTER
SOCIETY

IEEE

Contents

List of Figures

List of Tables

Part I

Introduction to Software Safety and Reliability

We live in a world today where software is pervasive. Software touches nearly every aspect of our lives, from software-controlled subways, air traffic control systems, nuclear power plants, and medical equipment to more mundane everyday examples such as software-controlled microwave ovens, gas burners, elevators, automated teller machines, the family car, and the local 911 service. In the past, many of these items relied upon established safety and reliability principles from electrical, mechanical, and/or civil engineering which developed over several decades if not longer. Today items like these are controlled by software.

When examined it its totality, the magnitude of the software safety and reliability challenge facing us today makes the Y2K problem look minuscule by comparison. Hence, it is time to acknowledge the discipline of software safety and reliability and its importance to everyday life. Some people and organizations are starting to understand and respond to this challenge. For example, the FBI recently established a National Infrastructure Protection Center to protect safety-critical systems and software [6]. Unfortunately, many still remain blissfully unaware of the situation or deny its existence. Contributing to the problem is the small number of universities that offer courses in software safety and reliability.

We hear a lot about the global economy today. Technology has less respect for state or national borders than do market forces. The software safety and reliability challenge is a global challenge. Products, such as cars and medical devices, are built in one jurisdiction and sold worldwide. Air traffic control systems must interoperate safely and reliably among multiple countries, for example along the long borders between the U.S., Canada, and Mexico. Accordingly, the first part of this book introduces the concept of software safety and reliability, the techniques and approaches used to achieve and assess it.

Chapter 1

Introduction

1.1 Background

The inherent complexity of software—its design, development, assessment, and use—is and has been increasing rapidly during the last decade. The cycle time between new versions of system and application software has decreased from a number of years to a number of months. The evolution and discovery of new design techniques and development methodologies are proceeding at an equally rapid pace. Consequently, the debate about what constitutes the standard body of knowledge for Computer Science professionals continues [8, 11].

Accompanying this is the ever broadening role that software plays in electronic products. A study performed in the U.K. in 1990 [3] estimated that the market for the development of safety-related software was $.85B per year and that it was growing at a rate of 20 percent per year. This is due to the fact that software is replacing discrete hardware logic in many devices. Some common examples include air traffic control systems, nuclear power plant control systems, and radiation therapy systems. In addition, advanced electronics with embedded software controllers are being incorporated into a variety of new products, such as laser surgical devices, automobiles, subways, and intelligent transportation systems.

As such the role of software has moved from simply generating financial or other mathematical data to monitoring and controlling equipment which directly affects human life and safety. In fact, it was reported by Donald Mackenzie that "the total number of people killed by computer system failures, worldwide, up to the end of 1992, is between 1000 and 3000 [5]." A sampling of the evening news reinforces this observation:[1]

- During 1994 a NASA shuttle launch was halted, under software control, at T minus .9 seconds after an improper mixture of gases was detected in the fuel tanks.

- During 1995, following a software "upgrade" a major automated teller machine (ATM) bank card system deducted double the cash amount actually withdrawn from customers' accounts.

- In June 1996 a Washington, D.C. Metro subway driver was killed when a train on automatic control crashed into a wall instead of stopping at the last station.

---

[1] For a complete list of reported software related anomalies see Chapter 2, "Computer Related Risks," by Peter G. Neuman [9].

- On July 24, 1996 *National Public Radio* (NPR) reported that six of the eight New England Yankee nuclear power plants were shut down during the first half of 1996 because simulated testing showed that they could reach unsafe states.

- On August 9, 1996 *WTOP News* reported that 50,000 pieces of mail sent to the U.S. Patent and Trademark Office (USPTO) had been "returned to sender." During the previous week an "upgrade" had been made to a U.S. Postal Service information system and the USPTO's zip code had been accidentally deleted.

- On September 17, 1996 *WTOP News* announced that an estimated one billion dollar contract had been awarded by the U.S. Federal Aviation Administration (FAA) to Raytheon and its bidding partners to modernize the air traffic control systems at U.S. airports. A major part of this upgrade effort will be to convert much of the system's functionality to software control.

As a result, a more thorough and widespread understanding of and familiarity with the specialized techniques used to achieve and assess the safety and reliability of software are needed in academia, industry, and government [3]. This is also true since many legal issues related to software liability are evolving [4].

1.2 Purpose

While the general concept of safety and reliability is understood by most parties, the specialty of software safety and reliability is not. The understanding of electronic component reliability and electrical safety has been evolving since the 1940s. In contrast, software safety and reliability is a relatively new discipline that only a few understand well or at all. Hence, the overall goal of writing this book is to improve the state of the art of software safety and reliability, both its understanding and practice. This goal is achieved through three objectives.

The first objective of this book is to serve as a "consciousness raising" about the importance of software safety and reliability and the attention this subject warrants in mission critical systems. As more and more functionality is shifted from hardware to software, two common scenarios occur. First, managers and technical personnel involved in mission critical projects are generally very knowledgeable about optics, radiation physics, mechanical engineering, and so forth. However, they are sometimes at a loss when it comes to knowing: 1) what to do about software safety and reliability; 2) the skill set that is needed to adequately address software safety and reliability; and 3) sometimes even that this subject warrants serious attention [7]. Second, today there are many excellent Computer Science and Software Engineering programs at universities throughout the world. Unfortunately very few of them offer any courses on software safety and reliability or on software engineering standards.[2] A student may acquire a thorough background in software engineering

---

[2]For a successful example of teaching software engineering through standards see Abran [1].

without being exposed to the field of software safety and reliability. Given the shift in technology to software controlled products, this is unfortunate because today's students will be tomorrow's safety and reliability practitioners. This book has been written to serve as a "consciousness raising" for both scenarios. As such, it includes many illustrative everyday examples about the importance of software safety and reliability, particularly in Chapter 2.

The second objective of this book is to provide practical information about the current methods used to achieve and assess software safety and reliability. This is accomplished by a comprehensive discussion of the current approaches promoted by key industrial sectors and standards organizations to software safety and reliability. Since most practitioners were not taught software safety and reliability in school, it is all the more imperative that they be made aware of current software safety and reliability standards. As a rule, standards are written in a very terse style. A phrase or sentence may be very meaningful to the committee members who spent years writing the standard, but the same phrase leaves the average reader in the dark. Accordingly, Parts II and III of this book have been written in the style of an application guide—"how to" read, interpret, and implement a given standard. While theory is not entirely neglected, the emphasis in on practical information.

The third and final objective of this book is to bring together, for the first time, in one volume the contemporary thinking on software safety and reliability so that it can be compared and analyzed; thereby leading to the improved understanding and practice of this field in the future.

1.3   Scope

This book is limited to a presentation and analysis of the methods used to achieve and assess software safety and reliability. In mission critical systems safety and reliability are paramount. This fact is recognized by the statement in the American Society of Quality (ASQ) Code of Ethics, "1.1 Will do whatever I can do to promote the reliability and safety of all products that come within my jurisdiction [2]." Accordingly, the standards discussed in Parts II and III are limited to software safety and reliability standards. Furthermore, they are limited to widely available national and international consensus standards which were developed in the last decade. Proprietary standards were excluded. This is not an exhaustive sample but a representative sample of current software safety and reliability standards which cross multiple industrial sectors.

Likewise, general purpose software engineering standards, such as ISO/IEC 12207, were excluded.[3] The text discusses the safety, reliability, and risk management activities that occur during the software development lifecycle. Since volumes have already been written about the generic activities that occur during any software development lifecycle, that information is *not* repeated here. Instead, this text focuses on the *additional* activities

---

[3]It is understood that in mission critical systems a software safety and reliability standard will be used in conjuction with a general purpose software engineering standard. In fact, as we will see in Parts II and III the structure of many of the standards promotes such a "layering" concept.

that are needed to achieve and assess software safety and reliability. As we will see in Parts II and III some standards integrate safety, reliability, and risk management activities in a single generic development lifecycle; while other standards promote a distinct safety lifecycle.

It is not within the scope of this book to endorse one standard over the other; instead their strengths and areas for improvement are discussed with an emphasis on the practicality of implementation.

1.4 Intended Audience

This book is written for engineers, scientists, managers, regulators, and policy makers involved in the design, development, acquisition, and certification of safety-critical systems. In particular:

- Manufacturers of safety-critical systems in the aerospace, defense, power plant, transportation, and biomedical industries;

- Government agencies responsible for overseeing safety and reliability of mission critical systems; and

- Independent laboratories responsible for certifying the safety and reliability of such systems.

Managers and technical personnel will find the abundant practical "how to" information, examples, templates, and discussion problems most useful. This book assumes a basic understanding of software engineering; however, no previous background in software safety or reliability is expected.

1.5 Organization

This book is organized in four parts and twelve chapters. Part I, Chapter 1 puts the book in context by explaining the rationale and purpose for which the book was written. It defines limitations on the scope of the book's subject matter, identifies the intended audience for whom the book was written, and discusses the organization of this book. This chapter concludes by acknowledging those individuals and organizations who made significant contributions during the book's development.

Part I, Chapter 2 sets the stage for the rest of the book by providing an introduction to and overview of the basic concepts related to software safety and reliability.[4] This is accomplished by examining five fundamental questions:

---

[4]Chapter 2 is intended for individuals who are relatively new to software safety and reliability. Those with more experience in this field may want to proceed directly to Chapter 3.

- What is software safety?

- What is software reliability?

- Why is software different?

- How can software safety and reliability be achieved?

- What is the role of standards?

The information in Chapter 2 establishes the basic principles necessary to understand and evaluate the approaches promoted by key industrial sectors and standards organizations, discussed in Parts II and III, to software safety and reliability. By design, at this introductory stage informal "practical working definitions" are provided in order to convey the basic concepts of software safety and reliability. Later, in Parts II and III the formal definitions promulgated by each of the standards are provided. As we will see, the standards do not always agree.[5] Consequently, Chapter 2 takes a middle of the road approach, rather than endorsing one standard over the other.

Part II (Chapters 3–7) examines in detail the approaches promoted by key industrial sectors (transportation, aerospace, defense, nuclear power, and biomedical[6]) to software safety and reliability. Collectively they represent the broadest possible spectrum of technology and mission critical systems. The approaches promoted by these industrial sectors are examined against a standard template. Each section opens with a brief discussion of how the standard was developed and a definition of its scope or applicability. A detailed description of the standard's approach to software safety and reliability is next. This description, which comprises approximately 80 percent of each chapter, focuses on:

- practices recommended and required by the standard;

- interaction between this standard, system safety, and other standards;

- designated roles, responsibilities, and qualifications of project members;

- data items which are produced when following the standard;

- how compliance to the standard is assessed; and

- the ability (or inability) of the standard to be scaled to match the size and complexity of a project.

---

[5]For a side by side listing of the differing definitions see van der Muelen [10].

[6]The IEC standards warrant particular attention. Following an affirmative IEC ballot, these standards generally proceed to a European Committee for Electrotechnical Standardisation (CENELEC) ballot. Once approved by CENELEC, they become an EN or European Normal standard. For example IEC 601-1-4 has been designated as EN 60601-1-4. Within the European Union countries, the EN standards are generally required to be followed during the development of applicable products, whether they are manufactured in or exported to an EU country, unless a special waiver is granted.

A discussion of the strengths of the standard, areas for improvement, and the results observed to date follow, such as an examination of how successfully the standard has been moved from theory to practice. Each chapter concludes with a summary of the information presented, discussion problems, and pointers to other relevant information resources.

Part III, Chapters 8–11, examines the approaches promoted by non–industry specific software safety and reliability standards in detail, using the same template that was used in Part II.

Part IV, Chapter 12, presents observations and conclusions about the similarities and differences in these standards and their approach to achieving and assessing software safety and reliability. Potential new and hybrid approaches are explored. Areas for improvement and further research are also identified.

Two annexes provide supplemental information. Annex A lists contact information for obtaining copies of the standards discussed in Chapters 3–12. Annex B lists a sampling of the automated software safety and reliability analysis tools currently being marketed.

1.6   Acknowledgments

The author would like to acknowledge the significant contributions made by the technical reviewers and production and editorial staff: Cheryl Baltes, Denise Hurst, Deborah Plummer, and Kathryn Sanders, during the development and formal review of this book.

The author would like to thank the American National Standards Institute (ANSI), British Standards Institution (BSI), Professor Robin Bloomfield of Adelard, Professor Bev Littlewood of the Centre for Software Reliability (CSR), Dr. R. Ciaschi and Lothar Winzer of the European Space Agency (ESA), Oliver Christ of the EuroSpec Institute of Equipment Safety, Dave Balderston of the Federal Aviation Administration (FAA), Dee Simons of the Health Industries Manufacturers Association (HIMA), Charles Jacquemart of the International Electrotechnical Commission (IEC), Institution of Electrical Engineers (IEE), Institute of Electrical and Electronics Engineers (IEEE), Gary LeBlanc of the Indiana Medical Devices Manufacturers Council (IMDMC), Lois Ferson of the International Society for Measurement and Control (ISA), Dr. Richard Mellish of the Medical Devices Agency, Dr. David D. Ward of the Motor Industry Research Association (MIRA), Kathryn Kemp-Greenly of the National Aeronautics and Space Administration (NASA), Nuclear Regulatory Commission (NRC), John Harauz of the Ontario Power Generation, Inc., Requirements and Technical Concepts in Aviation, Inc. (RTCA), Dr. David E. Peercy of Sandia National Laboratories, the U.K. Ministry of Defense (MoD), U.S. Department of Defense (DoD), and Dorothy Deutch of the U.S. Patent and Trademark Office (USPTO) for their willingness to share the information which is presented and analyzed in this book. Hopefully we can all continue to work together to move the state of the art for software safety and reliability forward.

Additional Resources

[1] Abran, Alain. "Teaching Software Engineering Using ISO Standards," *StandardView*, Vol. 4, No. 3, Sep. 1996, pp. 139–145.

[2] ASQ Certification: Certified Software Quality Engineer (CSQE) brochure, July 1996.

[3] Bloomfield, R. E. *SAFEIT: One Overall Approach—A Government Consultation on the Safety of Computer-Controlled Systems*, Adelard, 1990.

[4] Kaner, Cem. Legal Issues Related to Software Quality, Software Quality, ASQ, Dec. 1997, pp. 1–11.

[5] Kletz, Trevor. "Reflections on Safety," *Safety Systems*, May 1997, Vol. 6, No. 3, pp. 1–3.

[6] Lawson, H. W. "Infrastructure Risk Reduction," *Communications of the ACM*, Vol. 40, No. 6, June 1998, p. 120.

[7] Leveson, N. *Safeware: System Safety and Computers*, Addison-Wesley, 1995.

[8] Martin, C. D., Huff, C., Gotterbarn, D., and Miller, K. "Implementing a Tenth Strand in the CS Curriculum," *Communications of the ACM*, Vol. 39, No. 12, Dec. 1996, pp. 75–84.

[9] Neuman, Peter G. *Computer Related Risks*, Chapter 2, Addison-Wesley, 1995.

[10] van der Muelen, M.J.P. *Definitions for Hardware/Software Reliability Engineers*, Simtech b.v., 1995.

[11] Walker, H. M. and Schneider, G. M. "A Revised Model for a Liberal Arts Degree in Computer Science," *Communications of the ACM*, Vol. 39, No. 12, Dec. 1996, pp. 85–95.

Chapter 2

Software Safety and Reliability Basics

> Its mistakes of commission have been legion; and its mistakes of omission have been even greater. It has all too often done nothing when it should have realized that problems cannot be avoided by refusing to admit that they exist.

Harry S. Truman
U.S. Senate Special Committee to Investigate the National Defense Program
January 1942

This chapter sets the stage for the rest of the book by providing an introduction to and overview of the basic concepts and definitions related to software safety and reliability. The information in this chapter establishes the principles necessary to understand and evaluate the approaches promoted by key industrial sectors (transportation, aerospace, defense, nuclear power plants, biomedical) and standards organizations to software safety and reliability that are discussed in Parts II and III. Both theoretical and everyday examples are included to highlight these concepts.

2.1 Software Safety Basics

Most of us have a general idea of what safety is: water is safe to drink, food is safe to eat, a car is safe to drive. When we say water is safe to drink or food is safe to eat, we imply the absence of harmful bacteria and other contaminants. Is the water or food 100 percent free of these items? No. The levels of these items, measured in parts per million (ppm), are below a certain threshold which has been determined to be safe.

An automobile presents a different scenario. It contains electronic parts, mechanical parts, and combustible energy sources. This creates many opportunities for potential hazards. A multitude of factors must be evaluated before a car can be determined to be safe. Is a car 100 percent safe? No. Again, thresholds have been established for braking response, bumper impact resistance, engine fire containment, and so forth.

The concept of safety thresholds is a well established principle of safety engineering; it is not unique to software or computer technology. The idea that there are various thresholds above and below which a product is, to a greater or lesser degree, considered to be safe, has been applied in the fields of microbiology, medicine, pharmacology, mechanical engineering, civil engineering, aeronautical engineering, chemical engineering, and electrical engineering for decades. As Leveson [55] and Littlewood [59] observe, the goal is to answer the question how safe is "safe enough" without over- or under-designing a product. As reported by Petroski [72], one of the earliest documented studies for determining safety thresholds occurred in 1849 when a Royal Commission was appointed in the U.K. to investigate the use of iron in railway bridges vis a vis girder strength. Therefore, thresholds must be established for each product, design, and use scenario. As will be seen in Parts II and III, these thresholds are often derived from risk based assessments and ongoing hazard analyses [55].

Webster's Ninth New Collegiate Dictionary defines safety as:

1) the condition of being safe from undergoing or causing hurt, injury, or loss (n);

2) a device designed to prevent inadvertent or hazardous operation (n);

3) to protect against failure, breakage, or accident (vt).

"To prevent... To protect..." How does this relate to software? As a starting point for this discussion, a "practical working definition" of software safety will be developed. Following that categories of software safety will be examined. Then the relationship between software safety and the broader concept of system safety will be explored.

2.1.1   Definition[1]

Software safety can be defined as:

- features and procedures which ensure that

    - a product performs predictably under normal and abnormal conditions, and
    - the likelihood of an unplanned event occurring is minimized and its consequences controlled and contained;

- thereby preventing accidental injury or death, whether intentional or unintentional.

Let's explore this definition line by line in order to discover its full meaning and intent.

2.1.1.1   Software Safety Features and Procedures

Notice that there are two components in this clause: features and procedures. Both are necessary to ensure safety; neither is adequate by itself. The first part of this expression refers to features which are designed into a product. It has been stated by Petroski [72] that

---

[1]In this introductory chapter informal "practical working definitions" are provided in order to convey the basic concepts of software safety and reliability. In Parts II and III formal definitions promulgated by each of the standards are provided. As will be seen, the standards do not always agree [87].

"engineering design has as its first and foremost objective the obviation of failure." A simple software example is range checks, which will prevent a system from doing something which would compromise safety; in this case operating on out of range or bad data. Another example would be to include displays which monitor operational parameters such as temperature, humidity, vibration, dust, and EMI/RFI to see if they are within specification and issue warnings and/or alarms when they are not. In most systems there are many opportunities to design in features which would enhance safety; unfortunately these opportunities are not always taken advantage of.

The second part of this expression refers to procedures to ensure that the system is used: 1) in an operational environment for which it was intended; and 2) for a task for which it was intended. Operational procedures should be developed and followed to regularly verify that the system is being used in an environment for which it was specified. Operational procedures should indicate whether a system was specified and designed for demand-mode or continuous-mode operation and verify that it is used accordingly. Demand-mode operation refers to systems that are used periodically or "on demand" when needed. An everyday example is a computer-controlled braking system in a car. Continuous-mode operation refers to systems which are operational continuously, twenty-four hours a day, seven days a week, such as power plants.

Likewise, it is equally important that a system be used to perform a task for which it was designed and not for tasks for which it was not designed. In medical terminology these two mutually exclusive states are known as "indications" and "contraindications." The most severe case of "contraindications" is known as "warnings." For example, an over-the-counter analgesic may be "indicated" for reducing pain, fever, and swelling. However, the analgesic will be of no use as a decongestant, since that is not an "indicated" use. Furthermore, labelling for the analgesic will contain "warnings" about using it for chicken pox or flu symptoms in children and teenagers because of concerns about Reye's syndrome.

Technology is also developed for specific "indications" or uses. However, too often general descriptions are given of what a system is designed to do and its intended operational environment (perhaps to maximize sales). A concise succinct description of the intended operational environment and use of a system is needed. This should be accompanied by a concise succinct description of how and under what conditions the system should not be used. In some situations, this information is needed at the system, subsystem, and subcomponent level as well; especially with the move toward greater re/use of off-the-shelf (OTS) components and object-oriented libraries. Without specific "indications," "contraindications," and "warnings," a system or component may be accidentally used for an application for which it was never intended, potentially leading to unsafe operation. As will be seen in Parts II and III, several of the standards levy specific requirements in regard to the use of OTS software.

An illustrative example of what happens when attempting to use software to perform a task for which is was not designed is the much maligned new Denver Airport automated baggage handling system. The original software was designed according to performance specifications for a single airline operating within a single terminal. The proposed new application for this OTS software was to accommodate multiple airlines operating out of multiple terminals. As was discovered very late in the project, the software would not function correctly without a total overhaul.

2.1.1.2 Predictable Software Behavior

In general, products are designed to perform under certain "normal" conditions. These normal conditions should be explicitly specified. They include but are not limited to characteristics of the operational environment, such as those identified above, and anticipated low, normal, and peak system loads; the number of simultaneous users; transaction rates; storage requirements; response times; data transmission rates; and so forth. Systems which affect human life and safety must also be designed to take into account performance under abnormal conditions. Abnormal conditions include operation during system overload, severe power fluctuations, hardware faults, and/or extreme environmental conditions.

The deployment of the Patriot Missile system during the 1991 Gulf War is a recent example of what happens when a system is used under abnormal conditions. This system was designed to be operational for a specified number of hours per day under a demand-mode operation scenario. After this number of hours, the system was to be shut down and preventive maintenance performed. However, during the war it was used under a continuous-mode scenario. As observed by Keene [52], "This defeated their deployment ability. This operational failure happened at a critical time and American casualties resulted. The system's operating environment compromised the missiles' ability to function as programmed."

Why the concern about operation under abnormal conditions? Because many systems which affect human life and safety are frequently required to operate under less than optimum conditions. Airplanes must fly during thunder storms. Automobiles and trucks must operate on slippery pavements. Medical equipment must operate during brownouts or while bouncing around in the back of an ambulance and being subjected to EMI/RFI. Public utilities must deliver controlled stable levels of power in all weather conditions. Such systems will inevitably have to operate under abnormal conditions; therefore, they must be designed to operate predictably in such situations. Criteria must be established to determine how the system should respond in every conceivable (and perhaps inconceivable) situation. Should it shut down (fail safe)?[2] Should it assume known safe default values? Should it continue operating under a safe but degraded-mode scenario (fail operational)?[3] Should it request further input from the operator to confirm commands? Should it reject further input until the system load is stabilized? How the system should respond in such scenarios should be specified so that a system will always be in a known safe state. (See Figure 2.1.)

If a product is designed to perform predictably under normal and abnormal conditions, in theory no unplanned events will occur. The major loophole, after environmental and operational considerations have been taken into account, is the user. Humans tend to make

---

[2]**Fail safe:** the system can be brought to a safe condition or state by shutting it down, for example, the shutdown of a nuclear reactor by a monitoring and protection system [63].

[3]**Fail operational:** the system must continue to provide service if it is not to be hazardous, for example, it cannot simply shut down—an aircraft flight control system [63].

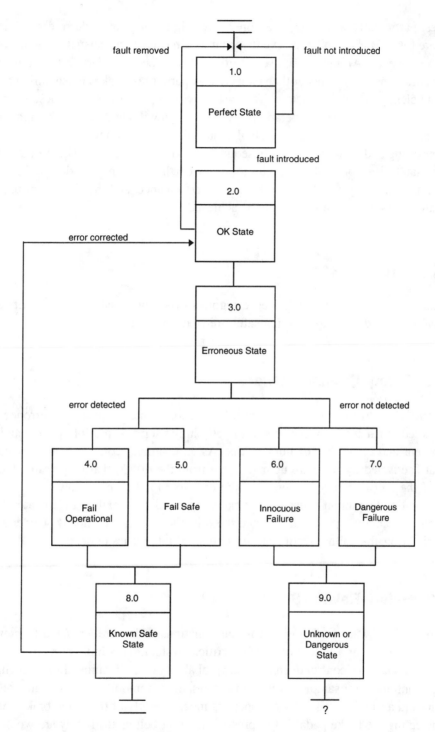

Figure 2.1: Model of system failure behavior. (*Source:* Adapted from Figure 5, page 8, Bishop, P.G. and Bloomfield, R.E., *The SHIP Safety Case Approach*, Adelard, Coborn House, 3 Coborn Road, London E3 2DA, UK, 1995, reprinted by permission.)

mistakes, particularly when they are bored, tired, in a hurry, or under pressure, as noted by Moore [66]. Many unplanned events occur as a result of an unusual sequence or combination of events. An unforeseen series of keystrokes occurs. Certain function keys are pressed simultaneously or faster than expected. A partial reset takes place during a critical event and clears certain parameters. The system will respond to each of these events, if in no other way than to suspend operations. A safe design will anticipate such anomalies and ensure that the system responds predictably, minimizing the likelihood of unplanned events and controlling and containing the consequences should they occur. The ultimate goal of software safety is to prevent accidental injury or death. Inherent safe design features, robust operational safety procedures, predictable performance, and the absence of unplanned events are all essential if this goal is to be achieved.

2.1.2   Categories

There are three commonly recognized categories of software safety: safety-critical software, safety-related software, and nonsafety-related software.

2.1.2.1   Safety-Critical Software

Safety-critical software performs or controls functions which, if executed erroneously or if they failed to execute properly, could directly inflict serious injury to people and/or the environment and cause loss of human life. As an example, consider automobile brakes which are activated by software upon a signal from the driver, that is, pressing the brake pedal. If the software failed to operate, the car would not stop or slow down. Under a benign situation this might cause a few tickets for speeding or failing to stop at red lights. This would be annoying to the driver and the driver's insurance company. Under a not so benign situation, this failure would cause a collision and injuries or death.

2.1.2.2   Safety-Related Software

Safety-related software performs or controls functions which are activated to prevent or minimize the effect of a failure of a safety-critical system. This indirect relationship provides a second layer of control to enhance the probability of maintaining the system in a safe state. To continue our example, assume that this same automobile had software controlled seat belts and air bags. This software operates independently of the failed brake software. Upon detecting the brake pedal being pressed, the seat belt control software would cause the seat belts to lock in position. Upon detecting an imminent collision, the air bag control software would trigger the air bag to inflate. In this case the safety-critical software failed, while the safety-related software minimized the consequences resulting from this failure.

2.1.2.3 Nonsafety-Related Software

Nonsafety-related software performs or controls other system functions which are not related to safety. In our automobile example, this would include the software activated climate control system.

Most mission critical systems include a combination of safety-critical, safety-related, and nonsafety-related software. In some systems the boundaries between them are distinct; in others they are not. As will be seen in Parts II and III, several standards promote isolating safety-critical, safety-related, and nonsafety-related software components. This practice is often referred to as partitioning.

2.1.3 Data Safety

Data safety is a distinct concern from software safety. As an analogy, we can consider data to be a noun while software is a verb; the software (or verb) acts upon the data (or noun). Consider the software logic which implements a calculation. No matter how accurate the logic is, if the data the calculation manipulates is faulty then the result is invalid. Faulty data can cause a system to operate unsafely and/or unreliably [84]. As Stalhane [82] observes, "the software system always communicates with its environment through data values, so dangerous events are ... connected to incorrect data values."

Data safety is concerned with: 1) correctly accessing the intended data; and 2) ensuring that the data has not been corrupted accidentally or intentionally [84]. Liddiard [57] points out that "it is easy to forget that an error in data can be just as disastrous as an error in executable software... Consider what would happen if a marine chart placed a rock in the wrong place, and that chart was used in an automated navigation system for a super tanker." Figure 2.2 highlights some important data safety issues.

- validity checks before acting upon critical data

- screening for illegal or out of range parameters

- correctly initializing, clearing, (re)setting, passing, and storing parameters

- validating addresses, pointers, indices, and variable names

- establishing correct relationships among files

- detecting and correcting errors during data communications

- protecting data from being overwritten

Figure 2.2: Examples of data safety issues [41].

2.1.4   Software as a Component of System Safety

Software safety is one component of many which determine overall system safety [55, 63, 84]. Software can contribute to or detract from system safety [55, 63, 84]. Likewise, electrical safety, mechanical safety, chemical safety, materials safety, radiation safety, and operational safety are all components of system safety. A system cannot be "safe" in and of itself, independent of the safety of each of these components [55, 63, 84]. The system component with the lowest level of safety determines overall system safety. As shown in Figure 2.3, system safety is a composite of the safety of each of its components. The same is true of the human body. A person is considered to be healthy if all of the structures, organs, and systems are healthy. A person may have a great cardiovascular system, but if his kidneys do not function he is not healthy. This analogy is apropos since the word safe is derived from the Latin word salvus which means healthy.

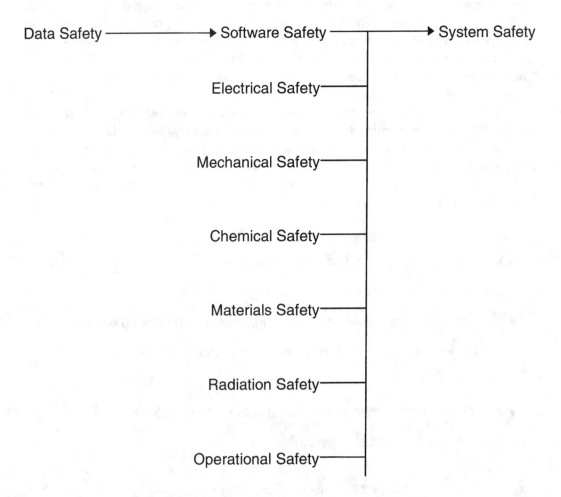

Figure 2.3: Software as a component of system safety [41].

The importance of software safety in relation to system safety can be deduced by answering the following questions:

- How does the software contribute to or detract from overall system safety and reliability?

- What safety-critical and/or safety-related function(s) does the software control or perform?

- What role does software play in hazard detection and prevention?

- How does the software reduce the likelihood and/or severity of potential hazards?

2.2   Software Reliability Basics

Returning to our safe water, safe food, and safe car example, we would want our water source, food source, and car to also be reliable. The terms software safety and reliability are often used interchangeably. However, they are distinct entities [55, 84]. Reliability infers that the ppm rating of harmful bacteria remains below the critical threshold consistently each time it is sampled and that the car's brakes, seat belts, and air bags deliver consistent performance each time they are used.

Webster's Ninth New Collegiate Dictionary defines reliability as:

1) the quality or state of being suitable or fit to be relied on; dependable (n);

2) the extent to which an experiment, test, or measuring procedure yields the same result on repeated trials (n).

The term reliability is derived from the Latin word religare, meaning to connect or tie back—yielding "connected" or consistent results. In Section 2.1 a "practical working definition" of software safety was developed. Now, a corresponding "practical working definition" of software reliability will be developed. After that, the categories of software reliability will be examined along with the different types of software reliability models.

2.2.1   Definition[4]

Software reliability can be defined as:

- a measure of confidence that the software produces accurate and consistent results

  - that are repeatable

---

[4]In this introductory chapter informal "practical working definitions" are provided in order to convey the basic concepts of software safety and reliability. In Parts II and III formal definitions promulgated by each of the standards are provided. As will be seen, the standards do not always agree [87].

– under low, normal, and peak loads

– in the intended operational environment.

In other words, a reliable system will produce correct responses every time a query, calculation, command, and so forth is executed even though different logic paths are taken or the system load varies. In simple terms, this means that a given software system will calculate that $2 \times 10 = 20$ under low, normal, and peak loading conditions; it will yield the same result, that $2 \times 10 = 20$, every time this calculation is performed. The system will also calculate that $4 \times 5 = 20$.

What does software reliability mean in regard to mission critical systems? It means that a radiation therapy system will deliver the exact dosage of radiation at the exact location in the exact time interval prescribed each time the system is used. It means that the system will not deliver more radiation one time, less the next; that the system will deliver the radiation to the "targeted" tumor, not the surrounding healthy tissues. It means that if instrument displays say an aircraft is flying at a certain altitude, direction, and speed the aircraft is in fact doing so; the instruments do not indicate that the aircraft is flying 10 percent higher or faster on one day and 10 percent lower or slower on the next; the results are accurate and repeatable.

2.2.2 Categories

Chronologically speaking there are two categories of software reliability: prerelease software reliability and postrelease software reliability. These two categories correspond to the dynamics of the marketplace and the regulatory environment.

For commercial systems, a manufacturer must determine when a product is "reliable enough" to market. Prerelease software reliability is an assessment of design integrity. It measures the robustness of the design features and procedures, evaluating how well preventive measures have been incorporated. A thorough assessment of premarket software reliability is essential for mission critical systems to prevent accidental injury or death. For mission critical systems, prerelease software safety and reliability assessments are a major component of the information that by law must be submitted to government regulatory agencies and/or third party certification laboratories. If and when this data is deemed accurate and adequate, a product may be marketed, but not beforehand.

In both the commercial and mission critical scenarios, actual data concerning performance once a product is fielded is also collected and analyzed; this information represents postrelease software reliability. Postrelease software reliability is an analysis of the type and source of errors found once a product has been fielded. It determines "what went wrong" and what corrective measures are needed, such as "lessons learned." This information is then fed back into the continuous process improvement cycle. This information is useful in preventing future accidents and injuries; unfortunately, it is too late to have prevented the accidents and injuries which occurred when the product was first released.

2.2.3   Software Reliability Models

There are three major types of software reliability models:

- quantitative models that are time related,

- quantitative models that are not time related, and

- qualitative models.

The first software reliability models developed and the most well known are quantitative time-related models. This type of software reliability model has been explored extensively by Musa [67] and Lyu [60]. Nontime-related quantitative models have been developed more recently. In general, quantitative models focus on product issues. Qualitative software reliability models are the newest models to be developed; they focus on process issues [55, 59].

There is an ongoing debate within industry, academia, and the international standards community on whether or not software reliability can in fact be quantified. Some standards promote a qualitative assessment of software reliability while others promote a quantitative assessment. In addition to the quantitative versus qualitative debate, there is also a debate on whether or not software reliability models should be time related. A common definition for hardware reliability is "the probability of operating failure free for a specified time under a specified set of operating conditions." Hence, hardware reliability models are quantitative and time related. If different types of models are used to assess hardware and software, this creates a challenge for the system engineer when trying to measure or estimate system reliability.

Traditional software reliability models from the 1980s are based on the number of errors found during testing and the amount of time it took to discover them. These models use various statistical techniques, many borrowed from hardware reliability assessments, to estimate the number of errors remaining in the software and to predict how much time will be required to discover them [60, 84]. These models provide metrics which are useful for project planning purposes, such as determining when to release a commercial product.

Traditional software reliability models do not distinguish between functional, performance, safety, or reliability errors. These models do not distinguish between the severity of the consequences of the errors (negligible, marginal, critical, catastrophic) found or predicted to be remaining in the software. Nor do they take into account errors found by analytical techniques other than testing. These limitations led to the development of some new software reliability models for mission critical systems.

Rees [78] has identified the main argument against a time-related software reliability model: "Software is susceptible to pattern failures that are not discovered until particular program or data sequences are processed." In other words, the failure will occur the first time the defective sequence is processed; however, this may have been preceded by weeks or months of testing. Hence, the time factor is irrelevant. This situation is often referred to as a latent defect. However, this is a misnomer since the defect was present from the beginning; a more accurate term would be the latent discovery of a defect.

Bieda has done some pioneering work in developing a quantitative nontime-related software reliability model. As Bieda observes [18]:

> ... it is the time element of the software reliability model which must be questioned... With software the amount of execution time or test time has no bearing on the functionality of the software... Software testing or mission simulation consists of verifying software output under varying input conditions. Thus, the simulation time is dependent on the verification rate which is not consistent among tests.

The Bieda model for software reliability analysis is derived in part by using the Taguchi design of experiments (DOE) technique. It focuses on the effectiveness of the test suite and meeting established reliability goals [18]: The first step is to determine what constitutes an effective test matrix by examining factors such as nominal, upper, and lower level operating specifications. Next the test effectiveness is calculated as the ratio of the number of input combinations in the matrix to the number of total possible input combinations. The probability of success is then measured as the number of successful tests divided by the number of input combinations in the test matrix. The results are plotted and compared against customer expectations and reliability goals. The process is repeated and corrective action is taken until reliability goals are met.

In addition to executing the model against the entire system, it is useful to execute this model against the safety-critical and safety-related software components in a mission critical system. These components can cause, minimize, and/or prevent serious injury, death, destruction of property or the environment. Hence, it is important to assess the reliability of these components individually.

Littlewood [59] has done some pioneering work in developing a holistic model for software reliability. As he observes, current software reliability estimation and prediction techniques do not take into account a variety of factors which affect reliability. Littlewood [59] contends that the "success [of these models] relates only to those cases where the reliability being observed is quite modest" and that "it is easy to demonstrate that reliability growth techniques are not plausible ways of acquiring confidence that a program is ultra-reliable." Instead, Littlewood promotes a holistic model which integrates many different sources and types of evidence to assess safety and reliability, as shown in Figure 2.4 [59]:

- **product** – metrics about the product, its design integrity, behavior, failure modes, failure rates, and so forth;

- **process** – metrics about how the product was developed and its safety and reliability assessed;

- **resources** – metrics about the resources used to develop the systems, such as the people and their qualifications, the tools used and their capabilities and limitations; and

- **human computer interaction (HCI)** – metrics about the way people interact with the system, which could be derived from formal scenario analysis and a HAZOP analysis.

Littlewood envisions that qualitative and quantitative information will be collected and analyzed throughout the development lifecycle. This model integrates metrics from all aspects of the P^3R (product, process, and people/resource) equation to yield a comprehensive software reliability assessment. (See Chapter 10 for a sample implementation of this model.)

2.3 Differences Between Hardware and Software Reliability

Increased use of firmware and embedded software is blurring the boundary lines between software and hardware. Regardless, software is not hardware and it has unique characteristics in relation to safety and reliability [55, 84]. As Walker [88] observes, "Many terms referenced in reliability discussions have a distinct meaning in the hardware engineering environment, but have a different meaning or no meaning in the software engineering environment and vice versa."

2.3.1 Comparison of Hardware and Software Reliability

Software safety is a component of overall system safety; likewise software reliability is a component of overall system reliability. In contrast to hardware, software does not fail, break, wear out over time, or fall out of tolerance [51, 55, 63, 84, 88]. Hardware reliability models are based on variability and the physics of failure—assembly lines mass producing something physical. Hardware reliability models do not apply to software since software is not physical. For example, as Walker [88] notes, it is not possible to perform the equivalent of accelerated hardware stress testing on software. Consequently, different paradigms must be used to evaluate software reliability [59]. Figure 2.5 summarizes the differences between hardware and software reliability, as described by Keene [51] and Walker [88].

2.3.2 Causes of Software Errors, Faults, and Failures

Unlike hardware, the cause of a software failure is always systematic, not random; either an error of omission, an error of commission, or an operational error was committed [41, 55, 63, 84]. Classifying errors into errors of omission (what was not done) and errors of commission (what was done wrong) has been a standard component of failure analysis for decades, as the quote at the beginning of this chapter demonstrates. This classification technique is not unique to software or computer technology, but instead is applied to many disciplines. The IEEE standard classification of software anomalies [8] illustrates this as items that are missing (omission) and items that are incorrect (commission).

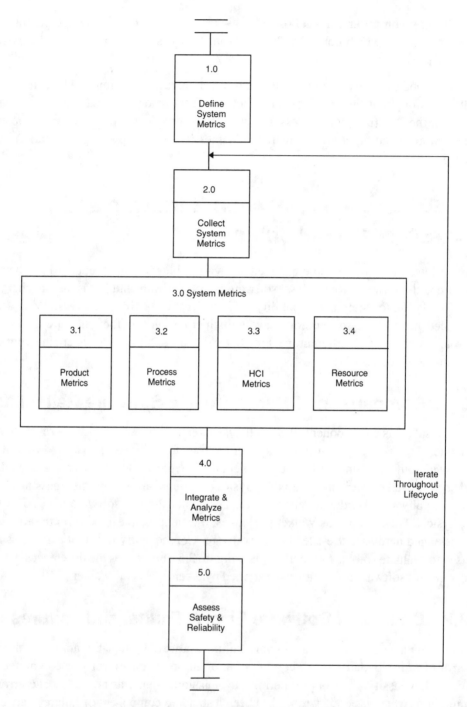

Figure 2.4: Littlewood holistic model for integrating disparate sources of evidence about the reliability and safety of a system. (*Source:* Adapted from Figure 1, page 218, Littlewood, B. "The Need for Evidence from Disparate Sources to Evaluate Software Safety," *Directions in Safety-Critical Systems*, edited by Felix Redmill and Tom Anderson, Springer-Verlag, 1993, reprinted by permission).

HARDWARE		SOFTWARE	
1.	Failures are caused by deficiencies in design, production, and maintenance.	1.	Failures are primarily due to design faults. Repairs are made by modifying the design to make it robust against conditions that can trigger a failure.
2.	Failures are due to wear or other energy-related phenomena. Sometimes a warning is available before a failure occurs.	2.	There is no wear-out phenomena. Software errors occur without warning. "Old" code can exhibit an increasing failure rate as a function of errors induced while making upgrades.
3.	Repairs can be made which would make the equipment more reliable; that is, through preventive maintenance.	3.	There is no equivalent to preventive maintenance for software.
4.	Reliability is time related. Failure rates can be decreasing, constant, or increasing with respect to operating time.	4.	Reliability is not time dependent. Failures occur when the logic path that contains an error is executed. Reliability growth is observed as errors are detected and corrected.
5.	Reliability is related to environmental conditions.	5.	External environmental conditions do not affect software reliability. Internal environmental conditions, such as insufficient memory or inappropriate clock speeds do affect software reliability.
6.	Reliability can be predicted in theory from physical bases.	6.	Reliability cannot be predicted from a knowledge of design, usage, and environmental stress factors.
7.	Reliability can usually be improved by redundancy.	7.	Reliability cannot be improved by redundancy, since this will simply replicate the same error. Reliability can be improved by diversity.
8.	Failure rates of components are somewhat predictable according to known patterns.	8.	Failure rates of software components are not predictable.
9.	Hardware interfaces are visual.	9.	Software interfaces are conceptual.
10.	Hardware design uses standard components.	10.	Software design does not use standard components.

Figure 2.5: Comparison of hardware and software reliability considerations. (*Source:* Adapted from Table 1, page 7, Keene, S.J., "Comparing Hardware and Software Reliability," *ASQ Reliability Review*, Vol. 14, Dec. 1994 and Table 1, page 4, Walker, E. "Bridging the Software/Hardware Reliability Gap," *RAC Journal*, Vol. 4, No. 2, 2Q96, reprinted with permission.)

2.3.2.1   Errors of Omission

Errors of omission are the primary source of software safety and reliability problems. An error of omission is an error that results from something that was not done, such as:

- incomplete or nonexistent requirements [80],

- undocumented assumptions,

- not taking constraints into account adequately,

- overlooking or not understanding design flaws or systems states [63],

- not accounting for all possible logic states, and

- not implementing sufficient error detection and recovery algorithms.

As shown in Figure 2.6, software quality requirements fall into five main categories:

- **functional** – requirements that describe what functions the system is supposed to perform;

- **performance** – the "how many, how fast" requirements that mandate response times, transaction rates, number of simultaneous users, and so forth as well as the operational environment;

- **safety** – requirements for maintaining the system in a known safe state at all times;

- **reliability** – quantitative and/or qualitative requirements for reliable system operation under specified conditions; and

- **security** – requirements for protecting and controlling access to the system and its data, as appropriate for company confidential, privacy act, or national security information.

As noted by Keene [52], "Very often software problems reveal requirements that were not previously recognized, stated, or understood." Software safety and reliability requirements are frequently overlooked [55]. Chen [31] points out that "Designers often fail to understand: (1) the contribution of software to the system risk factor; and/or (2) the differences between hardware and software reliability." This results in a serious error of omission. System developers are more familiar with and spend more time elucidating functional requirements, to the neglect of safety and reliability requirements. Functional requirements state what the system is supposed to do. As Leveson [55] observes, safety requirements should state what the product should *not* or *never* do. Safety requirements should detail at a minimum: 1) unauthorized states or sequences of events; 2) what action should be taken if an unknown state is encountered; 3) how to implement exception handling; and 4) the expected normal, peak, and overload conditions. This information is essential if mission critical systems are to operate continuously in a known safe state.

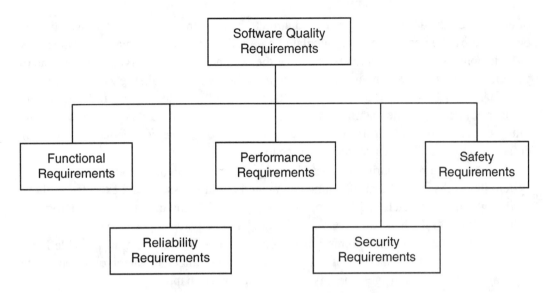

Figure 2.6: Types of software requirements.

Errors of omission often result from a communication gap between the functional domain specialist (such as a physician, pilot, nuclear physicist, or tank commander) and the software specialist [55]. Requirements that are understood, implied, or second nature to the functional domain specialist ("Everyone knows that...," "No one would ever...," "We always...") are not communicated or communicated inadequately to the software specialist. The same is true for undocumented assumptions. Incomplete or nonexistent requirements often lead to guessing on the part of the software specialist; especially if the "requirements analysis phase" has been reported as finished.

Personnel involved in eliciting requirements need to be aware that three types of knowledge exist within the application domain, which have been defined by Rugg [80] as: nontacit knowledge, semitacit knowledge, and tacit knowledge. Nontacit knowledge reflects basic common sense about a subject and is easily obtained by interviews and questionnaires. Rugg [80] describes semitacit knowledge as "elusive" or "taken for granted knowledge," such as the "everyone knows" comment above. As Rugg [80] observes, "Domain experts tend to take for granted things which are familiar to them, but which are usually not familiar to the person eliciting the requirements." Tacit knowledge is the most difficult for the requirements analyst to obtain. According to Rugg [80], tacit knowledge takes two forms: "compiled knowledge or knowledge which has become so familiar that an individual is no longer aware of it" [operating on 'auto-pilot'] and "implicit learning which occurs without an individual being aware of the principles learned" ['gut feel']. The importance of understanding these three types of knowledge cannot be overemphasized. As Rugg points out, wrong requirements can kill people.

As one example of the potential consequences of failing to communicate domain knowledge, consider a radiation therapy system which is intended to deliver multiple sequential doses of radiation at various "targets" on a tumor mass. The number of targets, the location of each target, the dosage, and type of radiation to be delivered are parameters which must be entered by the operator and/or calculated by a radiation treatment planning system. A radiation oncologist would "understand" that the normal number of targets is in the one to two digit range. However, in one system design, the software specialist set: minimum number of targets = 1 and maximum number of targets = 9999. If the operator failed to set the number of targets and the maximum number was used as a default, it is likely that serious injury or death would result from an overdose of radiation. Imagine what could happen if default values had also been set for target locations.

In another example, during simulated testing and evaluation of a ground-based missile system it was discovered that the launch command could be issued and executed without verifying if the silo hatch had been opened first. This is similar to taking a photograph without taking off the lens cap. Everyone "knows" that you are supposed to do that.

Another common error of omission is failing to take into account all possible logic states. With the ready availability of CASE statements and other equivalent logic constructs in today's computer languages, there is no reason for this to happen.

Figure 2.7 contains an example of a partial specification for a dialysis machine. There were two entities, the single needle mode and the blood pump switch, which could be in either an ON or an OFF state. This creates the possibility for the system to be in any of four possible states. However, the action to be taken was only specified for one of the four states. If the other three states were reached, the system entered an unknown or unspecified state. This is unacceptable in mission critical systems.

Single Needle Mode	Blood Pump Switch	State/Action
off	off	unspecified
off	on	unspecified
on	off	unspecified
on	on	legal

Figure 2.7: Sample partial specification for a dialysis machine [41].

This deficiency illustrates the types of problems which can arise when using human language specifications, rather than a formal specification. A simple truth table would have highlighted the missing information. However, it went undetected in paragraph form (and the subsequent code) which simply stated that if the single needle mode was ON and the blood pump switch was ON then the system should behave in the specified manner.

This error could have easily been avoided by the use of a CASE construct, as shown in Figure 2.8. In this example, all four possible known states are accounted for. An OTHERWISE clause is included to add an extra layer of prevention, following the defense in depth concept. This clause will leave the system in a known safe state should the system encounter an erroneous state or other exception. Suppose that the blood pump switch gets stuck between ON and OFF, for example due to a hardware-induced transient fault. That would yield another possible state. Without the OTHERWISE clause, you do not know for sure how the system will respond—the system is in an unknown and potentially unsafe state.

```
DO CASE
       CASE SINGLE NEEDLE OFF .AND. BLOOD PUMP OFF
           do...
       CASE SINGLE NEEDLE OFF .AND. BLOOD PUMP ON
           do...
       CASE SINGLE NEEDLE ON .AND. BLOOD PUMP OFF
           do...
       CASE SINGLE NEEDLE ON .AND. BLOOD PUMP ON
           do...
       OTHERWISE
           do...
ENDCASE
```

Figure 2.8: Sample corrected specification for a dialysis machine [41].

Mission critical systems should be designed with extensive error detection and recovery algorithms to leave the system in a known safe state at all times. Designers should adhere to the concept of defense in depth and assume that something is going to go wrong which they did not anticipate, that some unknown state is going to be encountered which was not planned for. The intent is not only to detect errors, but to also prevent as many errors as possible.

2.3.2.2 Errors of Commission

Errors of commission result from making a mistake or doing something wrong in a lifecycle activity. These types of errors are generally more well known and more visible during traditional testing and evaluation than errors of omission. Errors of commission include:

- logic errors,
- faulty designs [63],
- incorrect translation of requirements into software,
- incorrect handling of data, and
- faulty system integration.

Firmware and embedded software are generally developed in a different environment than the intended operational environment. Often timing constraints, response times, transmission delays, memory size, buffer limitations, required sequences of events, and other constraints are not adequately taken into account. The software will sail through testing and evaluation in the development environment and fail miserably in the operational environment. The system engineer can play an important role in preventing this type of error.

A brief discussion is in order about the different results obtained when using CASE constructs versus IF/THEN/ELSE constructs. In a CASE construct, each CASE specified is evaluated sequentially. Syntactically speaking, the statements need not be mutually exclusive. The instructions following the first CASE statement which is found to be true (or "matches") are executed, then control is returned to the first statement after the ENDCASE. If no "match" is found, control "falls through" to the first statement after the ENDCASE; unless an OTHERWISE clause is included, then it is executed. Suppose four separate IF/THEN/ELSE statements had been used in Figure 2.8 instead. Each of the four statements would be evaluated and executed sequentially if they matched. This is one example of the need to understand how different logic constructs will be evaluated and executed in mission critical systems, so that no unplanned events occur.

2.3.2.3   Operational Errors

Operational errors result from the incorrect use of a product. This can be accidental or intentional incorrect usage. Examples of operational errors include:

- induced or invited errors [30],

- illegal command sequences,

- using a system for a purpose or in an environment for which it was not intended,

- inhibiting safety features, and

- not following operational safety procedures [63].

Designers can minimize the opportunity for induced or invited errors by incorporating comprehensive human factors engineering[5] practices [55]. Extensive error detection and recovery logic will prevent execution of illegal command sequences. Adequate documentation about the intended operational environment and procedures, as discussed in Section 2.1.1.1, will reduce the likelihood of accidental operational errors.

2.4   Achieving and Assessing Software Safety and Reliability

As noted by Chen [31], accidents usually involve a complex interaction of incidents with multiple contributing product, process, and people/resource (P^3R) factors; hence the need

---

[5]Human factors engineering plays a critical role in safety engineering; however, it is not within the scope of this book. Instead, the reader is referred to: Bias and Mayhew [17], Brown [24], Carstensen and Sawyer [30], and Norman [68].

to promote a proper balance of emphasis on P^3R issues. This P^3R delineation is illustrated in the IEEE standard taxonomy for software engineering standards [1]. Recently there has been a tendency to emphasize one of these elements, usually process, almost to the exclusion of the other two. This is not only illogical, it compromises safety and reliability. As Littlewood [59] observes, "There is almost no empirical evidence to confirm that process-based standards alone can ensure safety." Hamlet and Voas [39] also state the case for not overemphasizing process issues:

> All of these ideas, from process definition and control to systematic testing have one failing in common: there is no established relationship between the method and quantitative assessment of the quality that method is supposed to engender.

The standards in Parts II and III specify adherence to various product, process, and people/resource criteria. The discussion that follows introduces techniques that can be used to satisfy these requirements. Design criteria, development and operational criteria, performance criteria, the use of previously developed software, and analysis and verification techniques are explored.

2.4.1 Design Criteria

The design of a mission critical system should be thoroughly analyzed to determine, then minimize through redesign, the likelihood of occurrence and the severity of the consequences of failures [55, 63, 84]. Software safety and reliability design criteria promotes the concept of "defense in depth," that is, multiple layers of preventive measures. The design team starts with the assumption that something will go wrong that was not planned for. By having multiple layers of preventive measures, the probability that a failure will be prevented is greater than if there was only one layer. Some common design techniques to implement these preventive measures and thereby enhance software safety and reliability include: block recovery, diversity, independence, information hiding, and partitioning [7, 19, 55, 63, 84, 85]. The use of coupling, recursion, re-entrant or self-modifying code should not be allowed in mission critical systems; in fact some standards prohibit it.

2.4.1.1 Block Recovery

Block recovery refers to design features which provide correct functional operation in the presence of one or more errors. There are three main types of block recovery: backward block recovery, forward block recovery, and n-block recovery.

In backward block recovery, if an error is detected the system is reset to an earlier known safe state. This method implies that internal states are saved frequently at well-defined checkpoints. Global internal states may be saved or only those for critical functions.

In forward block recovery, if an error is detected the current state of the system is manipulated or forced into a known future safe state. This method is useful for real-time systems with small amounts of data and fast changing internal states.

In n-block recovery, several different program segments are written which perform the same function. The first or primary segment is executed first. An acceptance test validates the results from this segment. If the test passes, the result and control is passed to subsequent parts of the program. If the test fails, the second segment, or first alternative, is executed. Another acceptance test evaluates the second result. If the test passes, the result and control is passed to subsequent parts of the program. This process is repeated for two, three, or n alternatives, as specified.

2.4.1.2　Diversity

Diversity refers to using different means to perform a required function or solve the same problem. For software, this means developing more than one algorithm to implement a solution. The results from each algorithm are compared and if they agree, the appropriate action is taken. Depending on the criticality of the system, 100 percent agreement or majority agreement may be implemented. If the results do not agree, error detection and recovery algorithms take control. Safety-critical and safety-related software is often implemented through diverse algorithms. In fact, some standards in Parts II and III require diversity and specify the extent of diversity required.

2.4.1.3　Independence

Independence carries the notion of diversity one step further by having the unique algorithms developed, verified, and validated by different project teams in order to minimize the likelihood of common cause failures (CCFs). CCFs "can stem from design errors in common or identical components and their interfaces [7]." Common cause failures can be the result of requirements errors, design errors, coding errors, HCI errors, and so forth. Independence also increases objectivity during assessment. As will be seen in Parts II and III, most standards specify the degree of independence required.

2.4.1.4　Information Hiding

Information hiding or encapsulation is a design technique developed by Dr. David Parnas. The goal of information hiding is to minimize the coupling and maximize the cohesion of modules. This is accomplished by making the logic of each module and the data it utilizes as self contained as possible. This reduces the likelihood of common cause failures, minimizes the potential for fault propagation, and facilitates future maintenance and enhancements.

2.4.1.5　Partitioning

Partitioning refers to isolating safety-critical, safety-related, and nonsafety-related software. The intent is to partition the software design and functionality to prevent nonsafety-related software from interfering with or corrupting safety-critical and/or safety-related software and data. This can be accomplished through logically and/or physically isolated procedure libraries and data regions. The partitioned safety-critical or safety-related software is often referred to as a "safety-kernel [54]." An additional benefit of partitioning is that it identifies the high risk areas in a system so that more effort can be concentrated on them. As will be seen in Chapter 10, partitioning is essential to using certain metrics, such as defect density and complexity, effectively in mission critical systems.

2.4.2   Development and Operational Criteria

Appropriate choices need to be made for the development and operational environments, because these choices will ultimately affect the safety and reliability of the system. These choices are particularly important when the development environment differs from the operational environment, as is the case with embedded software. Concerns about the development and operational environments include [84, 91]:

- operating system(s),

- compiler(s),

- platform(s),

- automated tool usage, and

- known system constraints.

There are many safety and reliability issues to consider in the selection of an operating system for a mission critical system. At a minimum the following questions should be asked. Is the operating system: real time, multiuser, single-user, multitasking, or single-tasking? Was the operating system developed and certified to a national or international standard? Is the observed reliability of the operating system acceptable for a mission critical application or only a commercial application? What effect will the use of one operating system in the development environment and another in the operational environment have on the assessment of and resultant safety and reliability? Has the operating system been optimized for the target hardware platform? How stable is the operating system in terms of the frequency of new releases and the availability of long term support? Is the development team proficient with this particular operating system?

Many of the same safety and reliability issues should be considered in the selection of a compiler for a mission critical system. Was the compiler developed and certified according to a national or international consensus standard? This is important because you want to be sure that the compiler is accurately and consistently translating the source code into object code. Different compilers may produce different results if they were not certified according to the same standard. Compilers are often chosen because the development team is familiar or comfortable with a given language. A compiler should be chosen because it is optimized for the target operating system, platform, and application such as scientific calculations, manipulating text or images, data communications, and so forth. Wichmann [91] has identified a variety of safety and reliability issues related to the selection of a computer language, including access to unset scalars and pointers, optional run-time checks, undefined features, default declarations, and inconsistent deallocation of memory and pointers.

Appropriate hardware platforms should be selected for mission critical systems. The platform needs to accommodate all known logistical constraints (physical size, weight, memory, interfaces, and so forth) as well as environmental tolerances. The functional characteristics of the platform (accuracy, speed, precision) must also be evaluated.

Computer automated software engineering (CASE) tools are often used to automate the design and development process and increase productivity. There are many different tools and types of tools available. However, at present there is no single tool or suite of tools from a single vendor which covers all phases of the development lifecycle. This raises concerns about the accuracy of outputs from and inputs to CASE tools throughout the development lifecycle; particularly when developers work in a nonintegrated or multivendor tool environment.

2.4.3   Performance Criteria

The third category of considerations is performance criteria. These criteria are used to assess the performance of a system against stated requirements before it is released. Some of the common techniques used include:

- modelling,

- timing analysis,

- emulation, and

- simulation.

Modelling is an effective tool to describe a real system or a system that is to be built, its characteristics, attributes, properties, and application views. A model may describe an entire system or some subset of it. Most models make use of graphical notation which facilitates communication of the model across application domains. System elements are portrayed by network diagrams which highlight the flow and interrelationships of processes, resources, constraints, and communications.

There are two basic categories of models: analytical and conceptual. Analytical models attempt to analyze mathematical and/or logical relationships in a system. These models seek to develop a precise unambiguous description of a system by analyzing real world constraints and conditions that are likely to occur during actual operation. Analytical models are useful in evaluating alternative designs and optimizing system performance and resource allocation.

Conceptual models incorporate qualitative aspects of a system. Conceptual models are often used to clarify, illustrate, or describe various relationships within a system. These models attempt to represent the processing of information, organization of information, and system behavior over time, taking into account the environment in which the system operates and external events. Conceptual models may be structural or behavioral, that is, they model entity topology or entity dependencies. Structural models are developed either horizontally or vertically. Behavioral models depict continuous or discrete events.

IDEF is a popular modelling tool. In IDEF two models are developed: IDEF0 the functional model which depicts activity nodes with inputs, outputs, mechanisms, and controls; and IDEF1x the information model which depicts relationships between types of information via entities and attributes. IDEF provides top-down models which can be repeatedly refined at lower levels of detail. IDEF also accommodates "as-is" (existing or legacy) and "to-be" (planned or future) system definitions. The popularity and widespread use of IDEF has prompted the IEEE to define standards for its use [9,10].

Modelling is a useful tool to evaluate whether specified requirements are correct and to identify missing requirements, especially safety and reliability requirements. Many automated modelling tools are available today, as shown in Annex B. However, remember that it is important to determine the validity and accuracy of any model before drawing conclusions from it.

These techniques are used to determine if a system will meet performance requirements in the intended operational environment under low, normal, and peak loading conditions. This evaluation may include an assessment of response times, the ability to control the sequence of critical events, identification of deadlock, race, and nondeterministic conditions [55,84]. Extensive timing analysis is particularly important for real-time, concurrent, parallel, embedded, and distributed systems. Emulation and simulation are useful tools with which to conduct timing analyses.

Electrical engineering uses error rates, both observed and predicted, to determine reliability. As shown in Figure 2.5, this is not feasible for software. Error rates or probabilities are a useful component of a comprehensive public safety assessment, but are not very meaningful by themselves. In addition, values supplied by vendors for the mean time between failures (MTBF) and mean time to repair (MTTR) are often misinterpreted [75,76]. Government agencies and others responsible for assessing public safety must take a holistic approach. A more complete assessment of public safety can be obtained from analyzing the following items in addition to error rates:

- a profile of the anticipated system usage per day;

- the number of people affected per system use; and

- the number of systems estimated to be used in a given country or group of countries.

To illustrate, recently it was announced on *WTOP News* that the doppler radar system at Washington National Airport had been "down" 27 times during the first six months of 1996. The radar system was intended to assist pilots detect and avoid potential hazardous wind shear conditions. Similar results were observed at other airports which had installed the radar. What does "down 27 times" mean? Knowing how many times a system is "down," how long it is down, and how long it takes to repair it provides statistically interesting data;

however it is incomplete. For this information to be useful to the government agencies responsible for assessing public safety, the following information is also needed.

For each airport, during the time the doppler radar system was down:

- How many flights landed and departed?

- How many passengers and crew members were on each of these flights?

- How many of these landings and departures took place during weather conditions conducive to wind shear?

A meaningful public safety assessment must acknowledge the fact that human lives are at stake. Isolated statistics about an inanimate system are only part of the picture.

2.4.4   Use of Previously Developed Software

The availability of COTS products, the desire for economies of scale, and increasing use of object-oriented design and development methodologies have led to software reuse becoming more commonplace. Software reuse may occur within and among companies and academia. When software is reused in a mission critical system, it should be subjected to the same rigorous verification activities as custom software to assess its safety and reliability. The IEEE and the Reuse Interoperability Group (RIG) are cooperating to develop a suite of standards which address the effective implementation of software reuse [11, 12]. These standards recognize the need for reusable software assets to be certified at different levels based on their criticality in a target system.

COTS software may be used to develop a mission critical system, as in the case of computer aided software engineering (CASE) tools, and/or incorporated into a mission critical system, as in the case of an operating system. Both scenarios raise concerns which should be addressed. As Petroski [72] points out:

> The computer is both a blessing and a curse for it makes possible calculations beyond the reach of human endurance while at the same time making it virtually beyond the hope of human verification. Thus far the computer has been as much an agent of unsafe design as it has been a super brain that can tackle problems heretofore too complicated for a human.

CASE tools can be used throughout the development lifecycle, from requirements capture and animation through testing to enhance productivity and thoroughness. However, they are not a panacea. First, there is no single suite of CASE tools which covers all phases of the development lifecycle. This leaves the opportunity open for errors to be introduced as information is translated from one CASE tool to the next throughout the lifecycle. Second, CASE tools themselves are software products and most likely contain errors. Since CASE tools are commercial products they are not developed to the same degree of rigor as mission critical systems; hence their integrity is less. This does not mean that CASE tools should not be used during the development of mission critical systems; rather it implies that developers should be aware of their limitations. To address these concerns the International Organization for Standardization (ISO) and the International Electrotechnical Commission (IEC) have issued a guideline for the evaluation and selection of CASE tools [13].

The use of COTS software products is being encouraged by industry. Solely performing verification on COTS software products is not sufficient for acceptance in mission critical systems. Verification activities should evaluate the safety, reliability, and integrity of the COTS product and its intended use in a mission critical system. As Kemp [53] points out, "Components (hardware or software) may be used in safety-critical systems although they were not designed for such applications and may have been intended for environments in which occasional failure is an inconvenience rather than a catastrophe."

During 1993 IPL, Ltd. conducted a study for the National Air Traffic Services (NATS) in the U.K. concerning the use of COTS software in safety-critical and safety-related systems. This study, documented by Liddiard [58], determined that the "use of COTS software components does constitute a risk to the integrity of a software system." Several problems encountered when incorporating COTS software into a custom system were cited [58]:

- development tied to a COTS product which became obsolete and was no longer supported;

- multiple memory allocation and deallocation conflicts;

- reuse of buffers by COTS products without checking first to see if the contents had been read;

- "COTS" product sold before it was actually developed—a prototype had been delivered to the customer;

- internal design changes were made from one version to the next of a COTS product which negatively affected the custom software.

The study concluded that the underlying problems with using COTS products are: (1) developers of the mission critical systems have no control over the development of COTS products; and (2) COTS products are not developed according to the same standards as mission critical systems. As Liddiard [57] summarizes, "COTS software products are overfunctional, undertested, and implemented using inappropriate technologies for high integrity and safety-related systems." The study also made a recommendation concerning the choice of language, which supports Wichmann's [91] findings:

Ada is the dominant language for the development of high integrity and safety-related systems, selected for its support of good software engineering principles, consistent standard of validation and consequent benefits for system integrity. Yet most COTS software components are developed in C, a language positively discouraged by standards for the development of safety-related software. The compatibility of COTS software components with high integrity and safety-related systems could be greatly improved if the components were developed in Ada [58].

2.4.5 Complementary Analysis and Verification Techniques

By using multiple static and dynamic, logical and functional techniques, as shown in Figure 2.9, a larger number and different types of errors will be uncovered; thereby enhancing software safety and reliability [41,44,55,84,92]. As Coy [32] points out, static analysis:

> ...gives you up-front information about code that:
>
> - would be difficult to maintain,
> - would be difficult to test,
> - is nonportable,
> - transgresses your coding standard,
> - transgresses the ANSI standard, and
> - contains known programming problems...
>
> The essential difference between static and dynamic testing is that static testing is about prevention and dynamic testing is about cure. As we all know, prevention is always cheaper than cure.

For example, in a study reported by Northern Telecom [33], one defect was found by traditional testing for every seven defects found by static analysis techniques. A similar study was conducted by Computer Sciences Corporation (CSC) [54] in 1994 which identified the type of error found and how it was found (Figure 2.10). Again, the majority of errors were found by static analysis techniques [54].

Traditional testing and other dynamic analysis techniques are best for uncovering functional errors. Static analysis techniques are best for highlighting safety and reliability problems. As observed by Salisbury [81], traditional testing is inadequate whenever a computer-based system can cause injury or death. As he states [81], "Conventional system testing can demonstrate reliability levels only up to about 10^{-3} or, exceptionally, 10^{-4} failures per operating hour, far too low for most safety-related systems." In fact, testing has been humorously described by Whitty [89] as "an ad-hoc exercise with little theory to guide it" and beta testing as "a con which no other engineers have been able to put over on their customers."

A variety of static analysis techniques exist to assess software safety and reliability. Some of these techniques are unique to software; others have been adapted from hardware or system safety and reliability analysis techniques [55,63,84]. The more common software safety and reliability assessment techniques are: cleanroom analysis, code inspections, critical path analysis, formal methods, formal scenario analysis, hazard and operability study (HAZOP), metrics, Petri nets, sneak circuit analysis, software failure modes effects analysis (SFMEA), software fault tree analysis (SFTA), and testability analysis [55,63,84,85]. A major advantage of these techniques, compared to traditional testing, is that they can be exercised early in the development lifecycle when it is easier and cheaper to fix problems

Analysis	FUNCTIONAL	LOGICAL

DYNAMIC	Traditional Testing:
	  module
	  subsystem
	  interface
	  system integration
	  stress
	  usability
	  regression
	  alpha
	  beta
		Boundary Value Analysis
		Branch or Path Testing
		Equivalence Classes
		Failure Assertion
		Fault Injection
		Structural Testing
		Trajectory or Statistical-
		  Based Testing

STATIC	Cleanroom Analysis
	Code Inspections (Fagan)
	Formal Scenario Analysis
	HAZOP Analysis (system
	  and software)
		Cause Consequence
		  Analysis
		Common Cause Failure
		  Analysis
		Critical Path Analysis
		Data Flow Analysis
		Decision/Truth Tables
		Emulation
		Formal Specifications/
		  Methods/Proofs
		Change Impact Analysis
		Petri Nets
		Simulation
		Sneak Circuit Analysis
		Software FMEA
		Software FTA
		Testability Analysis

Figure 2.9: Complementary analysis and verification techniques [41,44,92]. *Note:* not all techniques shown fall exactly in one quadrant of the chart; there is some overlap.

and iteratively throughout the development lifecycle as a product evolves from concept to reality. A question from the American Society of Quality (ASQ) certified software quality engineer (CSQE) study exam highlights this point [16]:

> "6. What happens to the relative cost of fixing software errors from the requirements phase through the test phase?
>
>   d. it increases exponentially."

Analysis Type	Cumulative System Errors	Error Type					
		Design	Code	HCI	I/F	Data	Performance
Static	~50–70%	~70%	~10%	~15%	~10%	~10%	~5%
Dynamic:							
unit test	~70–80%	~20%	~75%	~50%	~10%	~50%	~5%
module test	~80–90%	~5%	~10%	~15%	~50%	~30%	~20%
subsystem test	~90–95%	~4%	~2%	~15%	~20%	~5%	~50%
system test	~95–99%	~1%	~2%	~4%	~9%	~4%	~19%

Figure 2.10: Discovery of error types by type of analysis. (*Source:* Adapted from Figure 1, page 203, Lawrence, J.D., Persons, W.L., and Preckshot, G.G. "Evaluating Software for Safety Systems in Nuclear Power Plants," *Proceedings of the Ninth Annual Conference on Computer Assurance,* 1994, copyright IEEE.)

2.4.5.1   Cleanroom Analysis

Cleanroom analysis supports the measurement and analysis of prerelease software reliability. Cleanroom analysis emphasizes the prevention of errors, rather than just their detection and makes extensive use of formal methods and proofs. This technique takes a holistic view of software development by promoting top-down stepwise refinement of the total design, with correctness and verification of that design required at each step. Much research is being done in this area today, especially in comparing the results obtained from cleanroom analysis to those observed from traditional testing. For a complete discussion of the cleanroom technique see Dyer [34].

2.4.5.2   Code Inspections

Code inspections, or software inspections, are a formal rigorous examination of all software engineering artifacts, such as requirements, architecture, design, and code which are undertaken to prevent, detect, and remove defects as early as possible in the lifecycle. An inspection is conducted during each phase of the development lifecycle and the results are compared to the previous phase for consistency, correctness, and completeness. Inspections identify deviations from one phase to the next, and the cause and source of the deviation. The notion of a "code walkthrough" or "desk check" has existed for some time. However, this process was informal and conducted haphazardly at best. The pioneering work by

Michael E. Fagan formalized the software inspection process. See Graham and Gilb [38] for a discussion of the inspection process.

Figures 2.11 through 2.14 depict a sample error reporting and tracking form which can be used with formal code inspections throughout the development lifecycle. The modular design of the form facilitates automated collection and analysis of inspection information. It also enhances a project's ability to keep historical and current views of a system and to calculate various statistics. The different parts of the form are repeated as needed. Problems are characterized by source, effect, and severity. In addition, problem summary reports can be generated. This information, which is essential in mission critical systems, can be used to prioritize corrective action.

2.4.5.3 Critical Path Analysis

Critical path analysis is used to model a set of critical events that must take place and the conditions which must be fulfilled for safe and reliable operation of a system or task. The analysis is concentrated on paths through critical program control logic that contain logical junctions, decisions, and alternatives. Control can continue through the path if the condition is true or the critical event has taken place. If a vertex is reached, control is evaluated along all outgoing lines. A critical path is depicted diagrammatically, with a block representing a condition or an event [7].

2.4.5.4 Formal Methods

Formal methods provide a description of a system during specification, design, and development. Since the description is in a fixed notation based on discrete mathematics, it can be subjected to mathematical analysis to detect incompleteness, inconsistencies, and incorrectness. The description can be analyzed by computer, similar to the syntax checking of a source program by a compiler, to display various aspects of system behavior. Some of the more common formal methods used today include: Calculus of Communicating Systems (CCS), Communicating Sequential Processes (CSP), Higher Order Logic (HOL), Language for Temporal Ordering Specification (LOTOS), OBJ, Temporal Logic, Vienna Development Method (VDM), and Z. Most formal methods provide a capability for stating assertions for pre- and post-conditions at various locations in the program. The proof demonstrates that the program transfers preconditions into postconditions according to the set of specified logical rules [7, 22, 47].

As observed by Plat [73] and others, one of the main benefits of formal methods is that they enable larger and more complex software systems to be developed. His rationale for this statement points out that formal methods [73]:

- "provide for complexity control by offering extensive means to express representational and procedural abstraction;"

- "make unambiguous and consistent specifications possible at lower cost" through formal notations; and

System:[a] _____

Subsystem: _____ Component: _____

Part I – Identification[b]

1. Phase/Activity:
   a. reqts anal & spec   e. module demo & anal
   b. arch anal & spec   f. funct demo & anal
   c. design anal & spec   g. system integration
   d. development   h. system demo & anal

2. Item Reviewed:
   a. requirements spec.   i. risk analysis
   b. animated specification   j. V&V plans
   c. architecture spec.   k. emulation results
   d. algorithmic proof   l. simulation results
   e. design specification   m. V&V procedures
   f. prototype   n. V&V results
   g. data dictionary   o. user guide
   h. source code listing   p. installation instructions

3. Technique(s) Used:
   Dynamic: Static:
   a. module testing   q. cleanroom analysis
   b. subsystem testing   r. code inspections
   c. interface testing   s. formal scenario analysis
   d. system integration testing t. HAZOP analysis
   e. stress testing   u. cause consequence analysis
   f. usability testing   v. critical path analysis
   g. regression testing   w. data flow analysis
   h. alpha testing   x. decision/truth tables
   i. beta testing   y. emulation
   j. boundary value analysis z. formal specification/method/proofs
   k. branch or path testing   aa. change impact analysis
   l. equivalence classes   bb. Petri nets
   m. failure assertion   cc. simulation
   n. fault injection   dd. sneak circuit analysis
   o. structural testing   ee. SFMEA
   p. trajectory or statistical ff. SFTA
      based testing   gg. testability analysis

[a]This form is designed so that the appropriate items are circled or blanks are filled in to facilitate the automated collection and analysis of inspection information.

[b]Part I is repeated for each subsystem and component.

Figure 2.11: Sample error, fault, and failure reporting and tracking form (Part I).

Part II – Problem Characterization[a]

1. Problem Name/Identification:
2. Problem Description:

3. Problem Type:

Source		Effect	
a.	requirements	g.	functional
b.	design	h.	performance
c.	code	i.	safety
d.	interface	j.	reliability
e.	integration	k.	security
f.	HCI		

4. Problem Severity:[b]

a.	negligible	c.	critical
b.	marginal	d.	catastrophic

5. Recommended Corrective Action:
   a. description –

   b. estimated difficulty to implement –

   c. estimated time required –

6. Approval of Recommended Corrective Action:

   _____
                        name/date

7. Problem Resolution:
   a. description –

   b. implemented by:

   _____
                        name/date
   c. verified by:

   _____
                        name/date

---

[a]Part II is repeated for each problem. Initially the problem is identified. Later, information about the recommended corrective action and the actual resolution are added.

[b]This represents the severity of the consequences if this error occurred. The standards discussed in Parts II and III of this book provide definitions for these terms.

Figure 2.12: Sample error, fault, and failure reporting and tracking form (Part II).

Part III – Problem Summary[a]

1. Number of Problems Found by Type:

    Source   Effect
    a. requirements   _____   g. functional   _____
    b. design   _____   h. performance   _____
    c. code   _____   i. safety   _____
    d. interface   _____   j. reliability   _____
    e. integration   _____   k. security   _____
    f. HCI   _____

2. Number of Problems Found by Severity:
    a. negligible   _____   c. critical   _____
    b. marginal   _____   d. catastrophic   _____

3. Number of Problems Resolved to Date: _____

4. Number of Problems Unresolved to Date: _____

---

[a]This part can be kept as a 'running total' of the whole system and is repeated for each component and subsystem.

Figure 2.13: Sample error, fault, and failure reporting and tracking form (Part III).

Part IV – Team Participation[a]

1. Start Date/Time: _____

2. Finish Date/Time: _____

3. Team Leader: _____

4. Participants: _____   _____

                                _____   _____

                                _____   _____

                                _____   _____

---

[a]The part is repeated for each review activity.

Figure 2.14: Sample error, fault, and failure reporting and tracking form (Part IV).

- "facilitate formal verification of the correctness of design steps."

As noted by Harwood [40], "Formal methods promote verification as a progressive activity. A proof of correctness is built up as the result is built up." He identifies that the practical aspect of formal methods is they provide "tools for carrying out assurance of high integrity software development [40]." Since "the most costly and hardest to detect errors result from requirements and high-level design errors," Harwood [40] recommends "concentrating formal methods on the early stages of system development" for the best pay off; formal methods should be used to get the specification and architecture correct.

This recommendation is borne out by a study reported by Brookes [23] on the CON-FORM project, which conducted a "side-by-side" experiment with conventional and formal development methodologies. Two equally experienced teams developed the same system; one using conventional methods, the other formal methods. It should be noted that a complete suite of formal methods was not used. Instead, a subset was used—a formal specification was developed. The results reported by Brookes [23] indicate that there is little or no additional cost overhead from using a formal specification over the entire project lifecycle. While a higher cost was observed in the earlier stages of the project, when requirements were being analyzed and understood, the cost was lower in the later stages. The results also indicated that the use of a formal specification prevented one error which was not caught until the implementation phase by the conventional method. This single error increased the conventional implementation effort by 15 percent because of rework. (The 15 percent figure did not include any costs to correct supporting documentation; so, the actual total cost of rework is higher.)

As a result of the CONFORM project and others, British Aerospace identified six benefits from the use of formal specifications [23]:

1. "potential problems are highlighted [early] by the rigorous approach which formal specification forces upon the designer;"

2. "animated models of the design can be created [from a formal specification] which allows the system to be explored;"

3. "exception conditions can be identified clearly and catered for;"

4. "complex data can be defined in an implementation independent manner;"

5. "test cases can be generated very early in the design process;" and

6. "an executable specification is easier to validate against than an informal [human language] customer specification."

Although this study was conducted using VDM, it is expected that similar results would be observed using Z or other formal specification languages [21]. As will be seen in Parts II and III, many standards require the use of formal methods during the development of safety-critical systems.

2.4.5.5   Formal Scenario Analysis

Formal scenario analysis develops a scenario-based test model from the analysis of operational scenarios, user-views, and events. As Hamlet and Voas [39] point out, "without an accurate profile, there can be no validity to test[ing]." Scenarios are defined as concrete system usage examples that consist of an ordered sequence of events which accomplishes a functional requirement, as specified by the user. User-views are defined as a set of system conditions as seen by a class of users. Events are defined as specific stimuli that change a system state and/or trigger another event. Scenarios are recorded in a formalized "tree" and "forest" notation. The notation is similar to that for a finite state machine (FSM) and composite finite state machine (CFSM) and can be automatically analyzed to uncover deadlock, nondeterministic conditions, incorrect sequences, and incorrect initial and terminating states [45, 69]. Formal scenario analysis is particularly useful in identifying safety and reliability errors caused by faulty or incomplete understanding of semitacit and tacit domain knowledge.

2.4.5.6   Hazard and Operability Study (HAZOP)

HAZOP, a hazard and operability study, provides an interdisciplinary analysis of the number of ways in which a system can fail, accidentally or intentionally, and the severity of the associated consequences. A HAZOP can and should be performed at the system and software levels. The seven generic steps to a HAZOP are [85]:

1. defining the development lifecycle elements;

2. developing the parameters associated with each element;

3. predicting the potential for deviations from intended operations;

4. determining the consequences of potential deviations;

5. identifying the cause(s) of the potential deviations;

6. identifying the current risk control measures; and

7. identifying incorrect or inadequate risk control measures.

A HAZOP study is usually conducted by a facilitator with an interdisciplinary team. A study was conducted by British Aerospace to evaluate the practical experience gained from applying a HAZOP to an avionics software system and to a software controlled braking system. The final report stated the belief that HAZOP has wide applicability to software and provides a useful way to investigate the safety of a wide range of computer-based systems [62]. Burns [26] has developed a methodology for extending a standard HAZOP to programmable electronic systems (PESs).

2.4.5.7　Metrics

Metrics related to software are commonly classified into three groups: product metrics, process metrics, and project metrics. A subset of the available software quality metrics relate directly or indirectly to software safety and reliability; see Chapter 10 for a complete discussion. Two measurements are discussed here, lines of code (LOC) and function points (FPs), because they are referred to in the standards discussed in Parts II and III.

Software size can be measured in terms of lines of code (LOC), function points, or the amount of storage space (memory and/or disk space) needed for the software to operate effectively. Several problems arise from using LOC as a metric. First, there are inconsistent definitions concerning what constitutes an LOC. Does it measure source code or object code? Does it measure executable statements only or does it include data statements and comments? Does it measure logical lines or physical lines? Second, source code statements in different languages (Fortran, C++, Pascal, COBOL, Ada, and so forth) yield a different number of object code statements; they are not equivalent. Hence, LOC is not a uniformly meaningful metric.

The concept of function points was created to alleviate some of the problems associated with the LOC metric. The International Function Point Users Group (IFUG) standard defines a three step process to determine function points [4, 50]. Rather than simply counting lines of code, function points measure aspects of a system design and its functionality. The first step is to count the number of external inputs, external outputs, logical file interfaces, external interface files, and queries supported. This number is then multiplied by an assigned complexity weighting factor. The result is referred to as the number of function counts (FC).

The second step is to calculate the value adjustment factor (VAF) which evaluates and weights the importance of 14 system characteristics to successful system operation. The 14 characteristics evaluated include: data communications, online updates, distributed functionality, complex processing, response time(s), reusability, high system usage, installation ease, transaction rate(s), operational ease, online data entry, multiple installation sites, end-user efficiency, and facilitation of change. Lastly, the number of function points is calculated by multiplying FC by VAF. Discussions are continuing and refinements are being made to the function point (FP) calculation by IFUG and IEEE.

2.4.5.8　Petri Nets

Petri nets are often used to model relevant aspects of system behavior at a wide range of abstract levels. Some sources [85] consider Petri nets to be one of the most exhaustive and efficient methods of software safety analysis that exists today. The main advantage to Petri net analysis is its broad applicability; it can be used to model an entire system, subsystems, and/or subcomponents at conceptual, top level design, detailed design, and implementation levels.

Petri nets are a class of graph theory models which represent information and control flow in systems that exhibit concurrency and asynchronous behavior. Petri net models can be defined in purely mathematical terms, which facilitates automated analysis such as producing reachability graphs. A Petri net is a network of states and transitions. The states may be marked or unmarked. A transition is enabled when all the input places to it are marked. When enabled, it is permitted but not obliged to fire. If it fires, the input marks are removed and each output place from the transition is marked instead. Potential hazards can be represented as particular safe and unsafe states in the model. Extended Petri nets allow timing features of the system to be modelled and incorporate data flow into the model [27, 28, 49, 71]. They are useful for identifying race and nondeterministic conditions which could affect safety and reliability.

2.4.5.9   Sneak Circuit Analysis

Sneak circuit analysis is used to detect an unexpected path or logic flow within a program that could initiate undesired function(s), inhibit desired function(s), or cause incorrect sequencing/timing. Sneak circuit analysis can be used to evaluate combinations of hardware, software, and operator actions. Sneak circuits are latent conditions that are inadvertently designed into a system which may cause it to perform contrary to specifications. The unintended consequences of sneak circuits may affect safety and reliability.

The first step in sneak circuit analysis is to convert the source code into a topological network tree, identifying the patterns for each node of the network. The use and interrelationships of instructions are examined to identify potential "sneak circuits." Categories of sneak circuits that are examined include [85]:

- **unintended outputs** – sneak circuits which could cause current, energy, or logical sequence to flow along an unexpected path or in an unintended direction;

- **incorrect timing** – sneak timing in which events occur in an unexpected or conflicting sequence;

- **undesired actions** – sneak indications which cause an ambiguous or false display of system operating conditions and thus may result in an undesired action by the operator; and

- **misleading messages** – sneak labels which incorrectly or imprecisely label system functions, such as system inputs, controls, displays, and buses, and may mislead an operator into applying an incorrect stimulus to the system.

The last step in sneak circuit analysis is to recommend appropriate corrective action to resolve any unintended anomalies discovered by the analysis.

2.4.5.10   Software FMEA

Software FMEA follows the same procedure as a hardware or system FMEA. In fact, one of the advantages of a software FMEA is that it can be merged into a system-level FMEA. Like a hardware FMEA, a software FMEA identifies design deficiencies. This technique can and should be used iteratively throughout the development lifecycle. The output from a software FMEA can be used as input to a software FTA. The procedure for conducting a software FMEA is straightforward [5, 75, 76, 83]:

1. break the software into logical components, such as functions or tasks;

2. predict the potential failure modes for each component;

3. postulate causes of these failure modes and their effect on system behavior; and

4. conduct risk analyses to determine the severity and frequency of these failures.

The principle data elements to be collected and analyzed for each potential failure mode are: the failure, the cause(s), the effect of the failure, the criticality of the failure, the software component responsible, and the recommended change. Figures 2.15 and 2.16 illustrate a sample software FMEA for a radiation treatment system. Annex B lists automated tools which can be used in the production of FTAs and FMEAs.

Software Component: control_energy_release
Function Performed: control release of radiation

Part I – Identification

Potential Failure Mode(s)	Potential Cause(s)[a]	Effect of Failure	Current Controls
#1 – overdose	wrong beam type	serious injury or death	control 1a
	wrong beam duration	serious injury or death	control 1b
	wrong beam strength	serious injury or death	control 1c
#2 – wrong delivery location	calibration error	serious injury to healthy tissue/organ	control 2a
	operator error	serious injury to healthy tissue/organ	control 2b
	mechanical error	serious injury to healthy tissue/organ	control 2c
	data error	serious injury to healthy tissue/organ	control 2d
	location calculation error	serious injury to healthy tissue/organ	control 2e
#3 – underdose	wrong beam type	therapy ineffective, disease progresses	control 3a
	wrong beam duration	therapy ineffective, disease progresses	control 3b
	wrong beam strength	therapy ineffective, disease progresses	control 3c

[a]A failure may have multiple causes. Hence, each cause requires a control and has its own probability, integrity, and RPN value. The severity of each failure is independent of the cause.

Figure 2.15: Sample software FMEA for a radiation treatment system (Part I).

Part II – Assessment

Risk Assessment Current Controls				Recommended Corrective Action or Improvement	Action Taken	Risk Assessment New Controls			
P^a	S	D	RPN			P	S	D	RPN
p1a	s1	d1a	r1a	improvement 1a	action 1a	P1a	S1	D1a	R1a
p1b	s1	d1b	r1b	improvement 1b	action 1b	P1b	S1	D1b	R1b
p1c	s1	d1c	r1c	improvement 1c	action 1c	P1c	S1	D1c	R1c
p2a	s2	d2a	r2a	improvement 2a	action 2a	P2a	S2	D2a	R2a
p2b	s2	d2b	r2b	improvement 2b	action 2b	P2b	S2	D2b	R2b
p2c	s2	d2c	r2c	improvement 2c	action 2c	P2c	S2	D2c	R2c
p2d	s2	d2d	r2d	improvement 2d	action 2d	P2d	S2	D2d	R2d
p2e	s2	d2e	r2e	improvement 2e	action 2e	P2e	S2	D2e	R2e
p3a	s3	d3a	r3a	improvement 3a	action 3a	P3a	S3	D3a	R3a
p3b	s3	d3b	r3b	improvement 3b	action 3b	P3b	S3	D3b	R3b
p3c	s3	d3c	r3c	improvement 3c	action 3c	P3c	S3	D3c	R3c

where

p	=	probability that this failure will occur
s	=	severity of the effect of this failure should it occur
d	=	measure of software integrity to control this failure
rpn^b	=	risk priority number, (p $\times$ s $\times$ d), the higher the number the higher the priority for risk mitigation

---

[a]The standards discussed in Parts II and III define these terms and explain how to determine them.
[b]See Chapter 3 for a discussion of how the automotive industry calculates the risk priority number.

Figure 2.16: Sample software FMEA for a radiation treatment system (Part II).

2.4.5.11   Software FTA

Software FTA follows the same procedure as a hardware or system FTA to identify the root cause(s) of a major undesired event. Software FTA aids in the analysis of events, or combinations of events, that will lead to a hazard. Starting at an event which would be the immediate cause of a hazard, the analysis is carried out "backward" along a path. Combinations of causes are described with logical operators (AND, OR, IOR, EOR). Intermediate causes are analyzed in the same way back to root cause(s) [6, 75, 76].

Like a software FMEA, one of the advantages of a software FTA is that it can be merged into a system-level FTA. Again, a software FTA should be repeated iteratively throughout the development lifecycle. Figure 2.17 illustrates the symbols commonly used in an FTA.

Figures 2.18 through 2.23 illustrate an FTA for a radiation treatment system which uses the FMEA from Figures 2.15 and 2.16 as the starting point. Incorrect release of energy is identified as the top event to be analyzed. Three potential causes for the incorrect release of energy are identified. Then potential causes for each intermediate cause are identified in an iterative process. The FTA in Figures 2.18 through 2.23 is developed to three levels. The hierarchical relationship between events and causes is illustrated by the numbering scheme. This FTA demonstrates the ability to integrate hardware, software, and system events. Hence, different parts of the FTA may be developed by different project teams, who will decide to what level it is meaningful to carry the analysis. In this FTA it is interesting to note that some second level events share common lower level causes.

Both the FMEA and FTA are developed iteratively as more becomes known about a system and there is much interaction between them. First, Part I of an FMEA is developed for a system. This information is used as input to the system FTA. The identification of potential fault paths facilitates the design of appropriate robust risk control measures. Second, each fault path is analyzed as the system FTA is developed to lower levels of detail. From this analysis, the probability of the fault occurring (p) and the integrity of the control measures (d) are determined. Third, this information is then used to complete Part II of the FMEA.

Event Symbols   **Logic Symbols**

1. top event to be analyzed

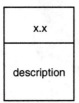

2. basic or lowest level event
   to be analyzed

3. undeveloped or unexpanded
   event

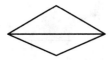

4. input event that is to occur

5. page connector to expanded path

6. AND gate: event occurs only
   if all input events occur

7. OR gate: event occurs if any
   one of the input events occurs

8. PRIORITY AND: event occurs
   only if all of the input events
   occur in the order from left to
   right

9. EXCLUSIVE OR: event expected
   occurs if one but not both input
   events occur

10. VOTING gate: event occurs if
    m of n input events occur

Figure 2.17: Common FTA symbols [6,75].

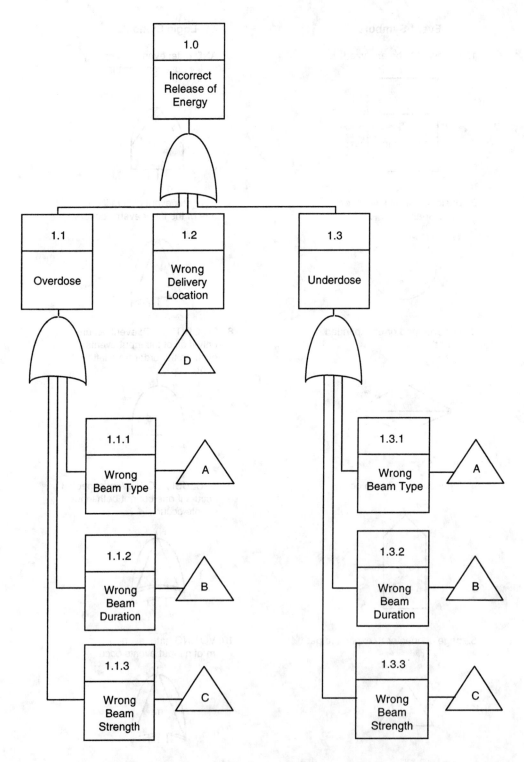

Figure 2.18: Sample software FTA for a radiation treatment system: Level 1.

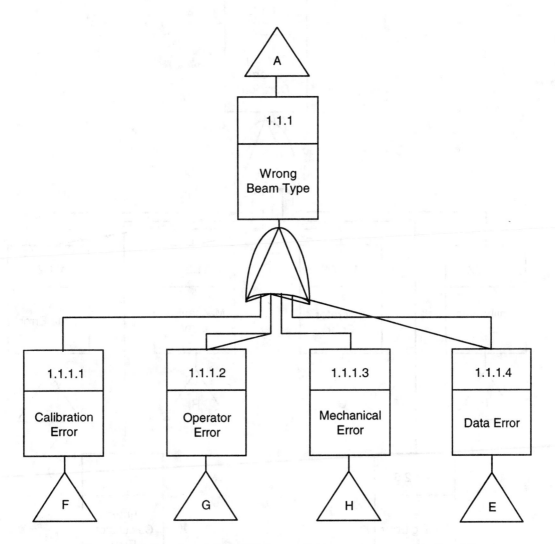

Figure 2.19: Sample software FTA for a radiation treatment system: Level 2.

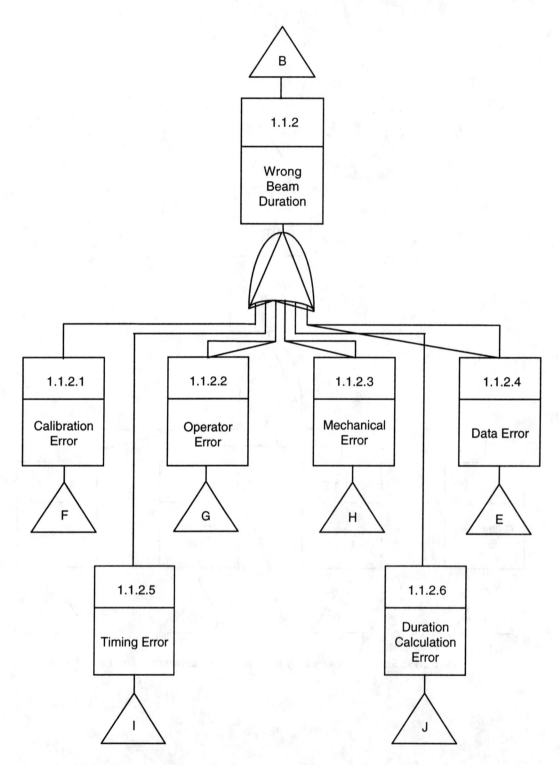

Figure 2.20: Sample software FTA for a radiation treatment system: Level 2 (continued).

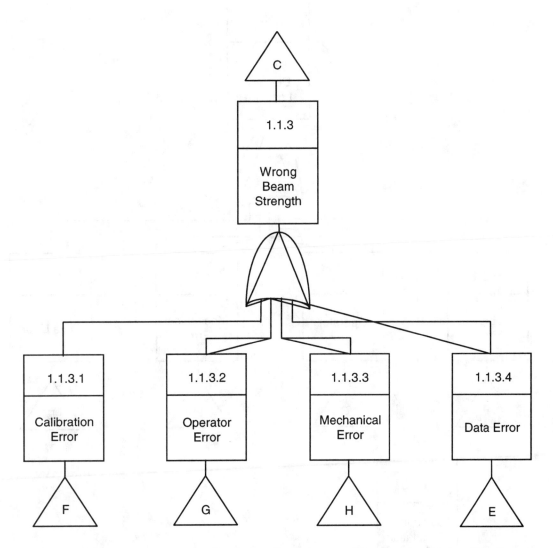

Figure 2.21: Sample software FTA for a radiation treatment system: Level 2 (continued).

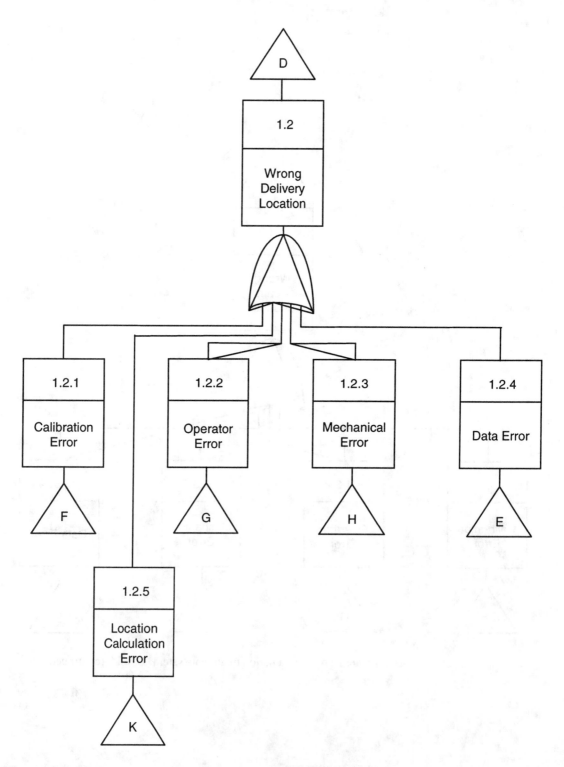

Figure 2.22: Sample software FTA for a radiation treatment system: Level 2 (continued).

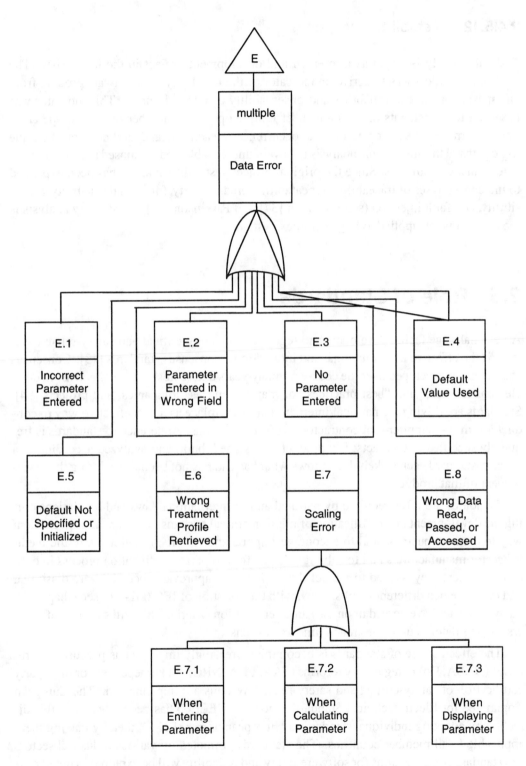

Figure 2.23: Sample software FTA for a radiation treatment system: Level 3.

2.4.5.12   Testability Analysis

Testability analysis began as a research and development project in the late 1970s. The goal of the project was to derive an indicator of the testability of a software product from an analysis of the controllability and observability of internal nodes. This indicator was based on measurements of the number of unique operators, number of unique operands, total occurrence of each operator, total occurrence of each operand, and number of unique logic paths. This algorithmic analysis uncovers unreachable nodes, unused nodes, and non-deterministic conditions. Since the original project, testability analysis has been expanded to include analyses of traceability, repeatability, predictability, functional testability, accessibility, and fault injection (see Friedman [37] and Parkinson [70]). Testability analysis is most useful when applied to large complex systems.

2.5   Role of Standards

A key challenge facing developers and regulators of safety-critical and safety-related systems is the effective use of national and international consensus standards [43]. Consensus standards are developed over the course of many years and represent the collective wisdom, "lessons learned," and "best practices" of many countries, companies, and projects [84]. Standards are driving the national/international marketplace as a cost effective way to conduct acquirer – supplier– subcontractor – certifier relations. Adherence to standards is frequently specified in contracts; if a product is designed, built, and analyzed according to a specific standard each stakeholder knows what has and has not been done during the development of that product.

Standards are often required by national and/or international laws and regulations during the development and certification of mission critical systems. They are also an efficient way to conduct business and to encourage imports and exports. Previously, in the medical sector manufacturers had to submit a device for a separate certification process in each country where they wanted to market the device. The approval processes were dissimilar and often yielded different results. Now, with the adoption of IEC 601-1-4 (see Chapter 7), many countries have agreed upon the same certification criteria. This will save manufacturers and regulatory authorities much time and expense.

The effective use of standards is becoming increasingly important as procurement reforms (NASA, DoD), regulatory reforms (FAA, FDA, NRC), and independent or third party certification of safety-critical and safety-related systems are implemented. The European Committee for Electrotechnical Standardisation (CENELEC) has been a leader in this direction by adopting individual standards as European norms (EN-x), thereby making them applicable to all member countries. The standards promoted by various industrial sectors and standards organizations for software safety and reliability will be explored in detail next in Parts II and III.

2.6   Concluding Remarks

A consensus is developing that general purpose software engineering skills are not enough when it comes to mission critical systems [55, 63, 84]. As observed by Chen [31] and others, people involved in the development, certification, and management of safety-critical systems must be qualified by training and experience to perform software safety engineering and risk management tasks, plus they need an understanding of the application domain. The underlying principle is that just as the activities associated with the development and certification of general purpose or commercial software are insufficient for the development and certification of safety-critical and safety-related software, so too is the associated skill set of the people performing these activities [55, 63, 84]. Additional specialized skills and expertise are needed. As will be seen in Parts II and III, many standards require special qualifications of people involved in the development and certification of safety-critical systems.

"All of this has nothing to do with me," you say. "All I do is build information systems and databases." Perhaps you should think again. Software safety and reliability issues do not only occur in high visibility systems such as airplanes and nuclear power plants. They also occur in many everyday scenarios: software controlled microwave ovens, software controlled elevators, software controlled 911 emergency dispatch systems, and medical databases [55]. For example, on July 16, 1996 a townhouse in the Old Towne part of Alexandria, VA exploded. Fortunately no one was home at the time. It was reported that employees of the gas utility were working in the area at the time of the explosion. The damage estimate was $365,000. On July 25, 1996 *WTOP News* reported the cause of the explosion: high pressure gas had been released into the house, but the house did not have a regulator. The gas utility employees were working from a computer generated report from a database which contained a data-entry error. The database had not been validated against the original hardcopy data. The database was nowhere near the townhouse, but it was the root cause of the explosion.

2.7   Discussion Problems

1. Consider a software controlled subway system. Under what conditions could it be safe but not reliable? Under what conditions could it be reliable but not safe?

2. Section 2.3.2.1 lists four items which should be defined as a minimum set of safety requirements. What other items might be appropriate to evaluate and define?

3. Section 2.4.2 lists several safety and reliability issues to evaluate during the selection of an operating system for a mission critical system. What other issues might be appropriate to be evaluated?

4. Develop a safety specification for a software controlled microwave oven in pseudocode or other standardized notation. Consider home and commercial use. Use one of the static analysis techniques in Figure 2.9 to prove that the specification is correct.

5. Develop a reliability specification for a software controlled clothes iron in pseudocode or other standardized notation. Consider home and commercial use. Use a static analysis technique from Figure 2.9 to prove that the specification is correct.

6. Develop diverse algorithms in a standardized notation for implementing software controlled brakes, seat belts, and air bags in an automobile. Determine what degree of diversity and independence is needed to ensure safety and reliability.

7. How could a software driven bank ATM network make use of information hiding?

8. Perform a formal scenario analysis for a software controlled elevator.

9. Consider a four-burner range that is software controlled. How would the software safety specification for a gas range differ from that for an electrical range?

10. How is diversity different from n-block recovery?

11. Since several software reliability models are not time related, develop an appropriate acronym to use in lieu of MTBF and MTTR.

12. Five groups of potential system hazards are listed below in Figures 2.24 and 2.25: energy hazards, biological hazards, device usage hazards, functional failure hazards, and environmental hazards. Examine these five groups and determine:

    a. Which of these hazards could be caused by software errors and how?

    b. Which of these hazards could be controlled and/or mitigated by software and how?

Potential Energy Hazards

- Excessive Electricity
- Excessive Heat or Cold
- Excessive Pressure
- Radiation
- EMI/RFI
- Erroneous Moving Parts
- Support Device Failure
- Unusual or Unwanted Vibration

Potential Biological Hazards

- Contamination
- Incompatibility
- Incorrect formulation
- Toxicity
- (Cross-)infection
- Pyrogenicity
- Inability to maintain hygienic safety

Potential Environmental Hazards

- EMI/RFI
- Inadequate/unreliable supply of power or cooling
- Operation outside of prescribed environment (dust, vibration, humidity, temperature, etc.)
- Incompatibility with other devices
- Accidental mechanical damage
- Contamination

Figure 2.24: Potential system hazards.

Potential Usage Hazards

- Inadequate labelling, instructions for use
- Overly complex instructions for use
- Inadequate specification for accessories
- Use by unskilled or untrained personnel
- Human error
- Insufficient warning of side effects
- Incorrect measurements
- Misrepresentation of results

Potential Functional Failure Hazards

- Inadequate performance characteristics for intended use
- Lack of maintenance/calibration specification
- Lack of method to determine end of useful device life
- Loss of mechanical integrity
- Inadequate packaging, contamination and/or deterioration

Figure 2.25: Potential system hazards (continued).

Additional Resources

Related Safety, System, and Software Engineering Standards

[1]   ANSI[6]/IEEE Std. 1002-1992. IEEE Standard Taxonomy for Software Engineering Standards.

[2]   ANSI/IEEE Std. 1012-1998. IEEE Standard for Software Verification and Validation Plans.

[3]   ANSI/IEEE Std. 1059-1994. IEEE Guide for Software Verification and Validation Plans.

[4]   ANSI/IEEE 1061-1998. IEEE Standard for a Software Quality Metrics Methodology.

[5]   IEC 60812:1985 – Analysis Techniques for System Reliability—Procedure for Failure Modes Effects Analysis (FMEA).

[6]   IEC 61025:1990 – Fault Tree Analysis (FTA).

[7]   IEC 61508-7: Functional safety of electrical/electronic/programmable electronic safety-related systems – Part 7: Overview of Techniques and Measures.

[8]   IEEE Std. 1044-1993, IEEE Standard Classification for Software Anomalies, and IEEE Std. 1044.1-1995, Guide to Classification for Software Anomalies.

[9]   IEEE P1320.2[7] Standard for Conceptual Modeling Language, Syntax and Semantics for IDEF1X97 (IDEFobject), 1998.

[10] IEEE P1320.2.1 Standard for Conceptual Modeling Language, User Guide for IDEF1X97 (IDEFobject), 1998.

[11] IEEE Std. 1420.1a-1996, IEEE Guide for Information Technology – Software Reuse – Data Model for Reuse Library Interoperability: Asset Certification Framework.

[12] IEEE Std. 1420.1-1995, IEEE Standard for Information Technology – Software Reuse – Data Model for Reuse Library Interoperability: Basic Interoperability Data Model (BIDM).

[13] ISO/IEC 14102:1995 Information technology – Guideline for the evaluation and selection of CASE tools.

---

[6]A standard listed as an American National Standards Institute (ANSI) standard has undergone an extra level of formal comment and review, as part of the consensus development process. Once approved, it is referred to as an American National Standard.

[7]An IEEE standard number that begins with the 'P' designation is still under development and has not been issued in final form. Once finalized, the 'P' is removed and the number stays the same.

[14] IEC 50-191(1990-12), International Electrotechnical Vocabulary (IEV) Chapter 191: Dependability and quality of service.

[15] ISO/IEC 9126(1991-12), Information Technology – Software product evaluation – quality characteristics and guidelines for their use.

Selected Bibliography

[16] ASQ Certification: Certified Software Quality Engineer (CSQE) brochure, July 1996.

[17] Bias, R. and Mayhew, D. *Cost Justifying Usability*, Academic Press, Cambridge, MA, 1994.

[18] Bieda, John. "Software Reliability: A Practitioner's Model," *Reliability Review*, Vol. 16, No. 2, June 1996, pp. 18–28.

[19] Bishop, P.G. et al. *Dependability of Critical Computer Systems*, Elsevier Applied Science, 1990.

[20] Bishop, P.G. and Bloomfield, R.E. *The SHIP Safety Case Approach*, Adelard, 1995.

[21] Bowen, J. *Formal Specification and Documentation Using Z*, International Thomson Computer Press, 1996.

[22] Bradley, P., Schackleton, L. and Stavridou, V. "The Practical Application of Formal Methods to High Integrity Systems—the SafeFM Project," *Directions in Safety-Critical Systems*, Springer-Verlag, 1993, pp. 168–176.

[23] Brookes, T. "CONFORM—A Comparison of Conventional and Formal Development Methodologies," *Software Reliability & Metrics Club Newsletter*, July 1995, pp. 5–8.

[24] Brown, C.M. *Human Computer Interface Design Guidelines*, Ablex Publishing Co., Norwood, NJ, 1989.

[25] Burdea, G. and Coiffet, P. *Virtual Reality Technology*, John Wiley & Sons, 1994.

[26] Burns, D.J. and Pitblado, R.M. "A Modified HAZOP Methodology for Safety Critical System Assessment," *Directions in Safety-Critical Systems*, Springer-Verlag, 1993, pp. 232–245.

[27] Buy, Ugo and Sloan, Robert H. Analysis of Real-Time Programs with Simple Time Petri Nets, Proceedings of the 1994 International Symposium on Software Testing and Analysis (ISSTA), ACM Press, pp. 228–239.

[28] Buy, Ugo Analysis of Real-Time Programs with Simple Time Petri Nets, Safety and Reliability for Medical Device Software, Health Industries Manufacturers Association (HIMA) Report No. 95-8, 1995, tab 5.

[29] Calvez, J.P. Embedded Real-Time Systems: A Specification and Design Methodology, John Wiley & Sons, 1993.

[30] Carstensen, P. and Sawyer, C.R. Human Factors and Software, Safety and Reliability for Medical Device Software, Health Industries Manufacturers Association (HIMA) Report No. 95-8, 1995, tab 12.

[31] Chen, B.H. and Ling Yang. "Design, Testing and Verification of Safety Critical Software," *Hazard Prevention*, 4Q95, Vol. 31, No. 4, pp. 22–28.

[32] Coy, R. Cutting development costs by automating the code inspection process, Software Reliability and Metrics Club Newsletter, Feb. 1998, pp. 6–8.

[33] Dale, C. Report of the 44th Club Meeting—How Much Does Quality Cost? Northern Telecom Experience (Dave Homan), Software Reliability and Metrics Club Newsletter, Mar. 1995, p. 7.

[34] Dyer, Michael. The Cleanroom Approach to Software Quality, John Wiley & Sons, 1992.

[35] Edwards, K. *Real-Time Structured Methods: System Analysis*, John Wiley & Sons, 1993.

[36] Falla, M. "Safety-Critical Software Professionals in the British Computer Society Industry Career Structure," *Safety-Critical Systems*, Chapman & Hall, 1993, pp. 181–192.

[37] Friedman, M.A. and Voas, J.M. Software Assessment: Reliability, Safety, and Testability. John Wiley & Sons, Inc. 1995.

[38] Gilb, T. and Graham, D. *Software Inspection*, Addison-Wesley, 1993.

[39] Hamlet, D. and Voas, J. "Faults on its Sleeve: Amplifying Software Reliability Testing," *Proceedings of the 1993 International Symposium on Software Testing and Analysis*, ACM Press, June 1993, pp. 89–98.

[40] Harwood, W. "Formal Methods is 'Correctness by Construction'," *Safety Systems*, Vol. 5, No. 2, Jan. 1996, pp. 11–14.

[41] Herrmann, D. "Software Safety and Reliability in the Regulatory Environment," *Safety and Reliability for Medical Device Software*, Health Industries Manufacturers Association (HIMA) Report No. 95-8, 1995, tab 8.

[42] Herrmann, D. "A Preview of IEC Safety Requirements for Programmable Electronic Medical Systems," *Medical Device and Diagnostic Industry*, June 1995, pp. 106–110.

[43] Herrmann, D. "A Methodology for Evaluating, Comparing, and Selecting Software Safety and Reliability Standards," *Proceedings of the 10th Annual Conference on Computer Assurance*, IEEE, June 1995, pp. 223–232.

[44] Herrmann, D. and Zier, D. "Using IEC 601-1-4 to Satisfy the Requirements of the FDA Software Guidance," *Medical Device & Diagnostic Industry*, Dec. 1995, pp. 104–107.

[45] Hsia, Pei. "Testing the Therac-25: A Formal Scenario Approach," *Safety and Reliability for Medical Device Software*, Health Industries Manufacturers Association (HIMA) Report No. 95-8, 1995, tab 6.

[46] Hyman, W., Lively, W., and Williams, C. "Safety Issues for Expert Systems Which 'Learn'," *Proceedings of the 10th International System Safety Conference*, July 1991, pp. 6.4-2-1 through 6.4-2-10.

[47] Ince, D.C. *An Introduction to Discrete Mathematics, Formal System Specification, and Z*, 2nd edition, Oxford, 1992.

[48] Jackson, D. "Target Qualities of Safety Professionals," *Safety-Critical Systems*, Chapman & Hall, 1993, pp. 139–152.

[49] Jensen, K. *Coloured Petri Nets: Basic Concepts, Analysis, Methods and Practical Use*, Springer-Verlag, Vol. 1, 1996, Vol. 2, 1995.

[50] Kan, Stephen H. *Metrics and Models in Software Quality Engineering*, Addison Wesley, 1995.

[51] Keene, Samuel J. "Comparing Hardware and Software Reliability," *Reliability Review*, Vol. 14, No. 4, Dec. 1994, pp. 5–21.

[52] Keene, Samuel J. "Modeling Software Reliability and Maintainability Characteristics," *Reliability Review*, ASQ, Part I, Vol. 17, No. 2, June 1997, pp. 5–28 and Part II, Vol. 17, No. 3, Sep. 1997, pp. 13–22.

[53] Kemp, A. "Yr 2000 and Embedded Systems," *Safety Systems*, Vol. 7, No. 1, Sep. 1997, pp. 18–19.

[54] Lawrence, J.D., Persons, W.L., and Preckshot, G.G. "Evaluating Software for Safety Systems in Nuclear Power Plants," *Proceedings of the Ninth Annual Conference on Computer Assurance*, 1994, pp. 197–207.

[55] Leveson, N.G. *Safeware: System Safety and Computers*, Addison-Wesley, 1995.

[56] Levi, Shem-Tov. *Fault Tolerant System Design*, McGraw Hill, 1994.

[57] Liddiard, J. "COTS software—can we trust it?" *Software Reliability and Metrics Club Newsletter*, Feb. 1998, pp. 1–3.

[58] Liddiard, J. *Using Commercial Off-the-Shelf Software in High Integrity and Safety Related Systems*, IPL Information Processing, Ltd., 1994.

[59] Littlewood, B. "The Need for Evidence from Disparate Sources to Evaluate Software Safety," *Directions in Safety-Critical Systems*, Springer-Verlag, 1993, pp. 217-231.

[60] Lyu, M. (ed.) *Handbook of Software Reliability Engineering*, McGraw Hill/IEEE Computer Society Press, 1996.

[61] Lyu, M. (ed.) *Software Fault Tolerance*, John Wiley and Sons, Inc. 1995.

[62] McDermid, J.A., Nicholson, M., Pumfrey, D.J. and Fenelon, P. "Experience with the Application of HAZOP to Computer-Based Systems," *Proceedings of the 10th Annual IEEE Conference on Computer Assurance*, June 1995, pp. 37–48.

[63] McDermid, J.A. "Issues in the Development of Safety-Critical Systems," *Safety-Critical Systems*, Chapman & Hall, 1993, pp. 16–42.

[64] McGettrick, A. "The IEE Draft Policy on Educational Requirements for Safety-Critical Systems Engineers," *Safety-Critical Systems*, Chapman & Hall, 1993, pp. 160–166.

[65] Melton, A. *Software Measurement*, International Thomson Computer Press, 1996.

[66] Moore, C. "Medical Radiological Incidents: the Human Element in Complex Systems," *Safety Systems*, Vol. 5, No. 2, Jan. 1996, pp. 4–6.

[67] Musa, J. *Software Reliability Engineering*, McGraw Hill, 1999.

[68] Norman, D. *The Psychology of Everyday Things*, Basic Books, 1988.

[69] Pant, H., Franklin, P. and Everett, W. "A Structured Approach to Improving Software-Reliability Using Operational Profiles," *Proceedings of the 1994 Annual Reliability and Maintainability Symposium*, Anaheim, pp. 142–146.

[70] Parkinson, J.S. "Classification of Programmable Electronic Systems Operation for Testability," *Directions in Safety-Critical Systems*, Springer-Verlag, 1993, pp. 67–83.

[71] Peterson, James L. *Petri-Net Theory and the Modelling of Systems*, Prentice Hall, 1981.

[72] Petroski, H. *To Engineer is Human: the Role of Failure in Successful Design*, St. Martin's Press, 1985.

[73] Plat, N., van Katwijk, J., and Toetenel, H. "Application and Benefits of Formal Methods in Software Development," *Software Engineering Journal*, Sep. 1992, pp. 335–346.

[74] Poulin, J. *Measuring Software Reuse: Principles, Practices, and Economic Models*, Addison-Wesley, 1997.

[75] Raheja, D. *Assurance Technologies: Principles and Practices*, Chapter 9, McGraw Hill, 1991, pp. 261–312.

[76] Raheja, D. "Software Failure Mode Effects Analysis (FMEA) and Fault Tree Analysis (FTA)," *Safety and Reliability for Medical Device Software*, Health Industries Manufacturers Association (HIMA) Report No. 95-8, 1995, tab 4.

[77] Redmill, F. and Dale, C. *Life Cycle Management for Dependability*, Springer-Verlag, 1997.

[78] Rees, R.A. "Detectability of Software Failure," *Reliability Review*, Vol. 14, No. 4, Dec. 1994, pp. 10–30.

[79] Reliability Analysis Center (RAC), *Introduction to Software Reliability: A State-of-the-Art Review*, 1997.

[80] Rugg, G. "Why Don't Customers Tell You Everything You Need to Know? or: Why Don't Software Engineers Build What You Want?," *Safety Systems*, Sep. 1995, Vol. 5, No. 1, pp. 3–4.

[81] Salisbury, N. "What is the Value of Independence?" *Safety Systems*, Jan. 1995, Vol. 4, No. 2, pp. 7–8.

[82] Stalhane, T. "Safety Analysis in SINTEF Information," *Safety Systems*, Vol. 7, No. 1, Sep. 1997, pp. 1–6.

[83] Stamatis, D.H. *Failure Mode and Effect Analysis: FMEA from Theory to Execution*, ASQC Press, 1995.

[84] Storey, N. *Safety-Critical Computer Systems*, Addison-Wesley, 1996.

[85] System Safety Society (USA), *System Safety Analysis Handbook*, 1993.

[86] Thomas, J. "An Industry View of Training Requirements for Safety-Critical Systems Professionals," *Safety-Critical Systems*, Chapman & Hall, 1993, pp. 173–180.

[87] van der Muelen, M.J.P. *Definitions for Hardware/Software Reliability Engineers*, Simtech b.v., 1995.

[88] Walker, E. "Software/Hardware Reliability—Bridging the Communication Gap," *RAC Journal*, Vol. 4, 2nd quarter, 1996.

[89] Whitty, R. "How Did Software Get So Reliable Without Proof?" *System Safety*, Vol. 4, No. 2, Jan. 1995, pp. 12–14.

[90] Wichmann, B. *Objective Test Criteria: Some Proposals for Bespoke Software*, National Physics Lab, U.K., NPL Report CISE 16/98, Mar. 1998.

[91] Wichmann, B. "Producing Critical Systems—the Ada 9X Solution," *Technology and Assessment of Safety Critical Systems*, Springer-Verlag, 1994.

[92] Zier, D. and Herrmann, D. "ODE Review of Software Development and Quality Assurance," *Proceedings of Indiana Medical Device Manufacturers Council (IMDMC) Software Validation Seminar*, May 16, 1995.

Part II

Approaches Promoted by Key Industrial Sectors to Software Safety and Reliability

Part II examines in detail current approaches to software safety and reliability promoted by key industrial sectors: transportation, aerospace, defense, nuclear power, and biomedical. Collectively these industries represent the broadest possible spectrum of technology and mission critical systems. The approaches promoted by these industrial sectors are examined against a standard template. Each section opens with a brief discussion of how the standard was developed and a definition of its scope or applicability. A detailed description of the standard's approach to software safety and reliability is next. This description focuses on:

- practices recommended and required by the standard;

- interaction with system safety and other standards;

- designated roles, responsibilities, and qualifications of project members;

- data items which are produced by following the standard;

- how compliance to the standard is assessed; and

- the ability (or inability) of the standard to be scaled to match the size and complexity of a project.

A discussion of the strengths of the standard, areas for improvement, and the results observed to date follow—in other words, an examination of how successfully the standard has moved from theory to practice. Each chapter concludes with a summary of the information presented, discussion problems, and pointers to related resources.

Chapter 3

Transportation Industry

Recently it was announced on *CBS Evening News* that automobile accidents will be the third leading cause of death for adults under the age of 45 by the turn of the century. In a related development Metro, the subway system serving the Washington, D.C. metropolitan area, experienced a 40-minute central computer crash during rush hour on April 23, 1998. The central computer system tracks train positions and controls signals and switches. It performs a safety-critical function when problems arise in which trains must stop in tunnels or between stations and/or switch to single track operations. As reported in *The Washington Post* [31], initially computer screens in the control room went blank, then they "began displaying double images for each train. ... workers were dispatched to locations throughout the [90-mile] rail system in case they were needed to manually operate signals and switches that guide trains." On April 29, 1998 *WTOP News* reported that the computer system had crashed 50 times between February 1997 and April 1998 and that the developer of the $21.5M system would not be paid.

As these examples illustrate, software has come to play an increasingly prevalent and important role in ground-based transportation systems, such as commuter trains and automobiles which are used daily by millions of people. Software performs many safety-critical control and monitoring functions in today's rail transit systems. Likewise, software controls many disparate safety-critical and safety-related functions in today's automobiles. Ground-based transportation exists in many forms, from subcompact automobiles to 18-wheel tractor trailers and commuter trains, as shown in Figure 3.1. (The discussion in this chapter excludes off-highway and similar vehicles. Current software safety and reliability standards do not apply to them.) There is also a wide variety in the types of operators of ground-based transportation systems, from occasional "Sunday drivers" to professionals, as shown in Figure 3.2.

Ground-based transportation systems have several unique software safety and reliability concerns compared to the aerospace (Chapter 4), biomedical (Chapter 7), and nuclear power (Chapter 6) industries. Since ground-based transportation systems operate in the natural environment, they must operate safely and reliably under extreme and unpredictable climatic conditions. Because of the speed at which such systems operate, the weight involved, space constraints, and the number of systems operating concurrently, response times and distances are crucial. There is a wide variety in the skill level for both operators and maintenance staff, particularly for automobiles. There are unique concerns when analyzing the cause of system failures and the subsequent cause of injuries.

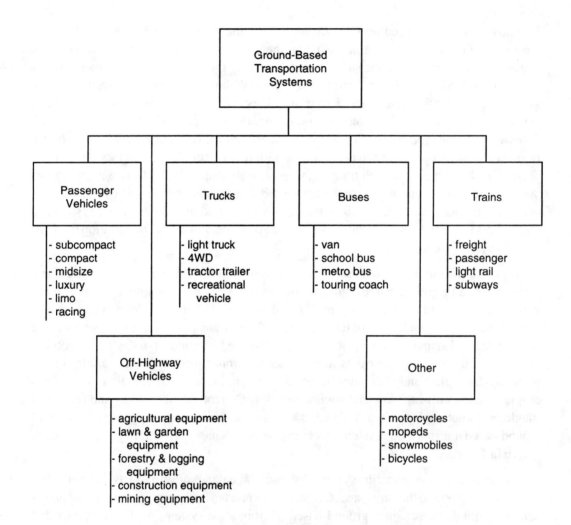

Figure 3.1: Types of ground-based transportation systems.

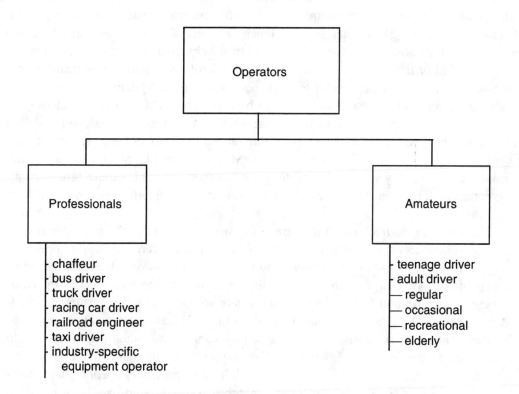

Figure 3.2: Types of operators for ground-based transportation systems.

Four high-level factors determine the safe and reliable operation of ground-based transportation systems:

1. road or track conditions;

2. weather conditions;

3. skill level and attentiveness of operators and maintenance staff; and

4. safety and reliability of the vehicle design.

As R. Rivett [26] observes, manufacturers can only address the design and construction of a vehicle; they cannot control the road infrastructure, weather, or the ability and behavior of a driver. Hence, designers and manufacturers of ground-based transportation systems can only address the fourth factor and then only when a system is new. Once a system is sold or fielded, manufacturers have no control over operation or maintenance. Accidents, sometimes fatal, are far too common in which the system design was not at fault, but rather inadequate maintenance had been performed. Research is underway to develop features which compensate for road conditions, weather conditions, and unskilled and unsafe operators. Many of these new features are software controlled; a recent example is the introduction of antilock braking systems. M. Lowson and C. Medus [24] agree that manufacturers can only address the fourth factor. As they point out manufacturers can try to compensate for the third factor, but risk hysteresis and legal liability concerns may deter or prevent their success.

Weather and road/track conditions are not a major concern for the safe operation of biomedical systems or nuclear power plants. Weather is a concern for the safe operation of aerospace systems, but not road/track conditions. Air traffic is very dense around major metropolitan airports; in some instances landings and takeoffs occur at 5 second intervals. However, centralized air traffic control systems monitor and direct flight patterns. In addition, commercial airplanes are equipped with collision detection and avoidance systems. There are no centralized car traffic control systems—cars are individually operated; nor do automobiles have collision detection or avoidance systems. Furthermore, in the aerospace, biomedical, and nuclear power industries the skill level of personnel operating and maintaining equipment is strictly regulated; this is not the case for ground-based transportation systems. Hence, ground-based transportation systems operate in a unique operational scenario.

Ground-based transportation systems have many unique technical concerns. The majority of ground-based transportation software is present in real-time embedded systems, which have minimal user interface instrumentation. R. Cook [20] describes the use of software in British Railways:

> ... software in data tables and program code is used extensively on modern railway systems. This includes systems regarded as the most essential to safety such as the signalling system, where it is crucial to the safety of the line. Most of the control functions employ software and substantial computing power exists at the service control centre and each station.

J. Tilloston [29] reports that, "In recent years most railway safety-related activities have been regulated and problems have moved from being purely technical to being more information driven." Many railway control and protection systems are configured by data. They are initialized from regulatory type-approved generic software and application specific data. Hence the software integrity depends on the correctness of the data, which may include information such as track layout, signal locations, speed limitations, and signalling control tables. J. Lindberg [23] cites other examples of computer-controlled railway systems used in the Swedish State Railways, such as computer-controlled interlocking systems and automatic train control systems.

This chapter discusses three standards which have been developed to address the unique software safety and reliability concerns of ground-based transportation systems:

- EN 50128:1997, Railway Applications: Software for Railway Control and Protection Systems, the European Committee for Electrotechnical Standardisation (CENELEC).

- Development Guidelines for Vehicle-Based Software, The Motor Industry Software Reliability Association (MISRA™), November 1994.

- JA 1002 Software Reliability Program Standard, Society of Automotive Engineers (SAE), 1998.

3.1 EN 50128:1997, Railway Applications: Software for Railway Control and Protection Systems

3.1.1 Background

EN 50128 was prepared by subcommittee (SC) 9XA of CENELEC technical committee (TC) 9X. It is part of a group of standards which address the safety and reliability concerns of railway systems, as shown in Figure 3.3.

CENELEC standards are recognized as "European Norms," as the "EN" designation implies. Member countries "are bound to comply" with CENELEC standards and give them "the status of a national standard without any alteration [1, 2]." Current member countries include: Austria, Belgium, Denmark, Finland, France, Germany, Greece, Iceland, Ireland, Italy, Luxembourg, Netherlands, Norway, Portugal, Spain, Sweden, Switzerland, and the U.K. A draft version of this standard, prEN 50128, was issued November 1995 for balloting by the member countries. Balloting closed May 15, 1996 and the standard was subsequently approved.

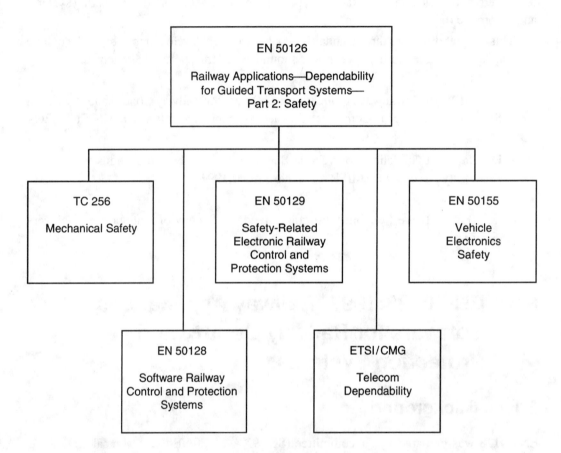

Figure 3.3: Structure of CENELEC Railway Dependability Standards [2].

3.1.2 Purpose and Scope

EN 50128 was specifically developed to identify "methods which need to be used in order to provide software which meets the demands for safety and integrity [1]." The EN 50126 group of standards were written and adopted for several reasons [2]:

1. to define a process for the specification and demonstration of dependability requirements for the railway industry.

2. to promote a common understanding and approach to the management of dependability.

3. to provide Railway Authorities and the railway support industry, throughout the European Community, with a process which will enable the implementation of a consistent approach to the management of reliability, availability, maintainability, and safety (RAMS).

4. to facilitate assessment of the dependability interactions between elements of complex railway applications.

The EN 50126 group of standards are intended to be used by the Railway Authorities and the railway support industry in CENELEC member countries. These standards apply to [1, 2]:

- the specification and demonstration of dependability for all railway applications, complete systems and routes and/or individual subsystems and components;

- all phases of the development and operational lifecycle;

- modification, extension, and decommissioning of applications in operation prior to creation of this standard;

- procedures and technical requirements for the development of programmable electronic systems (PES) used in railway control and protection systems, including safety-critical, safety-related, and nonsafety-related software; and

- software and the interaction between software and the wider system, including applications software, operating systems, support tools, firmware, and COTS software.

This group of standards does not specify RAMS targets for railway systems, certification rules to be used by the approving authority, or a particular software development lifecycle.

3.1.3 Description

EN 50128 is organized around the concept of software integrity levels (SILs). An SIL is equivalent to the level of risk associated with the use of a software system; that is, the SIL is allocated as part of the overall system risk. There are five qualitative SILs:

0 nonsafety related,

1 low,

2 medium,

3 high, and

4 very high.

According to the standard, the higher the SIL, the less likely it is that a dangerous failure of a software system will be caused by a software specification or design fault [1]. All modules are treated as though they belong to the highest SIL specified, unless partitioning can be demonstrated. The SIL for a particular system, subsystem, or component must be stated in the software requirements specification.

Since SILs correlate to risk, EN 50126 defines a detailed risk classification scheme which utilizes a combination of qualitative and quantitative measures. EN 50126 defines six probability levels [2]:

- **Incredible:** extremely unlikely to occur. It can be assumed that the hazard may not occur.

- **Improbable:** unlikely to occur but possible. It can be assumed the hazard may exceptionally occur.

- **Remote:** likely to occur at some time in system lifecycle. It can be reasonably expected for the hazard to occur.

- **Occasional:** likely to occur several times. The hazard can be expected to occur several times.

- **Probable:** will occur several times. The hazard can be expected to occur often.

- **Frequent:** likely to occur frequently. The hazard will be continually experienced.

EN 50126 defines four safety hazard severity levels in terms of both "consequence to persons" and "consequence to service [2]:"

- **Catastrophic:** fatalities and/or multiple severe injuries. Loss of one or more major systems.

- **Critical:** single fatality or severe injury. Loss of a major system.

- **Marginal:** minor injury. Severe system(s) damage.

- **Insignificant:** possible single minor injury. System damage.

EN 50126 correlates the hazard probability levels and safety hazard severity levels into four risk regions: intolerable, undesirable, tolerable, and negligible. The standard prescribes the appropriate response to each risk region. Risks in the intolerable region "shall be eliminated [2]." Risks in the undesirable region "shall only be accepted when risk reduction is impracticable and with the agreement of the Railway Authority [2]." Risks in the tolerable region are "acceptable with adequate control and the agreement of the Railway Authority." Risks in the negligible region are "acceptable with agreement of the Railway Authority [2]."

EN 50128 assigns lifecycle activities, techniques, and measures to be performed throughout the lifecycle based on the SIL to be achieved and assessed. The activities, techniques, and measures are grouped for SILs 1–2 and SILs 3–4 and listed as M - mandated, HR - highly recommended, R - recommended, NR - not recommended, and F - forbidden. Table 3.1 summarizes this information.

The standard points out that adherence to ISO 9001 and ISO 9000-3, while mandated, only result in SIL 0. The MISRA™ Guidelines make the same observations. Tilloston [29] reports the activities undertaken to make the British Rail Business Systems (BRBS), Ltd. compliant with ISO 9001 and EN 50128, which are listed below. He notes that these activities "have been built into the QMS as a strengthening of existing practices rather than as an extra level of imposed bureaucracy [29]."

- the whole system safety process for a project is overseen by an 'Assessor' who is independent of the software development part of the organization;

- planned and actual staff competencies are documented;

- a 'System Safety Requirements Specification' is produced before work starts—together with the corresponding verification plan;

- each safety-related project is ISO 9001 audited;

- more documentation is produced than for nonsafety systems;

- more attention is paid to formal verification and validation; and

- completed software is tested against System Safety Requirements.

EN 50128 does not specify or conversely prohibit a particular software development methodology. The standard identifies seven lifecycle phases: requirements specification, architecture specification, design and development, software/hardware integration, validation, assessment, and maintenance. Two activities are ongoing throughout these lifecycle phases: verification and quality assurance. The standard assumes that the software development lifecycle begins after system-level functional, performance, safety, reliability, and security requirements have been allocated to software.

Requirements Specification

The purpose of the requirements specification phase is to refine and decompose the system-level requirements allocated to software. EN 50128 references ISO/IEC 9126 to identify categories of requirements that are applicable to railway control and protection systems: functional, performance, safety, reliability, and security. Other characteristics to be evaluated include: maintainability, efficient use of resources, usability, and portability. The project team should ensure that the requirements address all of these concerns. EN 50128 states that requirements should have the following quality attributes: completeness, consistency, accuracy, unambiguousness, understandability, and verifiability.

The standard requires that the following activities be accomplished during the requirements specification phase. The SIL must be specified for all software components whether or not they are safety related. All interfaces (internal, external, software, and hardware) must be specified. All modes of operation, including normal, abnormal, degraded-mode, and failure mode must be specified. Hardware, software, and environmental constraints must be specified. The degree of hardware and software fault tolerance needed to achieve the stated SIL must be specified. In addition, the extent of continual and periodic monitoring of safety-critical and safety-related functions required must be specified.

The standard identifies the following techniques and measures to use during the requirements specification phase. The standard states that "one or more of these techniques shall be selected to satisfy the Software Integrity Level [1]:"

- Structured methodologies, such as: JSD, MASCOT, SADT, SDL, SSADM, and Yourdon are highly recommended for SILs 1–4.

- Formal methods, such as CCS, CSP, HOL, LOTOS, OBJ, Temporal Logic, VDM, Z and semiformal methods are recommended for SILs 1–2 and highly recommended for SILs 3–4.

The outputs of the requirements specification phase are the software requirements specification and the initial requirements traceability matrix (RTM). The RTM is updated throughout the lifecycle to demonstrate that all requirements have been met.

Architecture Specification

The purpose of the architecture specification phase is to analyze the feasibility of and options for achieving the stated SIL.

The standard requires that the following activities be accomplished during the architecture specification phase. Beginning with the requirements specification, each software component should be identified and labelled as new, preexisting, or proprietary software. The SIL of each component must be stated and an indication given of whether it is safety critical, safety related, or nonsafety related. The conditions under which preexisting software was validated should be documented. Above SIL 0, the use of preexisting software must be justified. This justification should include an analysis of the impact of using preexisting software on the rest of the system, particularly in regard to validation and verification

Techniques and Measures	SIL 1–2	SIL 3–4	Lifecycle Phase(s)
Structured Methodologies (JSD, MASCOT, SADT, SDL, SSADM, Yourdon)	HR	HR	Requirements Specification Design and Development
Formal Methods (CCS, CSP, HOL, LOTOS, OBJ, Temporal Logic, VDM, Z)	R	HR	Requirements Specification Design and Development Verification
AI Dynamic Reconfiguration	NR	NR	Architecture Specification
Safety Bags Recovery Blocks Retry Fault Recovery	R	R	Architecture Specification
Partitioning Defensive Programming Fault Detection and Diagnosis Error Detection Failure Assertion Diverse Programming SFMECA, SFTA	R	HR	Architecture Specification
Design and Coding Standards Data Recording and Analysis	HR	M	Design and Development Maintenance
Object-oriented Analysis and Design (OOAD)	R	R	Design and Development
Modular Approach	M	M	Design and Development
Static Analysis Dynamic Analysis	HR	HR	Verification
Software Quality Metrics	R	R	Verification
Functional Testing	HR	HR	Software/Hardware Integration Validation
Probabalistic Testing Performance Testing	R	HR	Software/Hardware Integration Validation
Modelling	R	R	Validation
Checklists Static Analysis Field Trials	HR	HR	Assessment
Dynamic Analysis SFMECA, SFTA Common Cause Failure Analysis	R	HR	Assessment
Cause Consequence Diagrams Event Tree Analysis Markov Modelling Reliability Block Diagrams	R	R	Assessment
Change Impact Analysis	HR	M	Maintenance

Table 3.1: EN 50128 assignment of techniques and measures by SIL and lifecycle phase [1].

requirements. A strong preference is stated for modules developed according to this standard.

The goal is to derive a strategy for developing software so that it meets the specified SIL by achieving a balance between avoiding and handling faults. The standard identifies the following techniques and measures to use or not use during the architecture specification phase [1]:

- The use of artificial intelligence and dynamic software reconfiguration is not recommended for SILs 1–4.

- Safety bag techniques, recovery blocks, and retry fault recovery is recommended for SILs 1–4.

- The use of partitioning, defensive programming, fault detection and diagnosis, error detection, failure assertion, diverse programming, software FMECA, and software FTA are recommended for SILs 1–2 and highly recommended for SILs 3–4.

It should be noted that all modules are treated as through they belong to the highest SIL specified, unless partitioning can be demonstrated. The outputs of the architecture phase are the architecture specification and the updated RTM.

Design and Development Phase

The purpose of the software design and development phase is to [1]: 1) design and implement software that meets the stated SIL, and 2) select a suitable set of tools to assist during verification, validation, assessment, and maintenance.

The standard requires that the following activities be accomplished during the software design and development phase. Beginning with the requirements specification, architecture specification, and quality assurance plan, requirements are further decomposed into modules which are analyzable, verifiable, maintainable, and understandable. The goal is to keep module size and complexity to a minimum. A design method should be chosen which facilitates abstraction, modularity, and complexity control. The design must clearly and precisely detail functionality, data structures, inter- and intra-module information flow, and the sequencing and timing of events including interrupt handling. The design should facilitate maintainability through modularity and the use of information hiding and encapsulation. Coding standards must be developed and used which specify good programming practices, describe procedures for documenting source code, and proscribe unsafe language features. Coding standards should be included in the Software Quality Assurance Plan. Module testing should be conducted to demonstrate whether or not specified functions and interfaces perform correctly.

The automated tool environment which will be used throughout the lifecycle is selected during the design and development phase. This includes but is not limited to the selection of a language, a compiler which implements that language, modelling tools, and automatic testing tools. The goal is to have an integrated suite of tools to minimize the introduction of errors when transferring information from one tool to the next. The choice of a language must be justified in the Software Quality Assurance Plan. The language should be appropriate for the design method, target architecture, and should facilitate error detection. The compiler selected must be certified to a national or international standard.

The standard identifies the following techniques and measures to use during software design and development and states that "a suitable set of techniques shall be chosen according to the SIL [1]:"

- A modular approach is mandated for SILs 1–4.

- Design and coding standards, data recording, and analysis are highly recommended for SILs 1–2 and mandated for SILs 3–4.

- Semiformal methods, structured methodologies (JSD, MASCOT, SADT, SDL, SSADM, and Yourdon), strongly typed programming languages, functional testing, performance testing, and interface testing are highly recommended for SILs 1–4.

- Formal methods (CCS, CSP, HOL, LOTOS, OBJ, Temporal Logic, VDM, and Z) are recommended for SILs 1–2 and highly recommended for SILs 3–4.

- Object-oriented programming is recommended for SILs 1–4.

The outputs of the design and development phase are: the software design specification, software module specification, software design test specification, source code and supporting documentation, software module test report, and the updated RTM.

Software/Hardware Integration Phase

The purpose of the software/hardware integration phase is to demonstrate that the software and hardware interact correctly to perform the specified functions and meet the specified SIL and safety requirements.

The standard requires that the following activities be accomplished during the software/hardware integration phase. A software/hardware integration plan must be developed from the specifications which were produced earlier in the lifecycle. The plan should allocate the software components into progressive integration levels. The types of tests to be performed at each integration level should be identified, along with the test cases, test data, test environment, and test completion and acceptance criteria. An analysis of the impact of making changes in response to incorrect testing results and the extent of reverification needed must be performed.

The results of the software/hardware integration phase must include:

- the results observed for each integration level;

- an indication of whether or not the success criteria was met;

- a list of failures and an analysis of their root causes; and

- the necessary evidence to support the above conclusions.

This information must be recorded in an auditable form.

The standard identifies the following techniques and measures to use during software/-hardware integration [1]:

- Functional testing is highly recommended for SILs 1–4.

- Performance testing is recommended for SILs 1–2 and highly recommended for SILs 3–4.

The outputs of the software/hardware integration phase are the software/hardware integration plan, the software/hardware integration report, and the updated RTM.

Software Validation Phase

The purpose of the software validation phase is to determine whether or not the integrated system complies with specified functional, performance, safety, reliability, and security requirements and achieves the stated SIL.

The standard requires that the following activities be accomplished during the software validation phase. A software validation plan must be developed using artifacts which were produced earlier in the lifecycle. The selected validation strategy should be justified in response to the stated SIL. The use of complementary static and dynamic, analytical and statistical, manual and automated techniques should be explained. The plan should identify how the adequacy of lifecycle artifacts to fulfill stated safety requirements and the SIL will be demonstrated. The required inputs, sequences, values, expected outputs, and acceptance criteria for all test cases, under normal and abnormal conditions, must be specified in the validation plan. The development of the validation plan should be coordinated with the assessor to ensure its completeness and accuracy.

The results of executing the plan must be documented in a software validation report, which is maintained in an auditable form. The software validation report should indicate whether or not the SIL and safety requirements have been achieved and acceptance criteria have been met. All failures observed should be recorded with an analysis of their root causes. Any discrepancies found and the corresponding corrective action taken should be recorded. The results of the validation phase should be analyzed and interpreted by an independent party, as required by the SIL.

The standard requires the following techniques and measures to be used during software validation [1]:

- Functional testing is highly recommended for SILs 1–4.

- Probabilistic and performance testing is recommended for SILs 1–2 and highly recommended for SILs 3–4.

- Modelling is recommended for SILs 1–4.

Software Assessment Phase

The purpose of the software assessment phase is to determine whether or not the software lifecycle processes and resulting products meet the stated SIL and are "fit for use" in the intended operational environment.

The standard requires that the following activities be accomplished during the software assessment phase. All lifecycle artifacts must be independently assessed, as required by the SIL, to ascertain whether or not they are fit for the intended purpose and respond correctly to safety issues. The assessment must determine if the appropriate techniques and measures have been selected and applied during each phase. Furthermore, the assessment must evaluate the effectiveness of the scope and content of the software validation plan; additional validation and verification activities may be asked for if needed. If any software components have been assessed previously, a determination must be made to confirm that the previous assessment satisfies the current SIL and operational environment; if not, those components must be reassessed.

A report must be produced for each assessment. This report should analyze and interpret the results observed without providing guidance on the corrective action needed. The report should highlight whether or not the stated SIL was achieved and list all nonconformities.

The standard identifies the following techniques and measures to be used during the software assessment phase [1]:

- Checklists, static analysis, and field trials are highly recommended for SILs 1–4.

- Dynamic analysis, software FTA, software FMECA, and common cause failure analysis are recommended for SILs 1–2 and highly recommended for SILs 3–4.

- Cause consequence diagrams, event tree analysis, Markov modelling, and reliability block diagrams are recommended for SILs 1–4.

The outputs of the software assessment phase are the software assessment plan, the software assessment report, and the updated RTM.

Software Maintenance Phase

The purpose of the software maintenance phase is to "preserve the required SIL and dependability when making corrections, enhancements, or adaptations [1]." As Cook [20] states, "No railway can be dependable ... unless dependability continues to be managed throughout the service life."

The standard states that "maintainability shall be designed into" products and that all maintenance activities shall be conducted in accordance with ISO 9000-3. Procedures must be established for: reporting errors; analyzing the impact of making changes; authorizing changes to be made; and verifying, validating, and assessing all changes made. Maintenance activities should be performed with the same "level of expertise, tools, documentation, planning, and management as the initial development [1]." The standard also requires that all maintenance activities be audited.

A software maintenance record must be produced for each item changed prior to its release. This record is required to include: the change request, references to all related software that was changed, an analysis of the consequences of the change, the test cases needed to support the revalidation and regression testing for the stated SIL, a complete software configuration history, and updated specifications.

The standard identifies the following techniques and measures to use during the software maintenance phase [1]:

- Change impact analysis and data recording and analysis are highly recommended for SILs 1–2 and mandated for SILs 3–4.

The outputs of the software maintenance phase are the software maintenance records, associated updated specifications, and updated RTM.

Software Verification Activity

The purpose of the software verification phase is to "... evaluate products of a given phase to ensure correctness and consistency with respect to the products and standards provided to that phase, as appropriate for the stated SIL [1]." The software verification activity is ongoing throughout the seven lifecycle phases.

The standard requires that the following tasks be accomplished throughout the software verification activity. A software verification plan must be written and executed to establish the verification strategies, techniques, and acceptance criteria for each phase. Methods to be used to establish the correctness and consistency of the inputs of each phase must be described. The use of automated tools and the roles and responsibilities of those involved in the verification process must be described. An analysis of how verification activities demonstrate whether or not functional, performance, safety, reliability, and security requirements and the stated SIL have been (or will be) achieved should be included in the plan.

A verification report must be written for each phase, as shown below, which documents observed errors, deficiencies, and nonconformances to specifications and the Software Quality Assurance Plan [1]:

- The software requirements verification report should record the adequacy of the derived requirements to satisfy the requirements allocated to software from the system requirements specification, system safety requirements specification, and the Software Quality Assurance Plan. It should also indicate whether or not the test specification is a complete and accurate representation of the software requirements specification.

- The software architecture verification report should document the ability of the architecture to fulfill the software requirements specification.

- The software design and development verification report should document the consistency and completeness of the design to meet the software requirements and architecture specifications. An evaluation of the feasibility of meeting performance, testability, readability, and maintainability requirements should be included. Conformance to coding standards should be assessed. The results of component testing should be documented, analyzed, and interpreted. A determination of whether the stated SIL will be met should be documented.

- The software/hardware integration verification report should document the results of integration testing and provide an analysis and interpretation of them.

The standard identifies the following techniques and measures to use during verification activities [1]:

- Static and dynamic analysis are highly recommended for SILs 1–4.

- Formal proofs and probabilistic testing are recommended for SILs 1–2 and highly recommended for SILs 3–4.

- The use of software quality metrics is recommended for SILs 1–4.

The outputs of the ongoing verification activity are the software verification plan, the software verification reports, and the updated RTM.

Software Quality Assurance Activity

The purpose of the software quality assurance activity is to "identify, monitor, and control all activities, technical and managerial, which are necessary to ensure that the software achieves the specified SIL" and functional, performance, safety, reliability, and security requirements [1]. The software quality assurance activity provides a qualitative defense against systematic errors and ensures that evidence, in terms of auditable reports and artifacts, is available for the validation and assessment phases.

The standard requires that the following tasks be accomplished throughout the software quality assurance activity. The railway support industry is mandated to be certified to ISO 9001 in accordance with ISO 9000-3. A Software Quality Assurance Plan is required which defines the lifecycle model, software development methodology, quality activities for each phase, and organizational responsibility for them. The Software Quality Assurance Plan should define the documentation tree and standards, review procedures, coding standards, and software quality metrics to be collected and analyzed. Furthermore, this plan should establish procedures for reporting problems and monitoring corrective action.

Software configuration management is mandated to be conducted in accordance with ISO 9000-3. The Software Configuration Management Plan should explain how unauthorized changes, duplication, and transfer of artifacts will be prevented, pre- and post-release, in order to maintain the integrity of versions, baselines, and builds.

The outputs of the software quality assurance activity are the Software Quality Assurance Plan, the Software Configuration Management Plan, coding standards, software development plan, software maintenance plan, audit and inspection reports, and quality assurance records.

Interaction with System Safety and Other Standards

As illustrated earlier in Figure 3.3, EN 50128 is part of a group of standards which were developed to specifically address safety and reliability concerns of railway systems. EN 50126 is the top or level one standard. EN 50128, which focuses on software concerns, is one of several existing or planned level 2 standards. EN 50128 includes the standards listed below as normative references. Normative references are incorporated by reference and form part of the standard which references them. This practice eliminates version control problems and the need to repeat information, since the latest version is always incorporated.

- EN 29001: Quality Systems – Model for quality assurance in design, development, production, installation, and servicing, CENELEC.

- EN 29000-3: Quality Management and Quality Assurance Standards; Part 3 – Guidelines for the Application of EN 29001 to the development, supply, and maintenance of software, CENELEC.

- EN 50126-2: Railway Applications: Dependability for Guided Transport Systems – Part 2: Safety, CENELEC.

- EN 50129: Railway Applications – Safety-related Electronic Railway Control and Protection Systems, CENELEC.

- ISO/IEC 9126: Information Technology – Software Product Evaluation – Quality Characteristics and Guidelines for their use.

- IEC 50(191): International Electrotechnical Vocabulary, Chapter 191, Dependability and Quality of Service.

EN 50126 assumes that the "Railway Authorities and railway support industry have business-level policies addressing quality, performance, and safety [2]." The standard is consistent with the quality management requirements in the ISO 9000 series and mandates adherence to ISO 9001 and 9000-3. EN 50128 is similar to IEC 61508 Part 3 (Chapter 8) in that it assigns lifecycle activities, techniques, and measures in response to the specified SIL; the foreword to EN 50128 acknowledges that early drafts of IEC 61508 Part 3 were consulted.

The risk classification scheme promoted by EN 50126 is similar to but does not quite match that of other standards, as the following examples illustrate. The qualitative hazard probability levels are the same as those used by IEC 601-1-4 and MIL-STD-882D. The quantitative values assigned to the probability levels do not match MIL-STD-882D. The names of the hazard severity levels do not match other standards. EN 50126 is unique in assigning quantitative values to hazard severity levels; other standards only assign qualitative values. EN 50126 classifies risk into four regions (intolerable, undesirable, tolerable, and negligible) compared to the three regions associated with the as low as reasonably practicable (ALARP) principle (intolerable, ALARP, and broadly acceptable). This standard is also unique in assigning specific actions in response to particular risk regions.

Roles, Responsibilities, and Qualifications of Project Members

EN 50128 defines requirements for personnel qualifications, organizational responsibilities, and independence of staff functions. The standard requires that all project personnel, including management, "have the appropriate training, experience, and qualifications [1]," which must be justified in relation to the SIL and documented in the Software Quality Assurance Plan. Specific areas of competence for which evidence must be supplied include: software engineering, computer system engineering, safety engineering, engineering skills associated with the specific application domain, and the associated legal and regulatory framework.

The standard stipulates two organizational requirements. First that the "safety process shall be implemented and under the control of the safety organization [1]." Second, the standard stipulates the degree of independence required between developers, verifiers, validators, and assessors according to SIL. Beyond SIL 0, the validation staff must be independent. At all SILs, the assessor must be independent.

Data Items Produced

The purpose of documentation according to EN 50128 is to "structure the development of the lifecycle into defined phases and activities," and "record all information pertinent to the software throughout the lifecycle [1]." A reference numbering schema is to be developed to maintain traceability between predecessor and successor artifacts. The same terminology, abbreviations, and acronyms should be used in all documents. The number of documents will vary depending on the size, complexity, criticality, and SIL of the software produced. Some documents can be combined, if there is no loss of detail, for small less complex projects. For large complex projects it may make sense to subdivide documents. This decision rests with the Railway Authorities. Table 3.2 presents a logical grouping of documentation by phase as specified in EN 50128.

Compliance Assessment

The standard does not provide guidance on how Railway Authorities should perform certification; however, it does specify how to determine compliance with its stated requirements. The standard declares that "...it must be shown that each of the requirements have been satisfied to the SIL defined and therefore the clause objective has been met [1]." For example, if highly recommended techniques and measures are not used the rationale for not doing so must be explained in the Architecture Specification and/or Software Quality Assurance Plan, as appropriate. Likewise, if a technique or measure is proposed for use that is not identified in the standard, its effectiveness and suitability for the prescribed SIL must be justified in the Architecture Specification and/or Software Quality Assurance Plan, as appropriate. Assessors are to determine compliance with the requirements of each particular clause and the techniques and measures applicable to the specified SIL by inspection of the required lifecycle artifacts and witnessing verification and validation activities. The assessment results must be documented in a Software Assessment Report.

PHASE	OUTPUTS
Requirements Specification	Software Requirements Specification Software Requirements Test Specification Software Requirements Verification Report Requirements Traceability Matrix (RTM)
Architecture Specification	Software Architecture Specification Software Architecture Verification Report Updated RTM
Design and Development	Software Design Specification Software Design Test Specification Software Design Verification Report Software Module Specification Software Module Test Specification Software Module Verification Report Source Code Software Module Test Report Updated RTM
Software/ Hardware Integration	Software/Hardware Integration Plan Software/Hardware Integration Report Software/Hardware Integration Verification Report Updated RTM
Validation Phase	Software Validation Plan Software Validation Report Updated RTM
Assessment Phase	Software Assessment Plan Software Assessment Report Updated RTM
Maintenance Phase	Software Maintenance Records Updated Specifications Updated RTM
Verification Activity	Software Verification Plan Software Verification Report (per phase) Updated RTM
Quality Assurance Activity	Software Quality Assurance Plan Software Configuration Management Plan Coding Standards Software Development Plan Software Maintenance Plan Audit and Inspection Reports Quality Assurance Records

Table 3.2: EN 50128 documentation requirements by phase [1].

Scaling

The standard does not address the issue of scaling in regard to the size, complexity, or duration of a project. Instead, the required lifecycle activities, techniques, and measures are scaled according to the specified SIL. These activities, techniques and measures are grouped in three categories:

- SIL 0: nonsafety related

- SIL 1–2: low and medium

- SIL 3–4: high and very high

It is assumed that more rigor is applied to execute and verify activities, techniques, and measures for SIL 2 than SIL 1 and SIL 4 than SIL 3.

3.1.4 Strengths

EN 50128 has several technical and regulatory strengths worth noting. Its major technical strength is the guidance provided about the techniques and measures to use to achieve specified SILs. The techniques and measures are grouped by lifecycle phase and activity. Each technique or measure is given a code prescribing its use for a given SIL: M - mandated, HR - highly recommended, R - recommended, NR - not recommended, and F - forbidden. Annex B of the standard provides brief descriptions of each technique and measure. In all cases there are several options to choose from and complementary combinations of techniques are highlighted. This eliminates the need for each Railway Authority and railway support company to research the effectiveness of these techniques and measures themselves. At the same time, the standard leaves open the possibility of using a technique or measure that is not mentioned so long as it is sufficiently justified in the Software Quality Assurance Plan. This feature will contribute to the longevity of the standard. The comprehensive list of recommendations is similar to IEC 61508-3:1998. No formal studies or data are provided in either document to support these recommendations; instead the recommendations represent an informal industry consensus of 'current best practices.' Lindberg's [23] study for the Swedish Railway System supports the recommendation for diversity: 10 to 20 percent more logical faults were found through the use of diversity; however, overall system availability was lower because of the increased number of restarts.

Another technical strength is that the standard allows developers to select the lifecycle model and software development methodology that is appropriate for their application. The standard specifies the informational content and types of documents to be developed while leaving the document outline and format to the developers. The standard supports the use of electronic and hardcopy documentation, so long as it is readily available for inspection.

EN 50128 promotes a common approach across the European community to achieving and assessing software dependability in railway applications. This simplifies the regulatory task of both the Railway Authorities and the railway support industry. It also facilitates the collection and analysis of consistent metrics by which to improve railway software products and the processes used to develop them.

3.1.5   Areas for Improvement

EN 50128 requires several data items to be developed and assessed throughout the system lifecycle. It would be helpful if the standard provided some guidance on the informational content of these data items, such as pointers to other standards which could be used to satisfy these requirements.

EN 50128 addresses the totality of RAMS, not just reliability. It would be useful if the standard provided guidance on how to assemble and present adequate evidence or proof that a system is safe and reliable; that is, the information needed for certification.

3.1.6   Results Observed to Date

The EN 50126 group of standards was issued during 1997 and 1998. Sufficient time has not been available to conduct a systematic study of the effectiveness of these standards.

3.2   Development Guidelines for Vehicle-Based Software, The Motor Industry Software Reliability Association (MISRA™), November 1994

3.2.1   Background

The Motor Industry Software Reliability Association (MISRA™) Consortium was created in response to an initiative of the U.K. Safety Critical Systems Research Programme. The U.K. Department of Trade and Industry and the Engineering and Physical Sciences Research Council funded the activities of the MISRA™ Consortium. The controlling members of the Consortium are: AB Automotive Electronics, Ltd.; AP Borg and Beck; Delco Electronics; Ford Motor Company; Jaguar Cars, Ltd.; Lotus Engineering; Lucas Enterprises; and Rover Group, Ltd. Rolls Royce and Associates, Ltd.; the Centre for Software Engineering, Ltd.; and the University of Leeds participated in the Consortium as consultants. The Motor Industry Research Association (MIRA) acted as the project manager, under the direction of Dr. David D. Ward.

The MISRA™ Consortium was established to address the unique safety and reliability concerns presented by software, compared to other automotive components. The Guidelines [3] provide several examples of these differences:

- software is not physical

- software has a greater capacity to contain complexity

- software is perceived to be easy to change

- software errors are systematic, not random

The Guidelines [3] also point out differences between automotive software applications and those of other industrial sectors: "...automotive software has an emphasis on data driven algorithms, parameter optimization, adaptive control, and on-board diagnostics."
Eight work groups were formed within the Consortium to address these concerns:

- diagnostics and integrated vehicle systems

- integrity

- noise, EMC, and real time

- software in control systems

- software metrics

- validation and verification

- human factors in software

- subcontracting automotive software

Each work group produced a detailed report [6–14] which provides background information and justification for the recommendations in the Guidelines. According to Rivett [26], the "MISRA™Guidelines represent the current definition of what is 'best practice' in the U.K. for automotive software development and have authority due to the large number of companies and organizations which endorse them."

3.2.2 Purpose and Scope

The MISRA™Guidelines [3] provide assistance to the automotive industry about software safety and reliability issues. While adherence to the Guidelines is voluntary, the goal is to promote a unified approach across the automotive industry. Furthermore, the Guidelines provide a much needed link between automotive engineering and software engineering, especially in relation to safety and reliability issues. Software engineers and managers responsible for the "creation, procurement, and maintenance of embedded vehicle software [3]" comprise the target audience.

As noted by N. Storey [28], "the automotive industry is ... moving toward an increased dependence on computer-based systems." Rivett [26] provides examples of current automotive software applications:

- power train systems

  - engine management
  - transmission control
  - cruise control

- body systems

  - exterior lights
  - wiper systems
  - central locking
  - electric seat controls
  - electric windows
  - security systems

- chassis systems

  - anti-lock braking
  - active suspension

- other

  - air bags
  - sound systems
  - instrument pack
  - heating and ventilation

Storey [28] concludes that "by their very nature most automotive subsystems are safety-related" and predicts "a dramatic increase in the volume of safety-critical software being used in the automotive industry." From their experience on the Computer-Based Automotive Suspension and Steering Systems (CBASS) project, J. Robinson and S. Merad [27] concur, "In any but the most simple automotive control systems, the reliability of the software component is central to the reliability of the system as a whole." The MISRA™ Guidelines were specifically developed to address these challenges.

3.2.3   Description

The MISRA™ Guidelines link software activities to the overall vehicle development life-cycle in an integrated approach. Seven key software activities are identified:

- project planning
- integrity

- requirements specification

- design

- programming

- testing

- product support

Project Planning

The Guidelines place major importance on project planning and view this activity as the time when several critical decisions are made. The project definition, often referred to as concept definition, should include a list of features and functions to be implemented and should identify which are optional, mandatory, and/or regulatory requirements. During project planning, organizational roles and responsibilities should be defined. Process definitions should be approved. The development, review, and approval procedure for life-cycle artifacts should be determined. A software development methodology and lifecycle should be defined and justified. The effect of using automated tools and previously developed software should be evaluated. A software development plan, software safety plan, and a software validation and verification plan should be developed and coordinated with relevant vehicle development plans.

Integrity

An integrity level is assigned per vehicle system and subsystem. The level indicates the system and/or software integrity needed to prevent [3]:

- harm to humans,

- damage to property or the environment,

- financial loss to the owner or manufacturer of a vehicle,

- traffic disruption, and

- laws from being broken.

Integrity levels correspond to the inherent risk from using a system or subsystem. They are derived from an analysis of potential hazards and failure modes and lead to the development of risk mitigation strategies. The MISRA™Guidelines use the same software integrity levels (SILs) as EN 50128 and IEC 61508. As Rivett [26] reports from the Certification and Assessment of Safety-Critical Applications Development (CASCADE) project, the correct assignment of an SIL is crucial.

Automotive software failure management techniques are based on the concept of controllability. The MISRA™Guidelines [3] define controllability as: "the ability of vehicle occupants to control the situation following a failure." Note that the definition refers to the vehicle occupants, not just the driver. Five controllability categories are identified: uncontrollable, difficult to control, debilitating, distracting, and nuisance. The SIL is determined by correlating the controllability of a hazard with the outcome and acceptable failure rate (see Table 3.3). The hazard with the highest controllability category determines the SIL of a system, unless adequate partitioning is demonstrated.

Predicting the outcome of a hazard is most difficult. As Dr. Ward [39] points out:

> In practice, given a particular hazard of a particular controllability category, an enormous range of outcomes are quite feasible (depending on road conditions, weather, other vehicles, pedestrians and a huge range of factors). Therefore it is not right to say that, for example, a "difficult to control" hazard will always lead to a "very severe" outcome. Sometimes (maybe often) there won't be an accident, or just vehicle damage; given particularly unfortunate and unlikely circumstances there might be a catastrophic pile up involving many deaths. The best we can say is that outcomes are "likely to be very severe."

Controllability Category	Definition	Most Likely Outcome	Acceptable Failure Rate	SIL
Uncontrollable	Human action has no effect	Most Likely Extremely Severe	Extremely Improbable	4
Difficult to control	Potential for human action	Most Likely Very Severe	Very Remote	3
Debilitating	Sensible human response	At Worst Severe	Remote	2
Distracting	Operational limitations, normal human response	At Worst Minor	Unlikely	1
Nuisance	Safety not an issue	Customer Dissatisfaction	Reasonably Possible	0

Table 3.3: MISRA™Guidelines correlation between controllability and SILs. (*Source:* Adapted from Table 1, page 18, *Development Guidelines for Vehicle-Based Software*, The Motor Industry Software Reliability Association (MISRA™), November 1994, by permission.)

The MISRA™Guidelines provide guidance for determining the correct approach for meeting and assessing SILs. They make very similar recommendations to those made by

EN 50128 and presented previously in Table 3.1. A few minor differences are worth noting. The Guidelines [3] state that the "...techniques, activities, and their rigour increase with the integrity level. Equally, the weight of the relevant recommendations increases." As a result, the Guidelines distinguish between SIL 1 and 2 and SIL 3 and 4 when making recommendations. For example, stress testing and analysis against deadlock is HR at SIL 3, in addition to the techniques for the software/hardware integration and validation phases. At SIL 4, 100 percent white box, requirements, and integration testing must be performed. All utilities, tools, and compilers must be formally validated and it must be proved that the object code accurately reflects the source code. The MISRA™ Guidelines require that software be designed to support degraded-mode operations; this requirement does not appear in EN 50128. The Guidelines caution against using compilers that are not certified to international standards because of the different ways in which the use of pointers, recursion, and other features can be implemented for the same language, causing unpredictable behavior. In fact, the Guidelines recommend using restricted subsets of compilers at SILs 2–3 and only certified compilers at SIL 4.

Robinson and Merad's [27] experience on the CBASS project supports the recommendation to use formal methods. They also note that "...commercial pressures may mean that some traditional aerospace techniques, such as software redundancy, may not be readily acceptable in automotive sectors." T. Vogel [30] makes a similar observation, "...systems are conceivable for automobiles whose safety requirements are certainly comparable to those for aircraft, even though... their cost may not be allowed to exceed that of a good radio."

Requirements Specification

Specification of requirements is the third key software activity for which the MISRA™ Guidelines make recommendations. The Guidelines emphasize that the software requirements specification is derived from and must be consistent with the system or vehicle specification. To accomplish this goal, the use of integrated product teams is encouraged during the development of the requirements specification.

The Guidelines recommend organizing software requirements into three categories: functional requirements, safety requirements, and nonfunctional requirements. Safety requirements are subdivided into functional safety requirements and safety integrity requirements, using the following hierarchy [3]:

1. functional requirements

2. safety requirements

    2.1 functional safety requirements

    2.2 safety integrity requirements

        2.2.1 error control

        2.2.2 fault avoidance

3. nonfunctional requirements

Functional safety requirements should identify the appropriate response to potential failure conditions. Safety integrity requirements should identify the need for partitioning, diversity, redundancy, condition monitoring, and other design techniques in order to meet error control and fault avoidance goals. Vogel [30] emphasizes the need to specify system limits in relation to software safety requirements. Traceability must be maintained between software safety requirements and the system safety requirements specification.

The Guidelines [3] advise including a thorough analysis of human factors during the safety analysis and provide examples of domain specific issues to evaluate: reaction times, intuitiveness, attentiveness, experience, risk hysteresis, potential subversion of system functions, mental and physical state of driver, and vision or hearing limitations. Vogel [30] provides similar examples of domain specific hazards to evaluate during the safety analysis: dimensioning errors in braking systems, insufficient temperature range in an rpm sensor, and faulty acceleration or deceleration.

The Guidelines provide some industry specific cautions to take into account when developing automotive software requirements. They concern vehicle control systems and electromagnetic conductance (EMC). The validation and verification plan developed during the project planning phase must require that the stability of all vehicle control systems be proved mathematically under all conditions. The software requirements specification should explain how the effects of errors in arithmetic systems, such as switching between fixed point and floating points systems, the accumulation of arithmetic errors, and converting to and from real numbers, will be dealt with to ensure safe and reliable performance. As Vogel [30] cautions:

> The capabilities of modern computerized control units are unquestioned, however they confront us with a number of new problems which have their cause in both the complexity of these systems and in the different failure characteristics of electronic versus mechanical systems... New failure and fault characteristics require new methods of avoiding, recognizing and verifying faults.

MISRA™ Report 3, Noise, EMC, and Real-time [9] presents an in-depth analysis of potential risks associated with EMC and proposes risk mitigation strategies. The software requirements specification must evaluate the impact of EMC on the SIL. As the Guidelines [3] point out, "The most important role that software has in relation to EMC is in providing a means of recovery from the effects of interference." To illustrate, the Guidelines provide the following examples of how software can be used to mitigate the risks of EMC [3]:

- filtering data digitally

- comparing data with constant values, or values inferred from related signals, to identify errors

- identifying and correcting corrupt data

- adjusting scaling factors dynamically to optimize the signal to noise ratio

- detecting and correcting corrupted communications processes and data

Design

Design is the fourth key software activity identified by the MISRA™Guidelines. The design should support traceability backward to the requirements and forward to the validation and verification activities. A detailed safety analysis should be performed while the design is being developed. As the Guidelines state [3]:

> Results from the preliminary safety analysis should be fed into the design at an early stage. The architectural design is at least as important as the detailed design stage in minimizing the effort required to meet safety requirements.

The software should be designed to support extensive fault management features. Integrity and availability requirements should guide the design for degraded-mode operations and determine whether a system should fail safe or fail operational. Partitioning, both physical and logical, and recovery blocks should be used to prevent fault propagation. The controllability category of a hazard should determine system defaults. As the Guidelines state [3]:

> Safety analysis of default states should consider driving situations and how combinations of default states interact with those situations. Safety analysis should also consider the effects of a system reset, so as to maintain a safe state.

The Guidelines recommend a robust design for on-board diagnostics. A combined software FTA and FMECA should be used as the basis for developing an on-board diagnostic strategy. Two types of on-board diagnostics are identified by the Guidelines: diagnostics that provide information to drivers and diagnostics that provide information to maintenance personnel. The diagnostics should relay information about failures such as incorrect sensor signals or actuators not performing as intended. The Guidelines recommend that diagnostic software be designed to transmit sensor data and fault codes on demand. At the same time, the Guidelines caution against overloading or unnecessarily alarming the driver with too much diagnostic information. Care should also be taken to display diagnostic information so that it is meaningful and easily and quickly understood.

Automotive software design should be consistent with system security requirements. Design features should prevent the possibility of unauthorized users having access to, tampering with, or making modifications to the software [3]. For example, only authorized users should be able to alter on-board parameters; the design should preempt attempts by unauthorized users to do so. The Guidelines also caution against the casual replacement of ROMs by unauthorized maintenance facilities. The concern is that they may not understand the system or software design in its totality and unknowingly introduce serious errors.

Automotive software systems operate in both demand-mode and continuous-mode scenarios. As Vogel [30] observes, "vehicles in the luxury class frequently feature more than 50 electronic control units with microprocessors which assist and protect by intervening in operational and driving processes." But there is no 'central computer' controlling, monitoring, or coordinating the execution of these functions.

The Guidelines strongly recommend the use of automated modelling, simulation, and emulation tools to validate the design and design assumptions. These tools are particularly useful in analyzing timing constraints, processor utilization, memory utilization, iterative processes, deadlock conditions, and interrupt handling.

Given the integrity level required for most automotive software, the Guidelines recommend the use of an international standard rather than a proprietary standard for bus communications, such as:

- ISO 11898, Road Vehicles – Interchange of digital information – Controller area network (CAN) for high-speed communication,

- ISO 11519, Road Vehicles – Low-speed serial data communication, and

- SAE Recommended Practice J1850 – Class B Data Communications Network Interface, August 1991.

The use of layered protocols, as promoted by the above standards, will help to isolate and/or alleviate some reliability concerns. As the Guidelines [3] point out, at the physical layer the primary concern is with interfaces, voltage, current, and pin assignments. Cyclical redundancy checks (CRCs), scheduling, and framing are the major issues at the transfer layer. Range checks, plausibility checks, receiving and/or transmitting errors are the key concerns at the application layer. Controller area networks (CANs) are commonly used in vehicles to link control units via a single bus system in order to reduce physical size and weight. However, as reported by Vogel [30], "at 20–30% utilization of bus capacity performance decreases markedly."

Programming

Programming is the fifth key software activity identified in the MISRA™ Guidelines. It is recommended that company standards be developed for module layout, module and data naming conventions, memory usage, interface conventions, software documentation including inline documentation, and design 'best practices.' These standards should be used by all developers working on the project. Adherence to these standards should be evaluated as part of the software inspection process. Project documentation should be developed with the goal of supporting validation and verification activities. A process should be defined for controlling both development and production baselines. In addition, the Guidelines recommend that a compiler be selected carefully; it should be optimized for the target platform and operational environment.

Testing

Testing is the sixth key software activity identified in the MISRA™ Guidelines. In this instance, the term testing encompasses both static and dynamic analysis techniques. The overall testing strategy should be defined in a test plan. The Guidelines [3] recommend that the test plan identify the "I/O conditions, acceptance criteria, limits of operations, likely failure modes, and timing constraints" for each functional requirement. A test strategy should be developed for each category of testing, such as: integration testing, system test, stress testing, safety and security testing, regression testing, and so forth. The Guidelines recommend the use of error seeding, equivalence class partitioning, boundary value analysis, and animated formal specifications during testing.

Product Support

Product support is the seventh and final key software activity identified in the MISRA™Guidelines. It includes in-house software maintenance and support provided by subcontractors and vendors. The Guidelines expect that the same standards, procedures, and degree of rigor will be applied to support activities as were applied during development.

Interaction with System Safety and Other Standards

It is expected that the MISRA™Guidelines will be used in conjunction with other standards. For example, suppliers must meet the requirements of a Quality Management System as defined by ISO 9001 and ISO 9000-3; however, they are reminded that this by itself only satisfies SIL 0. Suppliers and acquirers are expected to be knowledgeable about and to use related automotive standards developed by ISO, IEC, IEE, IEEE, and SAE, such as those mentioned previously for bus communications.

Roles, Responsibilities, and Qualifications of Project Personnel

The MISRA™Guidelines do not define specific responsibilities of project personnel; however, they do distinguish between the functions of supplier, acquirer, and assessor. Requirements for independence are defined which are consistent with EN 50128. The Guidelines are more concerned with personnel competency and present a detailed list of subjects in which project staff must have knowledge and experience: control systems theory, particularly for nonlinear systems; communications systems; software engineering; electrical engineering; mechanical engineering; human factors engineering; regulatory requirements; and professional responsibility.

Compliance Assessment

The Guidelines [3] state up front that "not all recommendations apply to all projects." It is expected, however, that any major deviations from the recommendations will be justified in appropriate lifecycle artifacts. Compliance can easily be verified by analyzing project documentation. As the Guidelines [3] state, "The recommendations given in both these Guidelines and the supporting Reports can be used as a basis of a [compliance] checklist."

Scaling

The Guidelines [3] do not specifically address the issue of scaling. Given the voluntary nature of the Guidelines, it is expected that during negotiations between supplier, acquirer, and assessor the relevant recommendations for a specific project will be identified. It should be remembered, however, that in this instance the primary driver for any scaling will be the target SIL(s), not the size of a project.

3.2.4 Strengths

The MISRA™ Guidelines have several strong points, both technically and programmatically. The Guidelines represent a wealth of domain specific knowledge and insights. The information and recommendations are organized in a logical and easy to understand manner, even for those new to software safety and reliability or automotive software. The Guidelines emphasize that software is part of the total vehicle design, not an end unto itself.

The Reports from the working groups [6–14] provide extensive backup material to support and justify the recommendations in the Guidelines. Report 3, Noise, EMC, and Real-time [9], is particularly noteworthy. It contains a comprehensive analysis of the effects of EMC on automotive software and provides guidance on risk mitigation strategies. Few other industrial sectors have conducted equivalent comprehensive analyses.

The Guidelines provide useful pointers to related automotive standards, such as the ISO and SAE standards for CAN communications. The Guidelines are structured to facilitate their use by suppliers, acquirers, and regulatory assessors. For example, the Guidelines can be used as the basis for a contract between an acquirer and supplier and as the foundation for a regulatory assessment of safety and reliability. This is advantageous because as Rivett [26] notes, "Although some vehicle manufacturers develop their own software, most [automotive] software is written by component suppliers."

3.2.5 Areas for Improvement

A major programmatic strength of the Guidelines is the voluntary nature of their adoption. The extent to which they have been adopted is a credit to and reflection of the composition of the MISRA™ Consortium and its efforts at consensus building. Consequently, the primary way to 'improve' the Guidelines would be to extend their usage outside of the U.K. At the time of writing, the Guidelines have been distributed within both the automotive industry and other sectors, both in the U.K. and elsewhere. They are certainly finding acceptance with European manufacturers and are starting to do so in the U.S.

3.2.6 Results Observed to Date

The MISRA™ Guidelines and supporting Reports were issued in November 1994. One year after the Guidelines were published, a survey was conducted which found that people were beginning to implement them. To date a systematic study has not been conducted of the effectiveness of implementing the Guidelines.

The MISRA™ Consortium has developed plans for future activities and guidelines. For example, in April 1998 a new report was added to the MISRA™ collection:

> Guidelines for the Use of the C Language in Vehicle-Based Software.

It is intended that the Guidelines will have a 10-year lifespan. In the meantime the Consortium is monitoring industry experience. To that end the MISRA™ Guidelines Forum has been established to promote an exchange of information among the automotive industries, automotive support industries, and government regulators. Notices about Forum membership and upcoming meetings are posted on the MISRA™ website:

> www.misra.org.uk

3.3   JA 1002 Software Reliability Program Standard, Society of Automotive Engineers (SAE), July 1998

3.3.1   Background

The G-11 Reliability, Maintainability, Supportability, and Logistics (RMSL) division was established to develop international consensus standards for RMSL, in response to DoD acquisition reforms. G-11 RMSL committees are staffed by international subject matter experts from industry, academia, government, and the military. A standard must undergo balloting within G-11 and by the Aerospace Council to become an approved SAE standard.

The G-11 software committee was chartered to develop two task guides, one for software reliability and another for software supportability. The software reliability task guide consists of:

- SAE JA 1002 Software Reliability Program Standard, 1998, and

- SAE JA 1003 Software Reliability Implementation Guide, 1999.

The software supportability task guide consists of:

- SAE JA 1004 Software Supportability Program Standard, 1998,

- SAE JA 1005 Software Supportability Implementation Guide, 1999,

- SAE JA 1006 Software Support Concept, 1999, and

- SAE AIR 5121 Software Supportability—An Overview, 1997.

The software supportability task guide is a collateral task guide to the software reliability task guide, for example, maintaining the level of reliability to which a system is certified is also a supportability issue. As another example, diversity may be used to enhance reliability during the software development lifecycle. At the same time diversity raises supportability issues during the in-service lifecycle, such as maintaining multiple baselines and performing upgrades in the field.

3.3.2 Purpose and Scope

The charter of the SAE G-11 SW committee was to develop a task guide that is consistent with the SAE G-11 system level reliability program standard, JA 1000, and contains the necessary software-specific information [4]. The standard acknowledges that software is an important component of many mission critical systems and "requires interpretation and variations on RMSL methods used by hardware [4]."

The standard is "intended to be used by industry to address market demands for reliable software products that improve system productivity, time to market, and cost-effective implementation [4]." The standard applies to the predevelopment, development, and the in-service phases of a system. The "JA" designation indicates that an SAE standard applies to both surface vehicles and aerospace applications.

3.3.3 Description

SAE JA 1002 defines the requirements for and structure of an effective software reliability program. The two key components are a Software Reliability Plan and a Software Reliability Case. The plan-case framework identifies the tasks and activities needed to achieve and assess a given level of software reliability, then closes the loop by providing the proof that it was indeed achieved. The software supportability task guide also uses a plan-case framework.

JA 1002 and JA 1003 are not tied to a specific software lifecycle or development methodology. Instead, they speak in terms of three main processes:

- determining customer requirements,

- meeting customer requirements, and

- demonstrating requirements satisfaction.

JA 1003 provides a dictionary of engineering analysis, design, and verification techniques and methods which can be used to achieve and assess software reliability and allocates them to these three processes. The intent is that techniques that are appropriate for the size, scope, complexity, duration, and risk of a project will be chosen and implemented.

SAE JA 1002 [4] makes the observation that:

> A mature software engineering process is necessary but not sufficient for the achievement of software reliability... To provide assurance that software products meet their reliability requirements, a software reliability program should be planned as a specific activity within the software development process.

The Software Reliability Plan covers the complete system lifecycle, from concept through decommissioning. This plan manages and coordinates the software portion of the overall System Reliability Program. It describes the management and technical activities necessary to achieve and demonstrate that stated software reliability requirements have been met. In particular, the strategy for achieving, measuring, monitoring, and reporting the attainment of or progress toward software reliability goals and objectives is explained in the plan.

The standard assigns the supplier responsibility for allocating system reliability requirements to software components. This flexibility is important—it allows the supplier to explore alternatives and, if requested, present the acquirer with options. The standard emphasizes that all requirements should be determined and validated with the acquirer as an interactive process. While analyzing reliability requirements, the developer should work with the acquirer to:

- determine safety-critical functions and their associated integrity requirements;

- identify potential failure modes, particularly those which are prohibited;

- assess the need for and feasibility of degraded-mode operations;

- develop reliability requirements for all known operational profiles, modes, and states; and

- devise a strategy for exception handling.

Throughout this exercise the focus should be on fault prevention and mitigation. As the standard [4] emphasizes, "the achievement and demonstration of software reliability should be design drivers." Since many automotive software control systems operate in demand mode, an accelerated testing strategy should be evaluated. Likewise, MTBFs and MTTRs should be developed for specific operational profiles.

The standard requires that the plan address two important issues which are gaining attention today: software reuse and personnel competency. The use of preexisting software, whether commercial or not, must be evaluated. An assessment must be made of the effect of using preexisting software on meeting reliability goals. Long term supportability issues must be considered. The effect of using preexisting software on a new hardware or software platform and/or in a new operational environment must be analyzed. Lastly, if the preexisting software underwent a prior safety or reliability assessment, a determination should be made about the relevance of that assessment to the proposed new implementation.

The standard requires that the Software Reliability Plan include activities related to personnel competency. This includes an evaluation of the education, experience, and certification needed for staff to perform effectively on a project with the stated reliability goals and objectives. The evaluation should include technical and management staff. Supplemental training requirements should be identified along with a training schedule.

Figure 3.4 provides a sample annotated outline for a Software Reliability Plan.

A Software Reliability Case, as required by JA 1002, captures and organizes the evidence necessary to prove that a software system meets specified reliability requirements. The Software Reliability Case justifies the approach taken in the Software Reliability Plan and proves that the plan has been executed. The Software Reliability Case must be accurate, current, and complete and presented in a convincing manner in order to obtain sign-off by the approval authority. It is a living document throughout all lifecycle phases defined by the standard: predevelopment, development, and in-service.

In general, a Software Reliability Case consists of five components:

- software reliability goals and objectives,

- assumptions and claims,

- evidence,

- conclusion and recommendation, and

- approval history records.

This information can be summarized at various levels as shown in Table 3.4.

The information in the Software Reliability Case must respond to the specified software reliability goals. The process by which the reliability goals were derived and apportioned to software should be described. The relationship between the system and software reliability goals should be explained. Any regulatory and/or contractual reliability requirements should be highlighted. In addition, the agreed upon validation and approval criteria should be noted.

All assumptions, such as citing existing systems or research, and claims made relative to achievement and assessment of the software reliability goals and objectives should be clearly stated and justified.

As Mitra [25] reports from the CASCADE project, an "argument can provide an effective means for documenting the view points of different parties (such as developers, operators, maintainers) in a single document." He lists types of evidence expected to support any claims of safety and reliability [25]:

- evidence to support the claim that due care has been taken by the developer to ensure the safety of the system;

- evidence that the above has been independently validated; and

1. **MANAGING THE SOFTWARE RELIABILITY PROGRAM ACTIVITIES**

   1.1 Define purpose, scope of plan, and program reliability goals and objectives

   1.2 Nomenclature and project references

   1.3 Program management functions, responsibility, authority, interaction between system and software reliability programs

   1.4 Resources needed, quantity and type

   1.4.1 Personnel education, experience, and certification

   1.4.2 Equipment

   1.4.3 Schedule showing when resources are needed

   1.4.4 Training Requirements

   1.5 Definition and approval of lifecycle processes

   1.6 Plan approval and maintenance

   1.7 Acquirer interaction/involvement

   1.8 Subcontractor management

2. **PERFORMING SOFTWARE RELIABILITY PROGRAM ACTIVITIES**

   2.1 Define lifecycle model and methodology, interaction with system engineering

   2.2 Identify specific static and dynamic analyses to be performed throughout lifecycle

   2.2.1 Metrics to be collected and analyzed

   2.2.2 Metrics to be reported

   2.3 Analysis of preexisting software

   2.4 SQM and SCM roles and responsibilities

   2.5 Transition to operational environment

   2.6 Training end users, operations and support staff

   2.7 Decommissioning

3. **DOCUMENTING SOFTWARE RELIABILITY PROGRAM ACTIVITIES**

   3.1 Lifecycle artifacts

   3.2 Software Reliability Case

Figure 3.4: Sample outline for a Software Reliability Plan.

System/Component: _____

Intended Use/Environment: _____

Phase/Date: _____

FAULT MANAGEMENT MEASURES	PRODUCT EVIDENCE/ SAFEGUARDS	PROCESS EVIDENCE/ SAFEGUARDS	PEOPLE/RESOURCE EVIDENCE/ SAFEGUARDS
Fault Avoidance	– software diversity – –	– formal proofs – HAZOP study –	– – –
Fault Removal	– – –	– SFTA – SFMECA – Peer Reviews	– certified ADA 95 compiler –
Fault Detection	– exception handling	– independence –	– –
Failure Containment/ Fault Tolerance	– partitioning – block recovery – information hiding	–	– hardware redundancy

Table 3.4: Sample summary of Software Reliability Case evidence.

- evidence that the system has been independently assessed by experts and that the evidence collected by them indicates that the system meets at least all statutory, technical, and administrative requirements.

Mitra [25] reports that this approach has been "favorably reviewed by several regulatory bodies, such as Her Majesty's Railway Inspectorate (HMRI, U.K.) and Agence de Certification Ferroviaire (ACF, France).

Three categories of evidence should be supplied in the Software Reliability Case file: product characteristics, process activities, and qualifications of people and resources that demonstrate achievement of software reliability goals. Product characteristics should include a description of the design features which contribute to enhanced reliability, such as partitioning, diversity, block recovery, information hiding, and system/software fault tolerance. This description should explain how the likelihood of common cause and common mode failures has been eliminated or reduced. The results of static and dynamic analyses should be recorded, along with an analysis of the effectiveness of fault management measures. During the in-service phase, root cause analysis and lessons learned should be derived from field data. Results from analyzing and interpreting product metrics should also be discussed.

Process activities should include a description of the selected lifecycle model and development methodology, including an explanation of how this model and methodology contribute(d) to the attainment and assessment of reliability goals throughout the lifecycle phases. Specific lifecycle activities that were used to assess software reliability should be called out, such as targeting specific types of software faults, performing iterative hazard analyses or using static analysis techniques. A justification should be provided for all automated tools used. The validation and verification strategy should be explained, including acceptance criteria. Suspected or confirmed reliability problems should be documented, along with the current status of their resolution. Results from analyzing and interpreting process metrics should be discussed.

An explanation of why the education, experience, and certification of the professional staff is appropriate for a project at the specified reliability level should be provided. A justification of why the hardware and software developmental and operational platforms, including automated tools, are appropriate for this project should be provided. Results from analyzing and interpreting people/resource metrics should be discussed.

The conclusion should summarize the information presented earlier to demonstrate whether or not the software reliability goals and objectives have been met. An accurate and complete chronological history of all approvals attempted should be maintained in the Software Reliability Case.

Figure 3.5 provides a sample annotated outline for a Software Reliability Case.

SAE JA 1002 and JA 1003 are meant to be used within the context of an overall system reliability program, as defined in SAE JA 1000, System Reliability Program Standard. SAE Recommended Best Practices for FMECA Procedures should be consulted about how to perform a software FMECA and integrate the results with a system or hardware FMECA. SAE J1739 [16] should be consulted for surface vehicles. It defines a 10-level hazard

1. **SOFTWARE RELIABILITY GOALS AND OBJECTIVES**

   1.1 What they are, overall and for individual components or partitions

   1.2 How they were derived and apportioned

   1.3 Relation to system reliability goals

   1.4 Regulatory and/or contractual requirements

   1.5 Agreed upon validation and approval criteria

2. **ASSUMPTIONS AND CLAIMS**

   2.1 Assumptions about current system and its development environment

   2.2 Claims based on experience with previous systems

3. **EVIDENCE**

   3.1 Product characteristics that demonstrate achievement of software reliability goals and objectives

      3.1.1 Predevelopment phase

      3.1.2 Development phase

      3.1.3 In-service phase

   3.2 Process activities that demonstrate achievement of software reliability goals and objectives

      3.2.1 Predevelopment phase

      3.2.2 Development phase

      3.2.3 In-service phase

   3.3 Qualifications of people and resources that demonstrate achievement of software reliability goals and objectives

      3.3.1 Predevelopment phase

      3.3.2 Development phase

      3.3.3 In-service phase

4. **CONCLUSION AND RECOMMENDATION**

5. **APPROVAL RECORDS**

Figure 3.5: Sample outline for a Software Reliability Case.

severity ranking criteria which is commonly used throughout the automotive industry.

SAE JA 1002 distinguishes two roles—that of supplier (or developer) and that of acquirer (or customer). In fact, the standard was written specifically for supplier/acquirer scenarios, consistent with the ISO/IEC 12207 philosophy. The standard does not levy specific responsibilities or qualifications of project members; instead it is expected that the Software Reliability Plan will define these items.

The Software Reliability Plan and the Software Reliability Case are the two primary data items produced by adherence to JA 1002. It is expected that the Software Reliability Plan will identify the other lifecycle artifacts that need to be developed.

SAE JA 1002 does not address the issue of compliance assessment.

SAE JA 1002 does not directly address the issue of scaling. However, since a Software Reliability Plan and the Software Reliability Case are developed for each project, by default they will be scaled to the appropriate size, complexity, duration, and risk of the project.

SAE JA 1002 is comprehensive yet practical. The standard is progressive in that it promotes the definition and assessment of software reliability throughout the entire lifecycle. This is accomplished by the execution of a Software Reliability Plan and creation of a Software Reliability Case. This approach is similar to and compatible with the development of a Software Safety Plan (Chapter 11) and Software Safety Case. The standard addresses people/resource issues which affect the achievement and assessment of software reliability and encourages active communication among all stakeholders; these issues are often overlooked in software reliability standards. The standard is primarily geared for use in supplier/acquirer scenarios. However, it could be easily adapted for in-house use.

SAE JA 1002 was published in the summer of 1998. SAE JA 1003 is scheduled for release in late 1999. Hence, it is too early to assess the effective implementation of these standards. SAE JA 1002 has been submitted for approval as an American National Standard (ANSI).

3.4 Summary

EN 50128, the MISRA™ Guidelines, and SAE JA 1002 represent the first three national and international standards to address the unique software safety and reliability concerns of ground-based transportation systems. EN 50128 is an industry specific implementation of IEC 61508-3 (Chapter 8). Both EN 50128 and the MISRA™ Guidelines are predicated on the concept of software integrity levels (SILs), with the MISRA™ Guidelines determining the SIL from the controllability of a hazard and its failure mode(s). Both standards assign activities, techniques, and measures to be performed during the lifecycle phases based on the specified SIL. Verification, validation, and assessment criteria for determining whether or not the specified SIL has been met (or maintained) continue into the operations and maintenance phase.

Of the four high-level factors affecting the safe and reliable operation of ground-based transportation systems, manufacturers can only address the fourth factor with any certainty [26]. Technology is or may soon be available to address the third factor; however risk hysteresis, legal liability concerns, and competitive pricing pressure may prevent it from being introduced.

Research is underway to develop personal ground-based transportation systems which address a major factor affecting safety and reliability: human error. Some examples include the Personal Rapid Transport (PRT) system research prototype reported by Lowson and Medus [24], the European Union Intelligent Vehicle Project which uses advanced transport telematics, reported by P. Barber and D. Smith [18], and the new standards being developed by IEEE for intelligent transportation systems, both railway and automotive (see [32–38]).

All three of the standards discussed in this chapter are new. EN 50128 was adopted in mid-1997. The MISRA™ Guidelines were approved in November 1994 and are currently undergoing a trial use period. SAE JA 1002 was published in mid-1998. Hence, it is too early to determine the effectiveness of introducing these standards.

3.5   Discussion Problems

1. Identify the major subsystems and functions in an automobile which currently are or could be controlled by software. Categorize them as safety-critical, safety-related, or nonsafety-related and provide a rationale.

2. Perform an SFTA and SFMECA of the safety-critical functions identified for problem 1.

3. Assign SILs to the subsystems and functions identified in problem 1.

4. Develop a plan for achieving and assessing the SILs identified in problem 3. List the specific techniques and measures to be used for SILs 2 and 3 during the design phase.

5. Identify the major subsystems and functions in a subway system which currently are or could be controlled by software. Categorize them as safety-critical, safety-related, or nonsafety-related and provide a rationale.

6. Perform an SFTA and SFMECA of the safety-critical functions identified for problem 5.

7. Assign SILs to the subsystems and functions identified in problem 5.

8. Develop a plan for achieving and assessing the SILs identified in problem 7. List the specific techniques and measures to be used for SILs 2 and 3 during the design phase.

9. What additional unique factors must be considered when performing a HAZOP for an automobile than for a railway system and why?

10. What additional unique factors must be considered when performing a HAZOP for a railway system than for an automobile and why?

11. Select a safety-related function from problems 1 and 5 above. Explain how, if properly designed and implemented, it could mitigate the risk associated with the safety-critical function.

12. Using Table 3.1, explain briefly which techniques and measures are complementary and which are redundant.

13. Identify techniques and measures which are not listed in Table 3.1 but could be useful in designing and/or assessing safety-critical and safety-related software. Provide a brief rationale.

14. Describe possible scenarios in which software could compensate for risky behavior on part of unskilled or inattentive automobile or railway system operators.

15. Most subway systems operate on automatic control with the driver having override capability. Because the work is repetitive, drivers often fall asleep. For example, it was reported on *WTOP News* June 9, 1998 that a Metro driver in the Washington, D.C. area had fallen asleep on the Green Line. The train was an automatic control, continued past the last station stop and crashed. How could software help to reduce this potential hazard?

16. What percent of the cost of a vehicle should be allocated to safety features? What percent of the cost of a vehicle should be allocated to creature comforts, such as air conditioning or sound systems? Explain your reasoning.

3.6   Acknowledgments

The author would like acknowledge the significant contributions made during the development and review of this chapter by Dr. David D. Ward, Head of Research for the Electrical Group at the Motor Industry Research Association (MIRA), U.K. and Dr. David E. Peercy, Sandia National Laboratories, U.S., Chair of the SAE G-11SW Committee which prepared the SAE standards discussed in this chapter.

Additional Resources

Primary Works Cited

[1]   EN 50128:1997, Railway Applications: Software for Railway Control and Protection Systems, CENELEC.

[2]   EN 50126:1997, Railway Applications: The Specification and Demonstration of Dependability, Reliability, Availability, Maintainability and Safety (RAMS), CENELEC.

[3]   Development Guidelines for Vehicle Based Software, The Motor Industry Software Reliability Association (MISRA™), November 1994, ISBN 0-9524156-0-7.

[4]   JA 1002 Software Reliability Program Standard, Society of Automotive Engineers (SAE), July 1998.

[5]   JA 1003 Software Reliability Implementation Guide, Society of Automotive Engineers (SAE), draft April 1999.

Related Safety, System, and Software Engineering Standards

[6]   Phase 1 Report – Sources of Information, The Motor Industry Software Reliability Association (MISRA™), February 1995.

[7]   Report 1 – Diagnostics and Integrated Vehicle Systems, The Motor Industry Software Reliability Association (MISRA™), February 1995.

[8]   Report 2 – Integrity, The Motor Industry Software Reliability Association (MISRA™), February 1995.

[9]   Report 3 – Noise, EMC, and Real-Time, The Motor Industry Software Reliability Association (MISRA™), February 1995.

[10] Report 4 – Software in Control Systems, The Motor Industry Software Reliability Association (MISRA™), February 1995.

[11] Report 5 – Software Metrics, The Motor Industry Software Reliability Association (MISRA™), February 1995.

[12] Report 6 – Verification and Validation, The Motor Industry Software Reliability Association (MISRA™), February 1995.

[13] Report 7 – Subcontracting of Automotive Software, The Motor Industry Software Reliability Association (MISRA™), February 1995.

[14] Report 8 – Human Factors in Software Development, The Motor Industry Software Reliability Association (MISRA™), February 1995.

[15] JA 1001 Software Reliability – An Overview, Society of Automotive Engineers (SAE), draft version 0.4, February 1998.

[16] J1739 Potential Failure Mode and Effects Analysis in Design for Manufacturing and Assembly Process Instructional Manual, SAE Surface Vehicle Recommended Practice, July 1994.

[17] Recommended Best Practices for FMECA Procedures, (draft), SAE, March 1998.

Selected Bibliography

[18] Barber, P. and Smith, D. "Effects of Technology on the Safety of Automotive Transport," *Safety-Critical Systems: The Convergence of High Tech and Human Factors*, Springer-Verlag, 1996, pp. 266–284.

[19] Branscomb, L.M. and Keller, J. (ed.) *Converging Infrastructures: Intelligent Transportation and the National Information Infrastructure*, MIT Press, 1996.

[20] Cook, R. "Management of Dependability: A Railway Perspective," *Safety-Critical Systems: The Convergence of High Tech and Human Factors*, Springer-Verlag, 1996, pp. 61–70.

[21] Edward, C. "Railway Safety Cases," *Safety and Reliability of Software Based Systems*, Springer-Verlag, 1995, pp. 317–322.

[22] Jesty, P. and Buckley, T. "Toward Safe Road Transport Systems," *Safety-Critical Systems*, Chapman & Hall, 1993, pp. 297–311.

[23] Lindberg, J. "The Swedish State Railways' Experience with n-Version Programmed Systems," *Directions in Safety Critical Systems*, Springer-Verlag, 1993, pp. 36–42.

[24] Lowson, M. and Medus, C. "Initial Safety Considerations for an Advanced Transport System," *Safer Systems*, Springer-Verlag, 1997, pp. 185–202.

[25] Mitra, S. "The Generalized Assessment Method for Safety Critical Railway Applications," *Safety Systems*, Vol. 7, No. 1, Sep. 1997, pp. 13–15.

[26] Rivett, R. "Is There a Role for Third Party Software Assessment in the Automotive Industry?" *Safer Systems*, Springer-Verlag, 1997, pp. 160–184.

[27] Robinson, J. and Menani Merad, S. "Developing an Environment for Computer-based Automotive Suspension and Steering Systems," *Directions in Safety Critical Systems*, Springer-Verlag, 1993, pp. 150–167.

[28] Storey, N. *Safety-Critical Computer Systems*, Addison-Wesley, 1996.

[29] Tilloston, J. "In the Foothills of System Safety," *Safety Systems*, Vol. 7, No. 1, Sep. 1997, pp. 11–13.

[30] Vogel, T. "System Safety—Challenge and Chance for Automotive Applications," *Safety and Reliability of Software Based Systems*, Springer-Verlag, 1995, pp. 96–106.

[31] *Washington Post*, "Metro Looks for Answers in Central Computer Failure Last Week," April 28, 1998, p. A10.

Related Standards Under Development

The following standards are also related to software safety and reliability in ground-based transportation systems. At the time of publication, they were too early in the standards development process to include in this chapter.

[32] IEEE P1473 Standard for Communications Protocol Aboard Trains.

[33] IEEE P1474 Standard for Communications Based Train Control.

[34] IEEE 1477-1998 Standard for Passenger Information Systems for Rail Transit Vehicles.

[35] IEEE P1483 Standard for Safety for Software Used in Rail Transit Systems.

[36] IEEE P1488 Standard Message Set Template and Data Registry for Intelligent Transportation Systems.

[37] IEEE P1489 Standard for Data Dictionaries for Intelligent Transportation Systems.

[38] IEEE P1512 Message Sets for Incident Management.

Correspondence

[39] Ward, D. Email correspondence, 24 September 1998.

Chapter 4

Aerospace Industry

The aerospace industry provides services to many different types of commercial, military, government, and scientific applications. Aircraft transport people, mail, and commercial products. Manned and unmanned spacecraft and satellites support scientific experiments and worldwide telecommunications services, including voice, data, and video transmission. The volume of passenger traffic has increased dramatically during the past decade and the trend is expected to continue. Likewise, more countries are participating in space exploration.

The commercial aerospace industry is regulated because of public safety concerns. Aircraft and spacecraft are safety-critical systems, which may, as R. Shaw [32] notes include 'ultra-high' reliability requirements for dangerous failure modes, for example, "a bound of 10^{-9} on the probability of failure per hour of flight in some flight critical systems." Air traffic control systems and ground radar monitor flights throughout the world. This requires coordination among the many government agencies involved. Laws, regulations, and standards have been developed to provide guidance about safety and reliability issues of airborne systems, on-board instrumentation, navigation systems, and maintenance equipment, records, and spare parts. In many of the newer aircraft and spacecraft 80–90 percent of the functions are controlled by software. Historically, the emphasis during investigations of aircraft accidents has been on pilot error, mechanical failures, and explosions. Given the dominant role that software plays in today's aircraft and air traffic control systems, this emphasis is slowly changing to include software.

Accordingly, this chapter reviews the standards developed by four key aerospace organizations to address software safety and reliability:

1. Requirements and Technical Concepts in Aviation (RTCA), Inc.,

2. European Space Agency (ESA),

3. U.S. National Aeronautics and Space Administration (NASA), and

4. American Institute of Aeronautics and Astronautics (AIAA).

4.1 Commercial Aviation: RTCA/DO-178B – Software Considerations in Airborne Systems and Equipment Certification

RTCA/DO-178B is the primary standard used to obtain regulatory certification of software used in commercial aircraft in the European Union and the United States. U.S. Federal Aviation Administration (FAA) Advisory Circular AC No.: 20-115B, dated 1 November 1993, announced that RTCA/DO-178B can be used:

> ... as a means, but not the only means, to secure FAA approval of digital computer software. The FAA may publish advisory circulars for specific FARs outlining the relationship between the criticality of software-based systems and the appropriate 'software level' as defined in RTCA/DO-178B. Those may differ from and will take precedence over the application of RTCA/DO-178B. [19]

While discussions are ongoing about updating RTCA/DO-178B, the standard is still widely used.

4.1.1 Background

Requirements and Technical Concepts for Aviation (RTCA), Inc. is an association of aerospace organizations from industry and governments. RTCA/DO-178B was jointly prepared by RTCA Special Committee (SC) 167 and the European Organisation for Civil Aviation Equipment (EUROCAE) WG-12. RTCA/DO-178B replaced an earlier version of the standard, RTCA/DO-178A(1985). It was approved on December 1, 1992.

4.1.2 Purpose and Scope

The standard [1] states that it was developed for two primary purposes: 1) "to provide the aviation community with guidance for determining, in a consistent manner and with an acceptable level of confidence, that the software aspects of airborne systems and equipment comply with air worthiness requirements," and 2) "to provide guidelines for the production of software for airborne systems and equipment that performs its intended function with a level of confidence in safety that complies with air worthiness requirements." This includes defining: objectives for lifecycle processes by software level, software development activities and design considerations, the types of evidence needed, and the documentation needed to form the basis for certification.

The standard points out that it provides guidelines developed through a consensus process, since RTCA has no regulatory authority. The standard also notes that SC-167 and WG-12 will periodically review and update the standard based on industry experience.

The standard applies to the production of software in airborne systems and equipment that requires air worthiness certification. It defines the relationship between system and software engineering lifecycles and certification processes. The standard states specifically that it does not apply to:

- operational aspects of software

- certification of user modifiable data

- use of the standard with specific national standards or regulations

- supplier/acquirer relationships

- roles, responsibilities, and qualifications of personnel

4.1.3 Description

RTCA/DO-178B is built around two major concepts: failure condition categorization and software level definitions. The standard uses the failure condition categories defined by FAA Advisory Circular 25-1309-1A and EUROCAE JAA AMJ 25-1309: catastrophic, hazardous/severe-major, major, minor, and no effect. They are defined as follows [1]:

- **catastrophic:** failure conditions which prevent the continued safe flight and landing of aircraft.

- **hazardous/severe-major:** failure conditions which reduce the capability of the aircraft or the ability of the crew to cope with adverse operating conditions; serious or potentially fatal injuries to some passengers.

- **major:** failure conditions which reduce the capability of the aircraft or the ability of the crew to cope with adverse operating conditions; discomfort and possible injury to passengers.

- **minor:** failure conditions which do not cause a significant reduction in aircraft safety.

- **no effect:** failure conditions which do not effect the operational capability of the aircraft or increase the crew's workload.

Software levels are defined as the "contribution of software to potential failure conditions as determined by the system safety assessment process [1]." A software level is assigned per software component or function, as appropriate. The software levels correspond to the failure condition categories:

software level	failure condition category
A	catastrophic
B	hazardous/severe-major
C	major
D	minor
E	no effect

The standard [1] notes that "if anomalous behavior of a software component contributes to more than one failure condition, then the most severe failure condition category of that component determines the software level for that software component." The standard [1] also cautions about reading too much into a software level assignment:

> Development of software to a software level does not imply the assignment of a failure rate for that software. Thus, software levels or software reliability rates based on software levels cannot be used by the system safety assessment process as can hardware failure rates.

In other words, software levels are qualitative. They relate to failure conditions, not failure rates. This is another example which highlights the differences between hardware and software reliability.

Dr. Samuel Keene has developed a model to predict latent fault density by correlating the maturity of the development process with the RTCA/178B software level, as shown in Table 4.1. However, Keene [21] points out that:

> It should be noted that the SEI ratings apply to a company's process capability. It is typically granted on an entire development facility. The safety certification levels are applicable to a particular software product that has been produced under rigorous development, test, and validation standards.

SEI SW-CMM Level	RTCA/DO-178B Software Level	Latent Design Fault Density per KSLOC (all severity levels)
V	A	0.5
IV	B	1.0
III	C	2.0
II	D	3.0
I	E	5.0
not rated	not rated	6.0 or higher

Table 4.1: Predicting software fault density from process maturity. (*Source:* Table 2, p. 28, Keene, S.J. "Modelling Software Reliability and Maintainability Characteristics," *Reliability Review*, Part I, Vol. 17, No. 2, June 1997, as updated March 17, 1998, reprinted by permission.)

RTCA/DO-178B focuses on six key software processes, instead of a software development lifecycle. The key processes are: software lifecycle planning, development, verification, software configuration management, software quality assurance, and certification liaison.

Software Lifecycle Planning Process

Software lifecycle planning identifies the tasks that need to be performed in order to meet air worthiness objectives. Tools, techniques, measures, standards, and other resources needed to perform software lifecycle activities are listed and scheduled to show when and for what intervals they are needed. Criteria are established for determining when a phase has been completed and the project is ready to transition to the next phase. Plans are developed which address:

- software aspects of certification

- software development methodology and environment

- software validation and verification strategy

- software configuration management

- software quality assurance

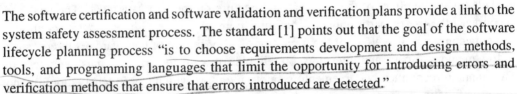

The software certification and software validation and verification plans provide a link to the system safety assessment process. The standard [1] points out that the goal of the software lifecycle planning process "is to choose requirements development and design methods, tools, and programming languages that limit the opportunity for introducing errors and verification methods that ensure that errors introduced are detected."

The standard [1] highlights that the "software development environment is a significant factor in the production of high quality software." The development environment should be chosen so that it minimizes risk associated with fielded software. The standard encourages the use of qualified tools and compilers. This will help to eliminate problems introduced as a result of compilers implementing language features differently and help maintain traceability between object and source code. The standard discourages the use of optional compiler features, again to maintain traceability and predictability in the object code. In addition it emphasizes that the validation and verification strategy must account for differences in the development and operational environment and differences between automated tools and the target platform.

Software Development Process

RTCA/DO-178B discusses the software development process in terms of five subprocesses: requirements subprocess, architecture subprocess, design subprocess, coding subprocess, and the integration subprocess. The standard includes information about general purpose software engineering activities, however that will not be discussed here. Instead, the additional activities needed to achieve and assess software safety and reliability are reviewed.

During the requirements subprocess safety and reliability requirements are allocated to software from the system requirements specification. Additional requirements are derived from preliminary risk analyses. Requirements are categorized as functional, performance, safety, reliability, or security requirements. All requirements are analyzed to ensure that they are correct, complete, unambiguous, consistent, and verifiable and that they do not contain undefined conditions.

On September 14, 1993 an Airbus A320-211 crashed in Warsaw killing two people. A variety of factors contributed to the hazardous consequences, including a software requirements specification error [20, 22, 32]. The aircraft hydroplaned causing only one wheel to touch the ground. The required speed to trigger the air-to-ground transition was not reached. As reported by M. Hohl and P. Ladkin [20], "the aircraft computer delayed deployment of spoilers and thrust reversers by 9 seconds, the braking commenced with the delay of an additional 4 seconds, and the deceleration decreased by 30 percent on the last 180 meters of the runway." A specification error required that both wheels reach the required speed and exhibit the required landing gear compression to trigger the proper air-to-ground transition. As the accident illustrated, these requirements will not be met when an aircraft hydroplanes. Aircraft software requirements must be valid for all weather conditions.

During the architecture subprocess alternative architectures are examined to determine which satisfies the requirements, in particular safety requirements, best. An assessment is made about the effect of the software architecture on the software level. The standard encourages the use of partitioning to minimize common cause failures, control coupling, and data coupling. The effect of the limitations and/or failure of hardware resources, such as I/O, memory, timers, and interrupts, on reliable software performance must be assessed. The standard recommends implementing safety monitors which continuously monitor and report on functions whose abnormal behavior could contribute to a failure.

Developers are cautioned about four specific architectural considerations: user modifiable software, option selectable software, use of COTS software, and field loadable software. User modifiable software should be designed to prevent unauthorized modifications. The verification strategy must demonstrate that unauthorized modifications cannot be made. Option selectable software should be designed so that only valid options and valid combinations of options can be selected. The verification strategy must demonstrate that invalid options and invalid combinations of options cannot be selected.

COTS software should be selected because it meets stated requirements without providing any additional or undocumented features. If the COTS lifecycle artifacts are deficient they must be upgraded to meet the requirements of this standard. The standard also addresses the issue of reused software. The intent to reuse software must be stated in the software architecture documentation and the plan for the software aspects of certification. The verification plan must explain how the reused software will be verified in its new environment. If the reused software is to be modified, all modifications must be made, verified, and documented according to this standard. Change impact analysis should be conducted to determine the effect of the modifications on the software level.

Field loadable software must detect incomplete, corrupted, or invalid load attempts as well as inadvertent enabling of load commands and unauthorized loading. The verification strategy must verify these capabilities.

The software design subprocess translates the design into low level requirements from which coding can begin. Design standards are developed and traceability is maintained between the design, architecture, and requirements. The standard encourages the use of design techniques, such as diversity, to preclude or contain failures. Likewise, the standard [1] strongly discourages overly complex designs:

> The current state of software engineering does not permit a quantitative correlation between complexity and the attainment of safety objectives. While no objective guidelines can be provided, the software design process should avoid introducing complexity because as the complexity of the software increases, it becomes more difficult to verify the design and to show that the safety objectives of the software are satisfied.

The standard provides some guidance about the qualification of automated software tools. The standard reminds developers that automated tools are software themselves and therefore prone to introducing or failing to detect errors. Developers should determine the types of errors that could be introduced by the tools and verify this by testing the tool under normal and abnormal conditions. Tools should be the appropriate integrity level for the software they are producing or analyzing. The standard also indicates that the certification authority must approve tool usage.

The software coding subprocess generates object and source code from the design. Traceability is maintained between the code, design, architecture, and requirements. The code is analyzed to verify that requirements were implemented correctly and that no features were implemented which are not stated in the requirements specification. Worst case timing analysis is performed to verify the correct timing and sequencing of safety-critical functions under all system states. The code is further analyzed to determine the potential for data corruption due to task or interrupt conflicts, the use of uninitialized variables and constants, resource contention, exception handling, and the resolution of floating point conversion/overflow conditions.

The importance of thorough timing analysis, under normal and abnormal operational scenarios, cannot be overemphasized. A timing change made to the HiMAT ground-based system and onboard uplink software caused it to land with its landing skids retracted. As reported by Rushby [30], the change had only been tested under normal conditions, not in the presence of an uplink failure.

The integration subprocess generates an executable load module from the object code, linked libraries, and utilities. Integration must take place on the target platform in order to yield bona fide results. Again traceability is maintained between the executable load module, source code, design, architecture, and requirements. The executable load module is analyzed extensively to determine if safety and reliability requirements have been met and if new hazards have been introduced during the development process. According to the standard [1], the software should be analyzed for the following conditions, at a minimum:

- incorrect initialization or passing of variables and constants

- incorrect timing or sequencing of events

- incorrect algorithm precision, accuracy, or performance

- stack overflow conditions

- failed or ineffective BIT

- missing software components

- memory overlaps

- incorrect addresses

- incorrect interrupt or exception handling

Software Verification Process

The software verification plan identifies and justifies the techniques that will be used to verify that safety and reliability requirements are being met and that the activities associated with each of the processes and subprocesses has been performed correctly. The purpose of the software verification process is to detect, report, and remove any errors that have been introduced during the development process. The verification process ensures that each process, subprocess, and activity was conducted in a technically correct manner and is complete and consistent with higher level activities and requirements.

The standard encourages the use of complementary static and dynamic analysis techniques during all lifecycle phases. These techniques should be used to verify that safety requirements are being or have been achieved and to provide confidence that the software performs safely and predictably under normal and abnormal conditions. State transitions, time related functions, equivalence classes, and boundary values must be tested. The standard [1] lists examples of testing under abnormal conditions: invalid values and ranges, initialization during abnormal conditions, errors on incoming data, arithmetic overflow conditions, and invalid state transitions. Any code which is identified as unused must be removed. The software architecture and design must prevent the execution of deactivated code. Annex A of the standard, pages 67–77, identifies features, such as partitioning integrity, which must be independently verified by software level.

The importance of adequate verification of software, prior to fielding it, cannot be overemphasized. On August 6, 1997 a Boeing B747-300 crashed on Guam, resulting in fatalities. There were several contributing factors to the crash, including software errors. Initially the crash was determined to be a controlled flight into terrain (CFIT). As P. Ladkin [24] states, "controlled flight into terrain (CFIT) accidents caused the deaths of 2,200 people, over half the air carrier fatalities, in the period 1988–1995, and is of great concern to aviation safety organizations." The contributing software problem concerned the minimum safe altitude warning (MSAW) system for the airport. Normally the MSAW system covered a 55-mile radius. However on the day of the accident it was restricted to a mile-wide circumferential strip. As reported by P. Ladkin [24], this error "was due to a bug introduced into the MSAW system by a software upgrade ... intended to reduce the number of false-positive alarms the system was generating... Investigators said that the lack of MSAW advisories did not cause the crash, but could have helped prevent it."

Software Configuration Management Process

Software configuration management (CM) activities are conducted without regard to software level. According to the standard [1] the purpose of the software CM process is to: 1) "provide a defined and controlled configuration of the software throughout the software lifecycle," and 2) "provide the ability to consistently replicate the executable object code for software manufacture or to regenerate it in case of a need for investigation or modification." The CM process controls changes, baselines, and builds and is responsible for labelling each configuration item and protecting them from unauthorized changes.

Software Quality Assurance Process

The software quality assurance (QA) process verifies compliance with project plans and standards and ensures that products are reviewed consistently. Under RTCA/DO-178B, responsibility for tracking and reporting errors and the need for corrective action is levied on the software CM process, not the software QA process like other standards.

Certification Liaison Process

The certification liaison process plans for the software aspects of certification. According to the standard [1], the purpose of the certification liaison process is to "establish communication and understanding between the applicant and the certification authority throughout the software lifecycle to assist the certification process." The standard recommends submitting the plan to the certification authority as early as possible. During the safety assessment the developer should provide evidence that the processes satisfy the plan, that the software levels have been achieved, and that they have complied with the standard. Developers are reminded that the "certification authority does not approve the software as a unique, stand-alone product [1]," but rather as part of an airborne system or equipment.

The standard does not place much confidence in quantitative time-related software reliability estimation and prediction models. The standard [1] discourages using these models as part of the evidence for the certification process:

> ...currently available methods do not provide results in which confidence can be placed to the level required for this purpose. Hence, this document does not provide guidance for software error rates. If the applicant proposes to use software reliability models for certification credit, rationale for the model should be included in the Plan for Software Aspects of Certification, and agreed with by the certification authority.

Data Items Produced

Nineteen data items are required by adherence to this standard. The standard lists the data items to be produced by each process and indicates that they can be maintained in an electronic and/or hardcopy format as long as they are available for "efficient retrieval and review." The standard provides guidance on the informational content of the data items, but not the format. Table 4.2 identifies the artifacts and process by which they are produced.

Process	Documentation Requirements
Software Lifecycle Planning	– Plan for Software Aspects of Certification – Software Development Methodology and Environment Plan – Software Validation and Verification Plan – Software Configuration Management Plan – Software Quality Assurance Plan
Software Development	– Requirements Specification – Design Standards – Coding Standards – Design Specification – Source Code – Executable Object Code
Verification	– Verification Cases and Procedures – Verification Results – Problem Reports
Software Configuration Management	– Lifecycle Environment Configuration Index – Software Configuration Index – Software CM Records
Software Quality Assurance	– Software QA Records
Certification Liaison	– Software Accomplishment Summary

Table 4.2: RTCA/DO-178B documentation requirements by process [1].

Five of the data items are of particular concern for software safety and reliability: Plan for Software Aspects of Certification, Software Accomplishment Summary, Software Verification Plan, Verification Cases and Procedures, and Verification Results.

The Plan for Software Aspects of Certification demonstrates that the chosen lifecycle is appropriate for the software level. The standard [1] requires that it contain the following information:

- system overview

- software overview

- certification considerations

- software lifecycle description

- software lifecycle data description

- schedule

- additional considerations

The Software Accomplishment Summary is used to demonstrate compliance with the certification plan. The standard [1] requires that it contain the following information:

- system overview

- software overview

- certification considerations

- software characteristics

- software lifecycle description

- software lifecycle data

- additional considerations

- software identification, part, and version numbers

- change history

- software status

- compliance statement

The Software Verification Plan identifies verification procedures, activities, and responsibilities. The standard [1] requires that it contain the following information:

- organizational responsibilities

- independence requirements

- verification method per activity

- verification environment and tools

- transition criteria

- partitioning considerations

- assumptions about compilers and utilities

The Verification Cases and Procedures discuss the review and analysis procedures, test cases, and test procedures. The Verification Results discuss the results observed during verification activities, whether or not the test was passed and why, and the configuration tested.

The standard does not cite any normative references; nor does it address the roles, responsibilities, and qualifications of project members, compliance assessment, or scaling.

4.1.4   Strengths

RTCA/DO-178B is a comprehensive well thought out standard. Its practicality is evidence of the fact that it was developed by a broad-based representation from industry and governments and is an update to an earlier standard. One of the major strengths of RTCA/DO-178B is that it focuses on processes, not just the software development lifecycle. Another major strength is that it links failure condition categories and software levels with required verification activities and independence requirements. In addition, the standard is written in a manner that facilitates use with national and/or international standards and regulations.

4.1.5   Areas for Improvement

RTCA/DO-178B could be improved in a few ways. The standard discusses qualitative failure conditions, qualitative software levels, and reasons not to use quantitative time-related software reliability models. For a risk assessment to be complete it must address the severity and probability of a hazard. Since the standard does not support quantitative software reliability models, it would be helpful to provide guidance regarding the use of qualitative models.

The standard makes clear that software is not certified alone, but is certified as part of a system. However it provides little guidance about how to link software safety assessments with system safety assessments or software engineering activities with system engineering activities. It would be helpful if the guidance in these areas was strengthened.

The standard could also increase its usefulness by addressing the issues of compliance assessment and scaling. (It is assumed that national standards and regulations that are used with RTCA/DO-178B will address roles, responsibilities, and qualifications of project members.)

4.1.6   Results Observed to Date

While RTCA/DO-178B has been used reasonably successfully since 1992, discussions are ongoing that it is time for an update. J. Penny [29] states that "some confusion exists in understanding the role software plays in aircraft systems, particularly high integrity systems." He cites examples such as confusion in certifying software, claiming software does not/cannot contribute directly to loss of an aircraft, and making untenable software reliability claims for Level A. He notes that EUROCAE WG 52 hopes to provide more guidance in this area, perhaps as an update/revision. WG 52 is focusing on four key areas: 1) previously developed software; 2) static/dynamic analysis; 3) use of service history in the certification process; and 4) ground-based aviation systems integration; since the current standard only addresses airborne software [29].

Likewise, B. Lawrence [27] observes that:

> Current certification practices in commercial aerospace will become inadequate due to the increasing use of complex computer systems which are phys-

ically modular, yet functionally highly integrated. The main attributes which distinguish these systems from current avionics systems are that they are software intensive and they share common resources.

Highly integrated systems are more complex, more difficult to validate and maintain, and have an increased probability of common cause and common mode failures. Certification techniques are needed which address both physical and logical interactions among system components. B. Lawrence is developing the Extended Common Mode Analysis (ECMA) technique to address this challenge. This technique, which builds upon root cause analysis, focuses on being able to "anticipate, identify, and prevent the initiating events which could generate" [27] common mode failures. The following steps summarize the ECMA process [27]:

1. establish potential common-mode points of failure from ANDed events in fault trees,

2. identify direct cause of event,

3. examine what events could initiate direct cause,

4. analyze result of event,

5. determine if a monitor would detect this result,

6. document the speed with which this could and would need to be detected to prevent a failure, and

7. check whether another monitor confirms the result.

4.2   European Space Agency (ESA)

In the spring of 1996 the Secretariat of the European Cooperation for Space Standardization (ECSS) issued a new set of product assurance standards for space systems and products, replacing the previous PSS series. The ECSS standards are layered in three tiers, as shown below:

Level 1

- Space Product Assurance: Policy and Principles, European Space Agency, ECSS-Q-00A, 19 April 1996 [2]

Level 2

- Space Product Assurance: Quality Assurance, European Space Agency, ECSS-Q-20A, 19 April 1996 [3]

- Space Product Assurance: Dependability, European Space Agency, ECSS-Q-30A, 19 April 1996 [4]

- Space Product Assurance: Safety, European Space Agency, ECSS-Q-40A, 19 April 1996 [5]

- Space Product Assurance: Software Product Assurance, European Space Agency, ECSS-Q-80A, 19 April 1996 [6]

Level 3

- ECSS-Q-80-2 Guidelines on Software Product Assurance Program Implementation

- ECSS-Q-80-3 Guidelines for Software Dependability and Safety Techniques

- ECSS-Q-80-4 Guidelines for Software Metric Program Definition and Implementation

The level 1 standard is the controlling document. The level 2 standards implement the goals and objectives of the level 1 standard within specific engineering disciplines, such as safety and dependability. A few level 3 standards have been developed to date. They "support implementation aspects of level 2 standards and will be defined whenever necessary [2]."

4.2.1 Background

The ECSS Space Product Assurance Standards are the result of a "cooperative effort between the European Space Agency (ESA), the national space agencies and European industrial associations... to develop and maintain common standards [2]." The ECSS Space Product Assurance Standards were developed by the ECSS Product Assurance Working Group, reviewed by the ECSS Technical Panel, and approved by the ECSS Steering Board. These standards, which are compatible with ISO 9000, focus on *what* needs to be done, not *how* to do it, particularly at levels 1 and 2.

4.2.2 Purpose and Scope

ECSS-Q-00A [2] states that the purpose of the standards is to "assure that Space Products accomplish their defined mission objectives and more specifically that they are safe, available, and reliable." ECSS-Q-00A [2] further states that the purpose of its safety program is:

> to ensure that space systems will not cause a hazard to, in order of priority: human life, the environment, public and private property, spacecraft and launchers, ground support equipment and facilities.

The standard includes an extensive discussion of the Product Assurance Management function. Organizational roles, responsibilities, authority, and interrelationships are defined for suppliers, acquirers, and certifiers. A comprehensive approach to integrating multiple engineering disciplines and coordinating management and technical functions throughout the lifecycle is presented. Resource and training requirements are identified.

The standards apply to "mission definition, design, development, production, and operation of space products, including disposal [2]." It is emphasized that the standards apply to developed or reused software.

4.2.3 Description

ECSS-Q-80A [6] "defines a set of requirements to be used in software product assurance for the development and maintenance of software for space systems." There is extensive interaction between ECSS-Q-80A and ECSS-Q-30A—Dependability [4] and ECSS-Q-40A—Safety [5]. ECSS-Q-30A and ECSS-Q-40A address systemwide safety and dependability issues, while ECSS-Q-80A is limited to software concerns. These standards define: 1) the quality management framework to be used on a project, by both suppliers and acquirers, 2) how processes and the associated lifecycle activities are to be defined, and 3) the required quality characteristics of products.

As K. Wright [33] points out, space systems face some unique safety risks, such as:

- the large amounts of energy which they contain and control,

- limited fault tolerance and performance margins due to severe mass constraints, and

- the frequent application of new and not necessarily mature technology.

The standard [5] requires a comprehensive four step risk management process. Potential hazards are identified through iterative risk analyses. Hazard severity and/or probability are reduced by design features and/or operational procedures. Design tradeoff analyses are conducted to compare alternatives for eliminating or mitigating hazards. Major risk contributors are identified and ranked. Wright [33] recommends performing a sensitivity analysis of the basic initiating event probabilities as well. Project resources are apportioned for risk reduction effectors. Residual risk is analyzed for compliance with safety targets and acceptability. The standard [5] makes an important point in regard to waivers related to residual risk and tailoring of the standard:

> The accumulated deviations and waivers which affect safety shall be assessed to ensure that the effects of individual deviations do not invalidate the rationale used for acceptance of other deviations.

Dependability analyses are conducted throughout the product lifecycle to optimize the system concept, design, and operation. Techniques are identified to minimize risks to meeting dependability goals. The standard [4] promotes qualitative and quantitative approaches. Functional analyses are used to determine critical functions and paths through the system. Reliability targets are apportioned among system and software components. Reliability, availability, and maintainability rates are predicted based on information from multiple sources: FMECA, FTA, failure rates, reliability models, and an analysis of hardware/software interaction. The system design and architecture is analyzed for potential common cause and common mode failures. Methods are identified for preventing, detecting, containing, limiting, diagnosing, and recovering from failures.

The standard [5] provides detailed guidance on the types of safety analyses to be performed. During requirements analysis, warning time analysis should be performed to determine time-critical detect-warn-react functions. Caution and warning analysis should be performed to determine required safing functions and emergency, warning, and caution parameters by operational phase. In fact the standard [5] states that "emergency, warning, and caution data and out of limit annunciation and safing commands shall be given priority over other data processing and command functions." Common cause and common mode failure analyses should be performed to determine requirements for fault tolerance. FTA and FMECA should be performed and integrated with system level models. Human dependability analysis should be performed to minimize the potential for induced or invited errors. The standard also recommends the use of sneak circuit analysis.

According to the standard [2], the safety and dependability organizations share joint responsibility for risk management activities. As Wright [33] points out "risk identification and evaluation is performed using reliability and safety analysis in a mutually supportive way." Reliability analysis identifies function criticality, failure effects, and qualitative and quantitative predictions of mission success. Safety analysis identifies hazardous conditions, their consequences, and qualitative assessments of risk likelihood. The standard encourages using both inductive and deductive, qualitative and quantitative approaches to risk analysis. For example experience from similar projects and the results from event tree analysis, FTA, FMECA, and interface analysis should be evaluated. Hazard likelihood and severity should be used to determine where risk reduction/mitigation measures can be applied most effectively in the system architecture.

The standard focuses on hazards that have catastrophic or critical consequences. Catastrophic hazards are defined as [5]:

- loss of life, life threatening or permanently disabling injury,

- loss of a manned flight system or launch system, and/or

- long term detrimental environmental effects.

Critical hazards are defined as [5]:

- temporary disabling, but not life threatening, injury,

- loss of or major damage to flight systems, major system elements or ground facilities,

- loss of or major damage to public or private property, and/or

- short term detrimental environmental effects.

Several fault tolerance requirements are specified by the standard. For example, neither critical hazards nor catastrophic hazards can result from a single failure or operator error, or a combination of two failures or two operator errors. Logical and physical partitioning is required for safety-critical functions. Diversity is recommended to prevent failure propagation. The standard requires that the crew and ground personnel be notified immediately of failure detection, redundancy switchover, or loss of operational redundancy. The software architecture must also provide a manual override capability for automatic safing and redundant switchover functions.

The standard [5] defines six lifecycle phases:

0: Mission Analysis, Needs Identification

A: Feasibility Analysis

B: Preliminary Definition

C/D: Detailed Definition, Production, and Qualification

E: Operational

F: Disposal

The software lifecycle is a subset of the overall system lifecycle and integrates with it. One or more safety reviews are held during each phase. These milestones assess whether the project is on track for meeting safety and reliability goals and should proceed. The standard [5] requires specific safety reviews per lifecycle phase, as shown below:

Phase	Safety Review
0	Mission Definition Review
A	Preliminary Requirements Review
B	System Requirements Review
	Preliminary Design Review
C/D	Qualification Review
	Acceptance Review
	Customer Safety Review
	Critical Design Review
E	Flight Readiness Review
	Operational Readiness Review
	Launch Readiness Review
	Commissioning Readiness Review
	In-Orbit Flight Reviews

Software safety and dependability activities begin by identifying the criticality of each software requirement, function, and component. The standard [5] defines safety-critical functions as "system functions that, if lost or degraded or that, through incorrect or inadvertent operation, would result in a catastrophic or critical hazardous consequence." The standard [5] requires that design features prevent safety-critical functions from being inadvertently executed. For critical consequences, two independent inhibits are mandated. For catastrophic consequences, three independent inhibits are mandated. Furthermore, the status of all safety-critical functions is required to be displayed continuously.

During the requirements analysis phase requirements are classified as functional, performance, safety, security, or reliability requirements. Safety requirements are categorized as safety critical or safety related. The criticality of software/software, software/hardware, and software/human interfaces is examined. A method is agreed upon between the supplier and acquirer for making and controlling changes to requirements.

Dependability requirements are also defined for system functions which are implemented in software and the interaction between hardware and software. Dependability requirements are used to optimize the system design and ensure a successful mission. The criticality analysis includes identifying functions and components which are critical to meeting dependability goals.

During the design and coding phases, methods and tools are applied to facilitate and measure progress in meeting safety and dependability goals. The standard [4] encourages the use of several design techniques to increase the likelihood of meeting safety and dependability requirements:

- design for hardware, software, and system fault tolerance

- fault detection, isolation, and recovery mechanisms

- worst case analysis

- monitoring and reporting critical parameters

- analysis of time needed to reconfigure a system

- defining design margins for time or memory critical operations

FMECA is performed to further the criticality analysis and promote fault isolation. Hierarchies and dependencies of control flows and information flows are analyzed. Design and coding standards are defined. Permitted languages and/or language subsets are defined. The use of compiler commands and features which can cause unpredictable behavior is prohibited. The standard also prohibits the use of shared memory. Complexity and fault density (see Chapter 10) are measured. The standard encourages the use of input verification, consistency checks, defensive programming, and formal methods for specification, design, and proofs. From his study of anomalies in digital flight control systems J. Rushby [30] concurs with the recommendation about formal methods. He states that it is:

> ...in satisfying the need for design descriptions which, in principle at least, would allow properties of the designs to be proved, that formal methods can make their strongest contribution to quality assurance for ultra-high dependable systems...

The standard promotes the use of partitioning to ensure that failures are contained and not propagated; specifically in instances where the failure of noncritical software could cause the failure of critical software. In addition, a checksum ID key is required per file to provide warnings about possible corruption.

Verification activities are ongoing throughout the product lifecycle. The standard [5] states that the focus of safety verification activities is to map each "hazard uniquely to unambiguous causes and controls." The status of all hazards must be tracked through to closure and presented at each safety review. Control measures must be witnessed and reports attesting to this signed and dated. Control measures for hazards with critical and catastrophic consequences must be independently verified. Dynamic analyses should evaluate nominal, contingency, and emergency operational modes.

The tools and techniques used and the verification goals per phase are specified in the verification plan, including test coverage goals. A verification report is required per phase which documents, analyzes, and interprets the results of verification activities, including reviews, inspections, and testing. Verification results are compared to the requirements traceability matrix. A statistical analysis of test results is recommended. Anomaly reports must be closed out before final approval of the verification activities. Final verification activities must be conducted in the intended operational environment. Highly critical software must be verified independently. Reused software must undergo the same verification activities as newly developed software.

The emphasis on complete validation and verification of reused software is, in part, a result of the Ariane 5 Flight 501 failure 4 June 1996, which exploded 40 seconds into flight. An independent inquiry board was established to investigate the failure. As reported by J. Lions [28], the root cause analysis performed by the board uncovered three major problem areas:

1. problems related to software reuse,

2. problems from implementing software redundancy instead of software diversity, and

3. a cultural bias toward addressing random hardware failures to the neglect of systematic software failures.

Lions [28] states that the software design of the Ariane 5 Inertial Reference System was nearly identical to that of the Ariane 4. This caused two requirements to be carried forward, untested, from the Ariane 4 to the Ariane 5 which were invalid. Differences in the timing of the software which performed alignment of the strap-down inertial platform and in the trajectories of the Ariane 5 and Ariane 4 were not captured in the Requirements Specification. The backup Inertial Reference System contained identical or redundant software, so it manifested the same errors. In addition, the software design exhibited insufficient exception handling—some Ada code was not protected from operand errors; because the software was reused it was assumed to be correct.

Lions [28] summarized the Inquiry Board's findings:

An underlying theme in the development of Ariane 5 was the bias towards the mitigation of random failure... The exception which occurred was not due to random failure but a design error. The exception was detected, but inappropriately handled because the view had been taken that software should be considered correct until it is shown to be at fault... The Board is in favor of the opposite view, that software should be assumed to be faulty until applying the currently accepted best practice methods can demonstrate that it is correct. This means that critical software—in the sense that failure of the software puts the mission at risk—must be identified at a very detailed level, that exceptional behavior must be confirmed, and that a reasonable back-up policy must take software failures into account.

During the operations and maintenance phase, the standard requires that software activities be undertaken with the "same degree of rigour" as during the development phases. Long term supportability issues, such as the accommodation of software and hardware upgrades should be evaluated.

Roles, Responsibilities, and Qualifications of Project Members

ECSS-Q-80A attaches a good deal of importance to organizational issues. According to the standard [6], the customer is responsible for ensuring that software product assurance requirements are correct, consistent, verifiable, complete, and unambiguous. The supplier is responsible for ensuring compliance with the ECSS standards, by prime and subcontractors, and that software dependability and safety requirements are correctly classified and met.

The standard [6] requires that a software product assurance manager be designated. This manager has primary responsibility for interacting with the safety and dependability managers about software issues. The software product assurance manager is responsible for verifying that the software product assurance plan is adhered to. The plan must be updated at each milestone. As part of the plan, product and process metrics are collected, analyzed, and reported for each milestone. Verification activities, acceptance criteria, and approval authority are described in the plan. Quality measures applied during the warranty phase are also described. The software product assurance manager is responsible for maintaining a matrix which demonstrates compliance with software product assurance requirements. S/he is also responsible for defining the software development and maintenance lifecycle, including the following items [6]:

- software development phases, activities, milestones

  - inputs and outputs of each phase
  - technical reviews required during each phase
  - approval needed to continue to next phase or activity

- methods and tools to be used during each phase

- technical characteristics and constraints of the project

- technical risk

- schedule risk

- financial risk

The software problem reporting and monitoring process is initiated and controlled by the software product assurance manager. In addition, the standard [5] requires that all personnel involved with safety-critical components complete training about basic and product specific safety engineering techniques.

Compliance Assessment

ECSS-Q-80A [6] is designed to facilitate compliance assessment. All mandatory requirements are labelled "RE" for easy identification. Requirements which must be verified independently have activities associated with them labelled "Assurance activities." Required outputs from each phase or activity are labelled "Required output."

Scaling

The standard encourages scaling for specific projects and contracts. It is the responsibility of the product assurance manager to ensure that all level 2 and 3 standards are scaled appropriately. Discussions about scaling should take place between the supplier and acquirer while software product assurance requirements are being defined. The standard recommends using software criticality levels and results of system level safety and dependability analyses as inputs to the scaling process.

Data Items Produced

Compliance with the standard [6] requires the production of several data items. They are associated with planning activities, ongoing activities, or a particular lifecycle phase, as shown in Table 4.3. The standard provides guidance on the content of the data items, not the format.

Of primary interest is the Safety Data Package. This data item, which corresponds to a safety case, contains the evidence needed by regulatory authorities and/or certifiers to grant approval to operate a system. The standard [5] requires that the Safety Data Package contain the following information:

- hazard analysis

- warning time analysis

- caution and warning analysis

- safety risk assessment

- FTA, FMECA

- design for minimum risk data

- software safety analyses

- supporting analyses, such as sneak circuit analysis and human dependability analysis

- safety-critical items list

- hazardous ground operations list and procedures

- waiver status log

- accident/incident status log

- safety review action items list

- conclusion

In addition, the standard requires that each project maintain a "lessons learned" file. The intent is that subsequent projects can use this information to improve their products and processes. The file should be readily available to project members and contain items such as [5]:

- an analysis of the impact of newly imposed requirements,

- an assessment of all malfunctions, accidents, anomalies, deviations, and waivers,

- an evaluation of the effectiveness of the project's safety strategy,

- a discussion of effective and ineffective verification activities,

- proposed changes to safety policy or strategy, along with a rationale, and

- results from using new safety tools and methods which have been developed and/or demonstrated.

Interaction with Other Standards

ECSS-Q-80A cites four standards as normative references:

- ECSS-Q-00A Space Product Assurance: Policies and Principles [2]

- ECSS-M-00 Programme Management

- ECSS-P-001 Glossary of Terms

- ECSS-Q-20A Space Product Assurance: Quality Assurance

While not normative references, ECSS-Q-80A interacts extensively with collateral level 2 standards and the level 3 standards derived from it.

Phase/Activity	Required Data Item(s)
Software Product Assurance Planning and Control	– Software Product Assurance Plan, including metrics, measures, and verification activities – Dependability Risk Management Plan – Compliance Matrix – Software Product Assurance Reports – Software Problem Reporting Procedures
Software Lifecycle Definition	– Software Development and Maintenance Lifecycle – Definition of Milestones
Ongoing Activities	– List of Critical Functions and Modules – Software Configuration ID File, Management Tools, and Methods – Milestone Metrics Reports – Verification Plan and Reports, including inspection and review schedule – Traceability Matrices – IV&V Plan and Report – Software Development Environment – Reused Software File
Lifecycle Phases:	
Requirements	– Software Requirements Specification
Design	– Methodology, Tools, and Design Standards
Coding	– Coding Standards and Tools – Language Justification – Complexity Measures and Metrics
Testing	– Test Documentation, including test analysis reports – Test Certification Report
Delivery, Installation, and Acceptance	– Installation Plan – Acceptance Test Plan – Acceptance Test Report
Operations and Maintenance	– Maintenance Plans and Procedures

Table 4.3: ECSS required data items by lifecycle phase and activity [6].

4.2.4   Strengths

The ECSS series of Space Product Assurance Standards have many strong points. The three tiered approach to specifying standards is very effective. It promotes a system perspective, rather than focusing on software alone, and integrates complementary engineering disciplines, such as safety and dependability. A robust risk management process is fostered by the standards. Specific design features and analysis and verification activities are assigned based on criticality. The ECSS Standards are compatible with ISO 9000. A comprehensive discussion of organizational roles and responsibilities is provided. The ECSS Standards facilitate compliance assessment by labelling mandatory requirements, required outputs from activities, and activities requiring independent verification. The informational content of a series of lifecycle artifacts is specified, but not the format. The standards are not tied to a specific software development lifecycle or methodology.

4.2.5   Areas for Improvement

There is one area in which the ECSS Standards could be improved. The standard supports both qualitative and quantitative measures. It would be useful if the standard would provide guidance on how to integrate the results from qualitative and quantitative analyses for hardware, software, and the system.

4.2.6   Results Observed to Date

The new ECSS series of standards were released in April 1996. To date a systematic study of their effectiveness has not been conducted.

4.3   National Aeronautics and Space Administration (NASA)

The U.S. National Aeronautics and Space Administration (NASA) has issued two software safety standards:

- NASA-STD-8719.13A: Software Safety, NASA Technical Standard, September 15, 1997 [7], and

- NASA GB-1740.13-96: NASA Guidebook for Safety Critical Software – Analysis and Development, NASA Glenn Research Center, Office of Safety and Mission Assurance, 1996 [8].

4.3.1   Background

NSS 1740.13 was issued as an interim standard July 19, 1994. During the first year after issue usage of the standard was voluntary. Since August 1995, usage is mandatory. NSS

1740.13 was prepared by the NASA Software Safety Standards Disposition Board, which included representatives from NASA headquarters, NASA centers, and the aerospace industry. The standard was developed in response to the National Research Council findings and recommendations about the shuttle flight software development process. The final version, NASA-STD-8719.13A, was issued September 1997. GB-1740.13-96 was developed by NASA Glenn Research Center. The two standards complement each other: NASA-STD-8719.13A addresses the *what* and *why* of software safety planning, development, and analysis; while GB-1740.13-96 addresses the *how*. In this section these two documents will be referred to jointly as "the standard."

4.3.2 Purpose and Scope

NASA views "software safety as an integral part of the overall system safety program [7]." As such, the purpose of the standard is to provide "a methodology for software safety programs at NASA" and describe the "activities necessary to ensure that safety is designed into software that is acquired or developed by NASA [7]." Software safety activities are undertaken by NASA to "ensure that software does not cause or contribute to a system reaching a hazardous state; that it does not fail to detect or take corrective action if the system reaches a hazardous state; and that it does not fail to mitigate damage if an accident occurs [7]." In this environment software includes airborne software, communications software, and software in ground control stations. The standard notes that it can be imposed contractually and emphasizes that it "shall be applied to government furnished software, purchased software (including COTS), and any other reused software [7]."

4.3.3 Description

The NASA standard uses a seven phase lifecycle to integrate software development activities with software safety activities. The seven phases, discussed below, are concept and initiation, requirements, architecture, detailed design, implementation, integration and test, and operations and maintenance. The standard does not promote or discourage any development methodology, as long as the specified activities are performed. Three activities are identified as "ongoing phase independent tasks:" 1) safety requirements traceability; 2) discrepancy reporting and tracking, in particular the safety impact of the discrepancy; and 3) configuration management change control.

Concept and Initiation

Software safety planning takes place during the concept and initiation phase. A software safety plan (see Chapter 11) is developed which describes:

- how this standard will be implemented;

- what software development and software safety activities will be conducted;

- interrelationships between system safety and software safety, as well as between system engineering and software engineering;

- how safety-critical requirements will be generated, implemented, tracked, and verified;

- what products will result from adherence to this standard; and

- a schedule of activities and milestone reviews.

Requirements

The purpose of the requirements phase is to develop complete, consistent, verifiable, and correct software safety requirements [7,8]. The standard notes that software safety requirements come from two sources: requirements that are allocated to software from the system safety specification and requirements that are derived from risk analyses. Software safety requirements should, at a minimum, address system limits, the interrelationship of limits, voting logic, failure recognition and tolerance, handling of hazardous commands, caution and warning interfaces, interrupts, inhibits, and protection of safety-critical software from being contaminated by nonsafety-critical software [7,8]. Software safety requirements are mapped to hazard controls and safety recommendations are made for the subsequent phases.

Requirements criticality analysis is performed to categorize requirements as safety-critical, safety-related, or nonsafety-related. The standard encourages identifying safety-critical and safety-related requirements in terms of "must work functions (MWFs)" and "must not work functions (MNWFs)." MWFs are described as "software that if not performed or performed incorrectly, inadvertently, or out of sequence could result in a hazard or allow a hazardous condition to exist [7]." This includes: "1) software that exercises direct command and control over potentially hazardous functions or hardware; 2) software that monitors critical hardware components; and/or 3) software that monitors the system for possible critical conditions or states [7]." Analytical decision support software for safety-critical or safety-related software would also fall in this category. MNWFs are sequences of events or commands that are prohibited because they would result in a system hazard.

Potential hazards are classified by the severity of the consequences, should they occur, and the probability of occurrence. Four qualitative severity levels are defined in the standard: catastrophic, critical, marginal, and negligible. Four qualitative probability levels are defined in the standard: probable, occasional, remote, and improbable. Hazard severity and probability are correlated to derive the risk index, as shown in Table 4.4. The risk index determines the priority for allocating risk management resources to hazard elimination and/or mitigation and the extent of safety analyses.

Oversight requirements are based on the risk indices, as shown below:

Hazard Severity	Hazard Probability			
	Probable	Occasional	Remote	Improbable
catastrophic	1	1	2	3
critical	1	2	4	4
marginal	2	3	4	5
negligible	3	4	5	5

Key:　1 - prohibited state
2 - full safety analysis needed
3 - moderate safety analysis needed
4 - minimal safety analysis needed
5 - no safety analysis needed

Table 4.4: NASA risk index determination [8].

risk index	degree of oversight
1	N/A—prohibited
2	fully independent IV&V plus full inhouse V&V
3	full inhouse V&V
4	minimal inhouse V&V
5	none

The standard establishes a hazard elimination priority for risk indices 2–4 [7, 8]:

1st - eliminate hazard by inherent safe (re)design

2nd - mitigate failure consequences by inherent safe (re)design

3rd - install safety devices and interlocks, both hardware and software

4th - implement thorough cautions and warnings

5th - develop safety procedures and administrative controls

The standard requires a minimum of one hazard control measure per cause and a minimum of one verification method per control measure per lifecycle phase. A hazard report is required per hazard/cause combination which contains the following information [8]:

- hazard description

- safety requirement

- cause

- hazard control measure

- hazard detection method

- hazard control verification methods (per lifecycle phase)

- status of verification activities

The standard identifies three high level factors that affect the development of safe and reliable software: 1) degree of control the software has over safety-critical functions; 2) complexity of the software; and 3) timing criticality of hazardous functions and control actions. These factors must be evaluated as software safety requirements are developed and analyzed. The standard emphasizes that safety analyses must be ongoing through the software lifecycle, with each phase providing input to the next.

Architecture

According to the standard, the safety objective of the architecture phase is to define a strategy for achieving the required level of failure tolerance, for the system as a whole and for individual components. A variety of architectural alternatives which meet the safety requirements are developed and analyzed on their technical and cost merits.

The standard provides a list of recommended techniques and approaches for developing and analyzing architectural alternatives. The standard notes that many of these techniques were borrowed from an early draft of IEC 61508 Part 3 (see Chapter 8). Other techniques may be used if it is proven that the results are comparable to the recommended techniques. The recommended techniques, which are discussed in Chapter 2, include [7, 8]:

- partitioning

- independence

- diversity

- block recovery

- sneak circuit analysis

- Petri nets

- hierarchy analysis

- control flow analysis

- information flow analysis

- simulation

- SFTA

- SFMECA

The final architecture should minimize coupling, prevent fault propagation, and promote fault containment regions. The standard emphasizes the need for timing and throughput analysis in aerospace applications and recommends that the following characteristics should be analyzed [7, 8]:

- memory usage versus actual memory availability

- I/O channel loading

- sampling rates versus actual parameter change rates

- adequacy of margins for system or operator response

- time interval needed to achieve fail safe or fail operational states

- time interval required for automatic safing with no human involvement

The standard lists several issues to be evaluated when selecting a real-time operating system. These features, which can affect system safety and reliability, are implemented differently by RTOS vendors [7, 8]:

- existence of a hardware memory management unit

- extent of determinism

- ability to bound priority inversion

- context switching time

- interrupt latency

- method of scheduling

- POSIX compliance

- synchronization

- intertask communication

The standard [8] cautions against the casual use of COTS software; it states that "use of COTS in safety-critical systems is an area of particular concern." As a result, the standard requires that all reused software, including COTS, be verified and certified according to this standard.

Flight tests of the X-31 demonstrated some of the pitfalls of software reuse. The reused air-data logic, originated in the 1960s, contained a divide by zero error. It is uncertain whether this error went undetected in previous systems or whether it was known and undocumented. The X-31 would not tolerate the error. As Rushby [30] states:

> This example ... points to one of the perils of reuse: just because a component worked in a previous application, you cannot assume it will work in a new one unless all of the relevant characteristics and assumptions are known and taken into account.

During architecture analysis, safety-critical components and design features are identified. Interfaces are analyzed to assess their criticality to safety-critical components. Planning is begun for how safety-critical features will be verified. Traceability is maintained to ensure that all safety requirements have been implemented in the architecture. Decisions are made about coding standards and using safe subsets of designated languages to minimize unpredictable compiler behavior, prevent memory conflicts, and protect critical memory blocks. A method should be developed for handling arithmetic errors that result from floating point conversions.

Hazardous commands and command sequences should be analyzed for stability and the likelihood of induced or invited errors. The standard requires that two or more unique operator actions are required to initiate a hazardous command. According to the standard, software interlocks and/or preconditions should be available to disable hazardous commands during unrelated mission phases or operational modes. In addition, an emergency override capability should be provided for all hazardous commands.

Detailed Design

During the detailed design phase the architecture is translated in a low level design from which software development can begin. Safety design features and methods are implemented. Safety-related information is incorporated into user manuals, cautions, and warnings. The detailed design safety analyses examine interfaces to safety critical modules, access to safety-critical data, execution control, interrupt characteristics, and error detection and recovery schemes [7, 8]. The initialization and synchronization of safety-critical modules and modules that interact with them are evaluated. The response to language generated exceptions and unexpected external inputs is assessed.

Design logic analysis evaluates equations, algorithms, and control logic to verify their correctness and completeness, in particular as related to safety-critical requirements [7, 8]. The standard indicates that "commercial automatic source code analyzers can be used ... but should not be relied on absolutely since they may suffer from deficiencies and errors, a common concern of COTS tools and COTS in general [8]."

Design data analysis evaluates the description, structure, and intended use of data for completeness, consistency, and correctness [7, 8]. For example the data dictionary for safety-critical data is compared with module design expectations for accessing and referencing data. The effect of interrupts, shared memory, dynamic memory allocation, unauthorized overwriting, and EMI on data integrity is assessed.

Design interface analysis examines control and data linkages. The methods by which data encoding, error checking, and synchronization are implemented are verified. The standard points out that "the sophistication of error checking implemented should be appropriate for the predicted bit error rate of the interface [8]." Parity errors, framing errors, timing errors, addressing errors, type mismatches, deadlock, and race conditions are identified by the standard as common interface problems to look for during design interface analysis.

Design constraint analysis evaluates how the proposed design will react in the "real world," especially in regard to meeting software safety and reliability goals. At a minimum, timing, sizing, I/O, sensor/actuator accuracy, noise, EMI, floating point conversion, weight, temperature, humidity, dust, and vibration constraints should be evaluated [7, 8].

The standard recommends using an SFTA to prioritize resources used to eliminate or mitigate potential hazards. The use of Petri nets is recommended to locate deadlock and race conditions. The standard notes that Petri nets are particularly well suited for finding problems that cross hardware/software/user interface boundaries.

The standard recommends the use of worst case analysis, dynamic flow graph analysis, Markov modelling, complexity measurement, formal methods, finite state machines, and formal inspections as part of the detailed design safety analysis. Dynamic flowgraph analysis is a new experimental technique that evaluates the dependability of software driven embedded systems by developing timed fault trees from state transition modes [8]. The standard reports that initial results from this technique are promising, but cautions that more work is needed. The standard supports using Markov modelling to determine system level RMA characteristics, but cautions against using it for software reliability modelling: "... attempting to apply these types of reliability modelling techniques to software is questionable because, unlike hardware, software does not exhibit meaningful random failure statistics [8]."

Implementation

During implementation the detailed design is translated into software. Safety features and methods are implemented using defensive programming. Code safety analysis verifies that safety requirements and safety-critical functions have been translated into code correctly. Potential unsafe states caused by language constraints are identified. Unused code is flagged for removal. The standard recommends extensive inline annotation to facilitate code safety analysis and subsequent maintenance. Many of the same techniques that were used to analyze the design are used to analyze the code: code logic analysis, data structure analysis, interface analysis, constraint analysis, SFTA, SFMECA, Petri nets, complexity measurement, and formal inspections. The analyses from the detailed design phase are updated to determine if new potential hazards have been introduced during the implementation phase.

Integration and Test

System integration and testing verifies the correct implementation of software safety requirements. This phase demonstrates that: 1) hazards have been eliminated, mitigated, or controlled; and 2) the system operates correctly in the intended operational environment, under stress conditions and in the presence of fault conditions. All safety-critical software components must be thoroughly tested. The standard [8] points out that "safety testing focuses on locating program weaknesses and identifying extreme or unexpected situations that could cause the software to fail in ways that would violate safety requirements." As noted earlier, the risk index will determine the extent of verification and validation activities and the need for independence.

Rushby [30] makes an observation worth noting concerning the discovery of software errors during flight tests:

> Flight test is for evaluating and tuning handling and controls, and the discovery of basic software problems indicates that the traditional methods of assurance are seriously deficient ... software problems discovered in flight test often concern redundancy management, coordination, and timing.

The standard reminds practitioners that a safety assessment certifies that a product is safe. In contrast, ISO 9000 certifies process consistency, not product safety. Certifiers are reminded not to rely on ISO 9000 certification alone to make a safety determination; because, as the standard states "ISO 9000 certified companies sometimes produce poor quality [that is, unsafe] products [8]."

Operations and Maintenance

Software changes that result from adaptive or corrective maintenance must follow the same process outlined in the standard for new software development. The standard [8] states that, "For every proposed software change, it is necessary to repeat each development and analysis task performed during the lifecycle steps previously used ... from requirements through ... test." Software safety change impact analysis must be performed to determine if the proposed change will [8]:

- invoke a new or known hazardous state,

- affect a hazard control,

- increase the likelihood of a hazardous state,

- adversely affect safety-critical software components, and/or

- change the criticality of a software component.

Thorough regression testing must be performed on all changes before they are fielded. All lifecycle artifacts are updated to reflect the change and brought under configuration management control.

Interaction with Other Standards

The standard cites three standards as normative references:

- NMI 2410.10B NASA Software Management Assurance and Engineering Policy, April 20, 1993

Lifecycle Phase	Milestone Reviews	Required Documentation
Concept and Initiation	– Software Concept Review – Software Management Plan Review – Phase 0 Safety Review	– Software Management Plan – Software Safety Plan – Software CM Plan – Software QA Plan – Risk Management Plan
Requirements	– Software Requirements Review – Phase 1 Safety Review	– Software Requirements Specification
Architecture	– Preliminary Design Review – Phase 1/2 Safety Review	–Preliminary Test Plan – Software Architecture Specification
Detailed Design	– Critical Design Review – Phase 2 Safety Review	– Final Test Plan – Software Design Specification
Implementation	– Formal Inspections and Audits – Phase 2/3 Safety Review	– Formal Inspection and Audit Reports
Integration and Test	– Test Readiness Review – Phase 3 Safety Review	– Test Reports, Problem/Failure Resolution Reports
Operations and Maintenance	– As Required	– Change Impact Analysis – Regression Test Results – Updated Lifecycle Artifacts

Table 4.5: NASA documentation requirements by lifecycle phase [7,8].

- NHB 1700.1(V1-B) NASA Safety Policy and Requirements Document, June 1993

- NASA-STD-2201-93 NASA Software Assurance Standard, November 10, 1992.

Roles, Responsibilities, and Qualifications of Project Members

The standard does not address the issue of personnel roles, responsibilities, or qualifications.

Data Items Produced

The standard does not dictate a specific format for lifecycle artifacts; instead the emphasis is on the information needed at each phase and milestone to monitor progress toward meeting software safety goals and objectives. Table 4.5 lists the required documentation by lifecycle phase.

Compliance Assessment

The standard does not address the issue of compliance assessment.

Scaling

The standard states that software safety activities may be tailored based on the inherent safety risk, as determined by the risk index, within the overall framework defined by the standard and in consultation with the NASA Center Safety and Mission Assurance organization [7]. Any deviations from this approach require waivers.

4.3.4   Strengths

The NASA software safety standards have several strengths. For example, the standards are not tied to a specific software lifecycle or development methodology. The standards focus on the information needed to monitor progress toward meeting safety goals and objectives, rather than on the format of lifecycle artifacts. The approach to risk analysis and control is comprehensive and fully integrated with software development activities. The results from preliminary risk analyses are used in several ways, for example to prioritize risk elimination and mitigation activities and to determine the extent and independence of verification and validation activities.

4.3.5   Areas for Improvement

There are some areas in which the NASA software safety standards could be enhanced. The standard states that it views software safety as part of the overall system safety program. However little guidance is provided on how to integrate the results of software safety analyses with hardware safety analyses or overall system safety analyses. The standard provides thorough guidance on dynamic analysis techniques; it would be helpful to balance this with more guidance on static analysis techniques. It would be helpful if the standard would address the issues of personnel qualifications and compliance assessment.

4.3.6   Results Observed to Date

NASA-STD-8719.13A was issued September 1997 as a replacement for NASA NSS 1740.13. NASA GB-1740.13-96 was released in 1996. NASA plans to conduct a systematic study of the effectiveness of these standards beginning in 1999.

4.4   ANSI/AIAA R-013-1992 Recommended Practice: Software Reliability

ANSI/AIAA R-013-1992 was developed by the American Institute of Aeronautics and Astronautics (AIAA) Software Reliability Working Group within the Space-Based Observation Systems Committee on Standards. R-013 was approved by the AIAA Standards Technical Council in November 1992 and approved as an American National Standard in February 1993.

ANSI/AIAA R-013 provides guidance in three specific areas: 1) estimating and predicting software reliability; 2) applying software reliability measurement to a project; and 3) collecting performance data needed to assess software reliability. It is applicable to in-house, commercial, and third party software projects. ANSI/AIAA R-013 does not follow the entire software development lifecycle. Instead, the standard states that it is "intended to be used from the start of the integration test phase through the operational use phase of the software lifecycle [9]."

In its present form ANSI/AIAA R-013 is limited to a discussion of an eight step process to select and implement quantitative time-related software reliability estimation and prediction models. The standard notes the differences between CPU time, execution time, and calendar time and cautions practitioners about integrating results from software reliability models which are based on CPU time or execution time with hardware reliability models that are based on calendar time [9]. The eight step process consists of the following activities [9]:

- defining project specific failure modes and their severity;

- characterizing the operational environment in terms of the system configuration, anticipated evolution of the system, and operational profiles;

- selecting a test suite which covers normal and abnormal usage;

- selecting appropriate software reliability models, based on their predictive validity, simplicity, capability, insensitivity to noise, quality of assumptions, and ease of parameter measurement;

- collecting data using methods which ensure its integrity, accuracy, and relevance;

- estimating parameters;

- validating the model; and

- performing the reliability measurement.

The standard concludes with a brief explanation of the standard categories of quantitative time-related software reliability models, like those discussed in Section 10.3.1.1.4.

In mid 1998 the process was begun to update ANSI/AIAA R-013, due to the many changes that have taken place in the field of software reliability since 1992. It is expected that the new version of this standard will include qualitative and nontime-related software reliability models.

AIAA has also published a guide for software reuse:

Reusable Software: Assessment Criteria for Aerospace Applications, AIAA Guide G-010-1993.

This guide is not specifically oriented toward software safety and reliability; however, it is one of the most comprehensive guides published on this topic to date. It promotes a methodology based on domain analysis to develop component assessment criteria and reuse library assessment criteria.

4.5   Summary

RTCA/DO-178B, ESA ECSS-Q-80A, NASA-STD-8719.13A, NASA GB-1740.13-96, and ANSI/AIAA R-013 are currently the predominant aerospace software safety and reliability standards. While there is some overlap, for the most part these standards take different approaches to achieving and assessing software safety and reliability. For example:

- ANSI/AIAA R-013 promotes the use of only quantitative time-related software reliability models. However, it does provide warnings about the difficulties of integrating hardware reliability models, which are based on clock time, with software reliability models which are based on CPU or execution time. NASA and RTCA caution against the use, particularly sole use, of quantitative time-related software reliability models, while ESA encourages the use of both quantitative and qualitative measures.

- The ECSS standards are compatible with ISO 9000. ANSI/AIAA R-013 and RTCA/DO-178B make no mention of ISO 9000. NASA cautions that ISO 9000 certifies process consistency, not product safety.

- ESA, NASA, and RTCA employ a robust risk management scheme. They further this concept by assigning design features and verification activities and prioritizing risk control efforts based on risk indices and software levels. Since ANSI/AIAA R-013 does not apply to the entire lifecycle, it does not address risk management.

- The ECSS standards are neatly organized into three tiers of standards which address product and process issues for individual components, such as software, as well as the entire system. The NASA, RTCA, and AIAA standards are for the most part standalone; they do not integrate with other system or safety standards.

The primary differences in the application domains of commercial aircraft and spacecraft are that spacecraft: 1) operate in greater climatic extremes; 2) have longer mission durations; 3) have greater interaction with ground control stations; and 4) can operate in an unmanned mode. However, these differences are not reflected in the standards. Given that NASA and ESA take a somewhat different approach to software safety and reliability, it would be interesting and useful to do a side-by-side comparison of the results obtained from using these standards, perhaps on the International Space Station project. From this comparison a hybrid standard could be developed.

Most notable however, is the fact that no standard addresses or applies to achieving or assessing the safety and reliability of commercial ground control, ground radar, or route control systems. It seems only logical that an equivalent amount of effort should be expended to specify, design, verify, and certify the safety and reliability of the systems which control, monitor, and report safety-critical information about commercial air traffic. To illustrate this situation, consider the following. R. Chandrasekaran and S. Barr [16] report that, "almost half of the [U.S.] FAA's 430 mission critical systems run the nation's air traffic control services... The air traffic systems have 23 million lines of computer code that are written in 50 different languages, some of them long obsolete and now known by only a handful of technicians."

4.6 Discussion Problems

1. Explain how the software levels defined by RTCA/DO-178B do or do not correspond to the SILs discussed in Chapter 3.

2. Discuss the limitations of associating failure conditions with software levels but not failure frequencies.

3. Why does RTCA/DO-178B not endorse quantitative time-related software reliability models?

4. Why does ANSI/AIAA R-013 endorse quantitative time-related software reliability models?

5. What are the two sources for software safety requirements?

6. What is the purpose of performing requirements criticality analysis?

7. Why are MNWFs specified?

8. How many hazard control measures are needed? How many verification methods are needed?

9. How can interface errors affect software safety and reliability?

10. What is the priority for techniques to eliminate or mitigate hazards?

11. How does the NASA risk index compare to that for EN 50126?

12. What are the advantages and disadvantages of using Petri nets?

13. Discuss the pros and cons of using Markov modelling for software reliability measures.

14. Discuss the problems encountered when trying to integrate the results from hardware and software reliability models.

15. Discuss the difference between ISO 9000 certification and software safety certification.

16. How did reused software contribute to the Ariane 5 Flight 501 failure?

Additional Resources

Primary Works Cited

[1]   RTCA/DO-178B: Software Considerations in Airborne Systems and Equipment Certification, December 1992.

[2]   Space Product Assurance: Policy and Principles, European Space Agency, ECSS-Q-00A, 19 April 1996.

[3]   Space Product Assurance: Quality Assurance, European Space Agency, ECSS-Q-20A, 19 April 1996.

[4]   Space Product Assurance: Dependability, European Space Agency, ECSS-Q-30A, 19 April 1996.

[5]   Space Product Assurance: Safety, European Space Agency, ECSS-Q-40A, 19 April 1996.

[6]   Space Product Assurance: Software Product Assurance, European Space Agency, ECSS-Q-80A, 19 April 1996.

[7]   NASA-STD-8719.13A: Software Safety, NASA Technical Standard, September 15, 1997.

[8]   NASA GB-1740.13-96 Guidebook for Safety Critical Software—Analysis and Development, NASA Glenn Research Center, Office of Safety and Mission Assurance, 1996.

[9]   ANSI/AIAA R-013-1992 Recommended Practice: Software Reliability, American Institute of Aeronautics and Astronautics.

Related Safety, System, and Software Engineering Standards

[10] Space Product Assurance: Electrical, Electronic, and Electromechanical (EEE) Components, European Space Agency, ECSS-Q-60A, 19 April 1996.

[11] Space Product Assurance: Materials, Mechanical Parts and Processes, European Space Agency, ECSS-Q-70A, 19 April 1996.

[12] Space Product Assurance: Programme Management, European Space Agency, ECSS-M-00, 19 April 1996.

[13] Space Product Assurance: Guidelines for Software Dependability and Safety Techniques, European Space Agency, ECSS-Q-80-3, 19 April 1996.

[14] Space Product Assurance: Guidelines on Software Product Assurance Programme Implementation, European Space Agency, ECSS-Q-80-2, 19 April 1996.

Selected Bibliography

[15] Aldea, F. and Sanchez, G. "Improving Reuse in Space," *Safety and Reliability of Software Based Systems*, Springer-Verlag, 1995, pp. 265–275.

[16] Chandrasekaran, R. and Barr, S. "FAA Lags in Fixing Crucial Systems," *Washington Post*, February 5, 1998, p. A15.

[17] DeWalt, M.P. "Comparison of FAA DO-178A and DOD-STD 2167A Approaches to Software Certification," *Proceedings of IEEE Software Engineering Standards Application Workshop*, San Francisco, 1991.

[18] Draper, J. "Applying the B-Method to Avionics Software: An Initial Report on the MIST Project," *Safety and Reliability of Software Based Systems*, Springer-Verlag, 1995, pp. 288–304.

[19] FAA Advisory Circular AC No.: 20-115B, dated 1 November 1993.

[20] Hohl, M. and Ladkin, P. "Analyzing the 1993 Warsaw Accident with a WB-Graph," *RVS*, Technische Fakultat, Universitat Bielefeld, Germany, Article RVS-000-97-09, 8 September 1997.

[21] Keene, S. "Modelling Software R&M Characteristics," *Reliability Review*, Part I, Vol. 17, No. 2, June 1997, pp. 5–28 and Part II, Vol. 17, No. 3, September 1997, pp. 13–22.

[22] Ladkin, P. "The X-31 and A320 Warsaw Crashes: Whodunit?" *RVS*, Technische Fakultat, Universitat Bielefeld, Germany, 28 January 1996.

[23] Ladkin, P. "Reasons and Causes," *RVS*, Technische Fakultat, Universitat Bielefeld, Germany, 1 February 1996.

[24] Ladkin, P. "The Crash of Flight KE 801, a Boeing B747-300, Guam, 6 August 1997: What We Know So Far," *RVS*, Technische Fakultat, Universitat Bielefeld, Germany, Article RVS-J-97-06, September 1997.

[25] Ladkin, P. (compiled by). "Computer-Related Incidents with Commercial Aircraft: A Compendium of Resources, Reports, Research, Discussion and Commentary," *RVS*, Technische Fakultat, Universitat Bielefeld, Germany, October 1997, [ladkin@rvs.uni-bielefeld.de].

[26] Lano, K. "Applications of Formal Methods to Safety-Critical Transport Systems: the AFRODITE Project," *Safety Systems*, Vol. 4, No. 2, January 1995, pp. 10–12.

[27] Lawrence, B. "Safety Cases for Integrated Systems," *Safety Systems*, Vol. 7, No. 2, January 1998, pp. 8–10.

[28] Lions, J.L. "Ariane 5 Flight 501 Failure: Report by the Inquiry Board," Paris, 19 July 1996.

[29] Penny, J. "DO 178B—Time for a Change?" *Safety Systems*, Vol. 7, No. 3, May 1998, pp. 4–6.

[30] Rushby, J. *Formal Methods and the Certification of Critical Systems*, SRI-CSL-93-07, November 1993.

[31] Schiavo, M. *Flying Blind, Flying Safe*. Avon Books, 1997.

[32] Shaw, R. "Safety Cases—How Did We Get Here?" *Safety and Reliability of Software Based Systems*, Springer-Verlag, 1995, pp. 43–95.

[33] Wright, K.M. "Safety for European Space Agency Programs," *Directions in Safety-Critical Systems*, Springer-Verlag, 1993, pp. 17–35.

Chapter 5

Defense Industry

The defense industry worldwide has a long history in safety and reliability engineering. Rapid developments and interest in these fields occurred following World War II in response to the introduction of new technology into existing weapon systems (aircraft) and the development of new classes of weapon systems such as ballistic missiles, remote-piloted vehicles (RPVs), nuclear weapons, laser weapons, and advanced navigation systems. In fact, the concept of the battlefield of the future depends on software.

Weapon systems are designed for destructive purposes; however, they are intended to be operated for specific purposes only when authorized [28]. Because of their destructive capability, the safe and reliable operation of weapon systems is a primary concern. Consequently, the risk analyses for weapon systems include assessing hazards which could affect the system operators, the public, equipment, property, and the environment.

The defense industry was one of the first industrial sectors to promote the concept of software safety and it continues to be a major player in this field today. For example, USAF AFR 122-10,[1] which was issued in 1982, required that the practice of nuclear safety cross-check analysis, performance analysis test and evaluation (NSCCA/PATE) be applied to software in nuclear weapon systems. And, USAF AFR 122-17,[2] which was issued in 1987, required the identification of critical software components as part of certifying the safety of nuclear systems.

This chapter reviews two of the leading software safety standards currently used in the defense industry:

- MIL-STD-882D: Mishap Risk Management (System Safety), U.S. Department of Defense (DoD) Standard Practice, (draft) 20 October 1998;[3] and

- DEF STAN 00-55: Requirements for Safety Related Software in Defence Equipment, Part 1: Requirements and Part 2: Guidance, U.K. Ministry of Defence (MoD), 1 August 1997.

Several similarities will be noted in these two standards. That is due in part to the open exchange of ideas and experience among the two communities developing and using these standards.

---

[1] USAF AFR 122-10, Nuclear Surety—Safety Design and Evaluation Criteria for Nuclear Weapon Systems, 5 January 1982.

[2] USAF 122-17, Nuclear Surety—Critical Components and Certified Software, 26 January 1987.

[3] This standard, when final, will supersede MIL-STD-882C.

The defense industry, like other industries, is moving toward greater use of COTS software. This practice raises safety and reliability concerns, as explained in Chapter 2. As a result, this chapter also discusses the North Atlantic Treaty Organization (NATO) COTS standard:

- Commercial off-the-shelf (COTS) Software Acquisition Guidelines and COTS Policy Issues, Communications and Information Systems Agency, NATO, 10 January 1996, 1st revision.

5.1   MIL-STD-882D: Mishap Risk Management (System Safety), U.S. Department of Defense (DoD) Standard Practice[4]

5.1.1   Background

MIL-STD-882A[5] was issued by the U.S. Department of Defense (DoD) in 1977. The next version, MIL-STD-882B[6] which was issued in 1984, was the first to mention software safety. This version included a separate task (212) for software hazard analysis. The software hazard analysis, which was meant to be ongoing throughout the lifecycle, was specifically intended to:

- ensure that system safety requirements were accurately translated into software requirements;

- ensure that the software specification clearly identified the appropriate safe response to a situation, that is, fail safe, fail operational, or recovery;

- identify safety-critical software functions, modules, and interfaces;

- analyze safety-critical software functions, modules, and interfaces for events, faults, and scenarios which could cause or contribute to undesired events; and

- ensure that the software did not cause hazardous situations to occur, did not inhibit desired functionality, and effectively mitigated hardware anomalies.

MIL-STD-882B recommended using more than one technique to analyze software hazards, such as fault tree analysis, sneak circuit analysis, critical path analysis, and NSCCA/PATE. The standard also recommended analyzing the software architecture for cohesion, coupling, and sensitivity to the occurrence of multiple concurrent anomalous events, both hardware and software.

---

[4]This standard, when final, will supersede MIL-STD-882C.
[5]MIL-STD-882A, System Safety Program Requirements, June 28, 1977, U.S. DoD.
[6]MIL-STD-882B, System Safety Program Requirements, March 30, 1984, U.S. DoD.

An interesting side note is the lifecycle phases defined by MIL-STD-882B: concept definition, validation, full scale engineering development, and production. The system concept and requirements were fully validated prior to any development activities. Now, some 15 years later we are again slowly recognizing the need for validation and verification activities throughout the lifecycle, not just at the end.

MIL-STD-882C,[7] issued in 1993, deleted the software hazard analysis task. This version of the standard defined the system safety engineering tasks and activities to be performed, but did not assign them to specific components, such as hardware, software, or human computer interfaces (HCI). Instead safety engineering requirements were followed by a clause which stated their potential applicability as "including . . . and software, as appropriate."

MIL-STD-882D was released in draft form October 20, 1998 for a formal comment and review period. When final, this standard will supersede MIL-STD-882C. Significant changes were made in this latest version of the standard, starting with the change in title from "System Safety Program Requirements" to "Mishap Risk Management (System Safety)."

MIL-STD-882D, like its predecessor, does not provide specific guidance for software safety or reliability issues. In essence, there is no U.S. DoD software safety or reliability standard. To fill this gap, DoD has promulgated two handbooks which supplement MIL-STD-882D [9, 11]:

- Software System Safety Handbook: A Technical and Managerial Team Approach, Joint Software Safety Committee, U.S. DoD, September 30, 1997.

- System and Software Reliability Assurance, Reliability Analysis Center (RAC), U.S. DoD, September 1997.

In addition, the new SAE Recommended Best Practices for FMECA Procedures [12], which replaces MIL-STD-1629A, provides guidance on how to perform a software FMECA and integrate the results with hardware and system-level FMECAs. These four documents are meant to be used in conjunction with each other; so this discussion of MIL-STD-882D will refer to them collectively.

5.1.2 Purpose and Scope

The stated purpose of MIL-STD-882D is to provide an effective, systematic, and consistent approach for managing the [8]:

> environmental, safety, and health (ESH) mishap risks encountered during the development, test, acquisition, use, and disposal of Department of Defense (DoD) weapon systems, subsystems, equipment and facilities.

---

[7]MIL-STD-882C, System Safety Program Requirements, 19 January 1993, U.S. DoD.

Hence, the standard is applicable during the entire lifecycle of a weapon system. Since software is a major component of most modern weapon systems, the standard is applicable to the software in these systems. The standard applies to newly developed systems, upgraded systems, modified systems, and systems undergoing corrective, adaptive, or preventive maintenance. Compliance with the standard is mandatory for internal DoD activities.

MIL-STD-882D does not provide general purpose system engineering, hardware engineering, or software engineering guidance. Instead, the standard relies on other standards for these requirements. For example, IEEE/EIA 12207.1 [14] and IEEE/EIA 12207.2 [15], which replace MIL-STD-498, are to be followed for general software engineering requirements.

At this point it is important to review a few definitions in order to understand how these terms are used in MIL-STD-882D [8]:

safety-critical: a term applied to any condition, event, operation, process, or item whose proper recognition, control, performance, or tolerance is essential to safe system operation and support (such as safety-critical function, safety-critical path, or safety-critical component).

Hence, software that performs or controls critical system functions or contains critical interfaces (hardware/software and software/software) is considered safety critical. This term applies to critical hazard mitigation functions as well; for example, MIL-STD-882D does not distinguish between safety-critical and safety-related software or components.

system safety: the application of engineering and management principles, criteria, and techniques to achieve acceptable mishap risk, within the constraints of operational effectiveness, time, and cost, throughout all phases of the system lifecycle.

system safety engineering: an engineering discipline that employs specialized professional knowledge and skills in applying scientific and engineering principles, criteria, and techniques to identify and eliminate hazards, in order to reduce the associated mishap risk.

MIL-STD-882D acknowledges safety engineering as a specialty; as a result safety engineering activities are not to be performed by nonsafety engineers. While not stated exactly, we can assume that the same holds true for reliability engineers.

mishap risk: an expression of the possibility and impact of an unplanned event or series of events resulting in death, injury, occupational illness, damage to or loss of equipment or property, or damage to the environment in terms of potential severity and probability of occurrence.

MIL-STD-882D uses the term mishap risk to distinguish between this type of risk, that is, risk that has safety implications, and cost, schedule, or technical risk.

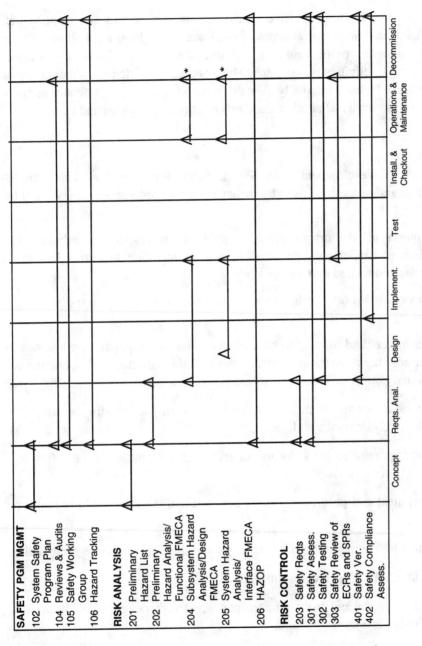

SAFETY PGM MGMT

102 System Safety Program Plan
104 Reviews & Audits
105 Safety Working Group
106 Hazard Tracking

RISK ANALYSIS

201 Preliminary Hazard List
202 Preliminary Hazard Analysis/ Functional FMECA
204 Subsystem Hazard Analysis/Design FMECA
205 System Hazard Analysis/ Interface FMECA
206 HAZOP

RISK CONTROL

203 Safety Reqts
301 Safety Assess.
302 Safety Testing
303 Safety Review of ECRs and SPRs
401 Safety Ver.
402 Safety Compliance Assess.

Generic Software Lifecycle

Concept · Reqts. Anal. · Design · Implement. · Test · Install. & Checkout · Operations & Maintenance · Decommission

* Modifications made during the Operations and Maintenance phase require change impact analysis and repeating earlier hazard analyses.

Figure 5.1: Relationship between MIL-STD-882D risk management activities and generic software lifecycle phases.

169

5.1.3   Description

MIL-STD-882D provides a comprehensive approach to mishap risk management, which includes management, risk analysis, and risk control activities. Figure 5.1 illustrates the relationship between these activities and a generic software lifecycle. This discussion will focus on applying these activities to software. The standard is written for the contractual environment, but it can be used internally as well. What MIL-STD-882D defines as tasks and activities can be viewed as what other standards refer to as processes and activities.

Management

The starting point is the development of the System Safety Program Plan. This plan describes the activities and tasks to be used by management to implement a safety program for a specific project [8]:

> This description includes organizational responsibilities, resources, methods of accomplishment, milestones, depth of effort, and integration with other program activities and related systems.

The standard gives examples of specific types of information to include in the plan, such as [8]:

- Analysis techniques and formats to be used in qualitative or quantitative analysis to identify hazards, their causes and effects, hazard elimination or risk reduction requirements, and how those requirements are going to be met.

- Verification requirements (such as test, analysis, or inspection) for ensuring that safety is adequately demonstrated.

- Certification requirements for software, safety devices, or other special safety features.

- Types of technical and programmatic reviews and audits to be conducted and the participants.

- Safety training for engineering, technician, operating, and maintenance personnel.

- Hazard reporting, tracking, and resolution.

- System safety technical and programmatic interfaces to other engineering disciplines, such as reliability and human factors.

As part of this plan, the standard recommends that a safety working group and a software safety working group be established, with representatives from all the organizations involved in the development, use, and maintenance of a weapon system. Working groups provide valuable insights about previous experience developing, using, and/or maintaining similar systems; promote the exchange of domain knowledge; and share responsibility for implementing the System Safety Program Plan [8,9].

Risk Analysis

The first risk analysis activity is to identify all potential hazards associated with the system, the severity of the consequences should they occur, and the likelihood of them occurring. K. Geary [28] notes that in defense systems safety implications of achieving or not achieving mission success must be considered in the hazard analysis.

Operational profiles should be developed to identify potential hazards as well as their likelihood. As the software reliability handbook [11] states, "the operational profile provides the foundation of a software reliability assessment." The handbook [11] recommends developing two categories of operational profiles:

- a user profile for each category or type of users; and

- a system profile for each system mode, that is, power-up, power-down, normal operations, abnormal operations, degraded-mode operations, maintenance mode, and so forth.

The hazard analysis should identify safety-critical software components, data, and interfaces so that they receive an adequate risk control, verification, and validation priority. In addition, as the software safety handbook [9] states, the hazard analysis:

... must determine the safety ramifications of loss of function, interrupted function, incomplete function, or the function occurring out of sequence.

Table 5.1 identifies software functions that are potentially safety critical.

The standard recommends conducting several types of hazard analysis activities: preparing a preliminary hazard list, a preliminary hazard analysis, a subsystem hazard analysis, a system hazard analysis, and a HAZOP study; the intent is that risk analysis be an ongoing activity. Previously developed software must be considered in the process of identifying hazards. J. Fragola [27] emphasizes the need to include potential human error during FTA, that is, mistakes (wrong response, wrong sequence of commands, and so forth) and responding too fast or too slow. Table 5.2 provides a sample software safety checklist to use during a subsystem hazard analysis/software inspection.

The information from the different types of risk analyses is integrated, kept current, and synthesized. Table 5.3 provides a sample format for reporting the results of a hazard analysis. The primary information to capture in hazard analysis reports includes: the potential hazards, the cause(s) of each hazard, the severity of the consequences should the hazard occur, and the likelihood of the hazard occurring. Particular attention should be paid to determining and isolating all intermediate and root causes of potential hazards. As the software safety handbook [9] notes:

This differentiation of causes assists in the separation and derivation of specific requirements that are attributed to the software. As the analysis progresses, for example, a hardware causal factor could subsequently be contributed to by software or hardware. A hardware component failure may cause the software to

- Any function which controls or directly influences the prearming, arming, enabling, release, launch, firing, or detonation of a weapon system, including target identification, selection, and designation.

- Any function which determines, controls, or directly influences the flight path of a weapon system.

- Any function that controls or directly influences the movement of gun mounts, launchers, and other equipment, especially with respect to the pointing and firing safety of that equipment.

- Any function which controls or directly influences the movement of munitions and/or hazardous materials.

- Any function which monitors the state of the system for purposes of ensuring its safety.

- Any function that senses hazards and/or displays information concerning the protection of the system.

- Any function which controls or regulates energy sources in the system.

- Software that handles or responds to fault detection and restoration of safety or correcting logic.

- Interrupt processing software, interrupt priority schemes, and routines which disable or enable interrupts.

- Software components that have autonomous control over safety-critical hardware.

- Software that generates signals which directly influence or control the movement of potentially hazardous hardware components or initiate safety-critical actions.

- Software that generates outputs that display the status of safety-critical hardware systems.

- Software used to compute safety-critical data.

Table 5.1: Sample safety-critical software functions [9].

1. Data

    - All variables are properly defined, named, and initialized. Data types are maintained throughout the program.

    - Data is not used prior to initialization or resetting.

    - There is no unused data.

    - Unintended and unauthorized modification of data is not possible.

    - Safety-critical data, processing, and interfaces are identified.

    - Array subscripts do not go out of bounds.

    - Variables are correct in procedure calls, for example, number, type, size, and order.

    - There are no memory conflicts for local or global data.

    - Common blocks are declared properly for each routine in which they are used.

2. Annotations

    - In-line code documentation, module headers, and prologues are accurate, current, and complete and include changes made as a result of engineering change requests and system problem reports.

3. Logic

    - Processing loops have correct and unambiguous starting and stopping criteria.

    - There is no self-modifying code.

    - There is no extraneous or unexecuted code.

    - Logical expressions are not nested beyond five levels.

    - Logical expressions are mutually exclusive and used correctly.

    - Processing control is not transferred into the middle of a loop.

    - Equations are encoded properly and accurately in accordance with specifications.

    - Exceptions are accounted for in all logical expressions and processed correctly, as specified.

    - Logical comparisons are made correctly.

    - The design implements robust error detection, correction, and containment features.

    - The design correctly implements all functional, performance, safety, reliability, and security requirements.

    - Safety features such as diversity, partitioning, information hiding, and block recovery have been incorporated into the design to reduce the likelihood and severity of a failure.

    - All software safety requirements have been correctly incorporated into the design and their implementation is compatible with system safety requirements.

Table 5.2: Sample safety-critical software inspection checklist [8,9].

react in an undesired manner leading to a hardware-influenced software causal factor. All paths must be considered to ensure coverage of the software safety analysis.

The handbook [9] recommends using fault tree analysis (FTA) to identify causal factors. J. B. Dugan [26] describes the value of FTA during the design process:

A fault tree analysis can help uncover the vulnerabilities of the system to particular classes of software failures and can guide the designer in choosing preventive or protective measures... A formal design review helps to insure that a software system *does* what it *should* do. A fault tree analysis helps to insure that a software system *does not do* what it *should not do.*

As discussed in Chapter 2, performing a failure modes effects criticality analysis (FMECA) in conjunction with FTA is an effective hazard analysis approach. FTA is a deductive top-down technique while FMECA is an inductive bottom-up technique. The two techniques complement each other; FTA concentrates on identifying causes while FMECA concentrates on identifying severity and likelihood. An advantage of both techniques is that they can be used to analyze hardware and software components.

The SAE FMECA procedures [12] recommend performing three types of FMECAs:

1. a functional FMECA, which is conducted during conceptual design to identify failure modes by function and their recovery requirements;

2. an interface FMECA, which is conducted to identify vulnerability to interface errors, hardware/software and software/software, timing dependencies, and transient faults; and

3. a detailed design FMECA, which is conducted to identify failure modes, single points of failure, error detection and recovery requirements, and the degree of fault isolation needed.

The SAE FMECA procedures [12] highlight the need to consider undetectable failures during these analyses. The FTA/FMECA process is ongoing throughout the system lifecycle. The results of the analyses uncover the need for changes in a design and/or more robust risk mitigation. The analyses are updated as new failure modes are identified. The SAE FMECA procedures [12] point out that the assumptions on which each analysis was based and the analysis procedures used need to be verified in order to ensure the accuracy and repeatability of the FMECA results.

The information shown in Table 5.3 is recorded for each hazard during the risk analysis process. During the risk control process a mitigation strategy will be devised, implemented, and verified.

The standard defines four severity categories [8]:

to provide a qualitative measure of the most reasonable credible mishap resulting from personnel error, environmental conditions, design inadequacies,

Hazard Analysis Report for the ABC Project
as of: 25 February 1999

I. Type of Hazard Analysis

____ preliminary hazard list	____ preliminary hazard analysis
____ subsystem hazard analysis	____ system hazard analysis
____ HAZOP	____ other (specify)

II. Lifecycle Phase in which performed

____ concept	____ requirements
____ design	____ implementation
____ test	____ installation and checkout
____ operations and maintenance	____ decommissioning

III. Risk Analysis

System/ Subsystem/ Unit	Hazard	Cause(s)	Severity	Likelihood or Software Control Category

IV. Risk Control

Hazard	Recommended Mitigation Strategy	Results of Recommended Mitigation	Status/ Verification	Residual Risk

Table 5.3: Sample hazard analysis report.

procedural deficiencies, or system, subsystem, or component failure or mal-function.

The four severity categories and their definitions are shown in Table 5.4. MIL-STD-882D uses the same severity category names as other standards discussed in this book; however the definitions differ. For example, MIL-STD-882D assigns dollar values to property losses. The standard permits some degree of flexibility for each project to tailor the severity definitions so that they fit their particular situation.

Category	Definition
I – Catastrophic	Could result in death, permanent total disability, property loss exceeding $1M, or irreversible severe environmental damage.
II – Critical	Could result in permanent partial disability, injuries, or occupational illness that may result in hospitalization of at least three personnel, property loss exceeding $200K but less than $1M, or reversible environmental damage.
III – Marginal	Could result in injury or occupational illness resulting in a lost work day, property loss exceeding $10K but less than $200K, or mitigable environmental damage.
IV – Negligible	Could result in injury or illness not resulting in a lost work day, property loss exceeding $2K but less than $10K, or minimal environmental damage.

Table 5.4: Sample MIL-STD-882D severity categories [8].

MIL-STD-882D defines five qualitative categories to express the likelihood of a hazard occurring. The standard [8] notes that this likelihood can be "described in terms of potential occurrences per unit of time, events, populations, items, or activity." This flexibility is particularly useful in the software domain. The standard is open to qualitative or quantitative likelihood measures but states a preference for qualitative likelihood measures during design [8]:

> Assigning a quantitative mishap probability to a potential design or procedural hazard is generally not possible early in the design process. A qualitative mishap probability may be derived from research, analysis, and evaluation of historical ESH data from similar systems.

The five likelihood categories and their definitions are shown in Table 5.5. Again, the standard permits some flexibility for tailoring the definitions so that they are appropriate for a specific project. This tailoring flexibility is useful for defining the likelihood for different types of subsystems, such as hardware and software.

Category	Definition
A – Frequent	Likely to occur often in the life of an item, with a probability of occurrence greater than 10^{-1}
B – Probable	Will occur several times in the life of an item, with a probability of occurrence less than 10^{-1} but greater than 10^{-2}
C – Occasional	Likely to occur some time in the life of an item, with a probability of occurrence less than 10^{-2} but greater than 10^{-3}
D – Remote	Unlikely but possible to occur in the life of an item, with a probability of occurrence less than 10^{-3} but greater than 10^{-6}
E – Improbable	So unlikely, it can be assumed occurrence may not be experienced, with a probability of occurrence less than 10^{-6}

Table 5.5: Sample MIL-STD-882D likelihood categories [8].

P. Clemens [22] makes a case for adding an additional hazard probability level, "F – impossible," to the standard to flag zero probability hazards. To date this recommendation has not been accepted.

The correlation of the probability and likelihood is used to assess the risk of individual hazards and determine their acceptability and/or the amount of risk reduction and control measures needed. The standard proposes using a risk assessment matrix, as shown in Table 5.6. Cells in the matrix are grouped to indicate the composite risk as either high, serious, medium, or low. F. Patterson [34] observes that different levels of decision makers have responsibility for the different levels of hazard risk:

- high or serious risk – Acquisition Executive

- medium risk – Program Executive Officer

- low risk – Program Manager

The standard points out some special considerations when assessing the risk for software controlled or software intensive systems [8]:

1. Software risk assessments cannot rely solely on severity and likelihood determinations.

2. Determination of the probability of failure of a single software function is difficult at best and cannot be based on historical data.

Likelihood	Severity			
	Negligible	Marginal	Critical	Catastrophic
Frequent	Medium	Serious	High	High
Probable	Medium	Serious	High	High
Occasional	Low	Medium	Serious	High
Remote	Low	Medium	Medium	Serious
Improbable	Low	Low	Medium	Medium

Table 5.6: Sample MIL-STD-882D risk assessment matrix [8].

3. Software is generally application specific and reliability parameters associated with it cannot be estimated in the same manner as hardware.

To compensate for this, the standard recommends assessing software risk as a function of the severity and the degree of control the software has over the hardware. Four software control categories are defined by the standard, as shown in Table 5.7, with category I being the highest degree of control and category IV the lowest. The concept of software control categories is similar to but not exactly the same as the software levels defined by RTCA/DO-178B. (See Chapter 4.)

The software safety handbook [9] and the software reliability handbook [11] recommend caution on the use of COTS software and point out that previously developed software must undergo the same safety and reliability analysis process as custom-developed software. The software reliability handbook [11] emphasizes that reliability experience with COTS software is only valid for the current project if the measurements were made in an identical operational environment. The rigor of the software verification and validation activities should correspond to the degree of control.

An equivalent software risk assessment matrix is derived by substituting the software control category for likelihood, as shown in Table 5.8. The higher the risk the more design and verification activities, both static and dynamic, are needed. The exact correlation of severity, likelihood, and control category which results in high, serious, medium, or low risk is defined by each project, so that "mission capabilities, social, economic, or political factors are taken into account [8]." The risk assessment matrix serves as a decision making tool to prioritize risk reduction and control activities.

After each iteration of risk analysis and control activities has been completed, the residual risk is assessed to determine its acceptability. The standard cites examples of unacceptable failures, such as [8]:

1. single component failure, common mode failure, human error, or design features that could cause a catastrophic or critical mishap

2. dual independent component failures, dual independent human errors, or a combination of a component failure and human error involving safety-critical command and control functions, which could cause a catastrophic or critical mishap

Category	Definition
I	Software exercises autonomous control over potentially hazardous hardware systems, subsystems, or components, without the possibility of intervention to preclude the occurrence of a hazard. Failure of the software or a failure to prevent an event leads directly to a hazard occurrence. Software interlocks that prevent a hazardous event should be an integral part of the design process and verified.
IIa	Software exercises control over potentially hazardous hardware systems, subsystems, or components, with time for intervention by independent safety systems to mitigate the hazard. However, these systems by themselves are not considered adequate.
IIb	Software item displays information requiring immediate operator action to mitigate a hazard. Software failures will allow, or fail to prevent, the hazard occurrence.
IIIa	Software item issues commands over potentially hazardous hardware systems, subsystems, or components, requiring human action to complete the control function. There are several redundant independent safety measures for each hazardous event.
IIIb	Software generates information of a safety-critical nature used to make safety-critical decisions. There are several redundant independent safety measures for each hazardous event.
IV	Software does not control safety-critical hardware systems, subsystems, or components and does not provide safety-critical information.

Table 5.7: MIL-STD-882D software control categories [8].

Software Control Category	Severity			
	Negligible	Marginal	Critical	Catastrophic
I	Low	Moderate	High	High
II	Low	Moderate	Medium	High
III	Low	Low	Moderate	Medium
IV	Low	Low	Moderate	Moderate

Table 5.8: Sample MIL-STD-882D software risk assessment matrix based on control categories [8].

3. generation of hazardous radiation or energy, when no provisions have been made to protect personnel or sensitive subsystems from damage or adverse effects

Software safety engineers need to be particularly concerned about common mode failures, common cause failures, and software induced or invited human errors.

An FMECA plays an important role in analyzing residual risk. For example, the SAE FMECA procedures recommend documenting FMECA results for each operational mode/profile, as shown below, to facilitate an analysis of residual risk [12]:

- operational mode/profile

    - local effect(s) of failure

    - next higher level effect(s) of failure

    - end level effect(s) of failure

    - severity

    - compensating provisions

    - detection method/monitoring

    - corrective action(s)

    - remarks

The residual risk of individual hazards is analyzed, as well as the aggregate residual risk of the system. The standard expects that all catastrophic and critical hazards will be elimi-nated or reduced to an acceptable level. Residual risk must be clearly documented so that: 1) an informed decision can be made about deploying the system; 2) personnel involved with the operation and use of the system are aware of this risk; and 3) the reason(s) why the risk(s) were not completely mitigated are recorded [8, 9]. The residual risk analysis report should be updated whenever corrective, adaptive, or preventive maintenance is performed.

The standard requires that a hazard log be maintained throughout the life of a system, which documents all known hazards, the risk associated with them, and their resolution or current status. A sample hazard log is presented in Table 5.9. The hazard log maintains a complete summary/chronological list of all hazards identified throughout the lifecycle and their status. The information shown in Table 5.9 is completed for each hazard.

**Hazard Log for XYZ Project
as of: 15 April 1999**

1. Hazard #: _____   name: _____
   a. date opened: _____
   b. description:

   c. severity category:
      ____ catastrophic   ____ critical
      ____ marginal   ____ negligible
   d. likelihood category or software control category:
      ____ frequent   ____ I
      ____ probable   ____ IIa or IIb
      ____ occasional   ____ IIIa or IIIb
      ____ remote   ____ IV
      ____ improbable
   e. current mitigation strategy:

   f. residual risk:

      severity: _____
      likelihood: _____ or
      software control category: _____
   g. current status:
      ____ open pending further analysis
      ____ closed pending verification of mitigation strategy
      ____ closed, verified on xx/xx/xx
      ____ determined not to be reducible, awaiting decision on residual risk
      ____ risk low enough, no further action needed
   h. responsible person/organization:

Table 5.9: Sample hazard log.

Risk Control

MIL-STD-882D promotes a comprehensive risk management process which includes the risk analysis activities discussed above and the following risk control activities. Interaction between risk analysis and risk control activities is an iterative process. As hazards are identified risk control activities are undertaken to eliminate or mitigate them. The risk analysis is repeated to determine if: 1) these hazards have been reduced sufficiently; and 2) if any new hazards have been uncovered or introduced in the meantime. This process is repeated until all hazards have been controlled to an acceptable level or eliminated. Risk control, as implemented by MIL-STD-882D, consists of three categories of activities:

- specifying safety and reliability requirements and their evaluation criteria;

- utilizing various techniques to eliminate and/or control potential hazards; and

- verifying the effectiveness of the mitigation strategies through a series of different assessments.

As the first risk control activity, the standard recommends specifying mishap risk requirements for the system. Examples of four types of system mishap risk requirements are given [8]:

- **ESH performance requirements** – specific ESH performance criteria established as a threshold or objective for the system;

- **Failure rates/modes** – acceptable quantitative failure rates by failure severity and mode;

- **Unacceptable failures** – objective requirements that specify which categories and types of failures are unacceptable; and

- **Compliance requirements** – requirements for the system and its design to comply with cited safety laws, regulations, and standards.

The standard states that the mishap risk management requirements should be "definitive." This is important for both safety and programmatic reasons. As the software safety handbook [9] points out:

> ...inadequately specified safety requirements ...leads to program schedule and cost impacts later when safety issues arise.

Table 5.10 lists sample software mishap risk requirements using these same four categories. Software safety requirements are documented in the appropriate system or subsystem specification along with specific objective criteria to verify that they have been met.

The software reliability handbook [11] recommends specifying reliability requirements at the system level, then allocating them to subsystems and components. For example, a reliability requirement should be apportioned between a software component and the hardware

1. **ESH Performance**

   - At least one safe state shall exist for each logistical and operational mode.
   - Safety-critical modules, data, and interfaces shall be partitioned from nonsafety-critical ones.
   - Prior to system operation, the software shall verify that safety interlocks are functioning.
   - A system error log and audit trail shall be maintained.
   - The system shall power-up and power-down into a safe state.
   - The system shall contain built-in continuous monitoring checks for race conditions, sequencing errors, and memory degradation.
   - Safety-critical functions shall be monitored by watch dog timers.
   - All input shall be verified by reasonableness checks and authenticated before acting upon it.
   - All modules shall contain only one entry point and one exit point, except for error handling.

2. **Failure Rates/Modes**

   - Software shall tolerate hardware and software faults and fail safe, fail operational, or attempt recovery, as specified.
   - System operation under unsafe conditions shall only be permitted with special authorization.
   - Comprehensive error handling shall be implemented which detects and recovers from system, user, and run-time errors.
   - The system shall provide adequate warnings and alerts before entering an unsafe state.

3. **Unacceptable Failures**

   - Software in control categories I and II shall not cause or contribute to catastrophic or critical failures.
   - The software shall not fail in a manner such that there is no manual override capability.
   - The software shall not allow energy of concentration x to be released. The software shall not allow energy of concentration y to be released for longer than 0.5 seconds.
   - The software shall not allow air speeds greater than x.
   - The software shall not allow the arming function to take place prior to the launch sequence.

4. **Compliance Requirements**

   - Software shall be developed according to MIL-STD-882D, the software safety handbook, the software reliability handbook, and the SAE FMECA procedures.
   - Procedures for installing, operating, maintaining, and decommissioning the software shall comply with PL 5201.3 and 17 CFR Part 200.

Table 5.10: Sample software mishap risk requirements [8,9].

on which it operates. Reliability requirements and their allocation need to take into account: 1) whether the system operates in demand mode or continuous mode; and 2) whether the software components execute concurrently, sequentially, or independently. These criteria have a significant impact on both the reliability allocation and measurement.

The next step is to utilize various techniques to eliminate and/or control potential hazards. The standard states an "order of preference" for activities to eliminate, reduce, or control risks. These four approaches should be used in conjunction with each other because they serve complementary purposes. This is particularly true when trying to reduce or control high risk hazards. As the software safety handbook [9] observes:

> ... most hazards have more than one design or risk reduction requirement unless the hazard is completely eliminated through the first (and only) design requirement.

The standard assigns first priority to eliminating or reducing risks through design or redesign efforts. As the standard states [8]:

> A safe design is a prerequisite for safe operations with the goal being to produce an inherently safe product that will have the minimum safety-imposed operational restrictions.

According to the standard, tradeoff studies should be conducted to analyze the different design options and the allocation of functions and features between hardware and software subsystems, to arrive at the optimal solution that satisfies safety, reliability, supportability, cost, and schedule concerns. N. Levenson[8] and N. Storey [41] also identify the need for tradeoff studies to arrive at the optimal design for both safety and reliability. As the software reliability handbook [11] points out:

> Design corrective actions may include structural changes in the system interrelationships... Design changes that result in a more robust design may allow reallocation of system reliability [and safety] requirements into lower-tiered software goals that are more achievable.

The standard assigns second priority to eliminating or controlling risks by incorporating safety devices or features in the system. As the standard states, safety features are to be designed into a system [8]:

> ... through a systematic application of standards, specifications, regulations, design handbooks, ESH design checklists, and other sources of design guidance.

In the case of software, this guidance comes from the software safety handbook [9], software reliability handbook [11], and the SAE FMECA procedures [12]. The standard lists examples of system safety features to incorporate to help control risk: hardware/software

---

[8]Leveson, N. *Safeware: System Safety and Computers*, Addison-Wesley, 1995.

interlocks, fail safe design, periodic functional checks of device safety, warning signals, and alerts. In the software domain this would also involve incorporating design features such as partitioning, diversity, information hiding, block recovery, and fault tolerance [41].

The standard assigns third priority to ensuring that the system provides adequate warnings and alerts to system operators. This implies that the software has robust error detection features which: 1) alert the operator when the system encounters an unknown or unstable state; 2) verify all command inputs before performing safety-critical functions; and 3) warn the operator when erroneous inputs or commands have been received, especially when they affect safety-critical functions.

The standard assigns fourth priority to providing thorough training and operational procedures to system operators, end users, and maintenance staff. All personnel involved with the operation and use of a system should thoroughly understand the potential risk associated with using a system and the consequences of not following standard procedures.

The standard requires several activities to be performed which assess different aspects of the effectiveness of the mitigation strategies, as shown in Figure 5.1. A safety assessment is performed to "document a comprehensive evaluation of the mishap risk being assumed [8]." A safety assessment should be performed at key milestones or decision points in the project, for example at the end of the design phase, at the end of the development phase prior to testing, or at the completion of testing and prior to deployment.

Likewise, software reliability is assessed at each key milestone. As the software reliability handbook [11] states:

> Software reliability prediction is performed at each phase of the software development process... Product and process metrics applicable to the goals of the project are collected and used to predict the failure rate that the software will exhibit ... at deployment.

The handbook provides detailed guidance on collecting and analyzing software reliability metrics similar to Chapter 10. That information will not be repeated here. This process provides an ongoing assessment of whether or not a project is on track for meeting specified safety and reliability goals.

The safety assessment report should assess the safety of the entire system. A few of the important software safety items to evaluate include [8, 9, 41]:

- the role of software in contributing to potential hazards;
- the role of software in controlling or mitigating potential hazards;
- the degree to which software safety requirements have been satisfied;
- the safety criteria and methodology used to classify and rank hazards, plus any assumptions on which the criteria or methodologies were based or derived, including the definition of acceptable risk;
- the results of static and dynamic analyses conducted to validate system and software safety; and

- an assessment of residual risk.

Any anomalies, hazards, or risk which must be resolved before proceeding to the next phase should be highlighted in the report.

Safety test and evaluation activities, both static and dynamic, are performed to ensure that safety is adequately considered during system testing and to provide the data (results) analyzed by other risk control tasks. Safety test plans and procedures should be developed from the safety requirements in order to demonstrate that the requirements are complete, the requirements have been satisfied, residual risk has been controlled to an acceptable level, and therefore the system is safe to operate in the intended environment [9, 41, 42, 44]. The software reliability handbook [11] offers some cautionary advice concerning testing results:

> ... many of the testing and reliability estimation techniques developed for hardware components are not directly applicable to software and care must therefore be taken when interpreting the implications of test results for operational reliability.

Proposed engineering change requests (ECRs) and system problem reports (SPRs) must be evaluated to determine the effect of their implementation on system safety and reliability. This evaluation is particularly important in the software domain, because it is a well-known fact that enhancements or corrections to one part of the system can unmask or introduce defects in another part of the system. Formal change control procedures must be followed throughout the system lifecycle with safety engineers as active members of the configuration control board.

Safety verification activities are performed to demonstrate through static analysis and dynamic analysis that safety-critical hardware, software, and procedures comply with ESH requirements [8]. These verification activities are conducted by an independent team as an adjunct verification to the safety test and evaluation activity. Testing conducted as part of the safety assessment, safety test and evaluation, and safety verification activities is quite different from normal functional testing. As the software safety handbook [9] points out:

> Testing to provide critical software assurance differs in emphasis from general software testing to demonstrate correct behavior. There should be a great deal of emphasis placed on demonstrating that, even under stressful conditions, the software does not present a hazard; this means a considerable amount of testing for critical software will be fault injection, boundary condition and out of range testing, and exercising those portions of the input space that are related to potential hazards.

The types of verification activities to be performed are defined based on the safety requirements and the intended operational environment. The standard recommends simulating known failure modes to verify the correct and timely system response. The adequacy of the design, safety features, error handling, fault tolerance, warnings, and alerts must be verified. The safety verification report should demonstrate traceability between the safety requirements, design, test plan and procedures, and pass/fail criteria. The results observed must be analyzed and interpreted in order to support the overall conclusion and recommendation of the report.

Safety compliance assessment activities are undertaken to ensure that the system, the processes by which it was developed, and specified operational procedures comply with all applicable safety standards. In the software domain, this would imply verifying compliance with:

1. the tasks in MIL-STD-882D that apply to software, as shown in Figure 5.1;

2. verifying that the guidance provided in the software safety handbook [9] and the software reliability handbook [11] was adhered to; and

3. verifying that guidance on how to perform a software FMECA and integrating the results with the hardware and system-level FMECA was followed [12].

Assessing compliance to general purpose software engineering standards is not part of the System Safety Program; responsibility for this lies with other program elements.

Interaction with System Safety and Other Standards

MIL-STD-882D follows a layered approach to standards, as shown in Figure 5.2. MIL-STD-882D, a safety engineering standard, relies on other general purpose engineering standards to address nonsafety engineering issues. At the same time, guidance documents are used to supplement and interpret MIL-STD-882D for the software domain.

Roles, Responsibilities, and Qualifications of Project Members

MIL-STD-882D recognizes system safety engineering as a professional specialty. As a result, during the procurement process qualifications for key safety engineering positions are required to be defined. For example, the software safety handbook [9] identifies "desired minimum qualifications" of software safety engineers as:

- B.S. in Computer Science or Computer Engineering

- System Safety Management course

- System Safety Analysis course

- Software Acquisition and Development course

- System Engineering course

- 2–5 years System Safety Engineering or Management

Level III: Software-Specific Safety and Reliability Guidance

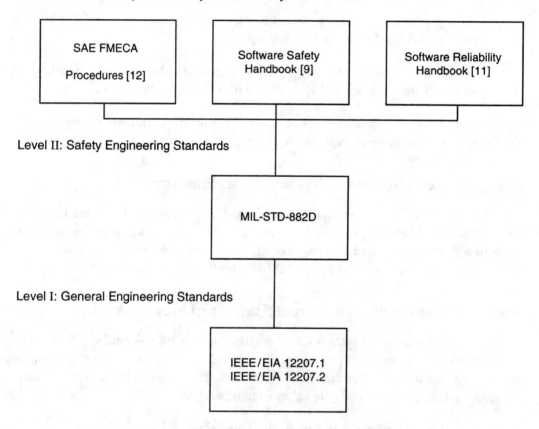

Figure 5.2: MIL-STD-882D software safety and reliability standards environment.

Data Items Produced

Several data items are produced by adherence to MIL-STD-882D. Those which may be applicable to safety-critical software projects are listed in Table 5.11. MIL-STD-882D is designed to be used in a contractual environment; hence, the contract will specify the exact format and content for presenting this information, usually by citing data item descriptions (DIDs).

- Software Safety Program Plan

- Preliminary Hazard List

- Preliminary Hazard Analysis

- Subsystem Hazard Analysis

- System Hazard Analysis

- HAZOP

- Risk Assessment Matrix

- Safety Requirements Specification

- Safety Requirements Assessment Report

- Safety Requirements Verification Report

- Hazard Log

- Residual Risk Report

Table 5.11: Software safety-related data items produced by adherence to MIL-STD-882D.

Compliance Assessment

Compliance with MIL-STD-882D is mandatory for all internal DoD activities. In fact, MIL-STD-882D includes a task, 402, which verifies compliance not only with this standard but all applicable "military, federal, national, international, and industry safety specifications, standards, and codes [8]."

Scaling

MIL-STD-882D is written specifically with tailoring in mind. For example, it states that [8]:

> The number of phases and decision points should be tailored to meet the specific needs of the individual program.

In addition, the standard permits some flexibility for each project to define hazard likelihood and severity categories and to select the appropriate data item descriptions (DIDs).

5.1.4   Strengths

MIL-STD-882D has several technical and programmatic strengths. First, MIL-STD-882D recognizes safety engineering as a specialty and requires that safety engineering functions be performed by safety engineers. Second, the standard requires a comprehensive set of risk management activities to be performed throughout the lifecycle. Software, hardware, and system safety activities are fully integrated. MIL-STD-882D is not tied to a specific software lifecycle or development methodology. Supplementary software-specific guidance is provided in the software safety handbook [9], software reliability handbook [11], and SAE FMECA procedures [12]. Third, the standard permits a degree of flexibility for hazard severity categories and quantitative or qualitative hazard likelihood categories to be defined which are appropriate for each project. Fourth, the standard acknowledges the differences between hardware and software reliability and recommends the use of software control categories in lieu of software hazard likelihoods.

5.1.5   Areas for Improvement

There are a few areas in which MIL-STD-882D could be improved. First, MIL-STD-882D is written in the form of numbered tasks and activities. To be consistent with current engineering initiatives like IEEE/EIA 12207.1, IEEE/EIA 12207.2, and the Software Engineering Institute (SEI) Capability Maturity Models (CMM), it would be more appropriate to talk in terms of processes and activities. Second, MIL-STD-882D is written for use within a large organization, as the discussion of different organizations involved and their roles implies. It would helpful if guidance were provided on how to implement these functions within a small organization. Third, MIL-STD-882D is very strong in the area of hazard analysis. However, it is weak in the area of discussing software safety design features or analysis techniques other than FTA, FMECA, and testing. Limited guidance is provided in the area of COTS and software reuse. Additional guidance in these areas would be helpful.

5.1.6   Results Observed to Date

Given its recent introduction, a comprehensive study of the effectiveness of MIL-STD-882D has not yet been undertaken. However, the standard takes into account the knowledge and experience gained from the earlier versions.

5.2 DEF STAN 00-55: Requirements for Safety Related Software in Defence Equipment, U.K. Ministry of Defence (MoD)

5.2.1 Background

DEF STAN 00-55 [3, 4] is one of a series of safety standards for programmable electronic defense equipment promulgated by the U.K. Ministry of Defence (MoD). As shown in Figure 5.3, DEF STAN 00-55 provides software safety engineering guidance. This standard builds upon DEF STAN 00-56 [1, 2], which provides system safety management guidance. DEF STAN 00-58, HAZOP Studies [5,6], DEF STAN 00-41, Reliability and Maintainability Procedures [7], and DEF STAN 00-42 Part 2, Reliability and Maintainability Guides: Software [13] provide guidance on how to apply specific safety and reliability techniques to software. Reference is made to ISO 9001 and ISO 9000-3 for general software quality engineering.

DEF STAN 00-56, Safety Management Requirements, makes the observation that safety is one of the most demanding technical risks a project manager has to deal with [1]. This is true, in part, because as the standard points out safety is not an absolute but rather a nondeterministic or somewhat subjective assessment that risk has been controlled to an acceptable level that is consistent with operational needs and societal norms [1]. As a result, a comprehensive approach to safety management is needed.

DEF STAN 00-56 [1,2] promotes a continuous evolutionary approach to safety management which begins during the concept/planning phase, supports the production of a safety case and continues through system disposal. The intent is to view safety in terms of operational effectiveness so that the likelihood of systems with unacceptable safety levels arriving in the field is minimized [1]. Management controls, such as prescribing design techniques, analysis techniques, and verification activities, are imposed to evaluate risks and reduce them to an acceptable level.

DEF STAN 00-56 provides the safety management framework for an entire system or project. The production and assessment of safety-related software, as defined by DEF STAN 00-55, melds into this framework. This process is described in Section 5.2.3.

Both DEF STAN 00-55 and DEF STAN 00-56 have been evolving over the last decade. DEF STAN 00-56 was issued as an Interim Defence Standard by the U.K. Ministry of Defence (MoD) 5 April 1991. The final full DEF STAN 00-56 was issued 13 December 1996 in two parts, Requirements and General Application Guidance.

DEF STAN 00-55 was issued by the U.K. MoD in two parts, Requirements and Guidance, for a trial use/comment period beginning 5 April 1991. A couple of rounds of comments were received and reviewed since then. The final full DEF STAN was issued 1 August 1997. As D. Saddleton [38] reports, the primary changes in the final version were: 1) the added requirement for and emphasis on producing a software safety case; and 2) the expansion of the standard to apply to all safety integrity levels (SILs), not just safety-critical

Level III: Guidance for Specific Techniques

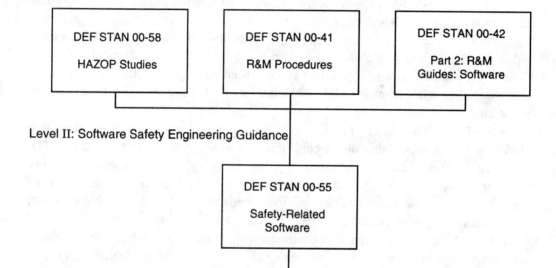

DEF STAN 00-58	DEF STAN 00-41	DEF STAN 00-42
HAZOP Studies	R&M Procedures	Part 2: R&M Guides: Software

Level II: Software Safety Engineering Guidance

DEF STAN 00-55

Safety-Related
Software

Level I: System Safety Management Guidance

DEF STAN 00-56

System Safety
Management

Figure 5.3: Relationship between U.K. MoD safety standards.

software (SIL 4). The title was also changed from "The Procurement of Safety Critical Software in Defence Equipment" to "Requirements for Safety Related Software in Defence Equipment." Contractual provisions were deleted and technical requirements clarified.

As indicated above, these two standards are meant to be used in conjunction with each other; hence they will be referred to collectively as "the standard."

5.2.2 Purpose and Scope

DEF STAN 00-55 was written to capture the current best practices for developing and analyzing safety-related software so that these techniques could be applied to defense equipment. The standard is applicable to all safety-related software in defense equipment. It is limited to software safety; hardware, human factors, and other system safety disciplines are dealt with in separate standards. DEF STAN 00-55 spans all lifecycle phases and safety integrity levels [3]:

> This standard places particular emphasis on describing the procedures necessary for specification, design, coding, production, and in-service maintenance and modification of safety-critical software (SIL 4). It also details the less rigorous approaches that are required to produce software of lower safety integrity levels (SILs 1–3).

DEF STAN 00-56 is applicable to all defense systems containing programmable electronics [1, 2].

At this point it is important to understand some of the terminology used by DEF STAN 00-55 [3]:

safety-critical software: software, including firmware, used to implement a function or component of safety integrity level 4.

safety-related software: software, including firmware, used to implement a function or component of safety integrity levels 1–4.

Safety-critical software refers to software of the highest integrity level (SIL 4); that is, a critical function or component in which a failure or design error could cause risk to human life. Safety-related software is a more generic term and applies to software of any safety integrity level above SIL 0, nonsafety related.

safety integrity: the likelihood of a safety-related system, function, or component achieving its required safety features under all the stated conditions within a stated measure of use.

In other words, safety integrity is a measure of confidence that all safety features will function correctly as specified. The degree of safety integrity needed drives the design, development, and assessment activities. The standard speaks in terms of safety integrity levels (SILs) 1–4, consistent with IEC 50128 (Chapter 3) and IEC 61508 Part 3 (Chapter 8). The probability of a dangerous failure per year per system is assigned by SIL [4]:

- SIL 4 $\geq 10^{-5}$ to $< 10^{-4}$

- SIL 3 $\geq 10^{-4}$ to $< 10^{-3}$

- SIL 2 $\geq 10^{-3}$ to $< 10^{-2}$

- SIL 1 $\geq 10^{-2}$ to $< 10^{-1}$

Formal Method: a software specification and production method, based on a mathematical system, that comprises: a collection of mathematical notations addressing the specification, design, and development phases of software production; a well-founded logical inference system in which formal verification proofs and proofs of other properties can be formulated; and a methodological framework within which software may be developed from the specification in a formally verifiable manner.

Formal Specification: part of the software specification written using the specification notation of a Formal Method.

proof obligation: mathematical statements arising during a formal design and development process that must be proved in order to verify the design or development step.

Formal Proof: discharge of a proof obligation by the construction of a complete mathematical proof.

DEF STAN 00-55 requires the use of a Formal Method, Formal Specifications, and Formal Proofs as part of the ongoing verification of completeness, consistency, correctness, and unambiguousness of software engineering artifacts, particularly the safety-related functions and features. The standard does not specify which Formal Method, that is, VDM, Z, B, and so forth to use; that decision is left to the discretion of the project team.

5.2.3 Description

The DEF STAN 00-56 safety management lifecycle consists of six primary processes [1,2]:

1. planning the system safety program;

2. defining system safety requirements;

3. performing a series of hazard analyses, that is, preliminary hazard analysis, system hazard analysis, subsystem hazard analysis, system change hazard analysis, and HAZOP studies;

4. allocating safety targets/requirements to system components, such as software;

5. assessing achievement of safety targets for each system component and the system as a whole; and

6. verifying that the resultant system safety is adequate and the individual and composite residual risk is acceptable.

The lifecycle iterates through processes 3–5 as the different hazard analyses are performed and the design and implementation is refined. Processes 3–6 are repeated until the system is determined to be "safe enough" and the residual risk is deemed acceptable.

The safety management approaches taken by DEF STAN 00-56 and MIL-STD-882D are very similar. Instead of repeating this information, the DEF STAN 00-56 safety management lifecycle will be summarized and the significant differences noted.

MIL-STD-882D and DEF STAN 00-56 promote similar sequences of hazard analysis: preliminary hazard analysis, subsystem hazard analysis, system hazard analysis, and HAZOP studies. DEF STAN 00-56 also requires a system change hazard analysis to assess the safety and reliability impact of proposed changes to the requirements, design, or implementation.

Hazard analyses are required to be conducted throughout the safety-related software lifecycle to [3]:

1. identify potential failures of safety-related systems that may cause new hazards or contribute to existing ones, and

2. establish the correct level of safety integrity for each software component.

Different types and levels of hazard analyses are conducted as the design and implementation become more detailed to evaluate the effectiveness of proposed risk control measures. Potential hazards and the sequence of events that could cause them are identified. The standard [1] notes the need to distinguish between random hardware failures and systematic software failures during this process. In the software domain the types of analysis performed would include [1, 2]:

- **functional analysis** – identifying hazards associated with normal operations, degraded-mode operations, incorrect usage, inadvertent operation, absence of function(s), and human error which causes functions to be activated too fast, too slow, or in the wrong sequence.

- **zonal analysis** – identifying hazards associated with usability on the part of the end users and maintenance staff, along with other human factors engineering concerns.

- **component failure analysis** – identifying the failure modes and rates of software components and the hardware on which they operate.

- **operating and support hazard analysis** – identifying hazardous tasks which must be performed by end users and maintenance staff and ways to reduce the potential for induced or invited errors.

DEF STAN 00-56 defines four hazard severity categories and six hazard likelihood categories as shown below [1, 2]. The definitions of the categories used by DEF STAN 00-56 and MIL-STD- 882D are quite similar.

Severity	Likelihood
catastrophic	frequent
fatal	probable
severe	occasional
minor	remote
	improbable
	implausible

DEF STAN 00-56 recommends developing a risk assessment matrix by correlating the hazard severity and likelihood, like MIL-STD-882D. However, the standard [1] recommends classifying risk acceptability into three levels (intolerable, undesirable, and tolerable) instead of four (high, serious, medium, and low). DEF STAN 00-56 does not broach the concept of software control categories; instead it recommends a qualitative assessment of the likelihood of systematic software failures, based in part on operational profiles [1].

DEF STAN 00-56 allocates safety targets by assigning a safety integrity level to each function and lower level function based on criticality. At the same time, reliability targets are allocated to system components including software. Software safety and reliability targets are derived from system level FMECA, FTA, and reliability block diagrams [13]. Safety and reliability targets should be specified for normal, abnormal, and degraded-mode operations. P. Bishop, R. Bloomfield, and P. Froome [17] note the need to consider whether architectural components operate in parallel or in series when allocating safety and reliability targets.

DEF STAN 00-41 points out that [7]:

> ...the consequences of system software should be taken into account, and allowances should be made for the contribution software may make to system failures. Reliability cannot be apportioned to software in the same way as hardware because failures due to software do not occur as a direct result of the passage of time. Also, there are no standard methods for the prediction of system reliability due to software faults.

B. Wichmann [44] concurs, with the observation that:

> ...one does not design to specific reliability targets but rather places more or less effort to achieve zero defects in the software.

The standard [1, 2] states that the process of allocating safety and reliability targets should foster design tradeoff studies and feasibility analyses to ensure that the most effective and efficient system architecture is pursued.

Design techniques to reduce, control, and/or eliminate risks and techniques used to assess the effectiveness of risk control measures are recommended according to safety integrity level, consistent with the approach taken by IEC 61508. (See Chapter 8, Table 8.4. That information will not be repeated here.)

In addition, the standard recommends reducing and controlling risks through respecification/redesign, designing in safety features, incorporating adequate warnings and alerts, and providing adequate training and operational procedures.

A safety compliance assessment report is produced at the end of the safety management lifecycle. This report determines whether: 1) hazard severity and likelihood targets have been met; and 2) the residual risk is acceptable, taking into account independent, dependent, and simultaneous failures.

Figure 5.4 illustrates the interaction between the MoD system safety and reliability standards (DEF STAN 00-56 and DEF STAN 00-41) and the software safety and reliability standards (DEF STAN 00-55 and DEF STAN 00-42 Part 2).

The DEF STAN 00-55 safety-related software lifecycle consists of seven primary processes [3,4]:

1. developing the software safety and reliability plans, as part of the system safety and reliability plans;

2. specifying software functional, performance, safety, reliability, and security requirements, based on the system requirements that were allocated to software;

3. developing a detailed design which implements these requirements;

4. translating the design into source code and executable object code;

5. verifying the correctness, completeness, consistency, accuracy, and unambiguousness of the code and its traceability to the design through Formal Proofs and other static analysis techniques;

6. verifying the correctness, completeness, consistency, accuracy, and unambiguousness of the code and its traceability to the design through dynamic analysis; and

7. validating that the software implements all requirements correctly as specified, the safety and reliability targets have been achieved, and the residual risk is acceptable.

The standard requires the use of complementary development and analysis methods to maximize the likelihood of producing safe and reliable software [3,4]:

- development of the software specification and design through Formal Methods;

- development of the software through structured methods; and

- verification of the specification, design, and software through static analysis, dynamic analysis, and Formal Proofs.

As DEF STAN 00-42 explains [13]:

> The philosophy embraced is one of improving system [safety and] reliability by early defect removal and continued defect prevention throughout the software development lifecycle.

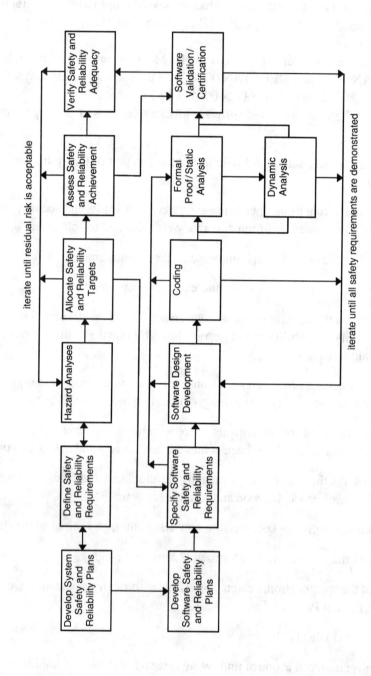

Figure 5.4: Relationship between MoD system and software safety and reliability standards [1,2,3,4,7,13].

198

In fact, the standard requires a safety assessment of the development process to analyze the potential for process failures which could lead to undetected hazardous defects being introduced into the software [4].

Processes 3–7 are repeated until all safety and reliability requirements are adequately demonstrated. The software safety and reliability engineering tasks in these processes are discussed below.

Software Safety and Reliability Planning

The first process is to plan the software safety and reliability programs and define how they will operate within the context of the system safety and reliability programs. In effect, these plans explain how DEF STAN 00-55 and DEF STAN 00-42 will be implemented on a specific project and the tasks and activities needed to do so. Organizational responsibilities, technical and managerial, should be clearly delineated. Resources needed to implement the plans, such as staff and their skills, automated tools, and training, and when they are needed must be identified.

The software safety and reliability plans should be traceable to the system safety and reliability plans. They should explain: 1) how safety and reliability requirements were allocated to software components and subcomponents; and 2) the strategies for achieving and evaluating software safety and reliability at key milestones. Specific safety and reliability measurements to be made should be agreed to by the Design Authority and MoD during the planning process [13].

The software safety and reliability plans should define the change control process that will be used on the project to identify and control baselines and maintain traceability between requirements and other software engineering artifacts. Change impact analysis must be conducted to evaluate the effect of implementing a proposed change on safety and reliability. Interaction between the change control process and the corrective action process should be defined. For changes that result from corrective action, an analysis should be undertaken to determine why the defect was not detected earlier in the lifecycle.

The standard [1] requires that a formal data reporting and corrective action system (DRACAS) be in place throughout the lifecycle. The plan should explain how this will be accomplished. A DRACAS is similar to a failure reporting and corrective action system (FRACAS); the difference is that a DRACAS also records successful results, performance, and maintenance data [7]. The software safety and reliability plans should be in place prior to developing the software requirements specification and updated at the beginning of each lifecycle phase.

The standard requires that a Code of Design Practice be developed as part of the planning process. This Code, which becomes a project standard, prescribes "specific procedures, methods, and techniques" to be used during the specification, design, development, and verification of safety-related software, such as [3,4]:

- which software lifecycle and development methodology will be used, that is, waterfall, spiral, Jackson structured design, object-oriented analysis and design, information engineering, and so on;

- which Formal Method will be used and how it will be used; for example, what formal notation will be used, how animation of specifications will be accomplished, how Formal Proofs will be constructed and evaluated;

- what programming language or restricted subset will be used, what language features can and cannot be used, what coding standards will be followed;

- what methodology will be used to distinguish between different sources, types, and severities of errors;

- what automated tools will be used on the project and during which phases, how their safety integrity, interoperability, usability, and maturity will be evaluated; and

- how preexisting software will be assessed according to the requirements of DEF STAN 00-55 and DEF STAN 00-42.

The standard requires that the selected implementation language(s) have the following characteristics [3,4]:

- strongly typed,

- block structured,

- formally defined syntax,

- predictable program execution, and

- a compiler certified to a national or international standard.

The justification for selecting a particular language must be included in the software safety case [41,43].

From his experience in the ISO group (ISO/JTC1/SC22/WG9) that is preparing guidelines for using Ada when producing high integrity systems, Wichmann [43] recommends classifying language features into:

- features that are included in the approved safe subset;

- features that are allowed, but not recommended if an alternative is available, that is, there are well known but understood problems associated with their use; and

- features that are excluded from use.

The British Computer Society (BCS) and Institution of Electrical Engineers (IEE) have developed guidance on how to select automated tools for use in developing safety-related software. They recommend comparing the required SIL with the level of influence the tool has on the safety of the target application (direct influence, indirect influence, V&V influence, or no influence) to determine the necessary tool integrity [20].

According to the standard, the Code should specify the acceptance criteria for each safety-related software engineering artifact. Procedures for dealing with unacceptable artifacts should also be defined, including capturing and tracking this information in the DRACAS.

The software safety and reliability plans should define a schedule for the formal safety and reliability reviews and audits to be conducted at each milestone and/or key decision point in the project lifecycle, how the reviews will be conducted, and what organizations/key personnel should participate. The results from formal reviews and audits are recorded in the DRACAS.

Specifying Software Requirements

The second process involves analyzing and specifying software functional, performance, safety, reliability, and security requirements and constraints which are derived from the system requirements that were allocated to software. Requirements should be decomposed to as low a level as possible to permit the design process to proceed without having to make assumptions about how to interpret the requirements. The standard requires that safety requirements be specified for each accident severity category and/or each identified hazard in terms of a qualitative probability of occurrence [2]. In some instances this will involve specifying unacceptable failures modes, rates, and states. The safety properties and attributes of software and data should also be specified.

DEF STAN 00-42 provides examples of characteristics to use when evaluating the completeness and accuracy of software reliability requirements [13]:

- Are failure modes known and their detection and handling specified?

- Is the software's response to out-of-range values specified for every input?

- Is a response specified if an input arrives when it should not, that is, too early, too late, before start up, while offline, or after shutdown sequence has begun?

- Are performance requirements specified for degraded-mode operations?

- Are sufficient delays incorporated into error recovery responses?

- Are data consistency checks performed before control decisions are made on that data?

The standard requires that the requirements be recorded in a Formal Notation Specification. A limited amount of English language commentary may be used to supplement or clarify the Formal Specification; however, the Formal Specification takes precedence. At first the dual specification approach may sound like redundant effort. However, when examined more closely it will be seen that this approach is very useful for capturing domain knowledge, communicating requirements to different types of stakeholders, and validating requirements at the earliest possible stage. It is well documented that most defects and re-work have as their root cause specification errors [41, 43]; hence the motivation for Formal Specifications which can be proven to be correct.

The standard requires that the Formal Specification be animated to demonstrate that all safety features, functions, and requirements have been specified correctly. Animation involves constructing an executable version of the Formal Specification, using the Formal Method tool, and exploring its behavior [17]. This is similar to producing a prototype to validate requirements. Formal Proofs are required to be constructed to prove that the specification is correct, complete, consistent, and accurate. These proofs are verified by the independent V&V team.

Table 5.12 provides a partial sample Formal Specification for a ground-based missile system. This specification identifies the two mutually exclusive modes in which the missile system can operate: ground operations or airborne operations; there are no other system modes. Ground operations is composed of two mutually exclusive states: standby or maintenance; there are no other ground operations states. Airborne operations is composed of five mutually exclusive states: launch sequence, targeting sequence, prearming sequence, arming sequence, and self destruct; there are no other airborne operations states. From this specification it is easy to tell that self destruct is not a valid ground operations state, nor maintenance a valid airborne operations state. As this example illustrates, the notation required by a Formal Specification creates a degree of accuracy, precision, and clarity far beyond that which is possible with natural languages.

MISSILEMODES
GroundOperations, AirborneOperations, AllModes: F MISSILEMODES

GroundOperations $\cup$ AirborneOperations = AllModes
GroundOperations $\cap$ AirborneOperations = 0
Standby $\cup$ Maintenance = GroundOperations
Standby $\cap$ Maintenance = 0
LaunchSequence $\cup$ TargetingSequence $\cup$ Pre-armingSequence $\cup$ ArmingSequence
      $\cup$ SelfDestruct = AirborneOperations
LaunchSequence $\cap$ TargetingSequence $\cap$ Pre-armingSequence $\cap$ ArmingSequence
      $\cap$ SelfDestruct = 0

Table 5.12: Sample formal specification for a ground-based missile system.

The Development Environment Specification is generally prepared as part of this process. The information in this specification falls into two main categories:

1. automated tools that will be used to implement the selected Formal Method, develop and analyze the design, trace requirements, perform static analysis, record and track the results of static and dynamic analysis, identify and maintain baselines, and so forth; and

2. hardware and software platforms used during development: processor(s), RAM, cache, disk storage, buses, interfaces, peripherals, operating systems, utilities, compilers, database management systems, and so forth.

This specification should identify these types of items which will be used on the project, what they will be used for, and when they will be used. Known limitations should also be identified to ensure that items are not used to perform tasks for which they are ill suited and to prevent overreliance on the accuracy of tool output during verification and validation. Differences between the specified development environment and the target operational environment should be highlighted.

The standard [3,7] requires a formal safety and reliability review of these specifications to ensure that they adhere to the Code of Design Practice, correctly interpret safety and reliability requirements, and are correct, complete, consistent, and unambiguous. Examples of requirements characteristics to evaluate during the review are given by the standard, such as [7]:

- have the requirements been validated by modelling?

- have all external interfaces been specified adequately?

- has the operational environment for transaction rates, event timing, and data volumes been defined?

- have areas of likely change been identified?

- are the requirements sufficiently complete to define system acceptance tests?

The review results and any necessary corrective action are recorded in the DRACAS.

The standard recommends conducting HAZOP studies, as defined in DEF STAN 00-58, as part of this process. In the software domain, the format and conduct of a HAZOP is similar to a joint application development (JAD) session. Representatives from all stakeholders participate in the HAZOP study: developers, end users, maintenance staff, the independent V&V team, and so on. A neutral facilitator guides the discussion. In a JAD session the group determines, clarifies, and refines requirements. In a HAZOP study, the facilitator guides the group through a discussion of system operation modes and states to identify potential hazards associated with using a system in the intended operational environment. Particular attention is paid to usability issues, operator actions, and capturing domain knowledge. A series of "guide words" are used to determine correct design values for system components, interconnection between components, and the attributes of these components, such as [5,6]:

- none/more/less

- as well as/part of

- reverse

- other than

- early/late

- before/after

The standard recommends recording the results of a HAZOP study in a tabular format with the following column headings [5,6]:

- system interconnection identification

- attribute evaluated

- applicable guide word

- consequence/implication

- indication/protection

- question/recommendation

- answers/comments

Table 5.13 illustrates a sample HAZOP study which is derived from the ground-based missile system specification in Table 5.12.

System Interconnection ID	Attribute	Guide Word	Implication	Indication/ Protection	Question/ Recommendation
Launch Sequence	initiation	part of before	Airborne Operations Targeting Prearming, Arming, Self Destruct	Software module x rejects the launch command if it is out of sequence	Verify correct launch command sequence through two independent means
		none	not while in Ground Operations		Verify that launch sequence initiation is prohibited while in maintenance or standby states

Table 5.13: Sample HAZOP study.

Software Design Development

During the software design development process the Software Design Description is prepared. The Software Design Description translates requirements from the Formal Software Specification into a design, using the agreed upon Formal Method. A limited amount of English commentary may be included to facilitate understandability. The standard recommends several design features to enhance safety and reliability [3, 4]: minimizing the use of interrupts; partitioning safety-related software, data, and interfaces; utilizing defensive programming techniques; and not allowing recursion. The standard requires that Formal Proofs be constructed to demonstrate that the design is correct and complete. These proofs are verified by the independent V&V team.

The standard recommends performing resource modelling as part of the design process to ensure that all system resources are utilized effectively and efficiently within specified performance constraints. Examples are given of items to model [3, 4, 13]:

- response times

- throughput

- low/minimum, normal, maximum, saturation/overload system loading scenarios

- minimum and maximum execution time of each module or group of modules

- context/mode switching times

- minimum and maximum database access times

- minimum and maximum communication delays and saturation points

- deadlock and race conditions

- memory management and potential conflicts

Efficient resource utilization is a prerequisite for safe and reliable system operation. As the standard states [13]:

> Both the achievement and demonstration of software [safety and] reliability should be design drivers ... to avoid delays and additional costs for the Contractor due to software [safety or] reliability problems.

A Software Target Downloading Specification, a corollary to the Software Development Environment Specification, is generally prepared as part of this process. The Software Target Downloading Specification addresses technical issues and concerns of the target operational environment and explains how the software will be transitioned from the development environment to the target operational environment. This specification identifies the steps and procedures necessary to build and install the executable application software, as well as any associated system software and utilities. In the case of firmware and programmable logic controllers (PLCs), this will include "burning-in" the chip set. In the client-server environment, this is the "push down" process. Table 5.14 provides a sample outline for a Target Downloading Specification.

The standard [3, 7] requires a formal safety and reliability review of the specifications to ensure that they are consistent with the Formal Software Requirements Specification and that they are internally consistent, correct, complete, and unambiguous. As part of this process the standard recommends conducting FTA, FMECA, and sneak circuit analysis. As P. Bishop, R. Bloomfield, and P. Froome point out [17]:

> Safety assessment should not be carried out in isolation, but as a key part of the design process. The early identification of potential problems should enable the design to be more easily modified, and should lead to a reduction in costs over safety-related projects where a less systematic approach is adopted.

Examples of design characteristics to evaluate during the formal safety and reliability review are given by the standard, such as [7]:

- Have mathematical proofs or algorithms and programs been constructed against formal requirements?

- Does the design implement diversity?

- Are data accessibility and validity checks performed?

- Does the design contain fault tolerant and fault containment features?

- Is the design structured and modular?

- Does the design contain watch dog timers?

- Does the design contain robust error detection and recovery features?

- Were group peer reviews of the design conducted?

- Has the software replication process been analyzed to verify that the process is accurate, errors are not introduced during this process, and the process is repeatable?

The review results and any necessary corrective action are recorded in the DRACAS.

Coding

During the coding process the Formal Software Design Description is translated into source code using the techniques and methods described in the Code of Design Practice. The standard encourages the use of diversity, defensive programming, and block recovery to enhance reliability [13]. If CASE tools are used to automatically generate code, they must undergo a thorough hazard analysis, per the requirements of DEF STAN 00-56 to evaluate

1. INTRODUCTION

   1.1 Purpose

   1.2 Scope

2. REFERENCES

   2.1 Normative

   2.2 Informative

3. INSTALLATION PLAN AND SCHEDULE

   3.1 Identification of Software to be Installed

   3.2 Key Installation Milestones

   3.3 Installation Schedule

4. INSTALLATION PREREQUISITES

   4.1 Hardware Platform: peripherals, end-user equipment, and interfaces

   4.2 Software Platform: operating system, databases, languages, utilities, and communications software

   4.3 Operational Requirements

   4.4 Production Control Requirements

   4.5 End-user Support Requirements

   4.6 Performance Management and Capacity Planning Requirements

   4.7 Security Requirements

5. INSTALLATION PROCEDURES

6. RISK MANAGEMENT

   6.1 Key Decision Points (Go/No Go)

   6.2 Assessment Criteria

   6.3 Key Decision Makers

   6.4 Fallback Position

7. ROLES AND RESPONSIBILITIES

   7.1 Organization Roles and Responsibilities

   7.2 Activity Coordination

Table 5.14: Sample outline for a target downloading specification.

their safety integrity [3]. According to the standard, compilers used to produce safety-related software must be certified to a national or international standard [3, 4, 13]. These evaluations are necessary to ensure that the object code is an accurate and reproducible interpretation of the source code. Formal Proofs are required to be constructed to demonstrate that the code is correct. The accuracy of these proofs is verified by the independent V&V team. Formal code inspections are required to be conducted to verify that: 1) the code adheres to the Code of Design Practice; 2) there is no redundant or unused code; and 3) the code is traceable to the design, complete, consistent, correct, and unambiguous [3, 4]. The standard gives examples of undesirable coding techniques to look for during a formal code inspection [7]:

- unconditional jumps

- backward jumps

- multiple entries to procedures

- self-modifying code

- recursion

The review results and any necessary corrective action are recorded in the DRACAS.

Formal Proofs and Static Analysis

The construction of Formal Proofs and the performance of static analysis techniques is an ongoing process throughout the software lifecycle. J. Draper [25] reports on the benefit of using Formal Proofs with static analysis, from his experience on the Measurable Improvement in Specification Techniques (MIST) project:

> Overall it was clear that proof, animation, and review complemented each other. Each discovered errors that were overlooked by the other processes.

The standard requires that Formal Proofs and other static analysis techniques be used throughout the software lifecycle to verify correctness and analyze characteristics of software engineering artifacts which affect safety and reliability. As mentioned earlier, Formal Proofs are required for the Formal Software Specification, the Software Design Description, and the source code. The Formal Proofs are constructed by the development team; the independent V&V team verifies their accuracy. Formal Proofs must be validated before proceeding to the next lifecycle phase.

The standard recommends using static analysis techniques to analyze, at a minimum, control flow, information flow, and data usage. In particular the standard [2–4, 13] recommends performing FTA, FMECA, HAZOP studies, event tree analysis, cause consequence analysis, common mode failure analysis, and Markov modelling and developing reliability block diagrams. Cleanroom techniques are recommended for critical software [13]. If emulation and/or simulation are performed as part of the static analysis process, the accuracy and repeatability of the results must be verified before they are acted upon. Metrics, such as those described in Chapter 10 should be collected and analyzed throughout the lifecycle to monitor progress toward achieving safety and reliability goals. The results of performing static analysis techniques and verifying the Formal Proofs are provided to the development team and recorded in the DRACAS, along with any necessary corrective action. These results, when analyzed and interpreted, may identify the need for changes in the requirements, design, and/or code.

Standard industry practice is to classify defects according to type, source, and severity. On the Hercules C-130J Static Code Analysis (SCA) project for the U.K. MoD, R. Granville and K. Harrison [29] report that defects were first classified according to whether: a) they could affect safety, b) they could affect safety in the presence of other defects, and c) they had no effect on safety. This two-level defect classification process allowed resources to be focused on defects affecting safety.

Dynamic Analysis

As the standard notes, dynamic analysis is conducted as a supplement to Formal Proofs and static analysis [4]. The dynamic analysis process, which begins as the coding process completes, involves unit, integration, usability, stress, interface, functional, structural, and regression testing. To the extent practical, testing should be conducted in the development environment and the target operational environment; differences in the results observed should be highlighted and evaluated. All test cases/procedures must be repeatable to ensure the accuracy and verifiability of the results [41].

The number, type, and severity of defects found during each testing exercise are recorded in the DRACAS and analyzed to identify common problem areas and trends. All defects must be resolved or waivers granted before proceeding to the next phase, as defined in the Code of Design Practice. The standard [3] requires that all safety functions be thoroughly tested; for example by exercising all statements, branches, cases within case statements including otherwise clauses, and loop initialization, execution, and termination. The criteria used to design test cases and the reasoning used to determine the extent of test coverage needed should be recorded in the software safety and reliability cases. Dynamic analysis is performed by the independent V&V team; the results are recorded in the DRACAS, along with any necessary corrective action.

Wichmann makes a case for conducting functional testing according to the user-manual to cross check against specification errors. As he observes [44]:

> If software is to be maintained over a long period, then after the first 'complete' release and acceptance, it may be that the user-manual will be the key document rather than the original specification. If this is the case ... testing judged against the user-manual is a long-term benefit.

Wichmann further identifies a set of metrics by which to measure the adequacy of structural testing [44]:

- number of components regarded as critical

- total number of statements and percent executed in critical components; percent not tested and rationale

- date of first issue of critical components and summary of error statistics logged since then, that is, defect type, severity, source, and time distribution

- number of components in total system

- percent of total components executed once during system test

Software Validation/Certification

The software validation process takes place in the target operational environment. During this process the independent V&V team verifies that the software satisfies all specified functional, performance, safety, and reliability requirements. They are responsible for assessing whether or not the specified safety integrity has been achieved. This may involve repeating previous static and dynamic analyses and performing new instances of these activities. The standard recommends paying particular attention to fault tolerant features, error handling features, and timing constraints during validation.

In accordance with the standard [3] the final step in the validation process, assuming it is successful, is certification and acceptance into service. This certificate indicates that all requirements of DEF STAN 00-55 have been met; all safety functions, features, and requirements are implemented correctly as specified; and the stated safety integrity has been achieved. The certificate is signed by the Design Authority and the Independent Safety Auditor. However, as the standard [3] points out the Design Authority retains the legal responsibility for the software's safety and reliability.

Prior to developing the certificate, the Design Authority and the Independent Safety Auditor review the information recorded in the DRACAS, the software safety case, and the software reliability case. A major component of the DRACAS is referred to as the safety records log. The safety records log, like the DRACAS, is a living compendium of verification and validation reports. As the standard notes, the safety records log provides [3]:

> ... comprehensive evidence that the safety integrity of the safety-related software has [or has not] been achieved, such as:
>
>   - results of hazard analyses and safety risk assessments,
>   - minutes from formal safety reviews,
>   - results of static and dynamic analyses,
>   - results from checking Formal Proofs, and
>   - in-service anomaly reports and their resolution.

DEF STAN 00-55 states that [3]:

> A safety case, which justifies the suitability of the software development process, tools, and methods, is required for software of all integrity levels ... and forms part of the equipment safety case required by DEF STAN 00-56.

A software safety case is a systematic means of reporting the data needed by contractual, regulatory, and/or certification authorities, in order to certify a system is safe to use in the intended operational environment. A software safety case organizes evidence to demonstrate that: 1) the activities, tasks, and measurements stated in the software safety plan were performed successfully; 2) software safety requirements are consistent with system safety requirements; and 3) software safety requirements have been achieved. It is a living document that records ongoing progress toward achieving and assessing software safety.

DEF STAN 00-55 expects a software safety case to be organized in four parts [3,4]:

- claims,

- assumptions,

- evidence, and

- arguments.

Claims and/or subclaims are made about the software in direct response to each software safety requirement. Assumptions, based on experience with preexisting systems, platforms, automated tools, and so forth are used to support the claims. Evidence from audits, formal reviews, static analysis, dynamic analysis, proof checking, and so on, as recorded in the DRACAS, is organized to support the claims. The ideal situation is to combine evidence from multiple diverse sources so that the cumulative weight of the evidence makes the case. The different types of evidence include:

deterministic – axioms, formal proofs, truth tables, state transition diagrams, prior research and experience;

probabilistic – failure rates, static analysis results, assumptions about independence; and

qualitative – design features such as diversity, partitioning, and information hiding; compliance with standards and industry best practices.

A logical argument links the assumptions and evidence to substantiate a claim or subclaim. DEF STAN 00-55 requires two or more diverse arguments to justify each claim about a safety-related software product or process. A software safety case is a quasi-legal document because system acceptance and certification is based on the evidence and reasoning it contains; hence great care should be taken to ensure the accuracy, completeness, and currency of the information.

A software safety case goes through three stages within the context of DEF STAN 00-55 [3,4]:

- preliminary software safety case,

- interim software safety case, and

- operational software safety case.

The preliminary software safety case is usually submitted during the proposal or best and final offer (BAFO) contractual phase. It presents a justification of the strategies to achieve and assess software safety as contained in the software safety plan; that is, logical reasoning that the required SIL will be achieved.

The interim software safety case is begun after the software requirements specification is written. It captures ongoing evidence from the different formal reviews and lifecycle phases to demonstrate that the project is (or is not) on track for meeting the required SIL. The final version of the interim software safety case supports the initial system certification.

The operational software safety case is begun prior to in-service use and updated whenever any corrective, adaptive, or preventive maintenance is performed. It highlights the risks associated with using a system and collects and analyzes information about in-service anomalies. The final version of the operational software safety case reflects the safety issues associated with decommissioning the system. Table 5.15 illustrates the relationship between contractual phases and software safety case stages.

A software reliability case, a parallel document to the software safety case, focuses on demonstrating the achievement of software reliability requirements. DEF STAN 00-42 Part 2 requires a software reliability case as a corollary to the software reliability plan; for example, proof that the combination of fault management strategies in the plan were effective. DEF STAN 00-42 expects a software reliability case to be structured the same as the software safety case [13]:

- claims,

- assumptions,

- evidence, and

- arguments.

The software reliability case forms part of the system reliability case.

Again, diverse types and sources of evidence should be provided:

deterministic – Formal Proofs, execution time analysis, FTA, FMECA, simulation results, software reliability product and process metrics like those discussed in Chapter 10

probabilistic – statistics from dynamic analysis and operational profiles

qualitative – design features such as fault tolerance, fault containment, block recovery; compliance with standards and industry best practices

A software reliability case also goes through three stages: proposal stage, development stage, and in-service stage, as shown in Table 5.15.

Contract Phase	DEF STAN 00-55 Software Safety Case Stage	DEF STAN 00-42 Part 2 Software Reliability Case Stage
I. Pre-Award Proposal, BAFO	Preliminary Software Safety Case: justification that approach in software safety plan will achieve required SIL	Preliminary Software Reliability Case: justification that approach in software reliability plan will achieve specified reliability requirements
II. Post-Award Development and Assessment	Interim Software Safety Case: ongoing evidence collection that indicates a project is on track for meeting the required SIL	Development Stage Software Reliability Case: ongoing evidence collection that indicates a project is on track for meeting specified reliability requirements
III. Transition to Maintenance Contract	Operational Software Safety Case: complete set of safety arguments and evidence that the required SIL was achieved and is being maintained	In-Service Stage Software Reliability Case: complete set of reliability arguments and evidence that the specified reliability requirements were achieved and are being maintained

Note: Software safety and reliability cases should be baselined at key project milestones, concurrent with the system safety and reliability cases.

Table 5.15: Relationship between contractual phases and software safety and reliability case stages.

Roles, Responsibilities, and Qualifications of Project Members

DEF STAN 00-55 identifies the key personnel/organizational roles during the development of safety-related software as [3]:

- MoD program manager,

- software design authority

  - software project manager
  - software design team

- independent verification and validation (V&V) team,

- independent safety auditor, and

- software project safety engineer.

The design authority is responsible for all aspects of the design, development, and safety engineering of the safety-related software, including certification and demonstrating compliance with the Code of Design Practice [3]. The design authority is required to demonstrate to the MoD program manager that personnel have the appropriate software safety engineering knowledge, skills, and experience to perform their assigned duties effectively. In fact, the standard requires that resumes be submitted to the program manager for approval prior to staff being employed on the project. The standard suggests citing competency requirements in the software safety and reliability plans. The standard provides examples of competency requirements to evaluate when selecting project staff members [4]:

- familiarity with the standards and procedures to be used,

- knowledge of the legal framework and responsibilities for safety,

- knowledge and experience in safety engineering,

- experience in the application domain,

- experience in software development,

- experience in the development of safety-related software,

- experience with the methods, tools, and technologies to be employed,

- education, training, and professional certification, and

- length, depth, and breadth of relevant knowledge and experience; applicability to the required SIL.

Data Items Produced

DEF STAN 00-55 identifies several data items which may be produced throughout the safety-related software lifecycle and assigns responsibility for them, as shown in Table 5.16. The design authority and MoD agree upon the documentation set, format, and content that is appropriate for a particular project. The standard supports paper and/or electronic documentation. Part 2 of the standard provides guidance on the informational content of some of the data items [4].

Compliance Assessment

Compliance with DEF STAN 00-55 is required for all MoD safety-related software projects. The design authority is responsible for demonstrating this compliance. This is accomplished in part through a compliance assessment matrix which maps the activities performed and the products produced to each subclause in Part 1 of the standard. The independent safety auditor is responsible for verifying the veracity and completeness of the compliance [3].

Scaling

The standard mentions the issue of scaling in two contexts. The first concerns tailoring the rigor with which activities are conducted, the amount of detail needed to substantiate them, and independence requirements to correspond to the required SIL. The second concerns tailoring the required documentation set, its content and format, so that it is appropriate for the project.

5.2.4 Strengths

DEF STAN 00-55 has several strong points which are derived from the fact that it is part of an overall safety standards framework. First, the safety-related software lifecycle is fully integrated with the system safety management lifecycle. Feedback between the processes of DEF STAN 00-55 and DEF STAN 00-56 ensures adequate evaluation of software safety and system safety. Second, additional technique specific guidance is provided by DEF STAN 00-41 and DEF STAN 00-58. DEF STAN 00-41 highlights the need to treat software reliability differently than hardware reliability and discusses techniques to enhance and evaluate software reliability. DEF STAN 00-58 explains how to conduct a HAZOP study. Third, design and assessment techniques are assigned based on software integrity requirements, similar to other standards discussed in this book. This allows resources to be focused on the most critical software components.

Safety-Related Software Lifecycle Phase	Data Item	Responsible
Software Safety and Reliability Planning	– Software Safety Plan – Software Reliability Plan – Software QA Plan – Software CM Plan – Code of Design Practice – Acceptance Test Specification – Software Development Plan – Risk Management Plan	– Design Authority
	– V&V Plan – Acceptance Test Specification	– Independent V&V Team
	– Software Safety Audit Plan	– Independent Safety Auditor
Specifying Software Requirements	– Formal Software Requirements Specification	– Design Authority
	– Specification Records	– Independent V&V Team
Software Design Development	– Software Design Description	– Design Authority
	– Design Records	– Independent V&V Team
Coding	– Source Code – Object Code	– Design Authority
Formal Proofs and Static Analysis	– Formal Proofs	– Design Authority
	– Safety Records Log	– Independent V&V Team
	– Safety Audit Reports	– Independent Safety Auditor
Dynamic Analysis	– Safety Records Log – Test Records	– Independent V&V Team
	– Safety Audit Reports	– Independent Safety Auditor
Software Validation/ Certification	– User Manuals – Maintenance Plan and Procedures – Configuration Records – Software Safety Case – Software Reliability Case – Safety Certificate	– Design Authority
	– Safety Records Log – Test Records – Acceptance Test Report	– Independent V&V Team
	– Safety Audit Reports – Safety Certificate	– Independent Safety Auditor

Table 5.16: Data items produced by adherence to DEF STAN 00-55 [3].

5.2.5   Areas for Improvement

It would useful if DEF STAN 00-55 provided more substantial guidance in the area of software reuse in general and COTS software in particular. At present the standard states that previously developed software must be reverse engineered to bring it into compliance with the standard; the reverse engineering activities being proportional to the required SIL.

5.2.6   Results Observed to Date

Studies are underway to evaluate the effectiveness of this standard and analyze the results observed. A few issues have emerged as part of this process.

DEF STAN 00-55 was one of the first standards to mandate the use of Formal Methods. As Saddleton [39] notes, DEF STAN 00-55:

> ... made a major contribution to pushing forward the technology for developing high quality software to provide the necessary assurance that the software meets the safety requirements demanded for safety-critical applications.

Reaction to the requirement to use Formal Methods has been mixed. In the eight years since the interim standard was issued, it appears that the greatest benefit seems to be derived from the rigor imposed by Formal Specifications [25, 35]. This is causing some to question whether it is necessary to require that Formal Methods be used throughout the lifecycle or just during requirements specification [38, 39, 41].

A second issue concerns the applicability of the standard to application specific integrated circuits (ASICs). While the safety engineering principles are the same, Saddleton reports that it was decided that the best approach would be to develop a separate safety standard for ASICs [38].

5.3   Commercial Off-the-Shelf (COTS) Software Acquisition Guidelines and COTS Policy Issues, Communications and Information Systems Agency, NATO

Recent acquisition reforms have led the defense industry to greater use of COTS software products. COTS products offer the potential advantages of reduced cost and development times. At the same time, as noted in Chapter 2, the use of COTS products in high integrity mission critical systems raises concerns about safety, reliability, interoperability, and long-term maintainability. The NATO COTS Software Acquisition Guidelines provide a practical approach to evaluating some of these risks.

The NATO COTS Software Acquisition Guidelines were developed for three specific reasons [10]:

1. to define a consistent COTS software acquisition strategy within NATO;

2. to identify the major issues associated with COTS software acquisition, in order to meet prioritized system requirements; and

3. to provide practical guidance through which COTS software components may be selected by careful vendor and product assessments.

The intent is that the Guidelines will become part of NATO's Software Management Policy.

The NATO Guidelines are to be applied only to COTS software, not to software reuse in general. As the Guidelines point out [10]:

> Whilst the use of all forms of off-the-shelf software involves the management and technical assessment of such issues as meeting requirements specification, architectural conformance, component integration, etc. the successful use of COTS components additionally requires detailed commercial market knowledge and vendor and acquisition risk assessment.

The Guidelines also clarify that COTS software products that are modified or customized are no longer COTS software.

COTS software is developed for the generic end user operating in a normal office environment, not high integrity mission critical environments. Commercial software products are not developed according to software safety, reliability, or security standards. Given the generic structure of COTS software, it is unlikely that a product will satisfy all requirements; safety, reliability, and security requirements being the most obvious examples [10]. The NATO Guidelines recommend clarifying, verifying, and prioritizing operational requirements prior to beginning the COTS selection process. The lack of software engineering artifacts accompanying commercial products makes it difficult to perform comprehensive verification and validation activities. In addition, there are the recurring problems associated with bugs, undocumented features, memory conflicts, and unexpected behavior. Hence, the use of COTS software is not a panacea. As the Guidelines note, there is a tradeoff between cost, reliability, and requirements satisfaction [10].

The Guidelines identify four primary risk areas associated with the use of COTS software products in defense equipment [10]:

1. complex integration problems, which may lead to a failure to meet requirements;

2. cost and resource escalation due to item #1;

3. vendor lock-in since the license relationship continues throughout the system lifecycle, risk of product being discontinued or no longer supported, and no control over release management; and

4. more complex configuration management due to the mixture of custom and COTS software.

To facilitate the assessment of these risks the NATO Guidelines identify assessment criteria for COTS software vendors and products, along with specific issues to be analyzed during each lifecycle phase. (See Tables 5.17 through 5.19.) While these checklists are not specifically written for safety-related software, they do raise important concerns and can easily be used with MIL-STD-882D and DEF STAN 00-55.

5.4 Summary

This chapter has reviewed two of the leading safety engineering standards used by the defense industry today. These two standards take similar approaches to system mishap risk management; however, there are differences in their approaches to achieving and assessing software safety and reliability.

MIL-STD-882D is a system safety standard which promotes a comprehensive risk management process. Programmatic details are emphasized as well as technical details. Software is viewed as a system component. Software specific safety and reliability guidance is provided through the software safety handbook [9], the software reliability handbook [11], and the SAE FMECA procedures [12].

DEF STAN 00-55 is one of a series of standards which address safety engineering concerns for programmable electronic defense equipment. The activities and processes of this standard fold into the DEF STAN 00-56 system safety management process. Software safety and reliability engineering activities are specified for each lifecycle phase. Design features and verification activities are specified according to the required safety integrity level. Formal Specifications, static analysis, and the production of a safety case are required.

Neither standard addresses the issue of COTS software in any detail. This is surprising given the emphasis on COTS software in order to deploy software intensive systems faster and cheaper, in response to acquisition reforms. Since both the U.K. and the U.S. are part of NATO, one can reasonably assume that their policies and practices concerning the use of COTS software in safety-critical or safety-related systems does not differ greatly from that provided by NATO.

1. General data on vendor's market status

    - name
    - legal type of organization
    - countries of representation
    - market status/standing
    - organization structure
    - size/number and qualifications of personnel
    - gross annual turnover
    - capital basis
    - customer references
    - position on the market
    - duration of establishment on the market
    - reputation of vendor in terms of product quality

2. Service-related data

    - domain(s) of company experience
    - domain(s) of major specialization
    - product line offered
    - product sale numbers per year
    - track record of secure products
    - customer base/size/track record
    - agreements with suppliers
    - participation in standardization activities
    - support capability

3. Contracting-related data

    - rates per hour
    - pricing policy
    - types of contracts
    - licensing policy
    - maintenance, support, training arrangements
    - release policy
    - company accreditation
    - warranty

Table 5.17: NATO assessment criteria for COTS software vendors [10].

1. Requirements Match

   - subset implementation, less functionality than required
   - superset implementation, more functionality than required
   - critical functional, performance, safety, reliability and security requirements met

2. Performance

   - general office environment
   - project specific environment
   - minimal performance capability

3. Security, Reliability, Maturity

   - product evaluated or under evaluation
   - how long on the market, number of users
   - NATO project experience with product
   - known problems and limitations

4. Conformance to Standards

   - NOSIP and NATO OSE compliant
   - proprietary standards used
   - data modelling, data dictionary standards, for example, UML compliant
   - portability, for example, platforms supported
   - scalability

5. Architectural Environment

   - required computer and network architecture
   - required operating systems
   - software dependencies
   - resource utilization requirements

6. Costs

   - actual product
   - documentation
   - maintenance and licensing
   - telephone and/or on-site support
   - training
   - cost per user

Table 5.18: NATO assessment criteria for COTS software products [10].

NATO Software Management Lifecycle Phase	COTS Issues/Analysis Needed
Needs Justification	− potential availability of COTS-based solutions assessed, along with inherent operational or technical constraints
Requirements Specification and Concept Development	− risk assessment of COTS solution: 1) satisfying essential requirements; and 2) compatibility with architectural framework − prototyping may be necessary to clarify these issues
Definition and Design	− decision to use/not use COTS based on: requirements satisfaction, COTS functionality, market surveys of vendors and products, assessment of integration difficulty, selection of suitable components and packages, availability of reliability data from vendor
Development	− integration with system software and custom application software − component verification and system validation − interoperability of COTS and custom software
Deployment	− site acceptance testing and certification − training of end users, operational and maintenance staff
Operations	− accommodating updates and new releases in the system − coordinating vendor support

Table 5.19: COTS software issues to be evaluated during each lifecycle phase, per NATO guidelines [10].

5.5 Discussion Problems

1. Which risk management activities are performed during the concept and requirements phase?

2. Discuss the advantages and disadvantages of Formal Specifications compared to natural language specifications.

3. Explain the difference between hazard likelihood and a software control category and the reason for this distinction. Identify situations in which it would be more appropriate to use likelihood than control category and vice versa.

4. What is the purpose of a software safety case? What is the purpose of a software reliability case?

5. What is a risk assessment matrix used for? When is it generated?

6. When should HAZOP studies be performed? Explain the difference between FTA and a HAZOP study.

7. How is the effectiveness of risk mitigation strategies evaluated?

8. What design techniques does DEF STAN 00-55 promote for safety-related software?

9. When and how is residual risk assessed? What criteria are used to determine its acceptability?

10. Discuss the advantages and disadvantages of using COTS software products in defense equipment.

11. Explain the difference between software functional requirements, safety requirements, and reliability requirements, and give examples of each.

12. Why are design tradeoff studies performed?

13. Is there any benefit to identifying intermediate cause(s) of hazards in addition to the root cause?

14. Explain the difference between a DRACAS and a FRACAS.

15. What situations lend themselves better to a qualitative assessment of hazard likelihood than quantitative and vice versa?

16. Explain the difference in evaluating the use of a COTS software product in a safety-related system compared to in-house software reuse.

17. Briefly discuss the links between the DEF STAN 00-56 safety management lifecycle and the DEF STAN 00-55 safety-related software lifecycle.

18. Explain how safety and reliability targets are allocated.

Additional Resources

Primary Source Documents

[1]   DEF STAN 00-56: Safety Management Requirements for Defence Systems Containing Programmable Electronics, Part 1: Requirements, UK Ministry of Defence,
(MoD), 13 December 1996.

[2]   DEF STAN 00-56: Safety Management Requirements for Defence Systems Containing Programmable Electronics, Part 2: General Application Guidance, UK Ministry
of Defence (MoD), 13 December 1996.

[3]   DEF STAN 00-55: Requirements for Safety Related Software in Defence Equipment,
Part 1: Requirements, UK Ministry of Defence (MoD), 1 August 1997.

[4]   DEF STAN 00-55: Requirements for Safety Related Software in Defence Equipment,
Part 2: Guidance, UK Ministry of Defence (MoD), 1 August 1997.

[5]   DEF STAN 00-58: HAZOP Studies on Systems Containing Programmable Electronics, Part 1: Requirements, UK Ministry of Defence (MoD), (interim) 26 July 1996.

[6]   DEF STAN 00-58: HAZOP Studies on Systems Containing Programmable Electronics, Part 2: General Application Guidance, UK Ministry of Defence (MoD), (interim)
26 July 1996.

[7]   DEF STAN 00-41: Reliability and Maintainability—MoD Guide to Practices and Procedures, UK Ministry of Defence (MoD), 25 June 1993.

[8]   MIL-STD-882D:[9] Mishap Risk Management (System Safety), U.S. Department of
Defense (DoD) Standard Practice, (draft) 20 October 19989.

Related Safety, System, and Software Engineering Standards

[9]   Software System Safety Handbook: A Technical and Managerial Team Approach,
Joint Software Safety Committee, DoD, September 30, 1997.

[10] Commercial off-the-shelf (COTS) Software Acquisition Guidelines and COTS Policy
Issues, Communications and Information Systems Agency, NATO, 1st revision, 10
January 1996.

[11] System and Software Reliability Assurance, Reliability Analysis Center (RAC), DoD,
September 1997.

---

[9]This standard, when final, will supersede MIL-STD-882C.

[12] Recommended Best Practices for FMECA Procedures, Society of Automotive Engineers (SAE) International, 1998.[10]

[13] DEF STAN 00-42 Reliability and Maintainability Assurance Guides, Part 2: Software, UK Ministry of Defence (MoD), 1 September 1997.

[14] IEEE/EIA 12207.1 Guide for Information Technology - Software Lifecycle Processes—Lifecycle Data, Industry Implementation of ISO/IEC 12207:1995, September 1, 1997.[11]

[15] IEEE/EIA 12207.2 Guide for Information Technology - Software Lifecycle Processes—Implementation Considerations, Industry Implementation of ISO/IEC 12207:1995, September 1, 1997.[12]

Relevant Publications

[16] Barnes, J. *High Integrity Ada: The Spark Approach*, Addison-Wesley Longman, 1997.

[17] Bishop, P.G., Bloomfield, R.E., and Froome, P. *Guide for Project Managers on Development Involving Safety-Critical Software*, Adelard, 1994.

[18] Bishop, P.G. and Bloomfield, R.E. *The SHIP Safety Case Approach*, Adelard, 1995.

[19] Bloomfield, R.E. *SAFEIT: One Overall Approach—A Government Consultation on the Safety of Computer-Controlled Systems*, Adelard, 1990.

[20] British Computer Society (BCS) and Institution of Electrical Engineers (IEE), *Guidance for the Adoption of Tools for Use in Safety Related Software Development*, 1997.

[21] Clayton, C. *A Checklist for Software Safety*, October 5, 1998, www.ssq.org/links/safety.html.

[22] Clemens, P.L. "MIL-STD 882 and the Case for Zero Probability," *Hazard Prevention*, 3Q95, Vol. 31, No. 3, pp. 22–25.

[23] Clemens, P.L. "Hazard Probalism and Good Old MIL-STD 882C," *Hazard Prevention*, 2Q96, Vol. 32, No. 2, pp. 9–13.

[24] Dorney, H.C. and Orr, J.D. "Working with MIL-STD 882," *Proceedings of the 11th International System Safety Conference*, August 1993, p. 3.A-4-1 through p. 3.A-4-6.

[25] Draper, J. "Applying the B-Method to Avionics Software: An Initial Report on the MIST Project," *Safety and Reliability of Software Based Systems*, Springer-Verlag, 1995, pp. 288–304.

---

[10]This guidance is intended to replace MIL-STD-1629A when final.
[11]This guidance replaces MIL-STD-498.
[12]This guidance replaces MIL-STD-498.

[26] Dugan, J.B. "Fault-Tree Analysis of Computer-Based Systems," *Annual Reliability and Maintainability Symposium (RAMS 99) Tutorial Notes*, IEEE, 1999, pp. Dugan 1–24.

[27] Fragola, J.R. "Human Reliability Analysis: Risk Assessment," *Annual Reliability and Maintainability Symposium (RAMS 99) Tutorial Notes*, IEEE, 1999, pp. Fragola 1–40.

[28] Geary, K. "Defence Standard 00-56: Background and Revision," *Safety-Critical Systems*, Chapman & Hall, 1993, pp. 312–322.

[29] Granville, R. and Harrison, K. "Use of Static Code Analysis to Support the Safety Certification of Airborne Software," *Industrial Perspectives of Safety-Critical Systems*, Springer-Verlag, 1998, pp. 169–183.

[30] LaMarca, J. "The Evolution of MIL-STD 882," *Proceedings of the 11th International System Safety Conference*, August 1993, p. 3.A-2-1 through p. 3.A-2-16.

[31] Lyu, M. (ed.) *Handbook of Software Reliability Engineering*, IEEE Computer Society Press, 1996.

[32] McKinlay, A. "Using the Software Risk Matrix of MIL-STD 882C," *Proceedings of the 11th International System Safety Conference*, August 1993, p. 1.A-1-1 through p. 1.A-1-8.

[33] Myhrman, G. "Developments for Safer Systems in the Swedish Defence," *Industrial Perspectives of Safety Critical Systems*, Springer-Verlag, 1998, pp. 82–91.

[34] Patterson, F. *The Accident Cycle*, U.S. Army Yuma Proving Grounds, September 1998.

[35] Plat, N., van Katwijk, J. and Toetenel, H. "Application and Benefits of Formal Methods in Software Development," *Software Engineering Journal*, September 1992, pp. 335–346.

[36] Pullum, L. "Software Fault Tolerance," *Annual Reliability and Maintainability Symposium (RAMS 99) Tutorial Notes*, IEEE, 1999, pp. Pullum 1–22.

[37] Richardson, J.E. "MIL-STD 882C and FAR 25 – Different Routes to the Same Place," *Proceedings of the 10th International System Safety Conference*, July 1991, p. 3.1-2-1 through p. 3.1-2-13.

[38] Saddleton, D. "What's Happened to the Infamous Interim Defence Standard 00-55?" *Safety Systems*, Vol. 6, No. 3, May 1997, p. 6.

[39] Saddleton, D. "Revision of Interim Defence Standard 00-55," *Safety Systems*, May 1995, p. 11.

[40] Shimeall, T., McGraw, R., Gill, J. "Software Safety Analysis in Heterogeneous Multiprocessor Control Systems," *Proceedings of the 10th International System Safety Conference*, July 1991, p. 6.4-4-1 through p. 6.4-4-15.

[41] Storey, N. *Safety-Critical Computer Systems*, Addison-Wesley, 1996.

[42] Taylor, J. "Developing Safety Cases for Command and Control Systems," *Technology and Assessment of Safety-Critical Systems*, Springer-Verlag, 1994, pp. 69–78.

[43] Wichmann, B. "Ada for High Integrity," *Industrial Perspectives of Safety-Critical Systems*, Springer-Verlag, 1998, pp. 70–81.

[44] Wichmann, B. "Objective Test Criteria: Some Proposals for Bespoke Software," National Physics Laboratory, U.K., *NPL Report CISE 16/98*, March 1998.

Chapter 6

Nuclear Power Industry

Today in most western countries nuclear power plants supply 30 percent or more of the electricity. Nuclear energy is one of the more environmentally friendly sources of energy. However, as the Three Mile Island accident in 1979 and the Chernobyl accident in 1986 demonstrated, the potential exists for catastrophic hazards with a long-term impact. As a result, the nuclear power industry is regulated by national governments to protect public safety.

The nuclear power industry has a long history in the area of safety and reliability engineering. Recently it is has expanded into software safety and reliability engineering, as the technology for instrumentation and control (I&C) systems has migrated to software control. For example, as stated in NUREG/CR-6293 [23]:

> Software may be required to validate operational channels, identify faulty channels to operators, perform automatic switching between channels to maintain the safety system operational after a fault has been diagnosed, and to initiate alerts when the safety system is no longer functional.

P. Joannou [39] reports that the nuclear industry expects to derive several long-term benefits from this switch to digital technology:

- higher reliability, availability, and safety,

- higher productivity, due to the above, and

- quicker design changes.

This chapter examines the two dominant standards that are representative of the approaches currently being taken to ensure the safe and reliable operation of software in nuclear power plants:

- IEC 60880:1986-09, Software for Computers in Safety Systems of Nuclear Power Stations, which is widely used around the world, particularly in the European Union, and

- CE-1001-STD Rev. 1, Standard for Software Engineering of Safety Critical Software, CANDU Computer Systems Engineering Centre for Excellence, January 1995, which is used in Canada.

6.1 IEC 60880:1986-09, Software for Computers in Safety Systems of Nuclear Power Stations, including the First Supplement, IEC 60880-1 (FDIS)

6.1.1 Background

The International Electrotechnical Commission (IEC) subcommittee (SC) 45A, which is responsible for nuclear instrumentation, prepared IEC 60880. IEC SC 45A produced its first standard IEC 568[1] in 1977 and is still active today. IEC member countries participated in the formal review and balloting process. IEC 60880, one of the first standards to address software safety and reliability in the nuclear power industry, was approved and issued in September 1986. It has undergone several revalidation cycles since then and remains in effect today.

IEC 60880 was written for the express purpose of interpreting and extending established hardware safety design principles to software used in nuclear power plants. For example, the standard states that [3]:

> ...special recommendations have been produced due to the unique nature of computer systems and their software [such as]:
>
> - a general approach to the development of highly reliable software,
> - a general approach to software verification and computer systems validation, and
> - procedures for software maintenance, modification, and configuration control.

Note that software is verified while a computer system is validated. The standard also emphasizes that it should be used in conjunction with the appropriate safety standards for nuclear power plant hardware and systems, such as those mentioned in Section 6.1.3 and listed under Related Safety, System, and Software Engineering Standards at the end of this chapter.

6.1.2 Purpose and Scope

The purpose of IEC 60880 is to provide guidance for the production, operation, and maintenance of [3]:

> ...highly reliable software required for computers to be used in the safety systems of nuclear power plants for safety functions... This includes safety actuation systems, safety system support features, and the protection systems.

---

[1]IEC 568(1977) In-core Instrumentation for Neutron Fluence Rate (flux) Measurements in Power Reactors.

Accordingly, the standard levies both product and process requirements throughout the development and operational lifecycle phases. As R. Tate [52] observes:

> The standard considers every facet of the design process and it is widely used and respected within the industry.

As mentioned in Chapter 2, the standards discussed in this book do not always agree on the definition for certain terms. Hence, before proceeding it is important to understand how IEC 60880 defines these four terms [3]:

defense in depth: provision of several overlapping subsequent limiting barriers with respect to one threshold, such that the threshold can only be surpassed if all barriers have failed.

fault tolerance: built-in capability of a system to provide continued correct execution in the presence of a limited number of hardware or software faults.

validation: the test and evaluation of the integrated computer system (hardware and software) to ensure compliance with the functional, performance, and interface requirements.

verification: the process of determining whether or not the product of each phase of the digital computer software development process fulfills all the requirements imposed by the previous phase.

6.1.3 Description

IEC 60880 is applicable to the entire software lifecycle, both during development and after the software becomes operational. The standard identifies seven lifecycle phases and assigns tasks and activities to each:

- software requirements analysis and specification,

- development, which includes design and coding,

- verification, which is ongoing throughout the lifecycle,

- hardware software integration,

- system validation,

- operations, and

- maintenance and modification.

Each phase ends with a 'critical review' of its products. A verification report is written which explains the analyses performed and the conclusions reached.

Software Requirements Analysis and Specification

IEC 60880 places a great deal of emphasis on the requirements analysis process and the elucidation of correct and complete requirements. As Tate [52] notes:

> The standard makes extensive reference to the specification of software reliability requirements and to the verification of those requirements.

One reason for the emphasis on correct requirements is the fact that, as N. Thuy and F. Ficheau-Vapne [53] point out, the average life span of software in nuclear power stations is usually very long. Software requirements for functions that are assigned to computer safety systems are derived from the System Requirements Specification. The standard states that requirements must be understandable, concise, nonredundant, current, unequivocal, testable or verifiable, and realizable [3]. The use of a formal specification language is recommended to enhance the clarity and completeness of the specification. Requirements should "describe the product, not the project" and be "free of implementation details;" that is, they should explain what is to be built, not how it is built [3]. Requirements should be labeled as mandatory or optional, to help prioritize implementation in view of the available resources. The standard points out that requirements should also include a statement of what the software must not do and address licensing concerns.

To help meet the goal of completeness, the standard encourages grouping the requirements into the following nine categories [3]:

- functional requirements,

- system performance requirements,

- reliability requirements,

- error handling requirements,

- continuous monitoring requirements,

- human computer interface (HCI) requirements,

- system interface requirements,

- operational environment constraints, and

- data requirements.

For each category of requirements the standard provides guidance on specific issues to be considered and concerns to be addressed. This information is captured in the Software Requirements Specification.

Functional requirements describe the system safety functions allocated to software. They should provide a complete list of all the functions performed by software. Each function should be described in terms of its purpose, required inputs, required outputs, interaction with other functions, and relation to system reliability. Functional requirements should be illustrated by graphical notation, mathematical notation, logic diagrams, and/or truth tables which depict activation conditions, task sequencing, functional verification, and error detection [3]. The input domain, input accuracy and noise limits, internal representations, output accuracy, and output range of required inputs and outputs should be defined in detail.

System performance requirements should explain how the system should perform under low, normal, peak, and above peak loading conditions. The standard states that mandatory volume, throughput, response times, communication synchronization, and accuracy requirements should be defined for each of these conditions [3].

Software reliability requirements may be derived from system reliability requirements or specifically allocated to the software in the System Requirements Specification; this will vary from project to project. Software reliability requirements must be linked to the operational environment and valid operational profiles. IEC 60880 concentrates on quantitative software reliability targets. This is understandable, because at the time the standard was originally issued the concept of qualitative software reliability measures was relatively unknown. However, Tate [52] and B. Jennings [38], among others, point out the difficulty of proving quantitative software reliability measures. As Jennings [38] states:

> System design is typically performed in a procedurally oriented or deterministic manner. Therefore, a qualitative view of reliability is more appropriate.

The standard recommends specifying reliability requirements for individual transactions, functions and sequences of transactions, specific disturbances, transients, and accident situations [3]. Reliability requirements should also be specified for changes in systems states, for example, startup, shutdown, graceful degradation, fail safe, and fail operational.

Error handling requirements are directly related to reliability requirements, since they specify how the software should detect, recover from, and/or respond to error conditions with the goal of preventing or containing accidents. Accordingly, initiation conditions should be specified for [3]:

- functions that prevent the release of radioactivity under accident conditions,

- emergency shutdown conditions, and

- functions that prevent plant damage.

Error detection requirements should be specified so that an error log is maintained and the operator is notified immediately of any degradation in the execution of any safety functions [3]. One particular error handling requirement levied by IEC 60880 is that [3]:

> No single failure shall be able to block directly or indirectly any function dedicated to the prevention of the release of radioactivity.

Continuous monitoring requirements drive error handling requirements because they provide the capability to detect anomalies and generate alerts. Continuous monitoring requirements should include a basic self-checking capability along with a robust capability to monitor the health of all safety functions, perform plausibility checks, and record failure details. Monitoring requirements should support the earliest possible detection of a failure or potential failure so that it can be contained and isolated. As the standard notes, requirements could be specified for a failure simulation tool which would help operators pinpoint potential failures very early. IEC 60880 levies two specific monitoring and testing requirements [3]:

1. Those parts of memory that contain code or invariable data shall be monitored to prevent any changes.

2. Essential functions of the whole safety system [shall] be testable during operation of the nuclear power generating station.

Human computer interface (HCI) requirements should explain in detail operator actions during system commissioning, startup, operation, and preventive, adaptive, and corrective maintenance. HCI requirements should specify what the operator should and should not do to maintain the system in a known safe state. All human input should be verified before the system acts upon it. Human interfaces and tasks which are safety critical should be highlighted in the specification. The standard recommends employing human factors engineering experts to analyze and refine these requirements so that the likelihood of induced or invited human error is reduced. Straightforward procedures should be specified for the introduction, modification, and display of system parameters [3]. Likewise, the standard encourages the use of menu techniques, consistent placement and scaling of parameters on menus, consistent and logical use of colors, flashing signals, and operator alerts. The standard requires that a manual override capability be provided for all failure modes. However, the standard makes it clear that "manual interaction shall not delay basic safety actions beyond specified limits [3]."

System interface requirements are to be specified for internal and external interfaces, current and future planned interfaces. System interface requirements should be specified so that they minimize coupling and the potential for common cause failures, while inhibiting failure propagation. The standard requires that detailed specifications be developed for [3]:

- communication protocols,

- interface failure checking,

- message formats,

- message throughput, timing, and sequencing, and

- I/O resource constraints.

Requirements related to operational environment constraints should highlight known limitations under which the software must operate. Some of these may be a restatement of requirements contained in the System Requirements Specification and/or the Hardware Requirements Specification. Operational constraints which should be specified include the target platform, target operating system, system reconfiguration options, arithmetic constraints, and the use of predeveloped software [3]. As part of the requirements analysis, the standard recommends conducting a study to determine whether or not hardware redundancy and/or diversity would enhance software and system reliability. An analysis should also be conducted to determine the effect of hardware timing limitations on software performance requirements. Known constraints should also be analyzed in view of planned or anticipated system expansion or adaptations.

Requirements should be specified for all data elements needed and their associated occurrence, precision, formatting, and manipulation requirements. Requirements should be specified for permitting and/or controlling access to individual data elements. This could be accomplished by specifying create, read, update, and delete privileges by use case for each data element. Relationships between data elements, if known at this time, should be specified. External sources of data should be identified and reconciled with system interface requirements. Online data backup, offline data backup, data archiving, offsite storage, data retention, and emergency data recovery requirements must also be specified.

Development

The production of software that is "error-free as possible ... and which can be easily verified" is the goal of the development phase [3]. IEC 60880 makes several specific recommendations, which are summarized below, to guide the design and coding process so that this goal will be achieved.

Design details are captured in the Software Performance Specification, which, as the standard points out, should be at a sufficient level of detail "so that program coding can proceed without further clarification [3]." The standard recommends the use of a formal design notation, set theory, mathematical notation, pseudo code, decision tables, logic diagrams, truth tables, and so forth to enhance the clarity and completeness by which the design is expressed. (See Table 6.1 for a sample decision table.) R. Blauw [28] concurs with this recommendation:

> Combinations of text and graphical techniques (e.g. logic diagrams, state transition diagrams, and truth tables) may be a vehicle to minimize the potential for specification faults.

Testability and reliability goals should drive the design, according to IEC 60880. As Thuy and Ficheux-Vapne [53] point out:

> For software testability means that one should be able to test software functions and software parts whenever necessary (after changes for example), in a reproducible manner, according to objective and sound sufficiency criteria and measures.

For this level of testability to be achieved, it must be designed in.

The standard [3, 4] strongly recommends the use of defense in depth, fault tolerance, software diversity, information hiding, and partitioning to increase reliability while decreasing the potential for common mode failures. According to W. Russell [49], in the U.S. the regulatory assessment includes an analysis of the effectiveness of implementing defense in depth and diversity as protection against common cause failures and common mode failures. Primary partitioning should be on the basis of criticality (safety critical, safety related, or nonsafety related); secondary partitioning should be on the basis of functionality. Jennings [38] states that experience on the ASIC project reinforces the use of partitioning beyond application software:

> Their report stressed the importance of using a rigorous, mathematically-based design process and the use of circuit partitioning to achieve exhaustive testing of all credible gate faults.

Likewise, the standard prohibits recursion and discourages the use of nested macros.

CONDITION STATEMENTS	1	2	3	4	5	6	7	8	9
temp = too_high	X			X			X		
temp = too_low		X			X			X	
temp = ok			X			X			X
pressure = too_high				X	X	X			
pressure = too_low							X	X	X
pressure = ok	X	X	X						
ACTION STATEMENTS									
activate shutdown				X	X				
trigger alert	X					X	X		
trigger warning		X						X	X
continue normal operations			X						

Table 6.1: Sample decision table.

Limited use should be made of interrupts; they should be inhibited altogether during the execution of critical sequences. J. Lawrence, W. Persons, and G. Preckshot concur with this recommendation [42]:

> The use of interrupts beyond a simple clock interrupt is considered a higher-risk implementation method because of the extra care required to ensure correct synchronization between interrupt code and interrupted code, and to ensure that interrupted code is correctly resumed.

Extensive error handling should be implemented, as defined in the Requirements Specification, to ensure that the system responds correctly to all conditions and states. The prevention and early detection of errors and anomalies should be a major consideration throughout the design. The design should contain robust features to support recovery from errors, containing or isolating errors, and transitioning to a fail safe or fail operational state. The standard recommends the use of watchdog timers for critical functions and interfaces. Blauw [28] points out the advantages of this approach:

> Use of various design techniques such as watchdog and deadman timers can be employed to identify a failure and provide an acceptable response (e.g. warn, alarm, or placement in the appropriate preferred failed mode.)

The likelihood of data errors should be minimized by implementing plausibility checks, reasonableness checks, parameter type verification, and range checks on input variables, output variables, intermediate parameters, and array bounds [3]. Data elements should be defined and used for a single purpose. Constants and variables should be separated in different parts of memory. Only one addressing technique should be used for each data type. Arrays should have a fixed, predefined length; dynamic structures should be avoided. The use of local variables should be maximized and the use of global variables minimized.

The standard states a preference for top-down software development methodologies and bottom-up verification activities. As part of the top-down approach, an analysis of alternatives should be conducted at each major decision point. In particular the effect on system risk of each of the alternatives should be analyzed. Functions which are likely to change over time should be highlighted so that they can be designed with modifiability in mind.

The standard recommends no more than 50–100 executable statements per module. Modules should have one entry point, one exit point (except for error handling), and one return point. Branches in a case statement should be exhaustive and preferably mutually exclusive; otherwise clauses should be used to trap error conditions. The standard emphasizes that the design should control the execution of critical sequences and verify that the software execution is synchronized, as specified with external programs or system functions. The design should also verify that the system performs correctly, as specified, under low, normal, peak, and abnormal loading conditions. Memory should be monitored to prevent and protect it from unauthorized reading, writing, or changing.

The standard makes recommendations regarding the selection and use of system software [3]: Operating systems should have a proven performance record with supporting quantitative reliability data. Newer versions of an operating system currently in use must be requalified. Access to operating system functions should be restricted to only those that are necessary and used.

Project specific coding standards should be enforced concerning [3]:

- the use (or prohibition from use) of language constructs and features,

- specification of parameter types and formats,

- the sequence for declarations and initializations,

- content, format, and location of comments and other nonexecutable code, and

- content and format of module headers or prologues.

Special requirements are levied on compilers, translators, linkage-editors, interpreters, cross compilers, and other system utilities [3,4]: Higher level languages are preferred over low level languages. Compilers and translators should be certified to a national and/or international standard. Input, output, and transient parameters should be syntactically distinct. Optional output features should be available during translation to aid verification. Exceptions must be triggered, without any attempt at correction, during translation should any of the following conditions occur [3]:

- array boundaries are exceeded,

- value ranges are exceeded,

- variables are accessed that are not initialized,

- assertions are not satisfied,

- significant digits are truncated,

- wrong parameter types are passed, or

- data type transfers are attempted.

This will help enhance data safety. The precision of floating point variables should also be determinable during translation.

Verification

Within the context of IEC 60880, verification activities are associated with each lifecycle phase. In fact, each phase is concluded with a critical assessment of the results of the verification activities performed. A Software Verification Plan is written to guide verification activities. This plan should define the verification criteria, strategies, tools, and techniques to be used during each lifecycle phase. For example, the specific static and dynamic analysis techniques which will be used to verify the correctness, completeness, and consistency of the requirements, design, and code should be defined [3]. The standard requires that verification activities be performed by an independent group; the responsibilities of this group and their relationship to the development staff must be explained in the Verification Plan. As Tate [52] points out:

> The standard has prescriptive requirements for independence during module verification, system integration, verification, and computer system validation.

The plan should also provide a methodology for recording, analyzing, and interpreting the results of verification activities. IEC 60880 does not specify a format for the Software

Verification Plan; however, a standard like IEEE Std. 1012-1998[2] could be used since it satisfies the informational content requirements.

The adequacy of software requirements is verified to ensure that they "fulfill safety systems requirements assigned to software [3]." Each category of requirements is analyzed to determine if they are complete, correct, consistent, unambiguous, understandable, verifiable, realizable, and traceable to the System Requirements Specification. As part of the process to verify requirements, IEC 60880 recommends including the following stakeholders:

1. the System Requirements Specification owners, to verify consistency and correctness;

2. the software design team, to verify understandability and feasibility; and

3. the Certifying Authority, to verify regulatory compliance.

The results of these activities are recorded in the Software Requirements Verification Report.

The design is verified by measuring its traceability to the Software Requirements Specification. The intent is to verify that the design incorporates all of the requirements but does not include any unspecified features. The design is assessed to determine its technical consistency, algorithmic correctness, and logical completeness. The design is analyzed to verify that [3]:

- it is feasible to implement the design as specified,

- the design is testable and/or verifiable,

- the design can be understood by the development and verification teams, and

- the design is maintainable without compromising safety or reliability.

In addition, the design is evaluated to ensure that it conforms to project design standards and good software engineering practices. The results of these activities are recorded in the Software Design Verification Report.

Code is verified by measuring its traceability to the Software Performance Specification (that is, design). The intent is to verify that the code implements the design correctly and completely without adding any unspecified functions or features. The standard encourages the use of static and dynamic analysis techniques to verify code; simulation, formal inspections, and mathematical proofs are mentioned in particular. The standard notes that the selection of techniques [3]:

> ...depends on the internal structure of a program, the level of reliability required, the demands imposed on it during plant operation, and the available testing tools.

---

[2]IEEE Std. 1012-1998 Standard for Software Verification and Validation.

The standard also makes the point that predeveloped software must be verified in the same manner as custom-developed software [3, 4].

As part of the dynamic analysis, formal test procedures are written to guide the different types and levels of testing. These test procedures define the test environment, test configuration, test cases, pass/fail criteria for each test case, and responsibilities of the test team and witnesses. The results of the various testing activities are recorded in the Software Test Reports. These reports track the status and resolution of anomalies, analyze design and performance deficiencies, and make recommendations for corrective action.

The standard promotes the use of both systematic testing and statistical-based testing. Systematic testing is used to verify functional and performance characteristics. Program behavior is verified under normal and abnormal conditions across the full input domain. Every path, branch operation, and statement is exercised at least once. Memory locations and references to memory locations which contain constants or variables are verified to ensure that there are no conflicts. All time constraints are verified, in particular during interrupt sequences. Statistical-based testing complements systematic testing by verifying reliability and availability. Statistical-based testing, as defined by IEC 60880, uses many of the techniques and metrics discussed in Chapter 10. (That information will not be repeated here.)

Hardware Software Integration

After the software has been successfully verified, it is migrated to the target platform and integrated with the other hardware and software components of the system. The standard expects the System Integration Plan to guide the integration activities which verify that the software operates correctly in the specified operational environment and that all system safety requirements have been achieved. The System Integration Plan defines the organizational roles and responsibilities, including independence, during integration, the procedural steps to be taken, and the system integration verification testing to be conducted. The System Integration Test Report records the results of integration activities, tracks the status and resolution of corrective action, and makes recommendations about the system in general and the efficacy of continuing to the next phase. The report must be maintained in an auditable form.

System Validation

System validation is conducted in accordance with the System Validation Plan by an independent team. Both static and dynamic analysis techniques are used to validate that system performance is safe and reliable under normal and abnormal conditions. According to the standard, validation activities should exercise all signal ranges, all calculated parameters, and all voting logic and ensure that accuracy and response time requirements are met [3]. Failure scenarios should be simulated to ensure that the system responds correctly, as specified. As the standard states [3]:

Each reactor safety function should be confirmed by representative tests of each trip or protection parameter singly and in combination.

The System Validation Report records the results of validation activities and assesses achievement of system requirements, in particular safety and reliability requirements. Recommendations for rework are included in the report.

Operations

IEC 60880 distinguishes between system operation activities and activities related to system maintenance and modification. System operation activities include planning for commissioning the system and making sure that operations and maintenance staff are thoroughly trained. A Commissioning Test Plan is prepared, which is similar to a site acceptance test plan with additional emphasis placed on safety and reliability. The results of the commissioning test are recorded in the Commissioning Test Report, along with a recommendation to (or not to) activate the system. The Certifying Authority's role in these activities and the final recommendation is defined by national regulations, not IEC 60880. Training is conducted and a User's Manual prepared. The training must emphasize the safety ramifications of following and not following established operational procedures. The User's Manual must be updated and training repeated whenever changes are made to the system.

Maintenance and Modification

Formal change control procedures are required by the standard for adaptive, preventive, and corrective maintenance. Joannou [39] explains their importance:

A planned and systematic software engineering process must be followed over the entire lifecycle of the software. Both the original development and any revisions must be treated as an integral, continuous and interactive process. Any changes must be verified to the same degree of rigor as the original development.

The change control procedures specify how and when change requests should be submitted and the information they should contain such as the reason for the request, the purpose or nature of the proposed change, the scope of the proposed change, and the originator. These procedures specify how change impact analysis will be conducted to analyze the feasibility of implementing the proposed change; assess the impact of the proposed change on system safety, reliability, and performance; and determine the extent of reverification and revalidation needed. The process for approving or rejecting change requests should also be explained in the change control procedures. Anomaly reports and/or new requirements may trigger a formal Software Modification Request. A Software Modification Report documents the results of a specific change request. The Software Modification Control History captures a chronological record of all maintenance and modification activities.

Interaction with System Safety and Other Standards

IEC 60880 was written to extend established nuclear safety design principles to the development and maintenance of software. As such IEC 60880 is intended to be used in conjunction with existing nuclear safety standards. The following seven standards are cited as normative references and are quoted throughout IEC 60880:

1. IEC 557(1982-01): IEC Terminology in the Nuclear Reactor Field.

2. IEC 639(1970-01): Nuclear Reactors. Use of the Protection System for Non-Safety Purposes.

3. IEC 643(1979-01): Application of Digital Computers to Nuclear Reactor Instrumentation and Control.

4. IEC 671(1980-01): Periodic Tests and Monitoring of the Protection System of Nuclear Reactors.

5. International Atomic Energy Agency (IAEA) Guide 50-SG-D3 (1980): Safety Guide.

6. IEC 960(1988-08): Functional Design Criteria for a Safety Parameter Display System for Nuclear Power Stations.

7. IEC 60987:1989-12, Programmed Digital Computers Important to Safety for Nuclear Power Stations.

Roles, Responsibilities, and Qualifications of Project Members

The standard does not address the topic of personnel roles, responsibilities, and qualifications other than to state independence requirements for validation and verification teams.

Data Items Produced

Several data items are produced by adherence to IEC 60880, as shown in Table 6.2. The standard identifies the items to be produced during each lifecycle phase and when and how they are verified. The standard encourages the use of graphical notation, mathematical notation, logic diagrams, truth tables, and so forth, wherever possible to enhance the clarity and completeness of the information presented. The software design documentation, which is referred to as the 'Software Performance Specification,' is the only item for which the standard provides a proposed content outline. Each project has to decide the appropriate informational content and format for the other data items; often the format and content will be decided by national regulations.

Data Item	Phase in which Developed	Verification
– System Requirements Specification	input to software development lifecycle	–
– Software Requirements Specification – QA Plan – Software Verification Plan	Requirements Analysis and Specification	– Software Requirements Verification Report
– Software Performance Specification (design) – Software Test Specification and Procedures	Development	– Software Design Verification Report – Software Test Reports
– System Integration Plan	Hardware Software Integration	– System Integration Test Report
– System Validation Plan	System Validation	– System Validation Report
– Training Plan – User's Manual – Commissioning Test Plan	Operations	– Training Results – Commissioning Test Report
– Software Change Control Procedures – Anomaly Reports – Software Modification Requests – Software Modification Control History	Maintenance and Modification	– Software Modification Reports

Table 6.2: Data items required by IEC 60880 [3].

Compliance Assessment

The standard does not specifically address the issue of compliance assessment. Some consider this to be a weakness of the standard. Viewed from another perspective, this flexibility allows the National Certification Authorities to determine which requirements in IEC 60880 are mandatory, desirable, and optional and to state this in their regulations.

Scaling

The standard only makes one limited statement in regard to scaling [3]:

> If practices differing from those of the Appendices are used, they shall be documented and auditable according to the requirements of the main part of this standard.

6.1.4   Strengths

IEC 60880 has several strong points, which explain why the standard is still in use. First, the standard is written in a manner which acknowledges the authority of national regulatory bodies. This facilitates the use of IEC 60880 concurrently with national standards and regulations. For example national standards can be used to define the content and format of the data items so that they comply with regulatory requirements. Second, IEC 60880 promotes a comprehensive approach to requirements analysis and specification. The standard identifies nine categories of requirements to be evaluated and specific issues and concerns to be evaluated for each. The guidance for reliability and HCI requirements is particularly strong. In addition, all stakeholders are involved in the process of verifying requirements. This attention to requirements will yield several important benefits; as discussed in Chapter 2 on average approximately 80 percent of software defects have as their root cause an erroneous requirement. Lastly, IEC 60880 is one of the few standards to address end-user safety in relation to training needs and the need for human factors engineering.

6.1.5   Areas for Improvement

There are a few areas in which IEC 60880 could be improved. First, a project would be hard put to follow IEC 60880 if doing object-oriented analysis and design or following a spiral lifecycle model. Guidance which addresses new developments in software engineering methodologies and lifecycle models would be useful. Second, as E. Leret [43] and others point out, IEC 60880 only applies to safety-critical software. Additional guidance is needed for safety-related and nonsafety-related software. In this way the same standard could be used for all software in a nuclear power plant. Third, the standard does not address decommissioning. This topic is of particular importance in the regulatory environment. Hence, it would be helpful if the standard would provide some guidance in this area as well.

6.1.6   Results Observed to Date

IEC 60880 was issued in 1986. Since then it has undergone several revalidation cycles and been used successfully in many countries, particularly within the European Union. Three initiatives are underway which may affect IEC 60880 in the future.

First, as mentioned in Chapter 8, the nuclear power industry was very active in the development of IEC 61508, including Part 3 which addresses software safety. At the time of writing it is unclear whether, in the long run, the nuclear power industry intends to migrate to IEC 61508 Part 3 or to update IEC 60880 to become an industry-specific implementation of IEC 61508 Part 3.

Second, IEC 60880-1 (FDIS), the First Supplement to IEC 60880, was submitted for balloting during the summer of 1999. The supplement provides additional detailed guidance on [4]:

- defense against common cause failures (CCFs),

- the use and qualification of computer aided software engineering tools to develop safety-critical software, and

- the use and qualification of previously developed software.

These topics have increased in importance in recent years, hence the motivation for the supplement. IEC 60880-1 (FDIS) notes that [4]:

> Software by itself does not have a CCF mode. CCF is related to system failures arising from faults in the functional requirements, system design, or software.

The potential for CCFs, including those resulting from faulty data, should be examined during design. The supplement recommends a combination of defense in depth and diversity (independent systems with functional diversity) as the best defense against CCFs.

IEC 60880-1 (FDIS) provides in-depth criteria by which to evaluate the use, guide the selection, and perform the qualification of automated software engineering tools. Central to this approach is the observation that [4]:

> The tools used in the development of software in safety systems in Nuclear Power Plants are required to be qualified to a level consistent with: the tool reliability requirements, the type of tool, the potential of the tool to introduce faults, ... and the ability to verify tool output.

IEC 60880-1 (FDIS) also provides criteria to guide the qualification of previously developed software. The guidance is not limited to COTS, but rather is applicable to software reuse in general. In summary, the supplement recommends evaluating the [4]:

- robustness of the design,

- process used to develop the software; especially how it compares to the requirements of IEC 60880,

- operational experience or history of the product,

- proposed change in the operational environment or use of the product,

- potential modifications needed, and

- suitability of the product for the given safety category.

The committee is proceeding cautiously for two reasons, according to C. Jacquemart, IEC Technical Officer [55]. First, IEC 60880 can be considered as the most important standard of SC 45A; any revision of or supplement to this standard has important implications in many existing software systems worldwide. Second, there is a need to establish a relationship between IEC 60880 and the classification levels defined in IEC 61226 [17] before initiating a revision or supplement.

Third, IEC 61940 Technical Report Type 3: A Review of the Application of IEC 60880 [18] was issued in 1998. As Leret [43] reports:

> The goal of this document ... is to provide pragmatic assistance, resulting from experience feedback in nuclear power plant instrumentation and control, for implementing a verification and validation programme supported by the techniques and tools (either static, dynamic, or based on dependability techniques).

Work is also underway within SC 45A to address nuclear power plant system safety concerns through IEC 61513 CDV [19] and software safety concerns of class 2 and 3 I&C systems [20].

6.2 CE-1001-STD Rev. 1, Standard for Software Engineering of Safety Critical Software, CANDU Computer Systems Engineering Centre for Excellence, January 1995.

6.2.1 Background

In December 1990, Ontario Hydro Nuclear and Atomic Energy Canada, Ltd. (AECL) issued AECL Standard STD-00-00902-001 [1], Standard for Software Engineering of Safety Critical Software, for a trial use period. This standard was the result of a joint project by Ontario Hydro Nuclear and AECL and reflected "experience gained in developing, licensing, and maintaining software for the Darlington Nuclear Generating Station Shutdown System Trip Computers, as well as other safety critical software [1]." J. Harauz [34] reports that the Darlington station, which was implemented with "two diverse reactor shutdown systems," was one of the first to make extensive use of digital technology.

Following the trial use period, CE-1001-STD Rev.1, Standard for Software Engineering of Safety Critical Software [2], was issued jointly by Ontario Hydro Nuclear[3] and AECL under the auspices of the Canadian Deuterium Uranium Nuclear Power Plants (CANDU) Computer Systems Engineering Centre of Excellence as a replacement for the earlier standard. The new standard, which is in effect today, incorporates real world experience and observations gained during the trial use period. In several ways CE-1001-STD Rev. 1 builds upon the strengths of IEC 60880 and updates it to reflect current technology and software engineering practices.

6.2.2 Purpose and Scope

CE-1001-STD Rev. 1 and its predecessor were developed for a specific mission: "to specify requirements for the engineering of safety critical software used in real-time protective systems in nuclear generating stations [2]." The standard states specifically that it [2]:

> ... applies to safety critical software which is part of a special safety system and which is directly required for the special safety system to meet its minimum allowable performance requirements.

The standard [2] identifies three categories of special safety systems: shutdown systems, emergency coolant injection systems, and nuclear generating containment systems.

The standard states that it is not applicable in three situations: 1) for software developed with nonprocedural languages, such as functional graphical languages; 2) for predeveloped software; or 3) for the modification of software that was not developed according to CE-1001-STD Rev. 1. The standard recommends tailoring to accommodate different language constructs for the first situation.

6.2.3 Description

CE-1001-STD Rev. 1 levies a minimum set of requirements on development, verification, and support processes. As Harauz [34] observes:

> Safety-critical software requires extremely rigorous methods to ensure that the probability of error introduction is very low and the probability of error detection is very high.

The software engineering lifecycle processes described in this standard are an integral part of the overall system and safety engineering lifecycle, as is evident from the interaction with the various processes and activities. CE-1001-STD Rev. 1 is to be followed throughout the entire lifecycle, "from inception until retirement of the software [2]."

The standard identifies specific quality objectives, quality attributes, and fundamental principles by which process outputs are evaluated to determine their acceptability. As Harauz [33] explains:

---

[3]Ontario Hydro Nuclear was renamed Ontario Power Generation, Inc. on April 1, 1999.

Quality objectives are 'what we want.' Quality attributes are how we measure whether we achieved the quality objectives and fundamental principles levy requirements on the process that lead to the development of a product with the required quality attributes.

Quality objectives are applied to the engineering of safety-critical software. They are categorized as primary objectives and secondary objectives [2, 33]:

Primary Quality Objectives

- Safety
- Functionality
- Reliability
- Maintainability
- Reviewability

Secondary Quality Objectives

- Portability
- Usability
- Efficiency

These are objectives that the system as a whole must satisfy; therefore the software component of a system must satisfy them also. For example, if a system is to meet stated safety, reliability, and maintainability goals the software in that system must meet the safety, reliability, and maintainability goals allocated to it.

Although often neglected, usability is an important quality objective for safety-critical and safety-related systems. Usability relates to the nature and scope of human computer interaction. B. Sherwood-Jones [50] recommends including "user analysis" to identify user characteristics, types of users, and high risk user groups, and "task analysis" to identify task design, user involvement, and workplace environment analysis, as part of the hazard analysis. This will help prevent induced or invited errors on the part of end users. Usability testing should be part of the verification process for any safety-critical or safety-related system that has human computer interfaces.

Efficiency is also often overlooked as an important quality objective for safety-critical and safety-related systems. Efficiency refers to the efficient use of system resources, such as memory, I/O channels, processor capacity, and other storage. For example, this means designing and implementing software that uses and references memory efficiently, partitions software into cohesive units, minimizes the use of global variables, and avoids recursive and self-modifying routines. Software that is designed and implemented efficiently is easier to verify, maintain, and generally less error prone.

CE-1001-STD Rev. 1 cites 11 quality attributes for safety-critical software, which are listed below [2]. Software engineering artifacts developed throughout the lifecycle are evaluated against these quality attributes.

Quality Attributes

- complete
- correct
- consistent
- modifiable
- modular
- predictable
- robust
- structured
- traceable
- verifiable
- understandable

These attributes correspond to the criteria defined in IEEE Std. 1012-1998[4] to verify process outputs.

The third criteria cited by CE-1001-STD Rev. 1 is referred to as fundamental principles. There are five specific engineering principles which must be applied at appropriate times during the lifecycle. Two of the fundamental principles are design features: information hiding and partitioning. As Joannou [39] explains:

> Information hiding is a software design technique in which the interface to each software module is designed to reveal as little as possible about the module's inner workings... In this way, if it is necessary to change the functions internal to one module, the resulting propagation of changes to other modules is minimized.

The standard expects that the design of safety-critical and safety-related software will incorporate the principles of information hiding (or encapsulation) and partitioning of safety-critical, safety-related, and nonsafety-related software. These design features help to enhance the operational safety and reliability of a software system, as well as its verifiability and maintainability.

A third fundamental principle concerns the use of formal methods. While not using the term formal methods per se, the standard requires the use of a formal mathematical notation to specify system behavior and to verify or prove that the specification, design, and code are correct and hence safe and reliable. Harauz [34] reports that the introduction of formal specifications at Ontario Power Generation, Inc. has resulted in more complete specifications with less errors. Joannou [39] provides one explanation for these results:

> Mathematical functions provide a mechanism for completely, precisely, and unambiguously specifying the behavior of the software... The requirements specification uses mathematical functions to specify the required behavior of the software system in terms of system inputs and outputs. The design description uses mathematical functions to specify the required behavior of each

---

[4]IEEE Std. 1012-1998 Standard for Software Verification and Validation.

program in terms of its program inputs and outputs. The code provides a representation of a mathematical function of the program outputs in terms of program inputs. The design description can therefore be mathematically verified against the requirements specification and the code can be mathematically verified against the design description.

The fourth fundamental principle requires that specific reliability goals be established for safety-critical software. These goals are reflected in the reliability requirements stated in the Software Requirements Specification. The standard defines a reliability requirement as [2]:

> A requirement specifying the probability of not encountering a sequence of inputs which lead to a failure.

As stated in the standard, these requirements must include quantitative and qualitative software reliability measurements which reflect actual operational profiles [2]. And as Pant [47] points out, developing operational profiles helps to determine a valid set of test cases and leads to more effective and efficient test cases.

Independence is the fifth and last fundamental principle. The standard levies independence requirements for staff involved in the development and verification of safety-critical software. In summary, the following independence restrictions hold [2]:

1. No one can verify or validate their own work.

2. Anyone can participate in the requirements verification review, except personnel who developed the requirements specification.

3. An independent verifier has primary responsibility for verifying the design, code, unit, and integration testing results.

4. An independent validator has primary responsibility for validating the hazard analyses, validation test results, and reliability qualification results.

CE-1001-STD Rev. 1 organizes software engineering activities into three high level process categories: Support Processes, Development Processes, and Verification Processes. These high level processes are composed of 12 subprocesses, each with specific inputs and outputs. Figure 6.1 illustrates how these processes correspond to generic lifecycle phases. Keep in mind that the standard considers this to be the minimum set of acceptable process requirements.

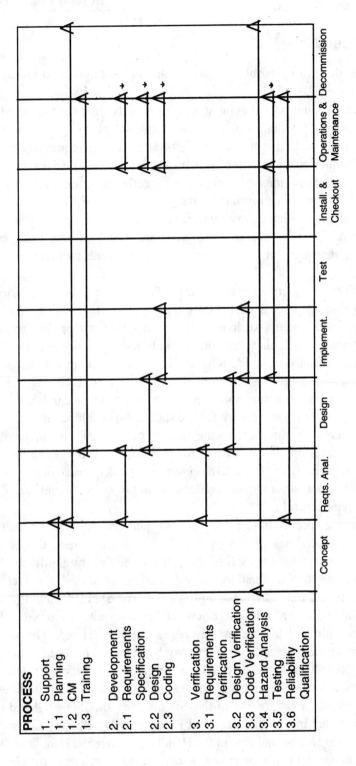

Figure 6.1: Mapping of CE-1001-STD Rev. 1 processes to generic lifecycle phases.

* Modifications made during the Operations and Maintenance phase require change impact analysis and repeating earlier hazard analyses.

251

Support Processes

The standard identifies three Support subprocesses: Planning, Configuration Management, and Training. (See Figure 6.2.)

The software planning subprocess begins with the products from the system planning process: the design input documentation and other system-level planning documents. Traditional planning concerns, such as schedules, budgets, and resource requirements, are addressed during the planning process. More importantly, several key decisions are made. First the scope of the project is defined. A software engineering lifecycle and development methodology are selected that are appropriate for the given project, target platform, and operational environment during both the development and operational phases. The standard does not endorse or prohibit any lifecycle or development methodology; its primary concern is that the lifecycle and development methodology contribute to meeting all requirements in the standard.

Second, the activities necessary to implement the development and verification processes are defined, including process goals and their required inputs and outputs. The Fundamental Principles and Quality Attributes, discussed earlier, are applied to the process outputs, as appropriate. Particular attention is paid to independence requirements for staff performing the hazard analyses, validation testing, and reliability qualification. Third, the organizational roles, responsibilities, structure, and communication channels are clearly defined. A clear organizational structure and open communications channels are essential for any project's success; they are imperative for the successful development, verification, and validation of safety-critical software and adherence to independence requirements. The information from these decisions is captured in the Software Development Plan. More mundane topics, like maintaining software development notebooks, is also discussed in the plan. This plan should be kept current, made available to all project staff, and placed under configuration management control.

Lastly, project specific "procedures, work practices, and conventions" are defined in a project Standards and Procedures Handbook [2]. The standard expects this handbook to include items such as standards for each of the software engineering artifacts, for example, Software Requirements Specification, coding standards, and design guidelines, in particular software safety and reliability design principles. The Standards and Procedures Handbook should explain how formal design reviews and peer reviews are to be conducted. A methodology for determining adequate test coverage should be defined. The use of automated software engineering tools and how they may be qualified for use on the project should be explained. Checklists should be developed to guide verification activities. (Tables 6.3 and 6.4 present sample checklists for unit testing and system integration testing.) If corporate standards already exist for any of these items, they should be tailored for the specific project and included in the Standards and Procedures Handbook. Contractually mandated standards should also be included in the Handbook. Once the Handbook is written two things should happen: 1) all project staff should be made aware of the Handbook and familiarized with its contents; and 2) the Handbook should be placed under configuration management control.

Evaluation Criteria	Responsible for Verification	Criteria Passed	Criteria Failed	Deficiencies Noted	Criteria N/A or Waiver Granted[a]
1. Was testing performed in accordance with the Test Specification and Procedures?					
2. Was the test environment correctly and completely defined in the Test Specification?					
3. Were all errors in the Test Specification and Procedures noted?					
4. Was the testing conducted by an independent test team?					
5. Was the testing witnessed?					
6. Was the testing conducted against a stable baseline?					
7. Were all test results recorded correctly, both correct results and anomalies?					
8. Were defects assigned a severity?					
9. Were all requirements tested: – functional – performance – safety – reliability – security					
10. Were all modules tested against the design specification?					
11. For every module and program, was the smallest executable function tested?					
12. Were all variables tested for valid, invalid, null, and boundary values?					
13. Were all algorithms tested? Were 'what if' conditions exercised?					
14. Were all logic paths through each program and module tested, including all branches and statements?					
15. Were modules with high defect rates identified?					
16. Were all detected errors corrected and retested?					
17. Were all software engineering artifacts updated to reflect changes made as a result of unit testing?					

[a]Signed waiver must be attached.

Table 6.3: Sample unit test checklist.

Evaluation Criteria	Responsible for Verification	Criteria Passed	Criteria Failed	Deficiencies Noted	Criteria N/A or Waiver Granted[a]
1. Was testing conducted in accordance with the Test Specification and Procedures?					
2. Were the Test Specification and Procedures complete, current, comprehensive, and correct?					
3. Was testing conducted against a stable baseline?					
4. Were all configuration options tested?					
5. Was testing repeated after corrections were made?					
6. Were software engineering artifacts updated to reflect changes made to correct defects?					
7. Were test results recorded accurately, for correct performance and for anomalies?					
8. Did the integrated software modules, hardware, and external interfaces operate correctly as specified?					
9. Was the severity of each defect identified?					
10. Were modules with high defect rates identified?					
11. Was the status and resolution of each defect tracked?					
12. Did the system meet performance requirements: – response times – speed – throughput – volume – loading					
13. Was the system tested to verify that maintenance, operational, and user manuals are correct?					
14. Were actual and expected results analyzed to determine whether test cases were successful or not?					
15. Was an assessment performed to determine if all acceptance criteria were met?					
16. If needed, have the necessary waivers been obtained?					
17. Did testing evaluate system performance under normal and abnormal conditions, with valid and invalid transactions?					
18. Was testing conducted to verify whether or not safety or security features could be subverted?					
19. Did all stakeholders have input to the Test Specification and Procedures?					

[a]Signed waiver must be attached.

Table 6.4: Sample system integration test checklist.

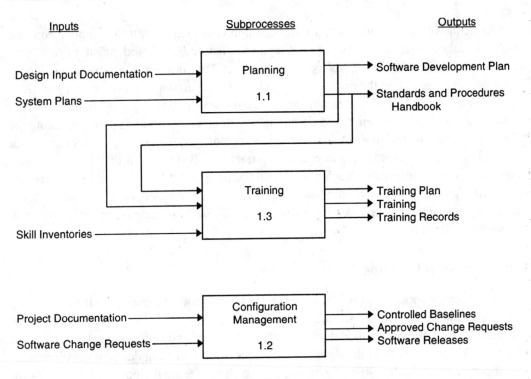

Figure 6.2: CE-1001-STD Rev. 1 support process.

One of the most comprehensive set of coding standards issued to date is that by NRC [25]:

NUREG/CR-6463, Rev. 1 Review Guidelines for Software Languages for Use in Nuclear Power Plant Safety Systems, final report, October 1997.

This document can be used as a set of coding standards and as the criteria for formal code inspections. It addresses safety and reliability issues related to the use of Ada 83, Ada 95, C, C++, Pascal, PL/M, and IEC 1131-3 ladder logic, sequential function charts, structured text, and function block diagrams.

The configuration management (CM) subprocess should be applied to all software engineering artifacts produced during the project and/or inherited from the system engineering process. The standard expects traditional CM functions to be performed, such as: identifying and controlling baselines, change impact analysis, evaluating change requests, change control management, and generating software builds. The CM Plan explains the process for performing these functions. The CM Plan should also explain how CM will be applied to predeveloped software. CM is responsible for maintaining an index of all internal and external software engineering artifacts associated with a project. This index should include entries for all versions of controlled artifacts. In addition, the standard assigns responsibility for performing defect causal analysis to CM, with the goal of continuously improving the Standards and Procedures Handbook and the products produced according to it.

As defined in the standard, the training subprocess begins with the outputs from the planning subprocess: the Software Development Plan and the Standards and Procedures Handbook, along with personnel skill inventories. This information is used to identify specific skills needed on the project; these are then compared against the existing skill set to deduce training needs. The Training Plan lists the types of training needed, the resources needed to conduct the training, and a training schedule. A methodology for evaluating the effectiveness of the training, such as the percentage of students passing each class and/or the ability to apply the training to real work situations, is defined in the plan. Minimum competency requirements for each position on the project are also defined in the Training Plan. The goal of the training process is to ensure that all project staff: 1) have the skills necessary to perform their tasks successfully; and 2) are familiar with the Standards and Procedures Handbook.

Development Process

The development process activities are defined in the Software Development Plan and the Standards and Procedures Handbook. These activities are distributed among three subprocesses: software requirements definition, software design, and code implementation. (See Figure 6.3.) All outputs of the development process are placed under configuration management as controlled baselines. Complete revision histories are maintained for all software engineering artifacts. Table 6.5 illustrates the quality attributes required in the development subprocess outputs.

Quality Attribute	Software Requirements Specification	Software Design Description	Code
complete	X	X	X
consistent	X	X	X
correct	X	X	X
modifiable	X	X	X
modular		X	X
predictable (behavior)		X	X
robust	X	X	X
structured		X	X
traceable	X	X	X
verifiable	X	X	X
understandable	X	X	X

Table 6.5: CE-1001-STD Rev. 1 quality attributes required in development process outputs.

The software requirements definition subprocess begins with the system requirements specification. Requirements allocated to software in the system requirements specification and derived requirements are analyzed, clarified, and refined. Specific requirements relating

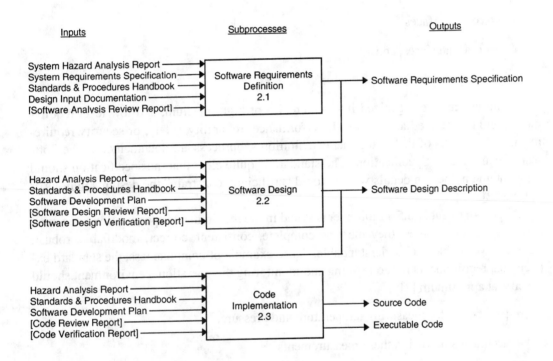

Inputs   Subprocesses   Outputs

System Hazard Analysis Report ⟶
System Requirements Specification ⟶   Software Requirements
Standards & Procedures Handbook ⟶   Definition   ⟶ Software Requirements Specification
Design Input Documentation ⟶   2.1
[Software Analysis Review Report] ⟶

Hazard Analysis Report ⟶
Standards & Procedures Handbook ⟶   Software Design
Software Development Plan ⟶   2.2   ⟶ Software Design Description
[Software Design Review Report] ⟶
[Software Design Verification Report] ⟶

Hazard Analysis Report ⟶
Standards & Procedures Handbook ⟶   Code
Software Development Plan ⟶   Implementation   ⟶ Source Code
[Code Review Report] ⟶   2.3
[Code Verification Report] ⟶   ⟶ Executable Code

Note: If deficiencies are found during verification activities, prior activities are repeated until the deficieinces are resolved. Deficiency reports are shown in square brackets: [ ]. The results of hazard analysis are used as inputs to all subprocesses.

Figure 6.3: CE-1001-STD Rev. 1 development process.

to the target platform and operational environment are also developed. The standard gives several examples of items which should be evaluated [2]:

- memory constraints,

- instruction set constraints,

- clock rates,

- I/O register limitations,

- internal interfaces,

- external interfaces, and

- accuracy limitations.

The requirements are organized into hierarchies of high, medium, and low level requirements, and categorized as functional, performance, reliability, safety, or security requirements. The results of the requirements definition subprocess are documented in the Software Requirements Specification. The standard is quite clear that the specification should not contain any design details which would "artificially constrain" the design solutions or options [2].

As shown in Table 6.5, requirements stated in the requirements specification must meet certain quality attributes; they must be complete, consistent, correct, modifiable, robust, traceable, verifiable, and understandable. As an example of completeness, the standard expects that requirements for controlling and monitoring the operational environment should specify, at a minimum [2]:

- parameters for measuring temperature and pressure,

- accuracies needed in these measurements,

- tolerances within the expected normal behavior range, and

- control actions to be taken for all system states.

Error handling actions should be specified for each failure mode, whether fail safe, fail operational, and/or attempted recovery. Interfaces should be specified by "type, format, valid range, and access method [2]." The standard requires mathematical functions to be specified in a mathematical notation. Requirements for reliability, fault tolerance, and degraded-mode operations must be highlighted in the specification. A unique requirement of the standard is to identify which requirements are "most likely to change in the future [2]." This requirement is levied in order to facilitate the quality attribute of modifiability in the requirements specification, design, and code.

The software design subprocess uses the Software Requirements Specification and the design guidelines in the Standards and Procedures Handbook to develop the Software Design Description. According to the standard, the Software Design Description [2]:

...is a representation of the software design. It describes the design to a sufficient level of detail so that no further refinement of the module structure, module interfaces, data structures, or databases is required in the code [subprocess].

As shown in Table 6.5, all 11 quality attributes apply to the Software Design Description. In addition, the design must incorporate the fundamental principles of partitioning and information hiding. Safety-critical, safety-related, and nonsafety-related functions must be partitioned. Likewise, the access to safety-critical, safety-related, and nonsafety-related data should be partitioned. Information hiding should be used to minimize the coupling and maximize the cohesion of modules. The standard endorses the concept of a single entry, single exit for each module; the exception being, of course, error handling actions. The use of interrupts should also be minimized. Information hiding, in addition to contributing to the safe and reliable operation of the software, also facilitates modifiability. According to Blauw [28]:

> An inherent element of the design process should be the identification and resolution of abnormal conditions and events (ACEs) which have the potential to defeat the safety related function. ACEs include external events as well as conditions internal to the computer hardware or software.

The software design description must satisfy all functional, performance, safety, reliability, and security requirements stated in the Requirements Specification. The design of mathematical functions is required to be proven through a formal mathematical notation [2]. Traceability to the Software Requirements Specification must be demonstrated. Requirements which cannot be satisfied are required to be identified [2]. An assessment is made of the effect of not implementing these requirements on the operational safety and reliability of the system. If the impact is moderate or higher, the system concept and design must be re-evaluated and a new hazard analysis is performed. At the same time, care must be taken to ensure that no new functionality or features are incorporated into the design that are not stated as requirements. The standard recommends documenting the following information, at a minimum, about each procedure [2]:

- unique procedure identifier

- procedure type: utility, I/O, calculation, UI, error handling, and so forth

- purpose/function

- called by/calls to

- dependencies: timing, sequencing, activation, data, and so forth

- internal and external interfaces

- algorithmic details

- local data definitions

- error handling and containment provisions

- preferred language for implementation

The code implementation subprocess uses the Software Design Description and the coding standards in the Standards and Procedures Handbook to produce the source code and executable code. All 11 quality attributes in Table 6.5 apply to the outputs of the code implementation subprocess.

The standard also emphasizes the importance of data safety. For example, it states that there should be no undefined or unused constants or variables. Data elements are to be referenced by "labels" or other symbolic constants rather than addresses [2]." Developers must ensure that the accuracy requirements for all variables in the Software Requirements Specification are met through correct data definitions and appropriate usage. Likewise, the data definitions in the source code must correspond to the data dictionary contained in the Software Design Description. In other words, traceability must be demonstrated between data requirements, the data dictionary, and actual data usage in the code.

The standard encourages the use of accurate, complete, understandable, and useful comments and procedure prologues to support verification, validation, and modification activities. Self-modifying and recursive code are prohibited by the standard. The code is required to implement error detection/correction features to protect against run-time errors, such as out of range indices and variables, potential divide by zero conditions, and stack overflow [2]. Likewise, the code implementation must accommodate all memory, I/O, timing, and other constraints stated in the Software Requirements Specification. Traceability must be demonstrated to the Software Design Description.

Verification Process

Six subprocesses comprise the verification process: software requirements verification, software design verification, code verification, hazard analyses, testing, and reliability qualification. Ten primary activities are associated with these subprocesses, the details of which are defined in the Software Development Plan. The output of each activity is a verification report. (See Figure 6.4.)

The verification reports should clearly state what baseline or version of each artifact was evaluated and when. The activities performed, the methods and tools used and the participants should be listed. The main part of the verification reports consists of a detailed description, analysis, and interpretation of the results observed, including any discrepancies and anomalies. The conclusion should make a recommendation for approval, conditional approval pending resolution of corrective action, or rejection of the software engineering artifact(s).

According to the standard, the software requirements review verifies that the Software Requirements Specification adheres to the guidance in the Design Input Documentation and the Standards and Procedures Handbook. The requirements are evaluated against the quality attributes to determine if they are complete, consistent, correct, modifiable, robust, verifiable, understandable, and traceable to system-level requirements. The expression of the requirements is examined to ensure that the design and implementation are not unduly constrained. A description of how these verification activities were conducted and their findings are documented in the Software Requirements Review Report.

The standard requires two design verification activities: the software design review and the systematic software design review. The software design review verifies that the design is consistent with the Software Requirements Specification, the Design Input Documentation, and the Standards and Procedures Handbook. The design is further evaluated to ensure that good software engineering practices, as defined in the Standards and Procedures Handbook, have been followed. An assessment is made to verify that the design does not implement any features or functionality that is not defined in the Software Requirements Specification. The results of these analyses are recorded in the Software Design Review Report.

In contrast, the systematic design verification activity analyzes the integrity of the design. A determination is made whether or not the design is complete, correct, and consistent. The design is analyzed to determine whether it is robust and will lead to predictable system behavior in all situations and that no unknown or unsafe states will be encountered. The modularity, structuredness, and understandability of the design is evaluated. An assessment is made of whether or not the design, in particular its safety, reliability, and immunity to common cause and common mode failures, can be verified. Modifiability is assessed to determine the feasibility of future enhancements. Lastly, the standard requires that the correct behavior of the design be proven mathematically through formal methods. The results of these activities are recorded in the Software Design Verification Report.

The Demonstration of Advanced Reliability Techniques for Safety Related Computer Systems (DARTS) project was undertaken in the U.K. to evaluate the cost/benefit of producing steam generating heavy water reactor protection systems via diversity. Four diverse channels were developed, two through formal methods and two using traditional development. As reported by G. Adams [26] the project demonstrated the benefit of diversity, formal methods, and the use of safe subsets of languages; the channels developed using these techniques took the same or less resources and were less error prone.

The standard requires two code verification activities: a code review and a systematic code review. The code review verifies that the code adheres to the coding standards in the Standards and Procedures Handbook, follows good software engineering practices, and meets the quality attributes in Table 6.5. In contrast, the systematic code review verifies the integrity of the code. As Harauz [31] points out:

> Formal design review mechanisms, alone, are not effective for software. Traditional verification techniques have to be tailored, replaced, or complemented by other defect detection and removal mechanisms, i.e. code inspections, walkthroughs, cross-reference matrices, in order to be effective for software.

The correctness of inputs and outputs, relative to asserted pre- and post-conditions, is mathematically proven. The standard expects that proofs will be developed "for the entire domain of the inputs [2]." As stated in NUREG/CR-6293 [23]:

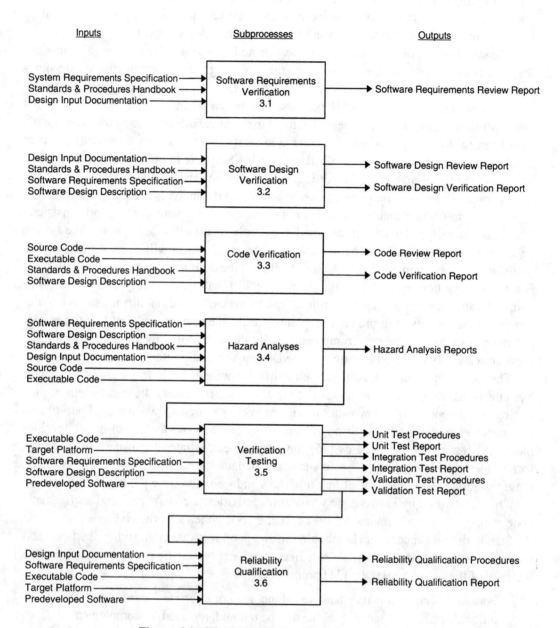

Figure 6.4: CE-1001-STD Rev. 1 verification process.

... the conditions most likely to induce software failure [in high integrity software] are combinations of unusual states or events, and exhaustive testing for these is impossible.

Hence, this is an area where formal methods/proofs and other static analysis techniques can and should be used to complement dynamic analysis. The results of the code review are recorded in the Code Review Report, while the results of the systematic code review are recorded in the Code Verification Report.

The hazard analysis subprocess is ongoing so that safety and reliability are continuously evaluated using standard risk analysis and risk management techniques, such as FMECA, FTA, and HAZOP. Combinations of sequences and events which could trigger a hazard are identified. As Beltracchi [27] points out:

... fault tolerance requirements for a computer-based safety system should be developed from hazard analysis and PRA studies.

The correct specification and efficient handling of system failure modes is verified at each milestone. As new failure modes, unsafe states, and potential single points of failure are identified, changes to the requirements, design, and/or code are recommended. The design is evaluated to ensure that the software safety design principles spelled out in the Standards and Procedures Handbook have been implemented to mitigate risk. The robustness of the design and code error detection, elimination, containment, and recovery features is evaluated. Changes to the requirements, design, and/or code are recommended which will enhance safety and reliability. The results of these analyses are recorded in the Hazard Analyses Reports.

The standard requires three verification testing activities: unit testing, integration testing, and validation testing. For each activity a set of test procedures and test results are produced. The objective of the testing process is to find software faults before a system is fielded. The test procedures should specify the complete test environment, including the inputs, outputs, expected results, pass/fail criteria, and conditions under which each test case will be executed. Testing should be conducted against an established baseline, following the specified procedures. Independent assessors determine what constitutes adequate test coverage. All tests should be repeatable by any test team. Results are analyzed and interpreted in the Test Reports.

The first verification testing activity is unit testing. Unit test procedures should contain a sufficient number of test cases so that all possible situations are exercised. The standard recommends [2]:

1. using boundary value analysis and equivalence class partitioning to determine the minimum set of test cases;

2. testing looping conditions against minimum, maximum, midrange, and out of range values; and

3. reading and writing variables and constants to every memory location used to ensure that there are no conflicts.

Unit test procedures should specify expected results and pass/fail criteria for each test case. They must also demonstrate traceability to the Software Design Description. The emphasis during unit testing is on verifying functionality. Unit testing verifies that each module and program performs correctly as specified on the target platform and that there is no unintended or unspecified functionality. Internal interfaces are also verified during unit testing. Unit test results are analyzed and interpreted in the Unit Test Report.

The second verification testing activity is integration testing. Integration test procedures must demonstrate traceability to the Software Requirements Specification to ensure that all functional, performance, safety, reliability, and security requirements are tested and verified. The integration test procedures must exercise all configuration options and all error handling scenarios. Test cases should verify that safety and security mechanisms cannot be bypassed. All integration test cases must be able to be repeated by different test teams.

The emphasis during integration testing is on verifying correct performance, as specified in the Requirements Specification, in the stated operational environment. The software is integrated with any predeveloped software on the target platform. Internal and external interfaces are verified, as is error handling. Integration testing verifies the safe and reliable operation on the system under normal conditions, overload situations, and abnormal usage. The correct response to all failure modes must be demonstrated. Integration test results are analyzed and interpreted in the Integration Test Report.

The third verification testing activity is validation testing. The standard defines validation as [2]:

> the process of determining the correctness of the final product with respect to the initial requirements.

The "initial requirements" in this case is, of course, the Software Requirements Specification. Validation test procedures must meet the same requirements as the integration test procedures, just discussed. Likewise, validation testing must meet the same requirements as integration testing. The primary difference is that greater independence requirements are applied to the validation testing team. The results of validation testing are analyzed and interpreted in the Validation Test Report.

The final verification subprocess is Reliability Qualification. The standard defines reliability qualification as [2]:

> A testing methodology in which a reliability hypothesis is demonstrated to the degree of confidence required.

Hence, the purpose of the reliability qualification subprocess is to demonstrate that specified reliability requirements and reliability goals are achieved (or not) when the software is integrated with the rest of the system in the target operational environment. The standard requires that reliability qualification testing be conducted against statistically valid operational profiles [2]. Particular attention is paid to time-related functions, response times, and system response to abnormal conditions. The independent assessor and/or Certification Authority will determine the degree of confidence needed in the reliability qualification results, which are analyzed and interpreted in the Reliability Qualification Report.

Interaction with System Safety and Other Standards

This standard is part of a set of standards, the Ontario Power Generation Inc. and AECL Software Engineering Standards (OASES), which address system engineering, software engineering, and safety engineering concerns of nuclear power plants. However, the other standards in this set are not cited.

Roles, Responsibilities, and Qualifications of Project Members.

CE-1001-STD Rev. 1 does not spell out the roles, responsibilities, and qualifications of project members. Instead, the standard requires that the Software Development Plan define the organizational roles and responsibilities and the communication channels. Minimum competency requirements for each position on the project are required to be defined in the Training Plan. In addition, as part of the Fundamental Principles, the standard defines independence requirements for staff involved in validation and verification activities.

Data Items Produced

The process outputs, illustrated in Figures 6.2 through 6.4, are the data items produced by adherence to this standard. The standard specifies minimum criteria for the informational content and the quality attributes these items must demonstrate, as illustrated in Table 6.5.

While developing the Darlington digital trip meter, Ontario Power Generation, Inc. kept track of the time spent on each activity. The results, which are shown below, are interesting. They show that 63 percent of the total project time was spent performing verification activities [33]:

Effort Expended on Software

Software Planning	13%
Software Requirements Specification	6%
Software Design Description	5%
Software Design Verification	12%
Code	5%
Code Verification	9%
Hazard Analyses	3%
Reviews	15%
Reliability Demonstration	7%
Testing	17%
Other	8%
	100%

Similar statistics were kept for the project as a whole [33]:

Effort Expended on Total Project

Software Engineering	21%
Hardware Engineering	15%
System Engineering	17%
Integration	16%
Contingency Planning	13%
Human Factors Engineering	1%
Monitoring	2%
Licensing	5%
Installation	6%
Project Management	4%
	100%

Compliance Assessment

While the standard does not specifically address the issue of compliance assessment, it states that "all the requirements which this standard imposes must be met [2]." Furthermore, the requirements for process inputs, activities, and outputs are specified in a very precise manner. This leads to a straightforward unambiguous assessment of compliance.

Scaling

The standard only mentions scaling in one context: scaling the standard for use with non-procedural or functional graphical languages. Therefore, it is expected that the standard will be applied in its entirety; project specific practices or conventions should be reflected in the Standards and Procedures Handbook.

6.2.4   Strengths

CE-1001-STD Rev. 1 has several strong points. CE-1001-STD Rev. 1 is one of the few standards to address both software safety and reliability concerns. It is also one of the few standards to emphasize the importance of data safety. The software development lifecycle is part of the system development lifecycle; the processes and activities are fully integrated. Rather than being spelled out in CE-1001-STD Rev. 1, project specific standards, such as coding standards, are recorded in the project Standards and Procedures Handbook. This enhances the usability and long-term applicability of the standard. The standard endorses the use of formal specifications and proofs, partitioning, information hiding, and independence. In addition the standard requires a comprehensive set of verification activities, not just testing.

6.2.5   Areas for Improvement

There are three minor areas in which CE-1001-STD Rev. 1 could be improved. First, the standard describes the inputs the software engineering process receives from the system engineering process. But, it does not describe the information the software engineering process feeds back to the system engineering process. Second, the standard maps the quality attributes to the outputs of the development process, but not the support or verification processes. Third, under the support process a Software Development Plan is written. It is mentioned in passing that this plan guides the activities in the development process, however it is not listed as an input to any of the development subprocesses. Additional guidance and clarification in these three areas would be helpful.

6.2.6   Results Observed to Date

The results achieved from the implementation of CE-1001-STD Rev. 1 since its introduction in January 1995 have been positive, in addressing both technical and regulatory concerns. As stated by Harauz [34] "detailed procedures and tools to support the methodologies have been produced" and successfully applied to several diverse projects:

- Darlington SDS1, which used a combination of Fortran and Assembler

- Darlington SDS2, which used a combination of Pascal and Assembler

- Pickering B Trip Meter, which was implemented in a subset of C

- Wolsong SDS1 PDC1 and PDC2, which was implemented in a functional block language

- Wolsong SDS2 PDC1 and PDC2, which was implemented in Modula 2

Verbal communication from J. Harauz in June 1999 indicated that the safety-critical software rewrite for the Darlington stations was completed on schedule and within budget. This accomplishment highlights the merits of CE-1001-STD Rev. 1. This success has led to some recognition [54]:

> The kind of software safety standards Ontario Hydro Nuclear and AECL have developed do not focus on perfection but preventing accidents. McMaster [University's Dr.] Parnas now considers Hydro the 'most advanced organization' in the field.

6.3   Summary

This chapter has presented the primary software safety and reliability standards in use in the nuclear power industry today: IEC 60880 and CE-1001-STD Rev. 1.

IEC 60880 was one of the first national or international consensus standards to address software safety and reliability in the nuclear power industry. It levies a comprehensive set of specific product and process requirements, from the beginning during requirements analysis and specification through operations and maintenance. For example, defense in depth, fault tolerance, software diversity, and partitioning are strongly recommended. Independence requirements are specified for verification activities, which are to include complementary static and dynamic analysis techniques. The standard promotes a comprehensive approach to the analysis and specification of nine categories of requirements. The importance of human factors engineering is also highlighted.

CE-1001-STD Rev. 1, which is derived from IEC 60880, is a process-oriented standard. Software engineering processes and activities are linked to system engineering processes. The standard does not have a separate software safety lifecycle. Process outputs are evaluated against quality attributes and objectives. Fundamental principles, such as partitioning, information hiding, and independence guide development, verification, and validation activities. The standard specifically calls out the need for defect causal analysis. A major advantage of this standard is that it incorporates the "lessons learned" from real world projects.

6.4 Discussion Problems

1. Develop a reliability hypothesis for a software controlled shutdown system. Assume the shutdown system operates in demand-mode and must perform a fail-safe operation within 10 seconds.

2. Which of these standards promote the use of formal specifications and formal proofs? Why do they do so?

3. Explain the difference between a design review and a systematic design review, a code review and a systematic code review.

4. What is the difference between the Software Requirements Specification and the Software Performance Specification in IEC 60880?

5. What effect does partitioning have on: the verification process, the safety assessment process, modifiability and robustness?

6. What design features does IEC 60880 require that CE-1001-STD Rev. 1 does not and vice versa?

7. Which CE-1001-STD Rev. 1 quality attributes apply to each development process output? To each verification process output?

8. What is the difference between criticality partitioning and functionality partitioning?

9. In CE-1001-STD Rev. 1, to which high-level process does quality assurance belong?

10. Which of the CE-1001-STD Rev. 1 fundamental principles apply to the design phase?

11. What compiler features could enhance or reduce data safety?

12. What is the benefit of identifying requirements that are likely to change in the future? Which of these standards require this?

6.5   Acknowledgment

The author would like to acknowledge the significant contributions made during the development and review of this chapter by John Harauz, Ontario Hydro Power Generation, Inc.

Additional Resources

Primary Source Documents

[1]   AECL STD-00-00902-001: Standard for Software Engineering of Safety Critical Software, Ontario Hydro Nuclear and AECL, December 1990, (issued for trial use period).

[2]   CE-1001-STD Rev. 1, Standard for Software Engineering of Safety Critical Software, CANDU Computer Systems Engineering Centre of Excellence, January 1995.

[3]   IEC 60880:1986-09, Software for Computers in the Safety Systems of Nuclear Power Plant Stations.

[4]   IEC 60880-1 (FDIS), First Supplement to IEC 60880:1986, Software for Computers in the Safety Systems of Nuclear Power Plant Stations.

Related Safety, System, and Software Engineering Standards

[5]   ANSI/ANS/IEEE Std. 7-4.3.2-1993, Application Criteria for Programmable Digital Computer Systems in Safety Systems of Nuclear Power Generating Stations.

[6]   International Atomic Energy Agency (IAEA) 50-C-D (rev 1):1998, Code on the Safety of Nuclear Power Plants: Design.

[7]   International Atomic Energy Agency (IAEA) Guide 50-SG-D3 (1980): Safety Guide.

[8]   International Atomic Energy Agency (IAEA) 50-SG-D8:1984, Safety Related Instrumentation for Nuclear Power Plants—A Safety Guide.

[9]   International Atomic Energy Agency (IAEA) 50-SG-D11:1984, General Design Safety Principles for Nuclear Power Plants—A Safety Guide.

[10] International Atomic Energy Agency (IAEA) 50-SG-QA6:1981, Quality Assurance in the Design of Nuclear Power Plants—A Safety Guide.

[11] IEC 557(1982-01): IEC Terminology in the Nuclear Reactor Field.

[12] IEC 639(1970-01): Nuclear Reactors. Use of the Protection System for Non-Safety Purposes.

[13] IEC 643(1979-01): Application of Digital Computers to Nuclear Reactor Instrumentation and Control.

[14] IEC 671(1980-01): Periodic Tests and Monitoring of the Protection System of Nuclear Reactors.

[15] IEC 960(1988-08): Functional Design Criteria for a Safety Parameter Display System for Nuclear Power Stations.

[16] IEC 60987:1989-12, Programmed Digital Computers Important to Safety for Nuclear Power Stations.

[17] IEC 61226:1993 Nuclear Power Plants – Instrumentation and Control Systems Important for Safety – Classification.

[18] IEC 61940:1998 Technical Report – Type 3: A Review of the Application of IEC 60880.

[19] IEC 61513 (CDV), Nuclear Power Plants, Instrumentation and Control for Systems Important to Safety, March 1999.

[20] IEC SC45A WG3 (draft), Nuclear Power Plants, Instrumentation and Control, Computer-based Systems Important for Safety, Software Aspects for I&C Systems of Class 2 and 3, March 1999.

[21] IEEE Std. 603-1991, Criteria for Safety Systems for Nuclear Power Generating Stations.

[22] NUREG-5930. High Integrity Software Standards and Guidelines, U.S. Nuclear Regulatory Commission (NRC), September 1992.

[23] NUREG/CR-6293: Verification and Validation Guidelines for High Integrity Systems, Vol. 1 – Main Report, U.S. Nuclear Regulatory Commission (NRC), March 1995.

[24] NUREG/CR-6293: Verification and Validation Guidelines for High Integrity Systems, Vol. 2 – Appendices A–D, U.S. Nuclear Regulatory Commission (NRC), March 1995.

[25] NUREG/CR-6463 Rev. 1, Review Guidelines for Software Languages for Use in Nuclear Power Plant Safety Systems, final report, October 1997.

Relevant Publications

[26] Adams, G. "Reliability Analysis of the DARTS Safety Critical Channels," *Software Reliability and Metrics Club Newsletter*, November 1994, pp. 2–7.

[27] Beltracchi, L. "NRC Research Activities," *Proceedings of the Digital Systems Reliability and Nuclear Safety Workshop*, NUREG/CP-0136, September 1993, pp. 31–46.

[28] Blauw, R.J. "A Utility Perspective on Digital Upgrades," *Proceedings of the Digital Systems Reliability and Nuclear Safety Workshop*, NUREG/CP-0136, September 1993, pp. 47–60.

[29] Byers, P.J. "The Role of Formal Methods in the Engineering of Safety-Critical Systems," *Technology and Assessment of Safety-critical Systems*, Springer-Verlag, 1994, pp. 247–258.

[30] Dobin, A., Clark, N., Godfrey, D., Harris, P., Parkin, G., Stevens, M. and Wichmann, B. *Reliability of SMART Instrumentation*, Parts 1–3, National Physics Lab and Druck, Ltd., 14 August 1998.

[31] Harauz, J. "Analysis of Implementation Difficulties with ISO 9001 and ISO 9000-3 Standards for Software Engineering," Draft Canadian Position Paper, CAC-JTC1/SC7/CAC-TC176, July 1993.

[32] Harauz, J. "ISO Standards for Software Engineers," *Standards Engineering*, July/August 1994, pp. 4–6

[33] Harauz, J. "The Ontario Hydro/Atomic Energy of Canada Ltd. (AECL) Software Engineering Process for Safety Critical Software," Safety and Reliability for Medical Device Software, Health Industries Manufacturers Association (HIMA) Report No. 95-8, 1995, tab 9.

[34] Harauz, J. "A Software Engineering Standards Framework for Nuclear Power," *StandardView*, Vol. 4, No. 3, September 1996, pp. 133–138.

[35] Harauz, J. "International Trends in Software Engineering and Quality Systems Standards: Ontario Hydro's Perspective, Part 1," *Software Quality Professional*, ASQ, March 1999, pp. 51–58.

[36] Harauz, J. "International Trends in Software Engineering and Quality Systems Standards: Ontario Hydro's Perspective, Part 2," *Software Quality Professional*, ASQ, June 1999, pp. 30–36.

[37] Jackson, W.E., Georgas, S., Harauz, J. and Lywood, M. *Guideline for the Use of Computer Software Tools by Professional Engineers and the Development of Computer Software Affecting Public Safety or Welfare*, Association of Professional Engineers of Ontario, 1993.

[38] Jennings, B. "Research into the Safety Issues Arising from Using ASIC Devices as a Potential Replacement Technology for Analogue Trip Amplifiers in Existing Reactor Safety Systems," *Industrial Perspectives of Safety-Critical Systems*, Springer-Verlag, 1998, pp. 222–232.

[39] Joannou, P.K. "Experiences from Application of Digital Systems in Nuclear Power Plants," *Proceedings of the Digital Systems Reliability and Nuclear Safety Workshop*, NUREG/CP-0136, September 1993, pp. 61–78.

[40] Joannou, P.K., Harauz, J., Tremaine, D.R. and Ichiyen, N. "The Ontario Hydro/AECL Approach to Realtime Software Engineering Standards," *Reliability Engineering and Systems Safety*, No. 43, 1994, pp. 143–150.

[41] Joannou, P.K. and Harauz, J. "Ontario Hydro/Atomic Energy Canada, Ltd. (AECL) Standards for Software Engineering—Deficiencies in Existing Standards That Created Their Need," *Proceedings 2nd IEEE International Software Engineering Standards Symposium*, August 1995, pp. 146–152.

[42] Lawrence, J.D., Persons, W.L., and Preckshot, G.G. "Evaluating Software for Safety Systems in Nuclear Power Plants," *Proceedings of the Ninth Annual Conference on Computer Assurance*, 1994, pp. 197–207.

[43] Leret, E. "Safety of Computerized I&C Systems: Projects of IEC Standards with Emphasis on Power Plant Sector," *Proceedings 2nd IEEE International Software Engineering Standards Symposium*, August 1995, pp. 18–22.

[44] Matsubata, T. "Does ISO 9000 Really Help Improve Software Quality," *American Programmer*, Vol. 7, No. 2, pp. 39–45, 1994.

[45] McDougall, J., Viola, M. and Moum, G. *Tabular Representation of Mathematical Functions for the Specification and Verification of Safety Critical Software*, Ontario Hydro, AECL, 1995.

[46] Mondal, U. and Viola, M. *Experience in Analog to Digital Upgrade of Reactor Protective Systems: Key Issues and How They Were Addressed*, Ontario Hydro/AECL, 1994.

[47] Pant, H., Franklin, P. and Everett, W. "A Structured Approach to Improving Software Reliability Using Operational Profiles," *Proceedings of the Annual Reliability and Maintainability Symposium (RAMS '94)*, IEEE, 1994, pp. 142–146.

[48] Plat, N., van Katwijk, J. and Toetenel, H. "Application and Benefits of Formal Methods in Software Development," *Software Engineering Journal*, September 1992, pp. 335–346.

[49] Russell, W.T. "Regulatory Perspective on Digital Instrumentation and Control Systems for Nuclear Power Plants," *Proceedings of the Digital Systems Reliability and Nuclear Safety Workshop*, NUREG/CP-0136, September 1993, pp. 21–30.

[50] Sherwood-Jones, B. "Human Factors—How Little Can You Get Away With and How Much Is Right?" *Safety Systems*, May 1997, Vol. 6, No. 3, pp. 12–14.

[51] Storey, N. *Safety-Critical Computer Systems*, Addison-Wesley, 1996.

[52] Tate, R.J. "Assessing Software Based Safety Systems Against the Requirements and Recommendations of IEC 60880," *Proceedings 2nd IEEE International Software Engineering Standards Symposium*, August 1995, pp. 153–164.

[53] Thuy, N. and Ficheux-Vapne, F. "IEC 60880: Feedback of Experience and Guidelines for Future Work," *Proceedings 2nd IEEE International Software Engineering Standards Symposium*, August 1995, pp. 117–126.

[54] Wade-Rose, B. "Danger, Software at Work," *Report on Business Magazine, Toronto Globe and Mail*, March 1995.

Correspondence

[55] Jacquemart, C. 11/11/97 Email.

Chapter 7

Biomedical Industry

7.1 IEC 601-1-4(1996-06), Medical Electrical Equipment – Part 1: General Requirements for Safety – 4. Collateral Standard: Programmable Electrical Medical Systems.

7.1.1 Background

The International Electrotechnical Commission (IEC), based in Switzerland, is a world-wide standardization organization comprised of IEC National Committees from 53 member countries. The purpose of the IEC "is to promote international cooperation on all questions concerning standardization in the electrical and electronic fields. To this end ... the IEC publishes International Standards [1]." Technical committees and subcommittees, composed of representatives from the National Committees, develop the International Standards and submit them to the IEC Central committee for official balloting and publication. IEC standards represent "an international consensus of opinion on the relevant subjects since each technical committee (TC) has representation from all interested National Committees [1]." IEC works closely with ANSI, CENELEC, IEEE, and ISO on harmonization issues.

In 1988 IEC published the second edition of IEC 601-1(1988-12) Medical Electrical Equipment – Part 1: General Requirements for Safety [2]; the first edition was published in 1977 [12]. This safety standard is the foundation for all standards in the IEC 601 medical electronics safety series and is applicable to all medical electrical equipment. The 601 series is organized in layers. Level one standards (IEC 601-1-x) are collateral safety standards that address safety issues, such as software safety and EMI/RFI, that are common to most medical electrical equipment. Level two standards (IEC 601-2-x) are device specific or "particular" safety standards. Level one standards incorporate the foundation standard as a normative reference. Level two standards incorporate the foundation standard and the applicable level one standards as normative references (see Figure 7.1). This modular layering approach is illustrated by the corresponding section numbers of the general and collateral standards. By the end of 1997, five Level one and ninety Level two medical electrical equipment safety standards had been published in the IEC 601 series.

IEC 601-1-4, the subject of this chapter, was prepared by IEC TC 62 which had representatives from Canada, France, Germany, the U.S., and the U.K. representing both the medical device industry and government agencies responsible for regulating the safety of medical devices. This standard was published as a collateral standard to IEC 601-1 in June 1996. IEC decided that this standard was needed due to the increased use of software to control safety-critical therapeutic and diagnostic medical equipment. Because of the complexity involved in such systems, the "standard goes beyond traditional testing and assessment ... and includes requirements for the processes by which medical electrical equipment is developed [1]." This was done in part because "ISO 9000-3 does not alone provide sufficient validation confidence [34]." In fact the standard states that "testing of the finished product is not, by itself, adequate to address the safety of complex medical equipment [1]." The standard, which contains one normative and five informative annexes, promotes risk management activities as an integral part of the software development lifecycle.

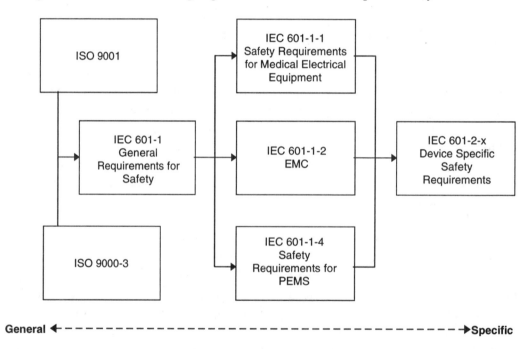

Figure 7.1: Organization of the IEC 601 series of safety standards for medical electrical equipment [22].

7.1.2 Purpose and Scope

IEC 601-1-4, referred to as the standard in this chapter, applies to all therapeutic and diagnostic medical electrical equipment that is controlled by software and/or incorporates software subsystems. This includes "devices containing software used to control delivery of treatment to a patient, to determine treatment delivery, or provide analytical support for the determination of treatment delivery [22]." The standard refers to such systems as programmable electrical medical systems (PEMS). Some examples include laser surgical devices, dialysis equipment, ventilators, and infusion pumps which are controlled by embedded software and radiation treatment planning systems. Conversely, the standard does not apply to hospital information systems that are used to maintain patient records or billing information.

The purpose of this standard is to: 1) specify "requirements for the process by which a PEMS is designed," and 2) serve "as a guide to safety requirements for the purpose of reducing and managing risk" in the end product [1]. The standard specifically does not address hardware issues, software replication, installation and commissioning, operations and maintenance, and decommissioning; it considers these topics outside of its scope.

The standard indicates that its intended audience is certification bodies, manufacturers of medical electrical equipment, and technical committees developing Level two device specific standards.

IEC 601-1-4 includes a glossary. It is worthwhile to point out a few terms to put the standard in the correct context [1]:

- the development lifecycle is defined to end after validation,

- risk is defined as the probability of a hazard causing harm and the severity of that harm,

- safety is defined as freedom from unacceptable risk,

- severity is defined as a qualitative measure of the possible consequences of a hazard,

- validation is defined as the process of evaluating a PEMS to determine if it satisfies requirements for its intended use, and

- verification is defined as the process of evaluating whether the product(s) of a given development phase satisfy specified requirements imposed at the start of that phase.

7.1.3 Description

The standard, building upon the foundation of ISO 9001 and 9000-3,[1] integrates a comprehensive risk management process with the software development lifecycle to address the additional needs of a class of software, that is, PEMS, whose failure would cause injury or death.

Recommended and Required Practices

A comprehensive risk management process, a combination of risk analysis and risk control activities which are ongoing throughout the development lifecycle, is required. The primary

---

[1]For a comprehensive description of how to satisfy the ISO 9001 and 9000-3 requirements of this standard see AAMI [11], Trautman [33], and Whitemore [35].

concern for PEMS is that: 1) appropriate risk management activities are undertaken; and 2) that they are undertaken with a degree of rigor consistent with the device's criticality. Figure 7.2 illustrates the IEC 601-1-4 risk management process.

Risk Analysis

Risk analysis, which is conducted in accordance with the project risk management plan (see Data Items Produced, below), begins with the identification of all potential hazards for the PEMS (step 1.0 of Figure 7.2). As Wingate points out, "risk analysis is used to prioritize validation" [34] activities. The standard requires that hazards be identified for normal, abnormal (accidental or intentional), and fault usage. "The last refers to degraded-mode operation; that is situations (i.e. life support) in which a device must continue to operate until it can be repaired or replaced [22]." Potential hazards that could affect "patients, operators, service personnel, bystanders, and the environment" are required to be identified [1]. Sequences of events and initiating causes are required to be evaluated, such as: human error, "hardware faults, software faults, integration errors, and environmental conditions [1]." The standard provides examples of common failure causes to scrutinize: compatibility of system components, human factors issues including inadequate or misleading warning and error messages and instructions for use, data integrity errors, and the use of third party or COTS software.[2]

A variety of inductive and deductive techniques should be used to perform the risk analysis. In general, different techniques will be used during different phases of the development lifecycle as more becomes known about the end product. The standard requires that the methods used and the results obtained from using them be documented in the Risk Management File (see Data Items Produced, below).

Next, the severity of each hazard, should it occur, is assessed (step 2.0 in Figure 7.2). The standard defines the four levels of severity as "a qualitative measure of the possible consequences of a hazard:

- **catastrophic:** potential of multiple deaths or serious injuries;

- **critical:** potential of death or serious injury;

- **marginal:** potential of injury; and

- **negligible:** little or no potential of injury [1]."

The method used to categorize the severity and the results obtained must be documented in the Risk Management File.

A system may have multiple potential hazards associated with it. Likewise, each hazard may have multiple potential causes. All potential causes for each software hazard should be identified (step 3.0 of Figure 7.2). For each hazard/cause combination the likelihood of

---

[2]See Chapter 2 for a discussion of potential safety and reliability problems associated with the use of COTS software.

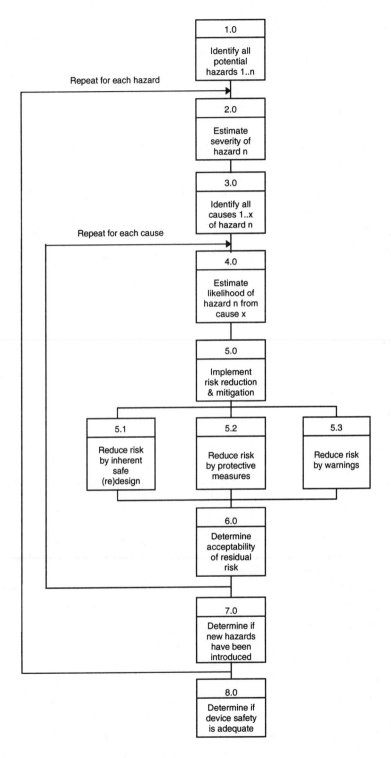

Figure 7.2: IEC 601-1-4 risk management process [22].

the hazard occurring is assessed (step 4.0 of Figure 7.2). The standard supports the use of either a qualitative or quantitative likelihood assessment as long as the method used and the results obtained are documented in the Risk Management File.

The standard identifies six categories of likelihood: frequent, probable, occasional, remote, improbable, and incredible. Recognizing the difference of opinion that exists within industry, academia, and the international standards community regarding the ability to predict software failures, which are systematic not random in nature, the standard does not define these terms. As Hughes observes, predicting software failures is not an exact science:

> The main difficulties... arise from the treatment of systematic (design) errors, common-cause failures (which limit the value of redundant and diverse elements), human error prediction, and ... the completeness of any analysis [26].

For reference purposes, MIL-STD-882D, discussed in Chapter 5, defines the categories of likelihood as:

- **frequent:** $x > 10^{-1}$
- **probable:** $10^{-1} > x > 10^{-2}$
- **occasional:** $10^{-2} > x > 10^{-3}$
- **remote:** $10^{-3} > x > 10^{-6}$
- **improbable:** $10^{-6} > x$
- **incredible:** not defined

The combination of the severity of a hazard and the likelihood of its initiating cause(s) occurring determine the risk of a PEMS. The standard does not provide specific guidance on what constitutes "acceptable risk" for a particular PEMS design or class of PEMS. Instead, the standard provides general guidance by stating that: "often, acceptable risk will be established on a case-by-case basis [1]." The standard also refers the reader to section 3 of IEC 601-1 which requires that single fault or single point of failure conditions not exist.

The general guidance provided by the standard makes use of the concept of three risk regions: intolerable, as low as reasonably practicable (ALARP), and acceptable. These regions represent the correlation of a hazard's severity and the likelihood of its initiating cause(s) occurring (see Figure 7.3). This concept was first promulgated by the U.K.'s Health and Safety at Work Act of 1974 [26]. Note that the risk region should be determined for all hazard/cause combinations. The highest risk region of any hazard/cause combination represents the device risk. This determination is made before and after risk control measures have been implemented.

The intolerable region depicts risks that are so severe that they would not be tolerated; the severity and/or likelihood must be reduced. The acceptable region depicts risks that have an extremely low severity and/or likelihood; risk reduction measures are not needed.

Between these two is the region known as ALARP. "Here the risk must be justified against the desirability of the benefits provided by the ... system and the cost of remedial action needed to reduce the risk to an 'acceptable' level [26]." In other words, risks in the ALARP region "are reduced to the lowest level practicable... Near the limit of intolerable risk, risks would normally be reduced even at considerable cost [1]."

Risk Control

The standard requires that risks associated with PEMS be controlled so that they are, at a minimum, in the ALARP region. Risk reduction and mitigation techniques are employed to control the severity of a hazard and/or the likelihood of it occurring. The order of precedence for risk control activities as stated in the standard is:

- reduce the risk by inherent safe design or redesign;

- reduce the risk by protective measures; and

- reduce the risk by sufficient warnings to users about residual risk. (Steps 5.0–5.3 of Figure 7.2.)

These activities are often used in conjunction with each other for high risk and/or complex systems. For example, "these techniques might include reallocating risk-control measures to architectural components, redesigning a system, or increasing the use of redundancy or diversity [22]."

The importance of adequate training and warnings to users about residual risk cannot be overemphasized [27]. Moore cites an incident at the University Hospital in Zaragoza, Spain during 1990 [28]:

> The hospital used an energy-selectable electron treatment unit. On December 5th faulty performance was expected and noted. December 7th the maintenance engineer, unable to find or fix the problem, overrode built-in security systems to make the system operational. December 10th the radiographer noticed a 36MeV electron output meter reading when the machine was turned off; he assumed that the meter was still jammed and continued using the machine as normal. December 20th regularly scheduled dosimetry checks were performed by the physicists. They found that regardless of the energy selection (7, 10, or 13MeV) the true energy output was always 36MeV. This led to "massive overdoses, up to 15 times the intended therapy. Ten of the twenty-seven patients treated during that interval died [28]."

The most well-known case of software induced fatalities by radiation overdosing is the Therac-25. (See Hsia [25] and Leveson [27].) This device was also responsible for underdosing, which received less attention [28]. In summary, the Therac failures were a result of deficient system/software engineering and risk management processes [27]. It is

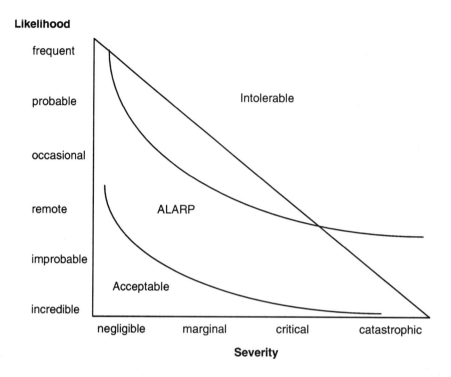

Figure 7.3: Risk regions correlate the likelihood and severity of a hazard occurring [1,22].

also likely that the operators were unaware of the device's residual risk—its ability to cause injury or death if operated incorrectly [27].

The next step is to determine the acceptability of the residual risk, that is, the risk remaining after risk reduction and mitigation techniques have been employed, by referring to Figure 7.3 (step 6.0 of Figure 7.2). Again, the risk region for each hazard/cause combination is determined. An assessment is then made as to whether the risk reduction and risk mitigation techniques have introduced any new hazards. If so, the risk management process is repeated (step 7.0 of Figure 7.2). Note that steps 4.0 through 6.0 of Figure 7.2 are repeated for each cause, while steps 2.0 through 7.0 are repeated for each hazard. After this a determination is made whether or not device safety is adequate. The Level two device specific standards provide some guidance in this area.

Several work products result from this iterative risk management process. To comply with the standard, a hazard analysis by itself is not sufficient; manufacturers and/or certifiers should also document:

- what hazard analysis techniques were used;

- what the estimated likelihood of each hazard occurring is and how it was estimated;

- what the estimated severity of each hazard is and how it was categorized;

- what risk reduction and mitigation techniques were implemented and how their effectiveness was assessed; and

- how verification and validation activities demonstrated correct implementation of safety and reliability features.

A generic risk management template, such as that shown in Figure 7.4, can be used to document this information. Sections 2 through 12 are repeated for each hazard, while Sections 5 through 11 are repeated for each cause.

Risk analyses should be performed for the system as an entity. Appropriate techniques must be chosen so that hazard analyses for the software, electrical, mechanical, biomaterials, chemical, and other components can be effectively integrated and analyzed at the system level.

Risk Management and the Development Lifecycle

The risk management process depicted in Figure 7.2 is an iterative process which is on-going throughout the development lifecycle. For example, hazard identification will begin during the requirements analysis phase. Likewise, risk analysis and control activities will be refined during each subsequent phase.

The standard requires that a development lifecycle be selected and justified. "It does not require that any particular development lifecycle be used, but it does require that the development lifecycle has certain attributes [1]." The primary concern for PEMS is that the development lifecycle is consistent and has the appropriate degree of rigor for the criticality of the system. The selected lifecycle model should have four particular characteristics:

1. distinct phases with well-defined inputs, outputs, and activities for each phase;

2. feedback of technical information among the phases and activities;

3. verification and validation activities return to the source of the error, not necessarily the previous phase, and look at adjacent and similar areas in the software for associated errors; and

4. development lifecycle and risk management activities are fully integrated.

A generic PEMS development lifecycle model is shown in Figure 7.5.

To comply with the standard, during the requirements phase risk-related functions are identified as part of the risk analysis. Each of these functions is so identified in the requirements specification, along with the safety integrity levels necessary to control them.

To comply with the standard, during architectural analysis and specification risk control measures are allocated to PEMS subsystems and components. The role of software in risk control measures should be defined. Architectural considerations such as redundancy, diversity, partitioning, information hiding, independence, error detection and recovery, and data safety issues should be analyzed. As Cosgriff observes, "since total reliability cannot

PART I – RISK ANALYSIS

1. Maximum tolerable risk allocated to software:_____

2. Hazard(s) identified:_____

3. Hazard analysis technique(s):_____

4. Severity category (negligible, marginal, critical, catastrophic):_____

    4.1 Can a failure be detected before a hazard occurs?_____

         During what interval?_____

    4.2 What techniques have been employed to reduce the severity of the hazard?_____

         _____

5. Software cause(s):_____

6. Likelihood (incredible, improbable, remote, occasional, probable, frequent):_____

    6.1 Does the hazard occur in the absence of a failure, in failure mode only, or in multiple
         failure mode only?_____

    6.2 What techniques have been employed to reduce the likelihood of the hazard?_____

         _____

7. Estimated risk/risk region:_____

    7.1 Initial:_____

    7.2 Residual:_____

PART II – RISK CONTROL

8. Risk Control Requirement:_____

    8.1 Minimum Acceptable:_____

    8.2 Implemented:_____

9. Analysis of Effectiveness of Risk Control Measures:_____

10. Resultant Safety Integrity:_____

11. Verification activities/results:_____

12. Validation activities/results:_____

13. Adequacy of Device Safety:_____

Figure 7.4: Risk management template [22].

be guaranteed, we have to rely on the designer to incorporate fail-safe features [13]." This decision making process should be documented to explain how and why these architectural considerations were incorporated. For example, how was diversity implemented and why; or why was it not incorporated.

To comply with the standard during the design and development phase, "the design shall be decomposed into subsystems, each having a design and test specification [1]." The decision making process should explain how and why specific design considerations were incorporated, for example: what software development methods were used, hardware platforms, automated tool usage, operating system and compiler selection, COTS software usage, and human factors issues.

As shown in Figure 7.5, verification activities are ongoing throughout the development lifecycle. A verification plan is required "to show how the safety requirements for each development lifecycle phase will be verified [1]." As Cosgriff points out, "safety-critical systems will be found in many corners of your local ... hospital... The software in commonplace treatment devices (e.g. drug infusion pumps, cardiac defibrillators) is usually embedded and operates in real-time. This presents particular problems ... in the area of testing [13]." Hence, multiple complementary static and dynamic analysis techniques should be used [21–24, 36]. That is why the standard uses the term 'verification activities' and not 'testing.' Likewise, the methods and results of verification activities should be documented, analyzed, and interpreted; for example, a discussion of why observed results were considered acceptable—not just that they passed.

A validation plan is required "to show that correct safety requirements have been implemented [1]." As Wingate observes, "it is just as important to provide evidence ... why certain software cannot affect ... product quality as justifying the level and priority of validation needed for software that can affect quality" [34] and thereby safety. During validation the observed results should be documented, analyzed, and interpreted to demonstrate that the PEMS has been adequately validated. Furthermore, the standard requires a limited degree of independence during validation:

- the validation team leader has to be independent of the design team;

- no one can validate their own work;

- organizational relationships of the validation and design/development team members have to be documented.

IEC 601-1-4 is one of the few standards to address modification and, by default, reuse [22]. The standard makes a short but concise statement regarding corrective or adaptive maintenance and enhancements [1]:

> If any or all of a design results from modification of an earlier design, then either all of this standard applies as it if were a new design or the continued validity of any previous design documentation shall be assessed under a modification/change procedure.

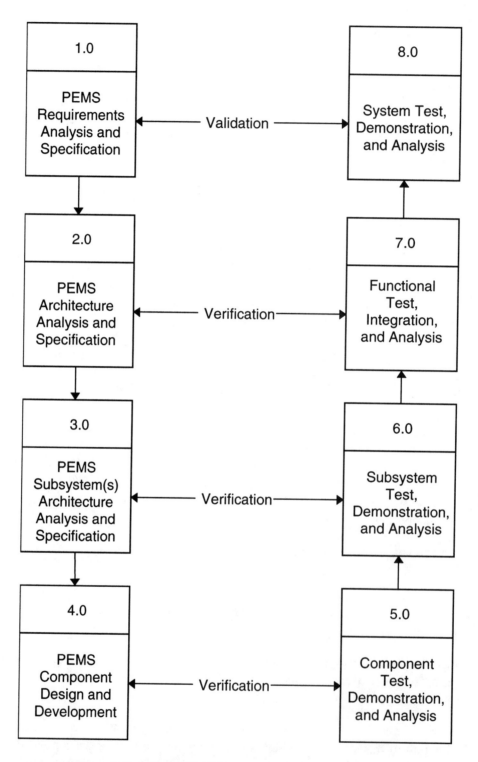

Figure 7.5: Generic PEMS development lifecycle model [22].

Modifications may take the form of requirements changes, design changes, corrections, enhancements, or software reuse. The primary concern for PEMS is the effect of the modifications on product safety and reliability. The extent and nature of the change will determine which set of activities applies. Note that the modification/change procedure must be in accordance with Section 4.5 of ISO 9001.

Examples of technology changes which should come under the purview of modification/change control procedures and be evaluated for their impact on safety and reliability include:

- **New hardware platform.** This could be migrating to a newer version of the same architecture family, such as from a i486 to a Pentium, or changing architectures, such as from i486 to a RISC workstation.

- **New operating system.** This could be migrating to a newer version of the same operating system, such as from Windows 3.1 to Windows 98, or changing operating systems such as from RTOS to UNIX.

- **New compiler.** This could be migrating to a newer version of the same compiler, such as from PASCAL 5.2 to PASCAL 6.0, or changing compilers such as from PASCAL to C++.

- **New functionality.** This includes new features and capabilities that are provided for the end user.

- **Design enhancements and corrections.** This includes changes to the internal software design that may or may not be visible to the end user. These changes are usually undertaken to improve software performance, safety, and reliability.

To illustrate, consider the evolution of a radiation treatment system. The original system design employed a single 8086 microprocessor and source code written in PASCAL. The new system design employed a combination of four i386/i486 microprocessors and source code written in Assembly and C++. Many functions that had been implemented in discrete hardware logic in the original system were now implemented in and controlled by software. To the end user, the functionality of the new system was identical. However, from the aspect of safety and reliability, it had to be evaluated as if it were an entirely new system since none of the original architecture or design remained.

Interaction with System Safety and Other Standards

This standard includes five standards as normative references:

- IEC 601-1(1988-12), Medical Electrical Equipment – Part 1: General Requirements for Safety, with IEC 601-1-am(1991-11) Amendment no. 1 and IEC 601-1-am(1995-03) Amendment no. 2.

- IEC 601-1-1(1992-06), Medical Electrical Equipment – Part 1: General Requirements for Safety – Section 1. Collateral Standard: Safety Requirements for Medical Electrical Systems.

- IEC 788(1984-01), Medical Radiology – Terminology.

- ISO 9000-3:1991, Quality Management and Quality Assurance Standards – Part 3: Guidelines for the Application of ISO 9001 to the Development, Supply and Maintenance of Software.

- ISO 9001:1994, Quality Systems – Model for Quality Assurance in Design, Development, Production, Installation and Servicing.

IEC designates a standard as a "normative reference" to convey that it is incorporated by reference; that is, these five standards form part of IEC 601-1-4 since they are incorporated by reference. This "layering" approach is common to all IEC standards. This approach eliminates the need to duplicate material common to many standards. It also eliminates version control problems; for example, the newest version of any normative reference is incorporated. Likewise, many Level two device specific standards include IEC 601-1-4 as a normative reference. Requirements in device specific standards generally take precedence over collateral standards.

Roles, Responsibilities, and Qualifications of Project Members

The standard makes the following statement: "The design and modification of a PEMS shall be considered as an assigned task in accordance with section 4.18 of ISO 9001 [1]." The standard is incorporating the clause in ISO 9001 which requires personnel to possess demonstrated and documented professional competence through the appropriate formal education, experience, licensing, and certification to perform assigned tasks. Hence, staff involved in the design and modification of a PEMS must possess demonstrated competence in:

- the application of the specific medical device,

- the development process(es) for medical devices,

- methods by which safety integrity is assured, and

- risk management techniques.

The staff as a whole must possess competence in all four areas. Individuals must be competent in a minimum of one of the areas.

Data Items Produced

"IEC 601-1-4 views documentation as a tool for verifying compliance [22]." The standard levies requirements for two categories of documentation: Instructions for Use and the Risk Management File. The standard purposely does not define the format of either, rather it concentrates on the informational content. This documentation may be maintained in hardcopy and/or on electronic media. Revisions, amendments, review, approval, and maintenance of documents must be done in accordance with a formal document control process as defined in Section 4.5 of ISO 9001 and Sections 6.2 and 6.3 of ISO 9000-3. These sections require that procedures be established and maintained for controlling, identifying, collecting, and organizing project documentation. Specific requirements include:

- review and approval for adequacy before issue;

- easy availability of current documentation;

- appropriate control, marking, and documentation of changes;

- maintaining accurate and current records to demonstrate that required quality objectives have been met; and

- maintaining records so that they are readily identifiable and available.

The requirements levied on the Instructions for Use, often referred to as "labelling" in the medical industry, are that they: 1) contain all relevant information regarding residual risk; and 2) be accurate, current, complete, and understandable.

A short discussion will amplify the importance of accurate, complete, current, and understandable Instructions for Use. Radiation treatment software systems are used to: 1) plan the actual treatment regimen based on advanced physical dosimetric models, graphical simulation, and tumor control goals for individual patients; 2) control the actual release of energy, which involves the 'targeting' information, beam-type, strength, and duration; and 3) monitor and record actual energy release in a treatment profile database. Moore reminds us that "... in radiotherapy ... underdosing, as much as overdosing, can lead to treatment failures ... the consequences of (which) can be terminal [28]." He reported an incident at the North Staffordshire Infirmary in 1991. A new treatment planning system was introduced in 1982. The radiographer continued to manually add in a distance correction factor as he had done for the previous system. However, the new system implemented an algorithm which already included the correction factor. This "led to the 5–30% underdosing of 989 patients (between 1982 and 1991) with the consequent increased risk of disease recurrence and mortality [28]."

The Risk Management File is the mainstay of the project safety documentation produced by adherence to this standard. This file contains the evidence needed to establish a "safety case" or proof that a device meets stated safety criteria and goals. This is the information that auditors, third-party certification bodies, and regulatory agencies will review before making a determination.

The standard provides a logical organization of the information required in the Risk Management File; the actual physical organization is left to the user. As shown in Figure 7.6, the major components of the Risk Management File are the risk-related lifecycle artifacts and the Risk Management Summaries.

The first item required is a Risk Management Plan. This plan should detail which development lifecycle model will be followed and the risk management activities, reviews, and management responsibilities associated with each lifecycle activity and phase. Next the method(s) used to identify hazards are documented, such as a SFTA, SFMEA, and/or HAZOP. The results obtained from using these methods are documented. The methods used to determine the severity of the consequences of a possible hazard are also documented in the Risk Management File; that is, an explanation is needed of why a consequence is considered marginal and not critical. The Risk Management File must include a description of the method(s) used to determine the likelihood of a hazard occurring. As noted earlier, the standard makes provision for the use of either qualitative or quantitative methods.

Requirements, architecture, and design specifications which detail risk-related functions and the corresponding risk mitigation/control measures for the PEMS and each of its subsystems must be included in the Risk Management File, along with the verification and validation plans. The last of the risk-related lifecycle documentation in the Risk Management File is a discussion of the validation methods used, an analysis of the results obtained during validation, the compliance assessment report, and an evaluation of the residual risk for each hazard/cause combination.

The Risk Management File also contains the Risk Management Summaries, which are prepared for each hazard. The Risk Management Summary identifies each hazard and its cause(s). For each hazard/cause combination, the risk is estimated and risk control requirements are identified. Later in the development lifecycle, an evaluation of the effectiveness of the risk control measures is added, along with an analysis of the verification results and residual risk. The template presented in Figure 7.4 could be used to capture this information.

For each of the items in the Risk Management File, it is expected that the amount of detail provided will correspond to the device's complexity and the consequences of its failure and/or misuse. If the documentation in the Risk Management File is developed in accordance with another standard, for example the Risk Management Plan follows IEEE Std. 1228-1994 (see Chapter 11), that should be noted.

Compliance Assessment

This standard includes mandatory requirements, which are indicated by the term "shall," and recommendations, which are indicated by the term "should." All mandatory requirements are followed by a statement which gives specific instructions on how to check compliance: "Compliance is checked by the inspection of ... " The standard states that an assessment shall be conducted to determine if all mandatory requirements of the standard have been satisfied and documented appropriately in the Risk Management File. This assess-

Risk Management File

- Risk Management Plan

- Hazard Identification Methods and Results

- Severity Categorization Methods

- Likelihood Estimation Methods

- PEMS/subsystem(s) Requirements Specifications

- PEMS/subsystem(s) Architecture Specifications

- PEMS/subsystem(s) Design Specifications

- Verification Plan

- Validation Plan

- Compliance Assessment Report

- Analysis of Residual Risk

. . . .

- **Risk Management Summaries (for each hazard)**
    - Identification of Each Hazard and Its Cause(s)
        - Risk Estimate (severity and likelihood for each hazard/cause combination)
        - Risk Control Requirements
        - Analysis of the Effectiveness of Risk Control Measures
        - Analysis of Residual Risk
    - Verification Results
    - Validation Results

Figure 7.6: Logical organization of the risk management file.

ment may be conducted by an internal or external audit, the results of which are required to be documented in an assessment report.

Scaling

IEC 601-1-4 gets high marks in the area of scaling. The standard recognizes that a "PEMS can be a very simple medical electrical device or a complex medical system or anything in between [1]." In a simple medical device the PEMS and the device are the same. In contrast, a complex medical device may have multiple electrical, electronic, electro-mechanical and software subsystems and components. Accordingly, "IEC 601-1-4 accommodates a wide spectrum of device complexity and supports top-down, bottom-up and spiral design methodologies," [22] as well as others.

Likewise, the standard is not overly prescriptive when levying requirements. For example, when listing the potential hazards to be considered, the potential initiating causes to be considered, or design requirements to be specified the standard includes the phrase "as appropriate" or "when appropriate."

A similar approach is taken in specifying documentation requirements: the logical structure and informational content is specified, not the physical structure. The standard relies on qualified and competent people to use the standard effectively in response to the size, complexity, and criticality of a PEMS.

7.1.4   Strengths

IEC 601-1-4 has many strong points which are advantageous to several classes of users: manufacturers, certifiers, and regulators. The standard builds upon the foundation of ISO 9001 and 9000-3 and the IEC 601 series. Many companies already have or are moving toward ISO 9000 certification. The standard provides a comprehensive risk management process as an integral part of the software development lifecycle. This is a major advantage over other standards which promote a separate safety lifecycle or only require a preliminary hazard analysis and provide the user no further guidance. "One of the standard's biggest advantages it its flexibility, which allows manufacturers to tailor it to individual devices according to (their size), complexity (and criticality. In addition,) by stating how compliance will be assessed, the new standard allows manufacturers and regulatory bodies to operate from the same baseline [24]."

The standard follows the ISO 9000 convention of specifying 'what' to do, not 'how' to do it; instead it relies on effective implementation by qualified and competent people. The following examples illustrate this fact. The standard does not specify a particular development lifecycle. Instead the user is to select and justify a development lifecycle which has certain attributes. Secondly, the standard does not specify what constitutes acceptable risk. Instead it provides general guidelines from which competent people are to make a case-by-case determination. Thirdly, the standard specifies the logical structure and informational content of project documentation. The physical structure and format are left to the user. In addition, the standard recognizes the difference of opinion regarding the ability to predict software failures and supports either qualitative or quantitative methods to assess the likelihood of a hazard occurring.

The strengths and flexibility just discussed will contribute to the long-term usefulness of this standard.

7.1.5 Areas for Improvement

A major way to improve IEC 601-1-4 would be to expand its scope to include two other safety-critical medical applications: 1) software that is used to control the manufacture of pharmaceuticals; and 2) software that controls management systems for bloodbanks and other biological products.

The production of pharmaceuticals is a safety-critical process because drugs must be manufactured to their approved and predetermined specifications; prescriptions and dosages are based on these specifications. Substandard products, resulting from an incorrect mixture or strength of materials, "can be detrimental to health care and at extremes can cause death [34]." Wingate et al. have studied this problem:

> Computer-related systems are being increasingly used for drug production to improve manufacturing performance (e.g. materials management, production control, and packaging). The complexity of (such) computer systems means they are susceptible to development and operational deficiencies, e.g. poor specification capture, design errors, and poor maintenance practice [34].

Software that controls management systems for bloodbanks and other biological products is also safety critical. These systems must accurately record, label, and retrieve products. Information recorded includes the blood type, Rh factor, other typing information, and the presence or absence of blood borne pathogens. This information must be recorded accurately and through the labelling and retrieval processes associated with the correct specimen. A data error in this environment could be fatal to the patient receiving the transfusion and/or transplant.

Similar problems can arise in diagnostic clinical laboratory systems if samples are not correctly labelled as to the patient they came from; incorrect data can lead to diagnosis and treatment (or nontreatment) for the wrong patient [18]. The National Council for Clinical Laboratory Systems (NCCLS) GP19-A standard [10] addresses some of these issues and can easily be used in conjunction with IEC 601-1-4.

In their study Wingate et al. uncovered that "there have been several prominent incidents" related to these types of medical software [34]:

- "... in 1989 a bloodbank management system (mistakenly) released HIV-infected plasma; and

- in 1991 there were incidents involving the sterilization, quality control, and labelling of anaesthetic, antimigraine, and eye-care products."

Their analysis of 300 unexpected computer system events in the pharmaceuticals industry showed the following error distribution [34]:

- 45% hardware or power supply failures

- 18.2% unknown cause, cleared after reboot

- 12.1% application software errors

- 11% user error, better instructions for use needed

- 9.9% system software errors

- 3.8% design errors

As this study shows, most software "suppliers to the pharmaceutical industry have typically been inexperienced in software validation," [34] particularly for safety-critical software.

It is obvious that the scope of IEC 601-1-4 should be expanded, perhaps as a supplement, to include these two additional categories of medical software.

7.1.6   Results Observed to Date

Although IEC 601-1-4 was only approved and published in June 1996, several companies and regulatory bodies have taken steps in preparation for its publication and implementation.

Siemens AG, Erlangen, FRG has developed a qualitative methodology for estimating the likelihood of a PEMS hazard occurring. This methodology is quite sophisticated in that it does not look at a single device as an entity. Instead, the methodology recognizes that, in general:

- multiple devices are sold throughout the world;

- a single device may be used multiple times during a day; and

- a single device may be used on more than one person per day.

These factors are accounted for in the likelihood estimation, as shown in Figure 7.7.

Siemens has also developed a risk analysis worksheet which captures all the information required in the Risk Management Summaries. (See Figure 7.8.) The likelihood and severity, both before and after risk control measures are implemented, are correlated to a risk region. The structure of this worksheet lends itself to being implemented in a relational database management system, which facilitates collecting the information and keeping it up to date.

Hewlett Packard, Boblingen, FRG has also developed tools to implement IEC 601-1-4. The first item is a Requirements Specification/Risk Table. This table not only identifies the cause(s) of a hazard, but also who or what is affected: patient, operator, and/or surroundings. Unlike the Siemens approach, residual risk is identified but not the residual severity and likelihood. (See Figure 7.9.)

Likelihood Factor	= 1	= 2	= 3
Number of installations per year (assume a 5 year device useful lifespan)	< 25	~ 150	> 1000
Number of patients per day per device or system	1	~ 20	> 50
Function use per safety function per patient	seldom	frequent	each patient
Resulting likelihood estimation	improbable	occasional	probable to frequent

Figure 7.7: Siemens AG application of IEC 601-1-4 likelihood estimation process to PEMS [29].

The risk table is linked to a test protocol which records and evaluates the effectiveness of risk control measures and verification procedures. Together, these two items could be used to satisfy the requirements for the Risk Management Summaries. (See Figure 7.10.)

An analysis of the recalls of medical devices between 1983–1991 showed the following [31]:

- medical device software quality problems by device type

  - 23% cardiovascular
  - 19% radiology
  - 18% in vitro diagnostic products
  - 14% anesthesiology
  - 11% general hospital
  - 10% other
  - 8% surgical

- medical device software quality problems by cause

  - 80% software design
  - 19% software design change control
  - 1% problems introduced during the manufacturing process

In other words, 61 percent of the recalls were in high-risk devices and 99 percent of the problems were due to deficient software engineering and risk management processes. These are exactly the types of problems IEC 601-1-4 was designed to prevent.

The U.S. Food and Drug Administration (FDA) had representation on IEC TC 62 from 1986 until 601-1-4 was published. The FDA and the United States voted in favor of adopting the standard during formal balloting in the spring of 1996. FDA also has representatives

Function:	
F#:	
Hazard:	
H#:	1.
Reason:	1. 2. 3.
Effect on:	1. 2.
Severity level:	1. 2. 3.
Likelihood:	1. 2. 3.
Risk region:	1. 2. 3.
Risk control measure:	1. 2. 3.
M#:	1. 2. 3.
Residual severity level:	1. 2. 3.
Residual likelihood level:	1. 2. 3.
Residual risk region:	1. 2. 3.
Status:	
Response:	

Figure 7.8: Siemens AG IEC 601-1-4 risk analysis worksheet [29].

Application or Malfunction:	
F#:	
Hazard:	
H#	
Cause/Reason:	
C#:	
Effect on:	
Severity level:	
Likelihood:	
Risk level:	
Risk control measure:	
M#:	
Residual risk level:	
Comments:	

Figure 7.9: Hewlett Packard implementation of IEC 601-1-4 risk analysis table [14].

on several other working groups in the IEC 601 series. FDA is governed by federal laws such as the Safe Medical Devices Act of 1990 and volume 21 of the Code of Federal Regulations (CFR). FDA implements these laws and regulations through policy and guidance documents. Standards, such as IEC 601-1-4, are viewed as a tool for the manufacturers to use to demonstrate and the certifier to use to verify compliance with regulations. Not surprisingly, there is a strong correlation between the information required in a premarket submission to the FDA and the contents of the Risk Management File required by IEC 601-1-4 (see Figure 7.11).

The main area of difference between FDA premarket submission requirements and IEC 601-1-4 concerns changes to a device:

> A submission covering device changes should contain a description of the changes, including what was changed, why it was changed, and how the changes affect safety and reliability. It should also contain a comparison of the design, functionality, operation, performance, and safety and reliability features of the new and predicate devices. At present, the new IEC standard does not address these two (regulatory) requirements [23, 24].

Review:	Phase:
Cause or Reason:	F#: H#: C#: M#:
Evaluation and realization of the risk control measure:	Phase: Milestone:
Verification Procedure: Validation Procedure:	Fab/SW: Version: Document: Designer: Date:
Evaluation of the effectiveness of the Risk Control Measure:	Version: Designer: Date:
Name: Signature: Department: Date:	Test: Successful: Repetition:
Notes:	

Key: F – application function or malfunction
      H – hazard and consequence number
      C – cause/reason number
      M – risk control measure number

Figure 7.10: Hewlett Packard implementation of IEC 601-1-4 risk control table [14].

FDA Software Guidance Requirements	IEC 601-1-4 Reference
Part I. New Submission	
Level of Concern – software and device – how it was determined	severity/likelihood estimation, 52.205.3.2 severity level categorization method, 52.204.3.2.3
Descriptive Data – development environment	design analysis & implementation considerations, 52.208.2
Labelling: – intended use – instructions for use – known nonhazardous anomalies	? instructions for use, 6.8.201 residual risk information, 6.8.201

Development Lifecycle Artifacts
– requirements spec
– architecture spec
– design spec
– test spec
– verification plan
– validation plan
– analysis of verification &
  validation results
– configuration management &
  change control
– compliance assessment report
	requirements spec, 52.206
	architecture spec, 52.207
	design spec, 52.208
	test spec, 52.208
	verification plan, 52.209.2
	validation plan, 52.210.2
	verification results, 52.209.3
	validation results, 52.210.6
	configuration management, 52.501.2 and
	modification/change control procedures, 52.211.2
	compliance assessment report, 52.212.1

Risk Management: – risk management plan – hazard analysis – hazard ID methods – risk likelihood estimation & estimation method(s) – severity estimation & categorization method(s) – risk control measures – evaluation of effectiveness of risk control measures	risk management plan, 52.202 hazard analysis, 52.204.3.1 hazard ID methods, 52.204.3.1.8 risk likelihood estimation & estimation method(s), 52.204.3.2 severity estimation & categorization method(s), 52.204.3.2.3 risk control methods, 52.204.4 evaluation of effectiveness of risk control methods, 52.204.6
Part II. Changes to a Device	
Description of Changes – what changed – why it was changed – impact on safety and reliability	?
Comparison of new and predicate device – design – functionality – operation – performance – safety and reliability	?
Traceability to previous development lifecycle & risk management activities	configuration management, 52.201.2 validation activities, 52.210.1 modification/change control procedures, 52.211
Revision History: – device/software – specifications – plans – procedures	configuration management, 52.201.2 modification/change control procedures, 52.211

Figure 7.11: Correlation of FDA documentation requirements for a premarket submission and IEC 601-1-4 [23,24].

7.2 Summary

IEC 601-1-4 "is the first international consensus standard to specifically address the issue of medical device software safety [24]." The standard, building upon the foundation of IEC 601-1, ISO 9001, and 9000-3, integrates a comprehensive risk management process with the software development lifecycle to address the criticality of PEMS. IEC 601-1-4 accommodates a variety of architectural complexities and is not overly prescriptive. Instead it concentrates on specifying 'what' to do, not 'how' to do it, and relies on effective implementation by qualified and competent people. This flexibility allows the standard to easily be used by manufacturers, certification bodies, and regulatory agencies and should contribute to its long-term usefulness.

The standard was approved during formal balloting by the 53 IEC National Committees in April 1996. The priority given to this standard is apparent from the fact that the European Committee for Electrotechnical Standardisation (CENELEC) conducted a parallel vote for adoption within the European Union (EU); CENELEC balloting usually follows IEC balloting by a year or more. Consequently, the standard has been concurrently published as harmonized European standard EN 60601-1-4. "In addition to the (United States and) European Union, Australia, Canada, and Singapore have indicated their intention to adopt all or part of the IEC 601 series of standards. Thus by complying with this standard, medical device manufacturers can demonstrate compliance with the regulatory requirements of multiple markets in North America, Europe, and the Pacific [24]."

7.3 Discussion Problems

1. Perform risk analysis, according to IEC 601-1-4, for a laser eye surgery device. Assume that software controls energy release (location, duration, beam type, intensity, and duration) and performs calculations necessary to determine the appropriate treatment. In addition, an accessory to the device maintains a treatment profile database.

2. What different factors must be considered when performing risk analysis for diagnostic devices versus therapeutic devices?

3. Why does IEC 601-1-4 levy additional requirements beyond ISO 9001 and 9000-3?

4. What additional information must be included in the architectural specifications to satisfy the risk management process of IEC 601-1-4?

5. Discuss the pros and cons of both qualitative and quantitative methods of estimating likelihood.

6. What development lifecycle methodology would not satisfy the requirements of IEC 601-1-4?

7. At what point during the development lifecycle is risk analysis performed?

8. Develop a Risk Management Summary for the PEMS described in question 1.

9. How many documents are produced by adherence to this standard?

10. How is compliance to this standard assessed?

11. Discuss the pros and cons of integrating or not integrating the risk management process with the development lifecycle.

12. Describe the attributes of personnel who are competent, according to IEC 601-1-4, to work on the design and development of a safety-critical PEMS.

13. If IEC 601-1-4 is used to develop the software for a hemodialysis device, what other standards must also be used during the development of this system?

Additional Resources

Primary Work Cited

[1] IEC 601-1-4(1996-06),[3] Medical Electrical Equipment – Part 1: General Requirements for Safety – 4. Collateral Standard: Programmable Electrical Medical Systems.

Related Safety, System, and Software Engineering Standards

[2] IEC 601-1(1988-12), Medical Electrical Equipment – Part 1: General Requirements for Safety, with IEC 601-1-am(1991-11) Amendment No. 1 and IEC 601-1-am(1995-03) Amendment No. 2.

[3] IEC 601-1-1(1992-06), Medical Electrical Equipment – Part 1: General Requirements for Safety – Section 1. Collateral Standard: Safety Requirements for Medical Electrical Systems.

[4] IEC 788(1984-01), Medical Radiology – Terminology.

[5] ISO 9000-3:1991, Quality Management and Quality Assurance Standards – Part 3: Guidelines for the Application of ISO 9001 to the Development, Supply and Maintenance of Software.

[6] ISO 9001:1994, Quality Systems – Model for Quality Assurance in Design, Development, Production, Installation and Servicing.

[7] ISO/IEC Guide 51(1990), Guidelines for Safety Aspects in Standards.

---

[3]Note: IEC plans to renumber this series to IEC 60601-x-x in the near future.

[8] IEC 513(1994-01), Fundamental Aspects of Safety Standards for Medical Electrical Equipment.

[9] IEC 50-191(1990-12) International Electrotechnical Vocabulary (IEV) Chapter 191: Dependability and Quality of Service.

[10] National Council for Clinical Laboratory Systems (NCCLS) document# GP19-A, Laboratory Instruments and Data Management Systems: Design of Software User Interfaces and End-User Software Systems, Validation, Operation, and Monitoring; Approved Guideline, 1996.

Selected Bibliography

[11] Association for the Advancement of Medical Instrumentation (AAMI), *AAMI Quality System Standards Handbook for Medical Devices*, ASQ Press, 1997.

[12] Christ, O. "Introduction to the EN60601 Series, Relationship of the General Standard and the Fourth Collateral Standard, IEC 601-1-4," *Proceedings EUROSPEC Institute Software Validation and Verification via EN60601-1-4 Seminar*, June 1995, Heidelberg, pp. 69–86.

[13] Cosgriff, P. "Quality Assurance of Software Used in Diagnostic Medical Imaging," *Safety Systems*, Vol. 5, No. 2, January 1996, pp. 1–3.

[14] Courtin, E. "Practical Tools for the Implementation of IEC 601-1-4 Requirements into the Design Process for PEMS," *Proceedings EUROSPEC Institute Software Validation and Verification via EN60601-1-4 Seminar*, Heidelberg, June 1995, pp. 97–108.

[15] Cowderoy, A. and Donaldson, J. "Quality: A Multimedia Perspective," *Software Reliability and Metrics Club Newsletter*, September 1997, pp. 8–10.

[16] Deshotels, R. Dejmek, M. and Ford, K. "Effective Hazard Analysis—What Level of Detail is Sufficient?" *Hazard Prevention*, 3Q96, Vol. 32, No. 3, pp. 6–10.

[17] Elliott, L. and Mojdehbakhsh, R. "A Process for Developing Safe Software," *Proceedings of the 1994 IEEE Seventh Symposium on Computer-Based Medical Systems*, pp. 241–246.

[18] Fink, R., Oppert, S., Collinson, P., Cooke, G., Dhanjal, S., Lesan, H. and Shaw, R. "Data Management in Clinical Laboratory Information Systems," *Directions in Safety-Critical Systems*, Springer-Verlag, 1993, pp. 84–95.

[19] Herrmann, D. "IEC (DIS) 601-1-4 Safety Requirements for Programmable Electronic Medical Systems." *Proceedings of 5th Annual Association for Advancement of Medical Instrumentation International Standards Conference*, Washington, DC, March 16–17, 1995, pp. 425–458.

[20] Herrmann, D. "IEC (DIS) 601-1-4 Safety Requirements for Programmable Electronic Medical Systems," *Safety and Reliability for Medical Device Software*, Health Industries Manufacturers Association (HIMA) Report No. 95-8, 1995, tab 3.

[21] Herrmann, D. "Software Safety and Reliability in the Regulatory Environment," *Safety and Reliability for Medical Device Software*, Health Industries Manufacturers Association (HIMA) Report No. 95-8, 1995, tab 8.

[22] Herrmann, D. "A Preview of IEC Safety Requirements for Programmable Electronic Medical Systems," *Medical Device and Diagnostic Industry*, June 1995, pp. 106–110.

[23] Herrmann, D. "How to interpret IEC 601-1-4 from the view of FDA," *Proceedings EUROSPEC Institute Software Validation and Verification via EN60601-1-4 Seminar*, June 1995, Heidelberg, pp. 141–158.

[24] Herrmann, D. and Zier, D. "Using IEC 601-1-4 to Satisfy the Requirements of the FDA Software Guidance," *Medical Device & Diagnostic Industry*, December 1995, pp. 104–107.

[25] Hsia, Pei. "Testing the Therac-25: A Formal Scenario Approach," *Safety and Reliability for Medical Device Software*, Health Industries Manufacturers Association (HIMA) Report No. 95-8, 1995, tab 6.

[26] Huges, G. "Safety Principles v. Safety Practice," *Safety Systems*, September 1995, Vol. 5, No. 1, pp. 5–7.

[27] Leveson, N. *Safeware: System Safety and Computers*, Addison-Wesley, 1995.

[28] Moore, C. "Medical Radiological Incidents: The Human Element in Complex Systems," *Safety Systems*, Vol. 5, No. 2, January 1996, pp. 4–6.

[29] Patzelt, K. "Requirements and Practical Aspects of 601-1-4: PEMS Structure, Development Life-Cycle, Risk Analysis," *Proceedings EUROSPEC Institute Software Validation and Verification via EN60601-1-4 Seminar*, June 1995, Heidelberg, pp. 87–96.

[30] Polaschegg, H.D. "Redundancy or Diversity?—Safety Integrity Concepts for the Design of Therapeutic Devices," *Proceedings EUROSPEC Institute Software Validation and Verification for Medical Devices Seminar*, March 1994, Vienna, pp. 119–136.

[31] Stettin, Dr. J., "FDA Requirements and Olympus Approach for Medical Information Systems and Medical Devices: Practical Experience," *Proceedings EUROSPEC Institute Software Validation and Verification via EN60601-1-4 Seminar*, June 1995, Heidelberg, pp. 159–184.

[32] Schwanbom, E. "Introduction to the Concept of Risk Analysis for Medical Devices Incorporating Software Controlled Programmable Electronic Systems (PES)," *Proceedings EUROSPEC Institute Software Validation and Verification for Medical Devices Seminar*, Vienna, March 1994, pp. 29–38.

[33] Trautman, K., *The FDA and Worldwide Quality System Requirements Guidebook for Medical Devices*, ASQ Press, 1996.

[34] Wingate, G., Smith M., and Lucas, P. "Assuring Confidence in Pharmaceutical Software," *Safety and Reliability of Software Based Systems*, Springer-Verlag, 1997, pp. 157–175.

[35] Whitemore, E. *Product Development Planning for Healthcare Products Regulated by the FDA*, ASQ Press, 1997.

[36] Zier, D. and Herrmann, D. "ODE Review of Software Development and Quality Assurance," *Proceedings of Indiana Medical Device Manufacturers Council (IMDMC) Software Validation Seminar*, May 16, 1995.

Standards Under Development

The following related standards are currently under development by the IEEE Engineering in Medicine and Biology Society:

[37] P1073.1.1 – Standard for Medical Device Communications – Medical Device Data Language (MDDL) – Common Definitions.

[38] P1073.1.1.1 – Standard for Medical Device Communications, Medical Device Data Language (MDDL) – Nomenclature.

[39] P1073.2.0 – Standard for Medical Device Application Profiles.

Part III

Approaches Promoted by Non–Industry Specific Software Safety and Reliability Standards

Part III, Chapters 8–11, examines in detail the techniques and approaches promoted by six standards to achieve and assess various aspects of software safety and reliability. In contrast to the standards discussed in Part II, these standards can and are meant to be used across multiple industrial sectors. In addition, these standards serve complementary purposes and are intended to be used in conjunction with each other and/or the standards discussed in Part II. Chapter 8 develops the concept of safety integrity levels, functional safety, and their assessment. Chapter 9 explores the unique software safety and reliability concerns of programmable logic controllers (PLCs), which arise independent of the application domain. Chapter 10 presents a suite of metrics to use to measure progress toward achieving software safety and reliability goals, throughout the development lifecycle. Lastly, Chapter 11 defines a model from which to develop software safety plans.

Chapter 8

IEC Software Dependability Standards

This chapter develops the concept of safety integrity levels and functional safety and their assessment by analyzing three new standards from the International Electrotechnical Commission (IEC):

- IEC 61508-3:1998 Functional safety of electrical/electronic/programmable electronic safety-related systems – Part 3: Software requirements

- IEC 300-3-9:1995-12, Dependability Management – Part 3: Application Guide – Section 9: Risk Analysis of Technological Systems

- ISO/IEC 15026:1998-04-29, Information Technology – System and Software Integrity Levels

IEC 300-3-9 and ISO/IEC 15026 amplify aspects contained in IEC 61508.

8.1 IEC 61508-3:1998-12 Functional Safety of Electrical/Electronic/Programmable Electronic Safety-Related Systems – Part 3: Software Requirements

8.1.1 Background

In 1987 IEC formed Technical Committee (TC) 65A with the charter to develop a standard that had an integrated approach to achieve and assess the functional safety of a system and all of its components. This committee was one of the first to acknowledge: 1) that safety is a system issue, and 2) the need for a harmonized approach to safety management across all system components. As stated in Part 3 [3]:

> In most situations, safety is achieved by a number of protective systems which rely on many technologies (mechanical, hydraulic, pneumatic, electrical, electronic, programmable electronic, ...). Any safety strategy must therefore consider not only all the elements within an individual system ... but also all the

safety-related systems making up the total combination of safety-related systems.

The result was IEC 61508, which contains seven parts:

- IEC 61508-1:1998 Functional safety of electrical/electronic/programmable electronic safety-related systems – Part 1: General requirements.

- IEC 61508-2:199x[1] Functional safety of electrical/elecronic/programmable electronic safety-related systems – Part 2: Requirements for electrical/electronic/programmable electronic safety-related systems.

- IEC 61508-3:1998 Functional safety of electrical/electronic/programmable electronic safety-related systems – Part 3: Software requirements.

- IEC 61508-4:1998 Functional safety of electrical/electronic/programmable electronic safety-related systems – Part 4: Definitions and abbreviations of terms.

- IEC 61508-5:1998 Functional safety of electrical/electronic/programmable electronic safety-related systems – Part 5: Examples of methods for the determination of safety integrity levels.

- IEC 61508-6:199x[2] Functional safety of electrical/electronic/programmable electronic safety-related systems – Part 6: Guidelines on the application of Parts 2 and 3.

- IEC 61508-7:199x[3] Functional safety of electrical/electronic/programmable electronic safety-related systems – Part 7: Overview of techniques and measures.

The first final versions of IEC 61508 Parts were published beginning in 1998; the rest are scheduled to follow shortly thereafter. Industry and government representatives from 10 countries participated in the work of IEC TC 65A. Representatives from the nuclear and offshore industries were particularly active in this process. All 53 countries who are currently members of IEC (the National Committees), participated in the formal comment, review, and balloting process.

The seven parts of IEC 61508 are meant to be used in unison. In summary, Part 1 establishes the standard's risk-based approach to safety management. Part 1 [1] requires that a hazard analysis be performed at the system and subsystem levels to determine the amount of risk reduction needed, the need for safety-related systems, the safety functions needed by each subsystem, and the safety integrity of each function. Parts 2 [2] and 3 [3] define the safety lifecycle processes and activities required for the prevention and control of random failures and systematic faults. The overall approach is based on a combination of

---

[1]Publication was pending as of August 1999.

[2]Publication was pending as of August 1999.

[3]Publication was pending as of August 1999.

fault avoidance and fault tolerance. Parts 4–7 [4–7] provide backup information and implementation details for Parts 2 and 3. This chapter will focus primarily on Part 3; appropriate references will be made to the other parts, when needed, for clarification.

8.1.2 Purpose and Scope

The primary purpose of IEC 61508 is to provide a "unified approach" for all safety lifecycle activities that is "rational and consistent [3]." As such, the standard [3] covers all lifecycle phases for all system components, from concept through decommissioning. The standard [2,3,7] promotes a "broad range of principles, techniques and measures" to achieve and assess functional safety; a fundamental premise being the risk-based determination of safety integrity levels (SILs).

The secondary purpose of IEC 61508 is to facilitate the development of industry specific standards, which has been successfully achieved. EN 50128:1997 (Chapter 3), the MISRA™ Guidelines (Chapter 3), and the SEMSPLC Guidelines (Chapter 9) are examples of application specific standards derived from IEC 61508. As the standard [3] notes this commonality should:

> ... lead to a high level of consistency (for example, of underlying principles, terminology, etc.) both within application sectors and across application sectors; this will have both safety and economic benefits.

IEC 61508 Part 3 applies to any safety-related software which, as defined by Parts 1 and 2, includes:

a) software that is part of a safety-related system;

b) software that is used to develop a safety-related system; and

c) the operating system, system software, communication software, human computer interface (HCI) functions, utilities, and software engineering tools used with (a) or (b) above.

8.1.3 Description

Two major concepts of IEC 61508 are safety integrity and functional safety. These terms are defined in Part 4 [4]:

- **safety integrity** – the probability of a safety-related system satisfactorily performing the required safety functions under all stated conditions within a stated period of time.

- **functional safety** – the ability of a safety-related system to carry out the actions necessary to achieve a safe state for the equipment under control or to maintain a safe state for the equipment under control.

The standard uses the term safety-related to refer to both safety-critical and safety-related systems: safety-critical systems are referred to as safety-related control systems while safety-related systems are referred to as safety-related protection systems.

The safety integrity of a system is said to be at one of four discrete SILs: 1 – low, 2 – medium, 3 – high, or 4 – very high. These levels signify the safety integrity requirements for the safety functions allocated to safety-related systems. According to the standard [1,3], the higher the SIL the lower the probability that the safety-related systems will fail. (An SIL of 0 refers to nonsafety-related systems.) As L. Tripp [33] states,

> ...the integrity level as a unifying concept provides a common integrity target for all constituent parts within the system hierarchy; presents a baseline process to determine critical applications defined by the relevant risk dimensions, and instigates a generic approach for determining the degree of rigor for software development and qualification methods.

Safety integrity levels account for all causes of system failure, random and systematic [3]. Hence the SIL for a system is a function of the hardware safety integrity and the systematic safety integrity. As R. Bell and D. Reinert [24] point out:

> The target safety integrity is subdivided into target values for hardware integrity and systematic integrity. These are required to be greater than or equal to the safety integrity target.

Hardware safety integrity relates to "random hardware failures in a dangerous mode of failure [4]." The hardware safety integrity corresponds to the overall failure rate for continuous-mode operations and the probability to operate on demand for demand-mode operations. An SIL should be established for demand-mode and continuous-mode operations. Random hardware failure rates can be quantified accurately; they are derived from established hardware reliability measures, factoring in the severity of the failure. IEC 61508 Part 1 [1] has established numerical targets for random hardware failure rates by SIL and mode of operation, as shown in Table 8.1. Demand-mode safety integrity is of major importance to the process industries, as noted by Bell and Reinert [24]:

> In the context of the process industries, safety-related protection systems are normally not actively controlling the equipment under control but, in the event of failure of the main control system, come into action and put the equipment under control into a safe state (e.g. an emergency shutdown system in a chemical plant, activated when the main process control system fails).

Systematic safety integrity relates to "systematic failures in a dangerous mode of failure [4]." Systematic failures are the result of errors of omission and errors of commission in safety lifecycle activities. Systematic failure rates are difficult to quantify; they are generally measured qualitatively. J. Brazendale [26] describes IEC 61508's approach to qualitatively measuring systematic integrity:

Continuous Mode Operation	Probability of a Dangerous Failure per Year
SIL 4	$\geq 10^{-5}$ to $< 10^{-4}$
SIL 3	$\geq 10^{-4}$ to $< 10^{-3}$
SIL 2	$\geq 10^{-3}$ to $< 10^{-2}$
SIL 1	$\geq 10^{-2}$ to $< 10^{-1}$
Demand Mode Operation	Probability of Failure to Perform Safety-Related Function on Demand
SIL 4	$\geq 10^{-5}$ to $< 10^{-4}$
SIL 3	$\geq 10^{-4}$ to $< 10^{-3}$
SIL 2	$\geq 10^{-3}$ to $< 10^{-2}$
SIL 1	$\geq 10^{-2}$ to $< 10^{-1}$

Table 8.1: Target hardware integrity failure rates by SIL [1,24,25,26,30,32].

This method is based on controlling the factors (techniques and measures) that influence achievement of safety integrity in software. These include: choice of engineering technique, software architecture, and rigour of quality assurance approach. This is the approach taken by Parts 2 and 3 of the standard which indexes these factors against the required safety integrity level.

Therefore, safety integrity of a system is a composite of quantitative and qualitative measures.

Software safety integrity is "a measure that signifies the likelihood of software in a programmable electronic system (PES) achieving its safety functions under all stated conditions within a stated period of time [4]." Software, as a component of a system, is assigned an SIL which specifies the safety integrity of software in a safety-related system. Since software failures are systematic, software safety integrity is part of the systematic safety integrity. As Tripp [33] observes,

Integrity levels serve as design targets for software development. They also provide a unified method for qualifying off-the-shelf software products for specific applications.

As will be discussed later, the software safety requirements specification is comprised of functional safety requirements and safety integrity requirements. These two types of requirements reinforce each other. Functional safety requirements specify the safety features and control measures to be implemented by a system, while the safety integrity requirements specify the degree of confidence needed that these functions will operate correctly. Together the functional safety requirements and the safety integrity requirements determine which design and development techniques and features and verification and validation activities and measures will be implemented. Brazendale [26] notes that in IEC 61508, "the emphasis is on preventing mistakes rather than finding them by testing."

IEC 61508 integrates the concepts of safety integrity and functional safety with the risk management process, as shown in Figure 8.1. (Note that this is an iterative process which interacts with the system safety lifecycle.) A risk analysis is performed on the software component of a system. The hazards that are identified, their cause(s), severity, and likelihood of occurrence are used to determine the software SIL. As N. Storey [32] notes, IEC 61508 uses the same four severity categories (negligible, marginal, critical, and catastrophic) and the same six likelihood levels (frequent, probable, occasional, remote, improbable, and incredible) that other IEC standards use. The software safety functional requirements and the software safety integrity requirements required to achieve the SIL are then defined. These requirements are captured in the software safety requirements specification. Risk control measures are initiated to eliminate, reduce, and mitigate potential hazards. Design features are chosen according to the software SIL from those specified in Annexes A and B of IEC 61508 Part 3 [3]. (The recommendations in IEC 61508 Part 3 Annexes A and B are discussed later in Table 8.4.)

The residual risk of the software is assessed to determine its acceptability, according to the specified SIL, software safety verification plan, the software safety validation plan, and functional safety assessment plan. The verification, validation, and assessment techniques and activities specified in these plans are selected according to the recommendations in Annexes A and B of IEC 61508 Part 3 [3] for the given SIL. (See Table 8.4.) As Bell and Reinert [24] observe,

> Determination of the tolerable level of risk takes into account the specific hazardous consequences for the application under consideration. In many instances, the tolerable risk levels are not defined as such, but are implicit in the consensus about what constitutes current good practice. However, where there is a lack of consensus, or insufficient experience to judge the value of current practice, more explicit analysis of the costs and benefits may need to be undertaken.

To effectively implement IEC 61508 it is essential to understand the interaction between SILs and the risk management process, as illustrated in Figure 8.1. To reinforce these concepts, a high-level hypothetical example follows.

Assumptions

1. The equipment under control is a laser eye surgery device. It includes an accessory which maintains a database.

2. Software controls:

   a. releasing energy

   b. targeting the beam

   c. determining the dosage

   d. maintaining the patient treatment profile database

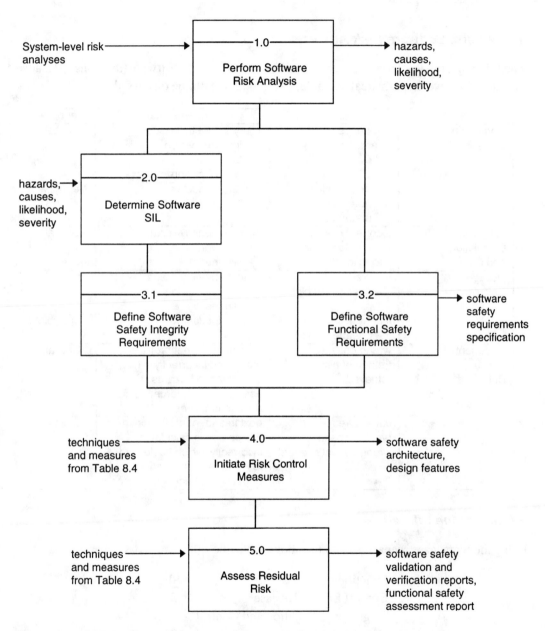

Figure 8.1: IEC 61508 Part 3 interaction between safety integrity, functional safety, and the risk management process.

3. Functions a and b operate in real time; c and d do not.

4. The device operates in demand mode.

1.0 Perform Software Risk Analysis

The following top level hazards were identified for each of the software functions. (Because this is a high-level hypothetical example, likelihood will not be discussed.)

Software Function	Hazard	Consequences	Severity
Control Energy Release	erroneous release of energy – overdose	injury to healthy tissue – impaired vision – blindness injury to operators	Critical
	erroneous release of energy – underdose	therapy ineffective	Negligible
Targeting Calculation and Control	incorrect calculation, energy delived to wrong location	injury to healthy tissue – impaired vision – blindness	Critical
Dosage Calculation	incorrect calculation – dosage too high	injury to healthy tissue – impaired vision – blindness	Critical
	incorrect calculation – dosage too low	therapy ineffective	Negligible
Treatment Profile Database	wrong patient's treatment history retrieved	current treatment profile calculated incorrectly, which could lead to hazards associated with targeting and dosage functions	Critical
	current treatment profile appended to wrong patient's record	next treatment profile for this person is calculated incorrectly, which could lead to hazards associated with targeting and dosage functions	Critical

2.0 Determine SIL

Using the worst case scenarios from the above table, the following SILs are assigned.

Function	SIL
Control Energy Release	3
Targeting Calculation and Control	3
Dosage Calculation	3
Treatment Profile Database	2

The Treatment Profile Database is assigned a lower SIL than the control functions because of the indirect relationship to the hazards. This rating is subject to debate and therefore should be clarified with the Certifying Authority.

3.1 Define Software Safety Integrity Requirements

These requirements become part of the Software Safety Requirements Specification.

1. The Control Energy Release function must operate correctly as specified 99.99 percent of the time. It must not release energy except under the exact conditions specified.

2. The Targeting Calculation and Control function must operate correctly as specified 99.99 percent of the time.

3. The Dosage Calculation function must operate correctly as specified 99.99 percent of the time.

4. The Treatment Profile Database must have a demonstrated data integrity of 99.99 percent.

3.2 Define Software Functional Safety Requirements.

These requirements become part of the Software Safety Requirements Specification.

1. The Control Energy Release function shall:

   a. verify the beam type through two independent means before operation
   b. verify the beam strength through two independent means before operation
   c. verify the beam duration through two independent means before operation
   d. be disabled during maintenance, testing, and upgrades
   e. verify against an established data table that the proposed beam type, strength, and duration are a valid and medically feasible combination

2. The Targeting Calculation and Control function shall:

   a. calculate the targeting parameters using three diverse software algorithms that implement a mathematical formula which is universally recognized in the biomedical community
   b. calculate and control the targeting parameters within .01mm of accuracy
   c. verify the targeting parameters through two independent means before operation
   d. verify against an established data table that the proposed targeting parameters are valid and medically feasible

3. The Dosage Calculation function shall:

   a. calculate the dosage using three diverse software algorithms that implement a mathematical formula which is universally recognized in the biomedical community

   b. verify against an established data table that the proposed dosage is within a valid and medically feasible range

   c. verify the dosage parameters through two independent means before operation

4. The Treatment Profile Database shall:

   a. maintain accurate, complete, and current treatment records for all patients

   b. store the dosage calculation parameters, targeting parameters, beam type, strength, and duration prior to treatment

   c. store the actual treatment parameters after treatment

   d. compare proposed treatment parameters with previous treatment history and generate an alert if there are major differences

   e. compare proposed treatment parameters with actual treatment parameters and generate an alert if there are major differences

   f. verify patient identification information through two independent means before recording or retrieving records

4.0 Initiate Risk Control Measures

Based on the SIL for each function, the following techniques and measures will be implemented.

1. A CASE tool will be used that supports requirements analysis, architecture specification, and design.

2. Function block diagrams and decision/truth tables, perhaps as an output of the CASE tool, will be used to clarify requirements.

3. The SADT methodology will be followed.

4. The four functions will be partitioned. The three control functions will each be implemented using diverse algorithms.

5. The company C++ coding standard will be followed.

6. An ANSI certified C++ compiler will be used.

5.0 Assess Residual Risk

Based on the SIL for each function and the device technology, the following verification, validation, and assessment techniques will be utilized.

1. Functional, performance, and interface testing will be performed.

2. Static analysis techniques will be used to verify the integrity of the software/design.

3. A HAZOP will be performed to verify that the device performs correctly in the operational environment.

4. Formal proofs will be used to verify the accuracy of all calculations and their correct implementation in software. The results of these activities will be documented in the software safety validation and verification reports and the functional safety assessment.

IEC 61508 promotes the safety lifecycle as a concurrent engineering endeavor. There is an overall safety lifecycle for a system and individual safety lifecycles for system components, all of which are coordinated and integrated.

IEC 61508 Part 3 [3] specifies the software safety lifecycle, which consists of eight phases:

- software safety requirements specification

- software safety validation planning

- software design and development

- system integration

- software safety verification

- software safety validation

- software functional safety assessment

- operation and modification.

The lifecycle is specified in terms of objectives and requirements for each phase and activity. General purpose software engineering activities, such as change management and version control, are expected to be consistent with ISO/IEC 12207.[4] The standard [3] emphasizes that, "quality and safety assurance procedures shall be integrated into safety lifecycle activities." If changes are initiated, for example as a result of validation or verification activities, prior lifecycle phases must be repeated.

Software Safety Requirements Specification

The first lifecycle phase is software safety requirements specification. The objective of this phase is to specify the software safety functional requirements and the software safety integrity requirements [3]. As the standard [3] notes, these functions are requirements which are derived from the system safety requirements specification and reflect the results of system safety planning activities, such as the assignment of an SIL to software. The software safety requirements specification should be written at a reasonable level of detail.

The standard [3] highlights several issues that must be addressed in the software safety requirements specification:

---

[4]ISO/IEC 12207:1995, Information Technology – Software Lifecycle Processes.

- all foreseeable modes of operation: normal, testing, maintenance, online and offline monitoring, set up, automatic, semiautomatic, manual, steady state, reset, shut down, and abnormal

- system capacity, response time, memory, and other known constraints

- interaction between safety and nonsafety-related functions

- detection, annunciation, and management of faults

- hardware/software, software/software, and human computer interfaces (HCI)

The effect of each of these items on achieving, assessing, and maintaining the specified software safety integrity and on the execution of software safety functions must be evaluated and documented. The standard recommends the use of safety integrity block diagrams to isolate specification errors, random failures, systematic failures, and common cause failures. In many respects safety integrity block diagrams are quite similar to the reliability block diagrams promoted by IEC 1078:1991.

B. Sherwood-Jones [31] expresses a concern that IEC 61508 does not adequately address human computer interface issues:

> It is generally accepted that 'human error' accounts for 60–80% of the risk exposure. Standards such as IEC 61508 are tightly bound to the 'software system' rather than the 'work system' and as such will not address more than 20–40% of the risk exposure.

To compensate for this, Sherwood-Jones recommends adding user analysis and task analysis principles to the risk analysis, design, and assessment activities.

The importance of a comprehensive and accurate software safety requirements specification cannot be overemphasized. As reported by Brazendale [26]:

> An analysis of 34 incidents for the ... Health and Safety Executive ... suggested that most control system failures may have their root cause in an inadequate specification. In some cases this was because insufficient hazard analysis of the equipment under control had been carried out; in others it was because the impact on the specification of a critical failure mode of the control system had not been assessed. Many of these failings can ultimately be traced back to a lack of safety management.

Software Safety Validation Planning

The second lifecycle phase is software safety validation planning. The objective of this phase is to develop a detailed plan which explains how software safety functional requirements and software integrity requirements will be validated. The standard [3] requires that the validation strategy, particularly the use or nonuse of manual/automated, static/dynamic, and analytical/statistical techniques, be defined and justified consistent with the SIL. The Software Safety Validation Plan specifies what validation activities will be conducted during each lifecycle phase, choosing from the techniques and measures cited in Table 8.4 [3]. The operational mode(s) and environment in which the validation activities will be conducted must be clearly stated. Expected results, objective pass/fail criteria, and guidelines for evaluating and interpreting actual results are an integral part of the plan. The standard [3] notes that the role of the certification authority in validation activities should also be described.

Software Design and Development

The third lifecycle phase is software design and development. The objectives of this phase are to design a software architecture that is optimized for the hardware platform and SIL and facilitates verification. The architecture should be developed with testability, modifiability, and supportability targets in mind. The standard [3] encourages partitioning safety-critical, safety-related, and nonsafety-related functions; in fact, unless partitioning is demonstrated, the highest SIL applies to all software. The architecture should support monitoring of critical data and control flows. Designers must be cognizant of timing, memory, I/O, and other constraints and dependencies during all design decisions [3].

Software engineering tools, system software and utilities, and compilers must be selected that are appropriate for the SIL throughout the lifecycle, including operations and modification; above SIL 2 certification is required [3]. The software engineering development environment must be consistent with the software development methodology and the application domain. It should promote the prevention and early detection of programming errors.

The standard [3] requires that coding standards be developed for each project that specify good programming practice, prohibit the use of ambiguous or unsafe features, and establish conventions for source code documentation. The coding standard should address topics such as:

- commenting source code;

- naming conventions for class names, method names, local and global variables, and constants;

- references to different types of files; and

- defining class structures.

The purpose of coding standards is to facilitate the comprehension of programs by all members of the development team and designated reviewers. They will also help to eliminate the possibility of some otherwise undetected latent defects. The standard [3] recommends using peer reviews to verify compliance with coding standards and traceability to design and requirements specifications.

The selection of a design methodology should be justified by demonstrating that it is appropriate for the hardware and software platforms, application domain, and SIL. The methodology should accommodate abstraction and modularity, clearly express functionality and design dependencies, use an unambiguous notation, and capture design assumptions while facilitating verification activities [3].

Architectural components should be identified as new or existing. The standard [3] encourages conducting architectural analysis, analysis of alternatives, and feasibility studies to determine the optimum combination of design features needed to achieve the specified SIL, such as diversity, information hiding, and partitioning. Likewise, all interface designs should be thoroughly analyzed to maximize their contribution to safe and reliable performance. Evidence must be supplied to justify the use of previously developed software; specifically proof is needed that the software has been certified for use in the current application domain at the specified SIL (or higher). Lacking this, previously developed software must undergo the same degree of validation and verification activities as custom developed software.

The standard [3] requires that module and integration testing be conducted to verify that the software only performs its intended function and no more, to verify that the software interacts correctly with other software components, and to identify the need for corrective action and failure analysis. Testing is to be conducted according to test specifications which identify:

- the test cases to be executed,

- the test data to be used,

- the environment in which the testing will be conducted,

- the use of automated test tools, and

- the exact software and system configuration for each test case.

The standard uses the term testing to refer to both static and dynamic analysis and expects that appropriate combinations of techniques will be chosen from those recommended in Table 8.4. For example, the standard [3] promotes the use of equivalence classes, boundary value analysis, control flow analysis, sneak circuit analysis, and formal proofs which assert pre- and post-conditions. The standard also emphasizes that change impact analysis must be performed before implementing corrective action.

Test specifications spell out the criteria used to evaluate results observed during testing, objective criteria to determine if a test passed or failed, the severity of a failure, and conditions for suspending, resuming, or repeating a test. A test analysis report should be produced which documents the number of test cases attempted, the number of test cases failed, and the severity of the failures. An assessment is made whether or not module testing and integration testing was successful. Table 8.2 illustrates a sample module test report form. Table 8.3 provides a sample integration test analysis summary report. All corrective action must be resolved at this point, unless a waiver is granted from the Certifying Authority. Failure analysis results are used to prevent similar defects from occurring, promote continuous process improvement, and uncover potential latent defects prior to deployment.

Page 1 of 1

Module Test Report Form

Test Date:_____

I. IDENTIFICATION

Class:	Class Operation:
Developer:	Supervisor:
Tester:	Witness:
Test Case:	Test Condition(s):

. . . .

II. RESULTS

Step	Description	Action	Data	Completion Status	Pass/Fail
1					
2					
3					
4					
5					
6					

. . . .

Table 8.2: Sample module test report form.

Integration

The fourth lifecycle phase is system integration. IEC 61508 includes a phase to integrate software with the target hardware platform. This reflects another aspect of the concurrent engineering approach promoted by this standard. At this point, the hardware safety lifecycle of IEC 61508 Part 2 is linked to the software safety lifecycle of IEC 61508 Part 3. This phase is important to safety management because it allows problems arising from differences in the development and operational environments to be identified and resolved prior to deployment. Particular attention is paid to interface compatibility, timing, capacity, and other performance requirements. Test cases that were performed separately on hardware and software components are repeated to verify correct results. Additional test cases are also executed to ensure successful integration, per the test specification. A test analysis report is produced which analyzes and interprets the results of system integration testing.

Test Analysis Summary Report
Test Date(s):_____

1. Test Identification

Test Technique(s)	Test Type(s)	Test Spec/Case Reference(s)	SIL Evaluated
static:	module _____		
_____	integration _____		
_____	interface _____		
_____	usability _____		
dynamic:	stress _____		
_____	regression _____		
_____	other _____		
_____			

2. Test Results

# Test Cases Attempted	# Test Cases Passed	# Test Cases Failed
	# %	# %

3. Severity of Failures

Negligible	Marginal	Critical	Catastrophic
# %	# %	# %	# %

4.1 Correction Action Requests (CARs)

CARs Closed	CARs Open
# %	# %

4.2 Severity of Open CARs

Negligible	Marginal	Critical	Catastrophic
# %	# %	# %	# %

5. Recommendation

_____ Approved
_____ Approved pending resolution of open CARs
_____ Approved, waiver for remaining open CARs
_____ Rejected, testing must be repeated

_____
signature/date

Table 8.3: Sample test analysis summary report.

Software Verification

The fifth lifecycle phase is software verification. The objectives of this phase are to verify that the outputs of each lifecycle phase are correct and consistent according to the software verification plan and the specified SIL. A software verification plan is developed which outlines the verification tools, techniques, strategies, and activities to be conducted during each lifecycle phase [3]. This plan provides guidance on how to evaluate and interpret results, handle nonconformances, perform failure analysis, and monitor corrective action. The standard notes that software verification activities should correspond to the size, complexity, duration, technology, and SIL of a project. Specific types of analyses are identified for each verification activity, as shown below [3]:

- The software safety requirements specification is analyzed to verify: 1) that it fulfills all safety requirements allocated to software; 2) that all requirements meet the characteristics of quality requirements, that is, they are complete, consistent, correct, unambiguous, and verifiable; and 3) that it adequately and accurately incorporates the results of software safety validation planning.

- The software architecture is analyzed to verify: 1) that it fulfills the software safety requirements specification; 2) that it contains adequate features to ensure the specified SIL, functional safety, testability, readability, modifiability, and maintainability; and 3) consistency between the software safety requirements specification, architecture, test specifications, and software safety validation plan.

- The software design is analyzed to verify: 1) that it is consistent with and traceable to the architecture; 2) that it contains adequate design features to ensure the specified SIL, functional safety, testability, readability, modifiability, and maintainability; and 3) consistency between the software safety requirements specification, architecture, design, test specifications, and software safety validation plan.

- Each software module is analyzed to verify: 1) that it is consistent with and traceable to the design; 2) that it implements adequate features to ensure the specified SIL, functional safety, testability, readability, modifiability, and maintainability; and 3) consistency between the software safety requirements specification, architecture, design, module design, test specifications, and software safety validation plan.

- The source code is analyzed to verify: 1) that it is consistent with and traceable to the module design specification; 2) that it implements adequate features to ensure the specified SIL, functional safety, testability, readability, modifiability, and maintainability; 3) consistency between the software safety requirements specification, architecture, design, module design, code, test specifications, and software safety validation plan; and 4) compliance with coding standards.

- The database design, if any, and data structures are analyzed to verify: 1) adequate protection against unauthorized access, alteration, and/or corruption, whether accidental or intentional; 2) adequate checks for invalid or undefined initiation and out of range values; 3) that critical data is validated before it is acted upon; 4) adequate detection of interface and other communication errors; and 5) that local and global data definitions are complete, consistent, and correct in relation to the algorithms that use them.

IEC 61508 expects that complementary validation and verification techniques will be used throughout the lifecycle. The techniques to be used in each phase are specified in the Software Verification Plan, Software Safety Validation Plan, and Test Specifications. The standard provides in-depth guidance in Annexes A and B of Part 3 [3] about what techniques and measures to use based on the lifecycle phase and SIL. The techniques are listed as M – mandatory, HR – highly recommended, R – recommended, NR – not recommended, and F – forbidden. The recommendations represent industry consensus of the technique's effectiveness at "preventing the introduction of systematic faults and controlling residual faults [3]." The standard expects that complementary combinations of techniques will be used during each lifecycle phase. In fact, the standard [3] states that:

> No single technique is likely to be sufficient. Appropriate techniques/measures
> shall be selected according to the safety integrity level.

Some techniques and measures are redundant; only one of them should be chosen. The standard [3] identifies the following groups of techniques as equivalent or redundant:

- semiformal methods and formal methods are considered equivalent;

- failure assertion, safety bags, diversity, and recovery blocks are considered equivalent.

Part 6 [6] provides additional guidance about selecting complementary combinations of techniques, while Part 7 [7] provides definitions of the techniques. Table 8.4 summarizes the recommendations from Annex A and B. There are slight differences between these recommendations and those made in the derivative standards, which were developed from early drafts of Part 3.

Software Safety Validation

The sixth lifecycle phase is software safety validation. The standard [4] defines validation as the "confirmation by examination and provision of objective evidence that the particular requirements for a specific intended use are fulfilled." The objective of this phase is to ensure that the integrated system as a whole satisfies the specified functional safety requirements, safety integrity requirements, and SIL. Software safety validation activities are conducted according to the plan that was developed during the validation planning phase. They "demonstrate that all software safety functions perform correctly, as specified" and that there are "no unintended functions [3]." At SIL 3 and 4, validation activities must be conducted independently. Results of validation activities are analyzed and interpreted in the Validation Analysis Report. Expected and actual results are compared. Corrective action requests, change requests, failure analysis results, and recommendations are also recorded in this report.

Techniques and Measures	SIL 1–2	SIL 3–4	Lifecycle Phase(s)

Computer Aided
  Software Engineering
  (CASE) Tools
	R	HR	–Requirements Specification
			–Archiecture Specification
			–Design and Development

Semiformal Methods
  (function block diagrams, finite state
  machine/state transition diagrams,
  timed Petri nets, decision/truth tables)
	R	HR	–Requirements Specification
			–Architecture Specification
			–Design and Development

Formal Methods
  (CCS, CSP, HOL, LOTOS, OBJ,
  Temporal Logic, VDM, Z)
	R	R/HR	–Requirements Specification
			–Architecture Specification
			–Design and Development

Safety Bags
Recovery Blocks
  forward
  backward
Retry Fault Recovery
	R	R	–Architecture Specification

Partitioning Defensive Programming Fault Detection and Diagnosis Error Detection/Correction Failure Assertion Diversity	R	HR	–Architecture Specification –Design and Development
Structured Methodologies (JSD, MASCOT, SADT, SDL, SSADM, Yourdon)	HR	HR	–Architecture Specification –Design and Development
AI Dynamic Reconfiguration	NR	NR	–Architecture Specification
Modular Approach (information hiding, 1 entry/1 exit)	HR	HR	–Design and Development
Design and Coding Standards Data Recording and Analysis	R/HR	HR	–Design and Development –Integration Test –Modification
Functional Testing	HR	HR	–Integration Test –Software Safety Validation
Probabilistic Testing Performance Testing Interface Testing Formal Proofs	R	HR	–Integration Test –Software Safety Verification –Software Safety Validation
Modelling Simulation	R	HR	–Software Safety Validation
Dynamic Analysis Software Quality Metrics Checklists Static Analysis	R/HR	HR	–Verification –Functional Safety Assessment –Integration Test
FMECA, FTA Common Cause Failure Analysis Cause Consequence Diagrams Decision/Truth Tables Reliability Block Diagrams Event Trees	R	R	–Functional Safety Assessment
Change Impact Analysis Regression Testing	HR	HR	–Modification

Table 8.4: IEC 61508 Part 3 assignment of techniques and measures by SIL and lifecycle phase [3].

Software Safety Functional Assessment

The seventh lifecycle phase is the software safety functional assessment. As the standard [6] states,

> ... assurance that the safety integrity target has been satisfied for systematic failures is gained by correct application of safety management procedures, use of competent staff, application of the specified safety lifecycle activities, including the specified techniques and measures, and an independent functional safety assessment.

The objective of this phase is to evaluate how well "functional safety is achieved by the safety-related systems and external risk reduction facilities [3]." Functional safety assessment activities are carried out in accordance with the Functional Safety Assessment Plan. The functional safety assessment is conducted during each lifecycle phase by an independent assessor. For SIL 1 an independent person is required. For SIL 2 an independent department is required. For SILs 3 and 4 an independent organization is required. The results are documented in a Functional Safety Assessment Report, which analyzes and interprets the results and makes a recommendation to accept, accept with conditions, or reject a system.

Operation and Modification

The eighth lifecycle phase is operation and modification. The objective of this phase is to maintain the system's SIL during corrections, adaptations, and enhancements. To achieve this objective, detailed Operation and Modification Procedures are needed which explain the actions and constraints necessary to maintain the system's functional safety and SIL during: installation, start-up, normal operations, testing, preventive maintenance, shutdown, and abnormal conditions [3]. The standard promotes a reliability centered maintenance effort which makes regular use of change impact analysis, FTA, and FMECA. All change requests must be authorized prior to implementation. They should contain information about the proposed change, hazards affected, and the reason for the change. Tables 8.5 and 8.6 provide a sample change request form.

Change request processing must return to the appropriate lifecycle phase and repeat appropriate activities. As emphasized by Brazendale [26],

> Where a modification of the safety-related control system is being contemplated, the Safety Requirements Specification should be reviewed to confirm that the proposed modification will not reduce the original safety integrity of the design.

A modification plan should be developed after the change request is approved. The modification plan should define the modification activities, the competency needed to perform them, and the required validation and verification activities, including any regression testing. Documentation should be prepared for each modification which identifies [3]:

Change Request #_____   **Date Opened:**_____

1. Identification

    a. System Name/Release:

    b. Submitter Name/Organization:

    c. Change Request Title/Description:

    d. Severity:

           Catastrophic:_____   Marginal: _____
           Critical: _____   Negligible:_____

    e. Affected Subsystems/Modules:

    f. Affected Requirements:

    g. Relevant Test Specifications/Cases:

2. Evaluation

    a. Impact of change on system performance, functional safety, and SIL:

    b. Evaluators' Response:

Response	Project Manager	System Architect	CM Manager	Initials/ Date
approve				
defer				
reject				
more info. needed				
hold CCB				

    c. Evaluators Comments:

Table 8.5: Sample change request form.

3. Solution

    a. Solution Implemented:

    b. Completion Date:

    c. Subsystems/Modules Modified:

    d. Documentation Prepared/Updated:

    e. Regression Testing Results:

Test Spec/Case	Pass	Fail	Initials/Date

    f. Acceptance Testing Results:

Test Spec/Case	Pass	Fail	Initials/Date

    g. SIL verification:

        signature/date:_____

    h. CM Build incorporating Change Request:

        signature/date:_____

Table 8.6: Sample change request form (continued).

- the change request,

- results of the change impact analysis,

- change control history,

- results of modification activities, including validation and verification, and

- a list of lifecycle artifacts which require updates and their status.

Interaction with System Safety and Other Standards

IEC 61508 Part 3 is intended to be used in conjunction with the other six parts of 61508. In fact this is required since the other six parts are cited as normative references, along with ISO/IEC Guide 51 [10] and IEC Guide 104 [11].

Roles, Responsibilities, and Qualifications of Project Members

Personnel requirements are specified in Part 1 [1]. In summary all project members, including management and operations staff, must be competent to perform their assigned duties. This competency must be demonstrated and documented through applicable formal education, experience, and certification. At a minimum, the staff should be competent in [3]: the specific engineering domain or technology, safety engineering, the specific legal and regulatory environment, and failure consequence analysis. As the standard [3] states, the greater the SIL, "more rigorous shall the specification and assessment of competence be."

Data Items Produced

IEC 61508 [1] views documentation as a tool that captures information which is needed to: 1) successfully perform lifecycle activities; and 2) accurately perform verification, validation, and functional safety assessments. Documentation may be maintained in electronic and/or hardcopy media as long as it is readily available to project members and assessors. Each data item is required to have unique identification and version control numbers. In addition, a documented approval, update, and change control process must be in place equivalent to that required by ISO 9001 and 9000-3. Table 8.7 summarizes the data items produced by adherence to IEC 61508 Part 3.

Compliance Assessment

Several factors have to be evaluated when assessing compliance to this standard. First, in addition to meeting the requirements of IEC 61508, the requirements of ISO 9001 must also be met. Actual ISO 9001 certification is not required, but the ability to demonstrate certifiability is. Second, it must be demonstrated that "each of the requirements have been satisfied to the required criteria specified" and that all "clause objectives have been met [3]."

Lifecycle Phase	Data Items Produced
Software Safety Requirements Specification	– Software Safety Requirements Specification
Software Safety Validation Planning	– Software Safety Validation Plan
Software Design and Development	– Software Architecture – Software Design Specification – Module Test Specification – Integration Test Specification – Coding Standards – Module Test Analysis Report
Integration	– Integration Test Analysis Report
Software Verification	– Software Verification Plan – Software Verification Report
Software Safety Validation	– Software Safety Validation Report
Functional Safety Assessment	– Functional Safety Assessment Report
Operation and Modification	– Software Operation and Modification Procedures – Change Impact Analysis Reports – Software Change History Log

Table 8.7: Data items required by IEC 61508 Part 3 [3].

In this case, the burden of proof lies with the developer or procurer, not the assessors. Third, if highly recommended (HR) techniques and measures have not been used an adequate explanation and justification is required. If techniques and measures have been used which are not listed in Annexes A and B of Part 3, a thorough justification of their suitability must be provided. The standard [3] states that compliance "...shall be assessed by the inspection of documents required by this International Standard and by witnessing tests."

Scaling

The standard permits a limited amount of scaling. As long as *all* of the requirements of the software safety lifecycle are met, the work products can be tailored to the complexity of a project and its specified SIL.

8.1.4 Strengths

IEC 61508 has several technical and programmatic strengths which will foster its widespread acceptance. First, the standard is applicable to multiple industrial sectors and has spawned industry specific derivative standards. Second, the standard focuses on safety as a system issue. Third, the software safety lifecycle is fully integrated into the system safety lifecycle. Design features, verification activities, and validation techniques are specified according to the lifecycle phase and SIL; extensive guidance is provided in this area.

These recommendations represent the consensus of multiple companies and countries as to what constitutes current 'industry best practices.' Complementary and redundant techniques are also noted.

8.1.5   Areas for Improvement

IEC 61508 has a few weaknesses, which most likely will be resolved by the next update cycle of the standard. First, IEC 61508 requires the development of a software safety validation plan and a functional safety assessment plan. But, it fails to require the development of a software safety case. Second, IEC 61508 states that systematic integrity can only be measured qualitatively. However, it provides limited guidance on how perform these measurements or how to integrate quantitative hardware safety integrity measures with qualitative systematic integrity measures. Additional guidance in this area would be useful. Third, the standard identifies the data items to be produced during each lifecycle phase. Pointers to standards which identify the informational content of these data items would be helpful.

8.1.6   Results Observed to Date

As the standard [3] states,

> If computer system technology is to be effectively and safely exploited, it is essential that those responsible for making decisions have sufficient guidance on the safety aspects on which to make those decisions.

IEC 61508 has done an exemplary job of providing this guidance, comprehensively and methodically, at the system level and at the software level. The first parts [1, 3–5] of IEC 61508 were formally published in 1998; the remaining parts [2, 6, 7] are scheduled for publication in 1999.

IEC 61508 is quickly gaining wide acceptance in the European community and elsewhere, as is evident from the Conformity Assessment of Safety-related Systems (CASS) project. The CASS project was begun in the U.K. in May 1998. The goal of the CASS project is to develop a standard set of conformity technical assessment schedules for all IEC 61508 lifecycle phases, processes, products, and competency requirements, along with models by which to implement the conformity schedules [28]. The dual purpose of the CASS project is to improve safety while reducing the cost of compliance with IEC 61508. Several pilot projects are planned. This project represents a collaboration of the computer-based safety-related systems industry, manufacturers, integrators, and end users. The project is organized in three functional groups: an Advisory Group, a Consultative Group, and the Technical Development Group. Eutech is serving as the project lead. Current participants include:

Advisory Group

Association for the Instrumentation, Control and Automation Industry; Engineering Equipment and Material Users Association; FRESCO Interest Group; Motor Industry Research Association; Energy Industries Council; Good Automated Manufacturing Practice Forum; Computer Services and Software Association; Federation of Electronic Industries; and Health and Safety Executive.

Consultative Group

Institute for Electrical Engineers, British Computer Society, Railway Industries Association, Institute of Measurement and Control, Safety and Reliability Society, Institute of Railway Signalling Engineers, Interdepartmental Committee on Software Engineering of Safety-Related Systems working group, the Association of British Certification Bodies, and the Airport Operators Association.

Technical Development Group

Eutech, Lloyds Registrar, Centre for Software Reliability, Ideo, National Engineering Laboratories, Health and Safety Executive, Honeywell, and SI Process Control.

Current information about the activities of the CASS project can be found at:

www.eutech.co.uk/cass

The CASS project will encourage the effective use and refinement of the standard, as will feedback of industry experience with the derivative standards.

8.2   IEC 300-3-9:1995-12, Dependability Management – Part 3: Application Guide – Section 9: Risk Analysis of Technological Systems

8.2.1   Background

The first edition of IEC 300-3-9 was issued in December 1995 by IEC TC 56. IEC TC 56 has been developing dependability standards since the 1970s. To date more than 40 international standards have been published by this committee which cover various aspects of system dependability, such as: reliability estimation, prediction, and growth; dependability design reviews; analytical dependability techniques; reliability centered maintenance; risk management; and lifecycle costing. The standards are organized in three layers:

1. dependability program management (IEC 300-1-x)

2. dependability program elements and tasks (IEC 300-2-x)

3. dependability application guides (IEC 300-3-x)

As noted by IEC TC 56 [40],

> Reliability is an important factor contributing to product quality and must be recognized in ISO quality management systems. IEC 300-1 has therefore also been issued as ISO 9000-4.

IEC 300-3-9 is part of the series devoted to the software aspects of dependability. Other standards that are planned for this series are listed in Related Standards Under Development at the end of this chapter.

8.2.2 Purpose and Scope

IEC 300-3-9 has narrowly defined its purpose and scope. The standard only applies to risk analysis; it does not cover risk management or risk control. Its stated purpose is to "provide guidelines for selecting and implementing risk analysis techniques," and to "ensure quality and consistency in the planning and execution of risk analysis [8]." This is accomplished by promoting current 'industry best practices.'

8.2.3 Description

According to the standard [8], the objective of risk analysis is to:

- identify risks and approaches to their solution;

- provide objective information, such as failure modes, rates, and severity, to support risk management decision making; and

- meet regulatory requirements.

The standard defines a six-step risk analysis process, which consists of: scope definition, hazard identification and consequence evaluation, risk estimation, verification, documentation, and analysis update. This six-step process corresponds to box 1.0 in Figure 8.1.

The scope of the risk analysis should be defined in the risk analysis plan. This plan should define the objectives of the risk analysis, any assumptions or constraints, the operational environment of the system being analyzed, the boundary of the system being analyzed, and the system success/failure criteria. Next, potential system hazards and their cause(s) are identified. The standard recommends the use of cause consequence analysis and root cause analysis in addition to the techniques traditionally associated with risk analysis, FTA and FMECA [8].

Risk is estimated before and after risk reduction techniques have been employed. The standard recommends estimating the frequency and severity of each hazard/cause combination based on the initiating events or sequences. Uncertainties and mitigating features must also be factored in. The frequency analysis should be based on a combination of historical data, analytical techniques, simulation, and expert judgement [8]. The standard supports a quantitative or qualitative estimate, as long as the approach is justified and documented.

Independent formal reviews and audits should be conducted to verify the integrity and repeatability of the risk analysis process and the accuracy and effectiveness of the results, as required by the standard. Given that the risk analysis process is iterative, the analysis and the work products resulting from it must be kept current.

The standard highlights the fact that risk analysis methods should be chosen that are appropriate for the technology and application domain. These methods must produce results that are repeatable and understandable by all interested parties [8, 32]. Techniques should be chosen so that it is easy to integrate the results from multiple analyses. Several common risk analysis methods are promoted by the standard [8]: event tree analysis, FMECA, FTA, HAZOP study, reliability block diagrams, sneak circuit analysis, common mode failure analysis, and simulation. These techniques are discussed in Chapter 2, while Annex B lists automated tools to support these analysis techniques.

The standard levies specific requirements on risk analysis documentation. For example, the standard [8] states:

> The risk analysis report documents the risk analysis process and should include or refer to the risk analysis plan and the initial hazard evaluation results. The presentation of technical information in it is a critical part of the risk analysis process. Risk estimates should be expressed in understandable terms, the strength and limitations of different risk measures used should be explained. and the uncertainties surrounding estimates of risk should be set out in language appropriate to the intended reader.

Too often, the risk analysis results are not recorded or presented in a logical, practical, or comprehensive manner. Weaknesses of techniques or assumptions are often ignored, leading to incorrect or unjustifiable conclusions.

8.3   ISO/IEC 15026:1998-04-29, Information Technology – System and Software Integrity Levels

ISO/IEC 15026 is a brief standard that provides additional guidance on how to determine software integrity levels. This standard corresponds to box 2.0 in Figure 8.1 and is a companion to IEC 61508 Part 5. ISO/IEC 15026 [9] defines integrity levels as:

> A denotation of a range of values of a property of an item necessary to maintain system risks within acceptable limits. For items that perform mitigating functions, the property is the reliability with which the item must perform the

mitigating function. For items whose failure can lead to a threat [hazard], the property is the limit on the frequency of that failure.

The standard [9] further defines software integrity levels as "the integrity level of a software item." This is a slightly different focus than IEC 61508. The orientation of IEC 61508 is toward functional safety, while ISO/IEC is oriented toward dependability. However, the two standards are compatible. (Note that ISO/IEC 15026 uses the term threat, where IEC 61508 uses hazard.)

ISO/IEC 15026 [9] promotes a three-step process for determining the software integrity level. The first step is to determine the system integrity level. Next, the software integrity level is determined, and from that software integrity requirements are derived. Both the system and software integrity levels should represent the worst case risk. ISO/IEC 15026 [9] defines four integrity levels, similar to IEC 61508:

Level	Risk
A	high
B	intermediate
C	low
D	trivial

The software integrity level represents properties of the software that are necessary to maintain a system within specified acceptable risk limits [9]. The standard recommends initially assigning software the same integrity level as the system. After analyzing the architecture/design, a determination is made as to whether the software integrity level can be lowered [9]:

- The software integrity level equals the system integrity level if the failure of a software subsystem or component occurs in isolation and will: 1) result in a threat, or 2) nondelivery of a mitigating function.

- The software integrity level may be lower than the system integrity level if the failure of a software subsystem or component *only* occurs in combination with other system states.

- Software subsystems and components whose failure modes cannot lead to a threat *and* whose functionality is not associated with a mitigating function should be assigned an integrity level of D.

All three of the examples demonstrate the necessity of partitioning and fault isolation.

The standard points out that software integrity requirements must be established based on each project's size, scope, complexity, technology, industrial sector, and risk. Software integrity requirements should include both product and process requirements, taken from the techniques and measures specified in Table 8.4; in fact, the standard makes similar recommendations to those in IEC 61508 Part 3. Integrity requirements for safety-related or risk mitigation software should emphasize ensuring reliability, that is, ensure that the mitigation software functions correctly and reliably as specified. Integrity requirements for safety-critical or control software should emphasize reducing the likelihood and the severity of the consequences of failures.

8.4   Summary

IEC 61508 provides a comprehensive and methodical approach to achieving and assessing safety and reliability at the system and software component level. IEC 300-3-9 and ISO/IEC 15026 amplify concepts contained in IEC 61508. The software safety lifecycle is fully integrated with the system safety lifecycle. Two key concepts of IEC 61508 are functional safety and safety integrity levels (SILs). SILs are determined based on risk analyses, then in turn determine which design features, verification activities, and validation techniques are implemented.

8.5   Discussion Problems

1. Develop and justify a recommendation for SILs 1 through 4 for using object oriented analysis and design (OOAD) during the requirements specification, architecture specification, and design and development lifecycle phases.

2. How is the integrity level for a system determined? How is the integrity level for software determined?

3. Consider a software controlled subway system. Define the software integrity requirements and functional safety requirements for this system.

4. Describe and compare the informational content of a Software Safety Verification Report, Software Safety Validation Report, and Functional Safety Assessment Report.

5. What design features are HR for an SIL 3 system? Which design features are NR for an SIL 3 system? Provide a rationale for this recommendation.

6. What verification activities are HR for an SIL 3 system? What verification activities are NR for an SIL 3 system?

7. Which design features are complementary for SIL 2; which are redundant?

8. What phases/activities of the software safety lifecycle intersect with the system safety lifecycle and how do they do so?

9. Describe the differences between the target failure rates established for continuous-mode operation and demand-mode operation.

10. Explain how and why systematic integrity is measured.

11. How does a traditional hazard analysis fit into the safety management scheme promoted by IEC 61508?

12. The SEI CMM, RTCA/DO-178B (Chapter 4), and IEC 61508 all promote the concept of levels related to software assurance activities. Briefly explain the similarities and differences in how each of these standards define and measure levels.

Additional Resources

Primary Source Documents

[1]   IEC 61508-1:1998 Functional safety of electrical/electronic/programmable electronic safety-related systems – Part 1: General requirements.

[2]   IEC 61508-2:199x[5] Functional safety of electrical/electronic/programmable electronic safety-related systems – Part 2:   Requirements for electrical/ electronic/programmable electronic safety-related systems.

[3]   IEC 61508-3:1998 Functional safety of electrical/electronic/programmable electronic safety-related systems – Part 3: Software requirements.

[4]   IEC 61508-4:1998 Functional safety of electrical/electronic/programmable electronic safety-related systems – Part 4: Definitions and abbreviations of terms.

[5]   IEC 61508-5:1998 Functional safety of electrical/electronic/programmable electronic safety-related systems – Part 5: Examples of methods for the determination of safety integrity levels.

[6]   IEC 61508-6:199x[6] Functional safety of electrical/electronic/programmable electronic safety-related systems – Part 6: Guidelines on the application of parts 2 and 3.

[7]   IEC 61508-7:199x[7] Functional safety of electrical/electronic/programmable electronic safety-related systems – Part 7: Overview of techniques and measures.

[8]   IEC 300-3-9:1995-12, Dependability Management – Part 3: Application Guide – Section 9: Risk Analysis of Technological Systems.

[9]   ISO/IEC 15026:1998-04-29, Information Technology – System and Software Integrity Levels.

---

[5]Publication was pending as of August 1999.
[6]Publication was pending as of August 1999.
[7]Publication was pending as of August 1999.

Related Safety, System, and Software Engineering Standards

[10] ISO/IEC Guide 51:1990 – Guidelines for the Inclusion of Safety Aspects in Standards.

[11] IEC Guide 104:1997 – Guide to the Drafting of Safety Standards, and the Role of Committees with Safety Pilot Functions and Safety Group Functions.

[12] ISO 9000-3:1991, Quality Management and Quality Assurance Standards – Part 3: Guidelines for the Application of ISO 9001 to the Development, Supply and Maintenance of Software.

[13] ISO 9001:1994, Quality Systems – Model for Quality Assurance in Design, Development, Production, Installation and Servicing.

[14] IEC 50(191):1990 – International Electrotechnical Vocabulary (IEV), Chapter 191: Dependability and quality of service.

[15] IEC 300-2, Dependability Management – Part 2: Dependability Programme Elements and Tasks.

[16] IEC 60812:1985 – Analysis Techniques for System Reliability—Procedure for Failure Modes Effects Analysis (FMEA).

[17] IEC 61025:1990 – Fault Tree Analysis (FTA).

[18] IEC 61078:1991 – Analysis Techniques for Dependability—Reliability Block Diagram Method.

[19] ISO/IEC 2382-1: Information Technology – Vocabulary: Part 1: Fundamental Terms.

[20] ISO/IEC 2382-20: Information Technology – Vocabulary: Part 20: System Development.

[21] ISO 8402: Quality – Vocabulary.

[22] IEEE/EIA 12207.1-1997: Guide – Industry Implementation of ISO/IEC 12207:1995, Standard for Information Technology, Software Life Cycle Processes, Life Cycle Data.

[23] IEEE/EIA 12207.2-1997: Guide – Industry Implementation of ISO/IEC 12207:1995, Standard for Information Technology, Software Life Cycle Processes, Implementation Considerations.

Relevant Publications

[24] Bell, R. and Reinert, D. "Risk and System Integrity Concepts for Safety-Related Control Systems," *Safety-Critical Systems*, Chapman & Hall, 1993, pp. 273–296.

[25] Brazendale, J. "Safety of Computer Based Systems, Main Requirements of IEC 1508: Functional Safety, Safety Related Systems," *Proceedings EUROSPEC Institute Software Validation and Verification via EN60601-1-4 Seminar*, Heidelberg, June 1995, pp. 121–140.

[26] Brazendale, J. "IEC 1508 Functional Safety: Safety Related Systems," *Proceedings 2nd IEEE International Software Engineering Standards Symposium* Aug. 1995, pp. 8–17.

[27] Cosgriff, P. "Quality Assurance of Software Used in Diagnostic Medical Imaging," *Safety Systems*, Vol. 5, No. 2, Jan. 1996, pp. 1–3.

[28] Eutech, *Conformity Assessment of Safety-Related Systems (CASS)*, www.eutech.co.uk/cass.

[29] Kelly, T. "Software Safety—by Prescription or Argument?" *Safety Systems*, Vol. 7, No. 2, Jan. 1998, pp. 6–7.

[30] Shaw, R. "Safety Cases—How Did We Get Here?" *Safety and Reliability of Software Based Systems*, Springer-Verlag, 1995, pp. 43–95.

[31] Sherwood-Jones, B. "Human Factors—How Little Can You Get Away With and How Much Is Right?" *Safety Systems*, Vol. 6, No. 3, May 1997, pp. 12–14.

[32] Storey, N. *Safety-Critical Computer Systems*, Addison-Wesley, 1996.

[33] Tripp, L. "International Standards on System and Software Integrity," *StandardView*, ACM, Vol. 4, No. 3, Sep. 1996, pp. 146–150.

Related Standards Under Development

The following standards are currently under development by IEC Technical Committee 56 and will undergo final balloting and publication in the near future. Consult the IEC Website for current information: http://www.iec.ch

[34] IEC 60300-3-6 (draft) – Dependability Management. Part 3: Application Guide. Section 6: Software Aspects of Dependability.

[35] IEC 61704 (draft) – Guide to Test Methods for Dependability, Assessment of Software.

[36] IEC 61713 (draft) – Guide to Software Dependability through the Software Life Cycle Processes.

[37] IEC 61714 (draft) – Software Maintainability and Maintenance Aspects of a Dependability Programme.

[38] IEC 61719 (draft) – Guide to Measures (metrics) to be Used for the Quantitative Dependability Assessment of Software.

[39] IEC 61720 (draft) – Guide to Techniques and Tools for Achieving Confidence in Software.

[40] IEC TC 56 Dependability Brochure, dated 12/97.

Chapter 9

SEMSPLC Guidelines, Safety-Related Application Software for Programmable Logic Controllers, IEE Technical Guidelines 8:1996

9.1 Background

In September 1996 the Institution of Electrical Engineers (IEE), U.K., published the Software Engineering Methods for Safe Programmable Logic Controllers (SEMSPLC) Guidelines [1]. These Guidelines are the result of a four-year research program funded by the U.K. Department of Trade and Industry and the Science and Engineering Research Council. A consortium of 16 diverse organizations, with different perspectives and orientations participated in the study. ERA Technology, British Gas, ICL, LDRA, Servelec, the University of York, and YSE were partners in the research program. CEGELEC Projects, Cincinnati Milacron UK, EUTECH Engineering Solutions, Gerrard Software, the Health and Safety Executive (HSE), ICI Engineering Technology, IDEC, Nestle UK, and Nuclear Electric were sponsors of the research program. The project was initiated in response to the rapid introduction of PLCs in safety-critical industrial machine and process control applications, in particular the offshore industry, as a replacement for electromechanical relays. Two trial projects were conducted using the SEMSPLC Guidelines at the end of the four-year study, but prior to their release to the general public. As reported by A. Canning [12], the trial projects "independently confirmed that use of the Guidelines leads to a reduction in the number of errors leading to unsafe PLC behavior."

9.2 Purpose and Scope

As stated in the Guidelines [1], their purpose is to:

> ...provide guidance on the development of PLC application software suitable
> for safety-related uses. The practices, methods, and techniques advocated by

these Guidelines help make visible the impact of the software on the system in terms of the hazards associated with the system.

The SEMSPLC Guidelines apply to the development of safety-related PLC application software. The Guidelines are not specific to any industrial sector. They represent an application specific implementation of IEC 61508 Part 3 (see Chapter 8). Required activities are split into two categories: 1) basic activities required to achieve SILs 1–2; and 2) extra activities required to achieve SILs 3–4. Like IEC 61508, the Guidelines focus on what needs to be done, not how to do it. In fact the Guidelines [1] state that: "the onus is now on the operating organization to demonstrate how safety has been achieved and continues to be assured."

It is emphasized that the SEMSPLC Guidelines only address PLC safety; they do not address safety of the entire system in which PLCs are used. The Guidelines are not applicable to COTS software or the deployment phase of the lifecycle. The term safety-related is used to refer to both safety-related and safety-critical software.

The SEMSPLC Guidelines issue several cautionary statements about reuse of PLC software, which are confirmed by A. Canning's [11] study:

> The second issue arising from the study is that little evidence could be found that reuse decreases the error rate of software, or increases the safety of the software.

9.3 Description

The SEMSPLC Guidelines are organized around management processes and software development lifecycle phases. Required activities are assigned to each based on the SIL. Three ongoing management processes are identified: Safety Management, Software Verification Management, and Quality Management. They are described in terms of objectives, inputs, outputs, procedure, verification, and authorization.

Safety Management Process

The Safety Management Process is responsible for: 1) producing the Software Safety Plan, Software Safety Justification, and the Software Safety Requirements Specification; 2) monitoring software development activities and their compliance with the Software Safety Plan; and 3) performing ongoing safety and risk analyses.

The Software Safety Plan defines an approach for achieving, assessing, and maintaining the required SIL. The plan should define the safe subset of the language to be used on the project, requirements for independent verification of activities, the corrective action monitoring and reporting system, and integrity requirements for software engineering tools. The plan should explain how software development activities are going to be monitored and what engineering analysis is needed during each lifecycle phase to demonstrate progress toward meeting software safety requirements. Furthermore, the plan should describe the requisite software safety engineering competency needed by project personnel [17]. The Guidelines point out that commitment to safety engineering practices is as important as competency. The Software Safety Plan is expected to follow the content and format specified in IEC 61508 Part 3.

The term Software Safety Justification is used to describe the component of the System Safety Case that discusses PLC software. The Software Safety Justification should summarize, analyze, and interpret information contained in the lifecycle artifacts. The SEMSPLC Guidelines note that while safety cases are required by several regulatory agencies, it is simply "good software safety management" practice to produce and maintain them. The Software Safety Justification presents the rationale for: 1) the assignment of SILs to software components; 2) the software architecture; 3) the design approach; 4) how partitioning was implemented; and 5) the types of verification techniques used. Results of risk analyses are discussed. The test analysis report is interpreted to prove that no adverse system behavior will occur. The Guidelines recommend an independent audit of the Software Safety Justification to ensure its accuracy.

Software safety requirements are categorized as functional safety requirements or safety integrity requirements, similar to the approach taken by the MISRA^{TM} Guidelines (see Chapter 3). Functional safety requirements address, at a minimum, system behavior in the intended operational environment and in response to known system hazards. Safety integrity requirements address risk management and verification activities necessary to demonstrate that the specified SIL has been or will be met. Software safety requirements are derived from the system safety requirements specification and the results of system hazard analyses.

The Safety Management Process performs ongoing safety and risk analyses and monitors software development activities and their compliance with the Software Safety Plan. Activities which are successful and those in which anomalies or discrepancies occur are documented in Observation Reports. The Guidelines [1] suggest that the Observation Reports contain the following information:

1. report name, number, and date

2. software/artifact name and version number

3. lifecycle phase

4. name and signature of person preparing report

5. description of problem (or successful activity)

6. rationale for rejection (or acceptance)

7. recommended corrective action

8. analysis of the impact of the corrective action on the SIL

9. approval signature(s) to perform corrective action

10. current status

11. closeout date and signature(s)

It would also be useful to capture:

4b. organization/process initiating report, and

5b. severity of the anomaly or discrepancy.

This would provide a more complete view of the situation and help to prioritize corrective action. Table 9.1 illustrates a sample Observation Report.

Another ongoing mechanism to monitor progress toward meeting stated PLC software safety and reliability goals is the Functional Safety Audit. The Guidelines recommend that the Functional Safety Audit be performed by an organization that is independent of the developers. The extent and thoroughness of the audit is proportional to the assigned SIL. The audit should inspect the design, detailed design, and/or code, depending on the life-cycle phase, to verify that software safety requirements and risk mitigation strategies have been implemented correctly as specified. The audit should verify that test specifications and procedures are correct, consistent, and adequate for assessing safety features. Prior to deployment an audit should be conducted to verify that safety issues have been adequately explained in operations and maintenance procedures. The results of Functional Safety Audits should be documented, including any findings, recommendations, and proposed corrective action. A format similar to that identified above for Observation Reports could be used. Again, the severity of open issues and nonconformances should be highlighted and the status of corrective action and other open issues monitored.

Software Verification Management Process

The Software Verification Management Process is responsible for ensuring that appropriate and adequate verification activities are undertaken. This is accomplished primarily through the development and implementation of the Software Verification Plan. According to the SEMSPLC Guidelines [1] the purpose of the Software Verification Plan is to "verify that the system requirements, especially the safety requirements, are met at each phase." Traceability between all lifecycle artifacts is verified. Specific verification strategies, activities, techniques, and tools are described. An assessment is made to determine if correct SILs have been assigned. Verification activities must demonstrate that the PLC software will not and cannot behave in an unexpected manner which could jeopardize safety. Above SIL 2, the Guidelines recommend using formal proofs of correctness. The results of verification activities are analyzed and interpreted to determine if safety and reliability goals are being achieved. The results are documented in Observation Reports, as discussed above.

J. Jacobson [16] makes some observations about validating systems containing PLCs based on his experience at the Swedish National Testing and Research Institute:

Observation Report: #023 – Audit of Test Results
15 September 1998

1. software/artifact: preliminary test results, dated 31 August 1998.

2. lifecycle phase/milestone: Test
                                                   Test Readiness Review 1

3a. person preparing report: Debra S. Herrmann

3b. organization/process: IV&V Contractor
                                             Software Verification Management Process

4a. description of problem: Forty-three percent of the tests failed. Test specifications do not trace to requirements. Expected results and actual results observed were not recorded.

4b. severity: major

5. rationale for rejection: The high percentage of failed tests would indicate that the design and software are unstable. Claims for passed tests are unsubstantiated since the testing is not tied to requirements and neither actual nor expected results were recorded.

6. recommended corrective action: Return to the design phase and revalidate design against requirements.

7. impact of the corrective action on the SIL: This action is necessary to ensure that the specified SIL is indeed met.

8. approval signature(s) to perform corrective action:

9. current status: open

10. closeout date and signature(s):

Table 9.1: Sample observation report.

The validation of safety of a machine control system should concentrate on the following...

- the existence of the required safety functions;
- the correctness of the implemented safety functions;
- the behavior at fault; and
- the safety principles implemented.

The validation and verification of a PLC is more complicated than that for its predecessors. As Canning [12] observes, a PLC:

...includes hardware and software at a complexity level higher than that of established control systems based on mechanical, hydraulic, pneumatic, or electromechanical components.

Quality Management Process

The Quality Management Process is responsible for ensuring repeatable quality in software development processes and products. The Quality Management Process assesses conformance to client's requirements through ongoing audits, inspections, reviews, and walk-throughs. Safety and reliability issues are not addressed by Quality Management. The Software Quality Plan, one of the major outputs of the Quality Management Process, describes the activities, techniques, and tools to be used to ensure product and process quality. The Quality Management Process includes four subprocesses: documentation, coding and design standards, configuration management, and software development process measurement. Observation Reports, as discussed above, are used to record findings, make recommendations for improving products and processes, and monitor the status of corrective action.

The Documentation subprocess is responsible for communicating information about products and processes. This information should be available and presented in a manner that promotes "lessons learned," supports inspections, audits, and reviews, and facilitates production of the Software Safety Justification.

The Coding and Design Standards subprocess is responsible for identifying the safe subset of the language to be used on a project, along with features which developers are prohibited from using. Coding standards ensure that similar techniques are used across a project. In this way all members of a project will be able to understand each other's work. Coding standards also facilitate software maintainability. The standards should specify the format and structure of modules. They should specify common: design techniques; defensive programming techniques; memory usage standards; exception handling standards; variable, constant, procedure, and file naming conventions; standard procedure header information, such as revision history; and standards for annotating code. These standards become part of the Software Quality Plan.

The Configuration Management subprocess is responsible for identifying and maintaining control of software baselines and the lifecycle artifacts associated with them. The Configuration Management subprocess maintains revision history logs and obtains the approvals necessary to freeze or modify a baseline. The Configuration Management subprocess is responsible for initiating change impact analysis for proposed changes to established baselines and identifying the revalidation and regression testing needed if they are approved. The SEMSPLC Guidelines [1] are quite clear that the change impact analysis must evaluate the impact of the proposed change on PLC safety:

> Every change to the design ... requires a revisitation of the hazard analysis for the preceding phase of the lifecycle. The effect of the changes on the safety of the software system needs to be reassessed, as do the assumptions on which the safe operation of the software is based.

According to the Guidelines [1] proposed changes should include the following information:

1. change request name, number, and date

2. name and signature of requestor

3. rationale for the change

4. description of the proposed change

5. list of software components and artifacts requiring changes

6. analysis of the impact of the proposed change on PLC safety integrity

7. discussion of revalidation and regression testing needed

8. approval signatures and dates

9. closeout signatures and dates

It is rarely possible to estimate the full extent of implementing and verifying changes. Hence, it would be useful to include the following information as well:

5b. actual software components and artifacts that were changed,

6b. actual impact of change on PLC safety integrity, and

7b. actual revalidation and regression testing conducted.

A sample initial change request is shown in Table 9.2.

The Software Development Process Measurement subprocess is responsible for demonstrating progressive improvement (or the lack thereof) in software safety and quality from one lifecycle phase to the next. Process measurement will highlight software development

Change Request:#37 – Provide Feedback on Redundant Switchover
21 July 1998

1. name of requestor: Debra S. Herrmann

2. rationale for change: The system operator should be informed when a switchover to the redundant backup system occurs. This will enable them to determine if the system should be shut down and/or any preventive maintenance and diagnostics performed, to determine why the switchover occurred.

3. description of the proposed change: Send alert to system operator the moment a switchover to the redundant backup system occurs. Include date and time of switchover and any available diagnostic information with the alert.

4a. software components/artifacts requiring changes:
    Software Requirements Specification
    Software Design Specification
    Software Detailed Design Specification
    Software Test Specifications
    Monitor_Backup_System module
    Alert_Operator module

4b. actual software components/changed:

5a. impact of the proposed change on PLC safety integrity: This change would enhance PLC safety integrity because the system operator would be notified a priori of potential system instability.

5b. actual impact of change on PLC safety integrity:

6a. revalidation and regression testing needed:
    All test procedures related to switching to the backup system.
    All test procedures related to monitoring the backup system.
    All test procedures related to monitoring the primary system.
    All test procedures related to shutting down the primary system.
    All test procedures related to alerting the system operator.

6b. actual revalidation and regression testing conducted:

7. approval signatures and dates

8. closeout signatures and dates

Table 9.2: Sample change request.

activities that are effective, ineffective, and need improvement. A software development process measurement report should be issued for each activity and phase, which includes an analysis of the measurements made and recommendations for improvement. Software process measurement should evaluate a variety of factors, such as the number, type, and severity of defects found, the phase or activity in which they were introduced, the phase or activity in which they were detected, and the phase or activity in which they were corrected. This may involve performing root cause analysis. Chapter 10 contains several examples of Software Process Measurement Reports.

Software Development Lifecycle

The SEMSPLC software development lifecycle complements the management processes. It consists of five phases: requirements, design, detailed design, coding, and testing. The Guidelines describe each phase in terms of: the objectives for the phase; its inputs and outputs; procedures; extra safety activities required for SIL 3 or 4; descriptions of phase outputs; verification; and authorization requirements.

Requirements Phase

To be useful, requirements must be accurate, consistent, complete, correct, unambiguous, and verifiable.[1] Requirements must take into account known system constraints, such as timing or memory size [20]. They also must be understandable by clients and developers [17].

PLC software applications operate in real time in both demand mode and continuous mode. The timing of events is critical; hence the need for a thorough timing analysis. Timing requirements for PLC software applications should be apportioned from system level timing constraints. All timing scenarios should be examined during the analysis, such as [20]:

- input to output timing

- input to input timing

- output to input timing

- output to output timing

- maximum allowable time

- minimum allowable time

- event duration

---

[1]IEEE Std. 1012-1998, Standard for Software Verification and Validation Plans.

PLC software requirements are derived from the system requirements specification and the system risk analysis. The Guidelines [1] recommend classifying software requirements into three categories:

1. Safety Requirements

    1.1 functional safety requirements

    1.2 safety integrity requirements

2. Nonsafety Functional Requirements

3. Nonfunctional Requirements

    3.1 performance requirements

    3.2 availability requirements

    3.3 reliability requirements

    3.4 security requirements

    3.5 maintainability requirements

The first category of software requirements is documented in the Software Safety Requirements Specification, which is produced by the Safety Management Process. The second and third categories of requirements are documented in the Software Requirements Specification, which is an output of the Requirements Phase. The Requirements Specification should explain software/software, software/hardware, and software/operator interfaces. A preliminary data dictionary should be developed during the Requirements Phase.

Each requirement should be assigned an SIL. This information can be determined by expanding the system level risk analyses to include PLC software. The SEMSPLC Guidelines recommend modelling the user interface, abnormal conditions, state transitions, and system inputs and outputs to ensure the accuracy of the requirements and to verify the understanding of requirements for safety functions and control measures. The Guidelines [1] make the practical observation "...that it may be necessary to plan to resolve conflicts between the target integrity requirement and the practical implementation."

During the requirements phase an analysis should be conducted to determine how system hazards affect or could be affected (positively or negatively) by software [17, 20]. The Guidelines recommend conducting both FTA and FMECA. An evaluation should be conducted of the PLC software in its intended operational environment to determine the need for fail-safe and/or fail-operational modes should undesirable states be reached.

In addition to the above activities, for SIL 3 or 4 the Guidelines recommend using a formal specification language, such as Z or VDM-SL, animated specifications, finite state machines, and Petri net modelling. These additional activities are recommended to ensure that the requirements, in particular the safety requirements, are accurate, consistent, complete, correct, unambiguous, and verifiable.

The importance of taking the time to develop thorough and accurate requirements specifications cannot be overemphasized. To illustrate, R. Shaw [19] reports that a 1995 Health and Safety Executive study of controller system failures exhibited the following error distribution:

- 44.1% failures due to specification errors

- 14.7% failures due to design and development errors

- 5.9% failures due to installation and commissioning errors

- 14.7% failures due to operations and maintenance errors

- 20.6% failures due to change management errors after commissioning

The outputs of the Requirements Phase specified by the Guidelines are the Software Requirements Specification, Data Dictionary, Software Requirements Test Specification, Factory Acceptance Test Specification, and Software Requirements Verification and Safety Report. Some guidance is provided on the content of each of these outputs. The format is to be specified by the client or applicable regulatory authority.

In addition to listing and categorizing requirements, the Software Requirements Specification should describe: the intended operational environment, hardware constraints, operational modes (including maintenance and failure), and error and exception handling [17,20].

The Software Requirements Test Specification should explain how all three categories of requirements (safety, nonsafety functional, and nonfunctional) will be tested and verified. The specification should provide guidance on how to evaluate test results and resolve any discrepancies.

According to the standard [1], the Factory Acceptance Test Specification should explain how the operational functionality and safety of the PLC software will be tested at the factory; while the Site Acceptance Test Specification should explain how the Factory Acceptance Test procedures will be verified at the customer's site, along with interfaces to the external plant.

The Software Requirements Verification and Safety Report documents how activities listed in the Software Verification Plan were conducted and whether or not they verified the correctness, completeness, consistency, accuracy, and unambiguousness of each requirement. All results and observations are recorded, analyzed, and interpreted. System, software, hardware, operational, and/or environmental dependencies are noted. System hazards that affect or are affected by software, positively or negatively, are highlighted. All open issues must be resolved before proceeding to the next phase, unless a waiver is granted by the Approval Authority.

Design Phase

The goal of the Design Phase is to develop a software architecture that satisfies the requirements and is feasible, testable, flexible, and understandable. The SEMSPLC Guidelines encourage modular designs with high cohesion, low coupling, and low complexity. The Guidelines recommend the use of several design techniques to achieve these goals, such as information hiding, abstraction, and partitioning. (See Chapter 2.) Logical and physical partitioning is encouraged to prevent nonsafety-related functions from corrupting safety-related functions. The Guidelines note that in some scenarios it may be useful to partition by SIL. The standard recommends the use of diversity and recovery blocks to increase fault tolerance.

Interface control diagrams, showing timing constraints, should be developed for internal and external interfaces. Interfaces between PLCs should be minimized. The modelling performed during the Requirements Phase should be repeated to verify that the design accurately reflects the requirements. The Data Dictionary developed during the Requirements Phase should be updated to include the name, type, and range of each data item, and an explanation of how the data item is used and/or changed by software programs.

PLCs generally have a proprietary system kernel to handle I/O. As N. Storey [20] observes, this complicates validation and verification:

> Although the hardware and software of PLCs are well tried, they are proprietary products and details of their design and development are not normally available to developers. This makes it impossible for manufacturers of safety-critical systems to verify the hardware or software.

The design specification must explain how hardware constraints, such as memory size, scan rate, power up/down, initialization/reset, and internal exceptions are accommodated by the design. The PLC configuration should be explained, including communication between PLCs, as appropriate.

Safety analysis, including FTA, FMECA, and HAZOP studies, should be performed to ensure that the design will perform as specified under all conditions [17,20]. The Guidelines recommend evaluating the effect of hardware and interface failures; for example processor failure, defective memory, bus errors, power supply failures, and I/O board errors. The design should specify how the software should detect and respond to each condition. Situations to evaluate include but are not limited to: 1) a software component that has stopped working; 2) the input to or output from a software component is received too early, too late, or not at all; and 3) the input to or output from a software component is incorrect. In the later case the erroneous input or output could be within the valid range or outside the valid range. The adequacy of alarms and the validity of alarm conditions should also be evaluated.

Storey notes that EMC is a major problem because of the normal operating environment for PLCs. He makes the following recommendation [20]:

> User programs are often stored in battery-backed RAM, although for safety-critical applications it is preferable to store such software in a form that is less easily corrupted, such as EPROM.

In addition to the above activities, for SIL 3 or 4 the Guidelines recommend the use of a formal design language, such as VDM-SL or Z, and formal proofs. All possible system states should be analyzed to determine the timing and sequencing criticality of events and that there are no unintended events. Plans for statistical-based testing and stress testing should be developed from the design specification.

In high integrity applications it is preferable to use fail safe PLCs and fault tolerant PLCs. J. Jacobson [16] states that "single standard PLCs should not be used in safety-related applications." He recommends the use of fail safe or fault tolerant PLCs. Storey [20] points out that fail safe PLCs protect against random hardware failures through redundant PLCs, I/O channels, and power supplies and the use of voting logic to determine if a system should be shut down. In contrast, he notes that fault tolerant PLCs employ triple modular redundancy and voting logic. C. Goring [13] concurs; he recommends using fail safe and/or fault tolerant PLCs for SIL 3, with 2 out of 2 voting for fail safe PLCs and 2 out 3 voting for fault tolerant PLCs. For SIL 4 designs Goring [13] recommends using fault tolerant PLCs plus diverse random testing, while Storey [20] recommends N modular redundancy. Both remind developers of the need to regularly check for "stuck on" conditions and that both fail safe and fault tolerant PLCs have limitations due to the potential for common cause failures.

The outputs of the design phase specified by the SEMSPLC Guidelines are the Software Design Specification, Software Operations and Maintenance Plan, Software Design Test Specification, and Software Design Verification and Safety Report. Some guidance is provided on the informational content of these documents. The format is to be specified by the client or applicable regulatory authority.

The Software Design Specification should describe the PLC software architecture. It should explain the PLC mapping, the functional and data models, and the required module sequencing, if appropriate. The Guidelines recommend including timing diagrams, interface control diagrams, and control flow models to illustrate the architecture. The design specification should state how SILs were assigned to software functions and components and what design techniques were used to ensure that they are achieved. A thorough discussion of error and exception handling should be provided. Traceability to the Software Requirements Specification and Software Safety Requirements Specification must be demonstrated.

The preliminary PLC Software Operations and Maintenance Plan should describe routine operation of the PLC software, from initial start up, and responses to abnormal conditions. Unique system safety procedures should be highlighted. The plan should explain change management procedures and responsibilities. Traceability to the software safety analyses must be demonstrated.

The Software Design Test Specification describes the procedures for verifying the software functionality, safety, performance, and interfaces against stated requirements.

The Software Design Verification and Safety Report describes how the activities described in the Software Verification Report were performed to verify the software design. The results observed are reported, analyzed, and interpreted. Particular emphasis is placed on the results of safety analyses of the design and efforts to verify the adequacy of risk control measures [17, 20]. All open issues must be resolved before proceeding to the next phase, unless a waiver is granted by the approval authority.

Detailed Design Phase

During the Detailed Design Phase comprehensive descriptions of each software module and its functionality are developed. These descriptions should contain sufficient detail so that no assumptions need to be made by the coder. All I/O, interfaces, timing, loading, and performance details should be specified. The Guidelines recommend defining conventions for distinguishing local and global variables and the use of a single entry and exit point per module. They also recommend the use of a fixed scan rate for each PLC program to reduce the likelihood of errors.

The safety analyses performed during the design phase should be updated during detailed design. Control flow, data flow, and information flow should be analyzed. Performing control flow, data flow, and information flow analysis is more difficult in PLC software than other applications. As A. Greenway [14] points out, "Control flow, data flow, and information flow analysis is feasible although . . . this suffers from lack of tool support and the lack of structuring by some languages."

The Guidelines encourage the use of defensive programming and parameter checking to minimize the likelihood of reaching undesirable system states. The Guidelines recommend conducting extensive walkthroughs, peer reviews, and inspections to detect and remove errors before coding begins. The Data Dictionary is also updated during the Detailed Design Phase.

In addition to the activities discussed above, for SIL 3 or 4 the SEMSPLC Guidelines encourage the use of a formal design language, formal proofs, dynamic and static analysis of all logic paths and I/O combinations, error seeding, and run-time checks. The intent is to uncover any errors which would cause the design to be unstable.

There are three outputs from the detailed design phase: the Detailed Design Specification, the Detailed Design Test Specification, and the Detailed Design Verification and Safety Report. Some guidance is provided on the informational content of these documents. The format is to be specified by the client or applicable regulatory authority.

According to the Guidelines, the Detailed Design Specification should provide a comprehensive description of module functionality, timing, loading, interfacing, I/O, and performance characteristics. Control flow, data flow, and information flow should be explained. Self testing, error handling, and exception handling logic should be described. Design features which support the SIL should be detailed. Traceability to the Design Specification must be demonstrated.

The Detailed Design Test Specification should describe how each module will be tested under normal and abnormal conditions.

The Detailed Design Verification and Safety Report should describe what activities listed in the Software Verification Plan were conducted to verify the soundness and suitability of the Detailed Design. The results observed should be recorded, analyzed, and interpreted. It must be demonstrated that the required SIL was achieved for each module. The results of the detailed design safety analyses must be discussed. All open issues must be resolved before proceeding to the Coding Phase, unless a waiver is granted by the approval authority.

Coding Phase

During the Coding Phase the actual executable PLC software is produced, using the specified safe language subset and coding and design standards. As the Guidelines note, several constraints must be taken into account during the development of PLC code [1]:

1. the order of execution of the program;

2. the order of evaluation of relays and functions within rungs and networks; and

3. the accuracy of floating point and integer operations.

Each of these constraints can have a significant impact on PLC software safety.

The Guidelines recommend developing a memory map which defines the type and scope of variables and their addresses to prevent potential memory conflicts. This information is also used to update the Data Dictionary. Traceability must be demonstrated from the code to the Detailed Design Specification.

In addition to these activities, for SIL 3 or 4 the Guidelines recommend formal proofs which demonstrate that the modules satisfy the Detailed Design Specification and that the constraints do not compromise safety. The Guidelines also recommend certifying that the object code accurately reflects the source code.

IEC 61131-3 [4, 6] was developed to standardize PLC programming languages. It defines five types of PLC languages, which range from low level languages to those that support a structured hierarchical notation:

- ladder logic or diagrams

- instruction lists

- function block diagrams

- structured text

- sequential function charts

The concept of ladder logic was carried forward from the predecessor to PLCs—electromechanical relays. Greenway [14] states that few PLC languages have an established safe subset. Storey [20] adds:

> Unfortunately, existing PLC languages do not satisfy many of the requirements of high integrity software. In particular it is often difficult to structure programs effectively and the widespread use of global variables makes effective isolation impossible.

This situation complicates the verification tasks and increases the importance of having comprehensive coding and design standards.

The outputs of the Coding Phase are the annotated source code, the object code, and the memory map.

Testing Phase

In this context the term testing is used to refer to all verification activities. Testing verifies that the activities of each phase were conducted as specified and that the outputs are correct. Testing verifies traceability from phase to phase using the test specifications that were developed for the requirements, design, and detailed design. A test report, produced after implementing each test specification, includes information about observed results, faults discovered, corrective action taken and its current status, requirements for revalidation and regression testing, ID and version number of the software or artifact, the person filing the report, and the person who witnessed the tests. At completion of the site acceptance test, a decision is made whether or not the PLC software is ready for deployment.

Interaction with System Safety and Other Standards

No normative references are cited in the SEMSPLC Guidelines. However, it is assumed that a quality management system, as required by ISO 9001/9000-3, is in place at the company developing the PLC software. As mentioned earlier, the SEMSPLC Guidelines are an application specific implementation of IEC 61508 Part 3. Appendix A of the Guidelines provides a mapping between the two standards.

Roles, Responsibilities, and Qualifications of Project Members

The roles, responsibilities, and qualifications of project members are to be defined in the Software Quality Plan. Organizational structures, interfaces, and controls should be defined in the plan and agreed to before development begins. Personnel are expected to have the appropriate experience, qualifications, and training to perform their duties. Specific competency requirements are derived from IEC 61508 Part 3.

Data Items Produced

Several data items are produced by adherence to the SEMSPLC Guidelines. As shown in Table 9.3, the data items are associated with a specific management process or lifecycle phase. The emphasis is on the informational content, not the format.

The main safety-related document is the Software Safety Justification, which is a component of the system safety case. The Software Safety Justification should be developed for a specific PLC software application and SIL. It should present a summary and analysis of information from lifecycle artifacts to demonstrate that adequate protective measures have been incorporated to prevent, minimize, and control hazards. The analysis should include qualitative information, quantitative information, and engineering judgement. The justification should be updated during each lifecycle phase and following each milestone review.

MANAGEMENT PROCESS	DATA ITEMS PRODUCED
Safety Management	– Software Safety Plan – Software Safety Justification – Software Safety Requirements Specification – Observation Reports
Software Verification Management	– Software Verification Plan – Observation Reports
Quality Management	– Software Quality Plan – Software Development Process Measurement Report – Coding and Design Standards – Observation Reports
LIFECYCLE PHASE	**DATA ITEMS PRODUCED**
Requirements	– Software Requirements Specification – Data Dictionary – Software Requirements Test Specification – Factory Acceptance Test Specification – Site Acceptance Test Specification – Software Requirements Verification and Safety Report
Design	– Software Design Specification – Software Operations and Maintenance Plan – Software Design Test Specification – Software Design Verification and Safety Report
Detailed Design	– Software Detailed Design Specification – Software Detailed Design Test Specification – Software Detailed Design Verification and Safety Report
Code	– Code – Memory Map
Testing	– Tested Code – Software Requirements Test Report – Software Design Test Report – Software Detailed Design Test Report – Factory Acceptance Test Report – Site Acceptance Test Report

Table 9.3: Data items required by IEE SEMSPLC Guidelines. (*Source:* adapted from Figure 2-1, page 20, IEE Technical Guidelines 8:1996, SEMSPLC Guidelines – Safety Related Application Software for Programmable Logic Controllers, by permission.)

Compliance Assessment

The SEMSPLC Guidelines do not address the issue of compliance assessment.

Scaling

For the most part the SEMSPLC Guidelines do not address the issue of scaling. The only comment made in this regard is that "smaller projects may not require both a design and a detailed design phase. The issues raised in each … still need to be addressed [1]."

9.4   Strengths

The IEE SEMSPLC Guidelines are methodical and comprehensive yet practical. They mesh management processes with lifecycle phases. The Guidelines are not tied to a specific software lifecycle, development methodology, or language. Required activities are grouped for SILs 1–2 and SILs 3–4. The Guidelines require the approval of data items, as a milestone, before moving to the next phase. The informational content of data items is emphasized, not their format. Given the nature of PLC software, emphasis is placed on using diagrams, graphics, and other nontextual notations in specifications, whenever possible. Additional guidance is provided in the appendices on related topics, such as language/compiler selection, development of coding standards, performing timing analyses, and the use of formal methods.

9.5   Areas for Improvement

The IEE SEMSPLC Guidelines could be improved in a couple of ways. The first would be to address the issue of compliance assessment. This would facilitate the use of the Guidelines by regulatory agencies and independent third-party certification labs. Second, more emphasis should be placed on the use of static analysis techniques, particularly those which can be used early in the lifecycle, when it is easier and more cost effective to detect and fix errors.

9.6   Results Observed to Date

The IEE SEMSPLC Guidelines were published in September 1996. Regular updates are planned, to incorporate industry experience. Since the release of the Guidelines a systematic study of their effectiveness has not been conducted. Two independent pilot studies were conducted prior to release, which confirmed that use of the Guidelines facilitated early error detection [12]. Information about the status of the Guidelines, industry experience, and updates is posted at:

www.iee.org.uk/PAB/Safe_rel/review.htm

9.7   Summary

The IEE SEMSPLC Guidelines are an application specific implementation of IEC 61508 Part 3 developed by a consortium of industrial, academic, and government organizations. The rapid introduction of PLCs in safety-critical industrial machine and process control applications prompted the development of the Guidelines. They provide specific guidance to address software safety engineering and the unique concerns of PLC software safety (such as the criticality of the timing and sequencing of events, unique programming languages, lack of tool support, and frequent unattended operation) through a comprehensive set of management processes and development activities. Pilot tests prior to the release of the Guidelines confirmed their merit [12].

9.8   Discussion Problems

1. How do the SEMSPLC Guidelines expect requirements to be categorized?

2. What position do the SEMSPLC Guidelines take on software reuse?

3. How is the Software Safety Requirements Specification different from the Software Requirements Specification? When is each specification produced and verified?

4. What is the difference between a safety case and a software safety justification?

5. What management processes or subprocesses make use of Observation Reports? Why?

6. How are Change Requests handled?

7. What scenarios should be considered when performing a timing analysis for a PLC software application?

8. What type of modelling is recommended and why?

9. When and why is a Data Dictionary produced?

10. What design techniques are recommended by the Guidelines?

11. What constraints must be taken into account during design? What constraints must be taken into account during coding?

Additional Resources

Primary Work Cited

[1]   SEMSPLC Guidelines, Safety-Related Application Software for Programmable Logic Controllers, Institution for Electrical Engineers (IEE) Technical Guidelines 8:1996.

Related System Safety and Other Standards

[2]   IEC 61131 – Programmable Controllers – Part 1:1992 General Information.

[3]   IEC 61131 – Programmable Controllers – Part 2:1992 Equipment Requirements and Tests.

[4]   IEC 61131 – Programmable Controllers – Part 3:1993 Programming Languages.

[5]   IEC 61131 – Programmable Controllers – Part 7:1999 Fuzzy Control Programming.

[6]   IEC 61131 Technical Reports, Guidelines for Users and Implementers of IEC 61131-3.

[7]   IEC 61609-4: Industrial Process Measurement and Control – Evaluation of System Properties for the Purpose of System Assessment – Part 4: Assessment of System Performance (FDIS 1997).

[8]   IEC 61609-5: Industrial Process Measurement and Control – Evaluation of System Properties for the Purpose of System Assessment – Part 5: Assessment of System Dependability (FDIS 1997).

[9]   IEC 61609-7: Industrial Process Measurement and Control – Evaluation of System Properties for the Purpose of System Assessment – Part 7: Assessment of System Safety (FDIS 1997).

Selected Bibliography

[10] Bell, R. and Reinert, D. "Risk and System Integrity Concepts for Safety-Related Control Systems," *Safety-Critical Systems*, Chapman & Hall, 1993, pp. 273–296.

[11] Canning, A. "Software Engineering Methods for Industrial Safety Related Applications," *Directions in Safety-Critical Systems*, Springer-Verlag, 1993, pp. 96–102.

[12] Canning, A. "Multi-Disciplinary Projects and Technology Exchange—The SEMSPLC Experience," *Safer Systems*, Springer-Verlag, 1997, pp. 275–284.

[13] Goring, C.J. "Methods and Techniques of Improving the Safety Classification of Programmable Logic Controllers Safety Systems," *Technology and Assessment of Safety-Critical Systems*, Springer-Verlag, 1994, pp. 21–30.

[14] Greenway, A. "A User's Perspective of Programmable Logic Controllers (PLCs) in Safety-related Applications," *Technology and Assessment of Safety-Critical Systems*, Springer-Verlag, 1994, pp. 1–20.

[15] Hung, Ng (ed.) *Safety, Reliability and Applications of Emerging Intelligent Control Technologies*, Pergamon, 1995.

[16] Jacobson, J. "Programmable Electronic Systems in Machine Control," *Safety Systems*, Vol. 7, No. 2, Jan. 1998, pp. 3–6.

[17] Leveson, N. *Safeware: System Safety and Computers*, Addison-Wesley, 1995.

[18] Maggioli, V.J. and Johnson, W.H., "An Industrial Approach to Integrity Level Determination and Safety Interlock System Implementation," *Directions in Safety-Critical Systems*, Springer-Verlag, 1993, pp. 270–277.

[19] Shaw, R. "Safety Cases—How Did We Get Here?" *Safety and Reliability of Software Based Systems*, Springer-Verlag, 1995, pp. 43–95.

[20] Storey, N. *Safety-Critical Computer Systems*, Addison-Wesley, 1996.

Chapter 10

ANSI/IEEE Std. 982.1-1989 and 982.2-1989 Measures to Produce Reliable Software

10.1 Background

ANSI/IEEE Std. 982.1-1989 provides a dictionary of metrics to produce reliable software. ANSI/IEEE 982.2-1989 is a supplement which provides general guidelines on how to use the metrics defined in 982.1. In other words, the two standards are meant to be used in conjunction with each other. Hence, the term 'the standard' will be used in this chapter to refer to these standards collectively.

The title 'measures to produce reliable software' is somewhat of a misnomer; a more accurate title would be 'measures to assess various aspects of software reliability.' This standard, unlike the other standards discussed in this book, does not follow a lifecycle methodology. Instead it presents a collection of metrics which can be used to measure various attributes that relate directly or indirectly to software reliability throughout the software lifecycle.

10.2 Purpose and Scope

This standard was written to establish consistent definitions of commonly used software reliability metrics. The stated intent of the standard is to provide a common foundation for researchers and practitioners, in order to promote a dialogue and meaningful exchange of data concerning the use and effectiveness of these metrics [1, 2].

The standard states that its use is "not restricted by the size, type, complexity or criticality of the software" evaluated. Hence, the standard is not specifically written for high reliability systems; it is equally applicable to commercial software.

10.3 Description

The metric definitions which follow make use of errors, faults, defects, and failures as their primitives and distinguish between them according to the definitions in IEEE Std. 610.12-

1990. All of these metrics are quantitative; many are time related. Automated tools are available which implement many of these metrics, as listed in Annex B.

While the standard presents these metrics in random order, this chapter discusses them in three major categories: product maturity assessment metrics, process maturity assessment metrics, and people/resource maturity assessment metrics.[1] Within these three categories, subcategories are identified. Furthermore, this chapter explains how to adapt these metrics so that they can be effectively used for mission critical systems. Many sample reports are provided which expand the single calculations in the standard into information that is useful to management and technical staff responsible for monitoring and assessing a system's development. Since no single metric by itself measures software reliability adequately, the intent of the standard is that multiple complementary metrics should be used throughout the software lifecycle. Collectively, the values resulting from these multiple complementary metrics will provide a more complete indication of a system's reliability. (This idea is expanded upon in Section 10.8.)

10.3.1   Recommended and Required Practices

Since the standard is composed of a dictionary and guidelines, none of the metrics are required. Instead, the standard recommends that multiple complementary metrics should be used by the system and software engineering staffs throughout the lifecycle to measure how the system is progressing toward stated safety and reliability objectives. In fact, the standard states that these measurements should not be made unless there is a plan for how to interpret, evaluate, use, and respond to this information!

Each of the three categories of metrics will be discussed next.

10.3.1.1   Product Metrics

Product metrics provide an assessment of the maturity of a product and an indicator of its operational readiness. The goal of collecting and analyzing product metrics is to ensure customer satisfaction. Some product metrics provide a snapshot of certain conditions at a given point in time. Other metrics estimate future behavior. There are four subcategories of product metrics that directly or indirectly relate to software safety and reliability: completeness and consistency metrics; complexity metrics; error, fault, and failure metrics; and reliability growth and projection metrics. (See Table 10.1.)

10.3.1.1.1   Completeness and Consistency Metrics

Completeness and consistency metrics measure various aspects of how completely and consistently specified requirements have been implemented in a system. Factors evaluated include missing information, inconsistent information, incomplete information, and undefined and unused functions and data.

---

[1]The standard uses a table to categorize the metrics. Many of the metrics are assigned to multiple categories. In this chapter they are discussed under only one category.

Attribute Measured	Metric	Applicable Lifecycle Phase(s)[a]	Source Definition
1. completeness & consistency	a. completeness	R D I OM	IEEE Std. 982.1,2
	b. requirements compliance	D I T IC OM	IEEE Std. 982.1,2
	c. requirements traceability	R D I T IC OM	IEEE Std. 982.1,2
	d. design integrity	D I T	new
	e. performance measures	D I T IC	new
2. complexity	a. cyclomatic	D I T OM	IEEE Std. 982.1,2
	b. information flow	D I T OM	IEEE Std. 982.1,2
	c. design structure	D	IEEE Std. 982.1,2
	d. generalized static	R D I	IEEE Std. 982.1,2
	e. number of entries and exits per module	D I T	IEEE Std. 982.1,2
3. error, fault, & failure	a. cumulative failure profile	R D I T IC OM	IEEE Std. 982.1,2
	b. defect density	R D I T IC OM	IEEE Std. 982.1,2
	c. defect indices	R D I T IC OM	IEEE Std. 982.1,2
	d. fault density	R D I T IC OM	IEEE Std. 982.1,2
4. reliability growth & projection	a. reliability growth function	T IC OM	IEEE Std. 982.1,2
	b. run reliability	T IC OM	IEEE Std. 982.1,2
	c. software maturity index	R D I T IC OM	IEEE Std. 982.1,2
	d. software purity level	D I T IC OM	IEEE Std. 982.1,2
	e. system performance reliability	D I T IC OM	IEEE Std. 982.1,2

[a]Lifecycle phases are defined as: R-requirements analysis, D-design, I-implementation, T-test, IC-installation and checkout, and OM-operations and maintenance. These may vary depending on the development methodology chosen.

Table 10.1: Product metrics [12].

Completeness

The completeness metric is used to determine the completeness (or incompleteness) of a software specification, such that [1, 2]:

$$CM \; = \; \text{completeness measure}$$

$$= \; \sum_{i=1}^{10} W_i D_i$$

where

$$W_i \; = \; \text{priority weighting factor of } D_i$$

$$D \; = \; \text{a factor derived from specification attributes, such that}$$

$$0 < D < 1$$

$$D_1 \; = \; \text{functions satisfactorily defined}$$

$$= \; (B_2 - B_1)/B_2$$

$$D_2 \; = \; \text{data references having an origin}$$

$$= \; (B_4 - B_3)/B_4$$

$$D_3 \; = \; \text{defined functions used}$$

$$= \; (B_6 - B_5)/B_6$$

$$D_4 \; = \; \text{referenced functions defined}$$

$$= \; (B_8 - B_7)/B_8$$

$$D_5 \; = \; \text{all condition options at decision points}$$

$$= \; (B_{10} - B_9)/B_{10}$$

$$D_6 \; = \; \text{all condition options with processing at decision points are used}$$

$$= \; (B_{12} - B_{11})/B_{12}$$

$$D_7 \; = \; \text{calling routine parameters agree with called routine's parameters}$$

$$= \; (B_{14} - B_{13})/B_{14}$$

$$D_8 \; = \; \text{all condition options that are set}$$

$$= \; (B_{12} - B_{15})/B_{12}$$

$$D_9 \; = \; \text{processing follows set condition options}$$

$$= \; (B_{17} - B_{16})/B_{17}$$

$$D_{10} \; = \; \text{data references have a destination}$$

$$= \; (B_4 - B_{18})/B_4$$

and

$$B_1 \; = \; \text{number of functions not satisfactorily defined}$$

$$B_2 \; = \; \text{number of functions}$$

B_3 = number of data references not having an origin

B_4 = number of data references

B_5 = number of defined functions not used

B_6 = number of defined functions

B_7 = number of referenced functions not defined

B_8 = number of referenced functions

B_9 = number of decision points not using all conditions or options or both

B_{10} = number of decision points

B_{11} = number of condition options without processing

B_{12} = number of condition options

B_{13} = number of calling routines with parameters not agreeing with defined parameters

B_{14} = number of calling routines

B_{15} = number of condition options not set

B_{16} = number of set condition options having no processing

B_{17} = number of set condition options

B_{18} = number of data references having no destination

This metric assumes the use of a formal specification language, such as VDM or Z, and/or a structured design language, such as PDL. It is useful for detecting mismatches between stated requirements and the corresponding design and implementation. This metric should be calculated several times within a phase and during different phases to determine if the completeness measure is improving. It is likely that during the design and implementation phases this metric will help identify missing requirements which will need to be refined or added to the specification.

The standard indicates that this metric can be used during the requirements, design, implementation, and operations and maintenance phases. The standard gives this metric an experience code of 2, indicating that it has received a moderate level of operational validity by industry.

This metric can be easily adapted for use in mission critical systems by calculating each of the ten D_x completeness parameters and the completeness measure CM for safety-critical, safety-related, and nonsafety-related software,[2] as well as for the entire system, as shown in Figure 10.1.

---

[2]See Chapter 2 for the definition of safety-critical, safety-related, and nonsafety-related software.

Completeness Metric Report
Phase/Date:_____

Type of Requirement	Goal	Reqts	Phase Des.	Impl	O&M
1. safety-critical					
D1					
D2					
D3					
D4					
D5					
D6					
D7					
D8					
D9					
D10					
CM	.99				
2. safety-related					
D1					
D2					
D3					
D4					
D5					
D6					
D7					
D8					
D9					
D10					
CM	.98				
3. nonsafety-related					
D1					
D2					
D3					
D4					
D5					
D6					
D7					
D8					
D9					
D10					
CM	.95				
4. total system					
D1					
D2					
D3					
D4					
D5					
D6					
D7					
D8					
D9					
D10					
CM	.96				

Figure 10.1: Use of completeness metric for mission critical systems.

Requirements Compliance

The requirements compliance metric measures three aspects of errors that occur during the interpretation and implementation of system requirements: inconsistencies, incompleteness, and misinterpretation, such that [1, 2]:

$$\text{inconsistencies} = N1/(N1 + N2 + N3) \times 100$$
$$\text{incompleteness} = N2/(N1 + N2 + N3) \times 100$$
$$\text{misinterpretations} = N3/(N1 + N2 + N3) \times 100$$

where

$$N1 = \text{number of errors due to inconsistencies}$$
$$N2 = \text{number of errors due to incompleteness}$$
$$N3 = \text{number of errors due to misinterpretation}$$

Inconsistencies are defined as system elements that do not accurately interpret or implement requirements as specified, for example, an inconsistent or conflicting interpretation of requirements. Incompleteness is defined as systems elements that do not completely interpret or implement requirements as specified, for example, a partial interpretation or implementation. Misinterpretation is defined as system elements that incorrectly interpret or implement requirements as specified, for example, a mistake in translating requirements into a design. This metric identifies what percentage of the requirements errors are due to these three aspects.

A fourth aspect, $N4$, could be added—specified requirements that are not implemented in any system element. This would identify not only requirements that are not implemented but also requirements that are not specified in a manner in which they can be implemented or verified. Hence, the percentage of requirements errors would be:

$$\text{requirements errors} = (N1 + N2 + N3 + N4)/\text{total number of requirements}$$

This metric assumes that the requirements have been validated; it does not measure incorrect or missing requirements.

The requirements compliance metric can be used during the design, implementation, test, installation and checkout (I&C), and operations and maintenance phases. The standard gives this metric an experience code of 1, indicating that it has received a limited level of operational validity by industry.

This metric can easily be adapted for use with mission critical systems, as shown in Figure 10.2, by calculating $N1 - N4$ for the safety-critical, safety-related, and nonsafety-related software and identifying the lifecycle phase in which the error was detected.

Requirements Traceability

The requirements traceability metric is used to identify requirements stated in the specification that have not been implemented in the software architecture. This metric also identifies

Requirements Compliance Report

Phase/Date:_____

Type of Requirements Error	Goal # %	Des. # %	Impl # %	Phase Test # %	I&C # %	O&M # %	Total to Date # %
1. Safety-critical							
inconsistent (N1)							
incomplete (N2)							
misinterpreted (N3)							
missing (N4)							
total errors							
2. Safety-related							
inconsistent (N1)							
incomplete (N2)							
misinterpreted (N3)							
missing (N4)							
total errors							
3. Nonsafety-related							
inconsistent (N1)							
incomplete (N2)							
misinterpreted (N3)							
missing (N4)							
total errors							
4. Total system							
inconsistent (N1)							
incomplete (N2)							
misinterpreted (N3)							
missing (N4)							
total errors							

Figure 10.2: Use of the requirements compliance metric for mission critical systems.

requirements that have been implemented in the software architecture that are not stated in the specification, a situation that is sometimes referred to as "requirements creep," such that [1, 2]:

$$TM = \text{requirements traceability}$$
$$= R1/R2 \times 100\%$$

where

$$R1 = \text{number of specified requirements met by the system architecture}$$
$$R2 = \text{number of original requirements in the specification}$$

The standard states that this metric can be used in the requirements, design, and operations and maintenance (O&M) phases. In fact, it can and should be used in all phases except the concept phase. The standard gives the requirements traceability metric an experience code of 3, indicating that it has received an extensive level of operational validity by industry.

To use this metric effectively, requirements in the specification should be assigned unique identifiers and counted. As the project progresses from phase to phase, the presence or absence of these requirements should be determined. Often a requirement may be implemented through a series of subrequirements. As more becomes known about a system in later phases, new requirements may be uncovered; if so, they should be added to the specification. The goal of this metric is to account for all requirements, those specified and those implemented. By default, the use of the requirements traceability metric encourages the specification of requirements that are verifiable.

For mission critical systems, the requirements traceability metric should be calculated by type of requirement (safety critical, safety related, and nonsafety related) and phase, as shown in Figure 10.3.

Requirements Traceability Report

Phase/Date:_____

Type of Requirement	# of Reqts	RT Goal	Reqts	Des.	Phase Impl.	Test	I&C	O&M
safety-critical		100%						
safety-related		100%						
nonsafety-related		100%						
total system		100%						

Figure 10.3: Use of requirements traceability metric for mission critical systems.

This book proposes two new product metrics: design integrity and performance measures.

Design Integrity

Design integrity measures how well the design has incorporated features to minimize the occurrence and consequences of potential failures. Specific design attributes evaluated include: forward/backward/n-block recovery, diversity, independence, information hiding, partitioning, defensive programming, fault tolerance, dynamic reconfiguration, error detection and recovery, fail safe/operational, and provision for degraded-mode operations, such that:

$$DI = \sum_{i=1}^{11} df_i$$

where

df_1 = 1 if forward/backward/n-block recovery is implemented

df_1 = 0 if forward/backward/n-block recovery is not implemented

df_2 = 1 if software diversity is implemented

df_2 = 0 if software diversity is not implemented

df_3 = 1 if independence is implemented

df_3 = 0 if independence is not implemented

df_4 = 1 if information hiding is implemented

df_4 = 0 if information hiding is not implemented

df_5 = 1 if software partitioning is implemented

df_5 = 0 if software partitioning is not implemented

df_6 = 1 if defensive programming is implemented

df_6 = 0 if defensive programming is not implemented

df_7 = 1 if software fault tolerance is implemented

df_7 = 0 if software fault tolerance is not implemented

df_8 = 1 if dynamic reconfiguration is implemented

df_8 = 0 if dynamic reconfiguration is not implemented

df_9 = 1 if error detection and recovery is implemented

df_9 = 0 if error detection and recovery is not implemented

df_{10} = 1 if the system is designed to fail safe or fail operational

df_{10} = 0 if the system is not designed to fail safe or fail operational

df_{11} = 1 if there is a provision for degraded-mode operations

df_{11} = 0 if there is not provision for degraded-mode operations

Weighting factors can be assigned to reflect the criticality of the software. For example, in a safety-critical system which cannot fail safe but must fail operational, primitives such as software fault tolerance, dynamic reconfiguration, and provision for degraded-mode operations may receive a higher weight than other design attributes.

Performance Measures

Performance metrics measure, or estimate depending on the lifecycle phase, the success in meeting stated performance criteria; the "how many how fast" type requirements. Specific performance criteria evaluated include: accuracy, precision, response times, memory utilization, storage utilization, and transaction processing rates under low, normal, and peak loading conditions, such that:

$$PM = \sum_{i=1}^{8} p_i$$

where

p_1 = 0 if accuracy goals not met

p_1 = 1 if accuracy goals met

p_1 = 2 if accuracy goals exceeded

p_2 = 0 if precision goals not met

p_2 = 1 if precision goals met

p_2 = 2 if precision goals exceeded

p_3 = 0 if response time goals not met

p_3 = 1 if response time goals met

p_3 = 2 if response time goals exceeded

p_4 = 0 if memory utilization goals not met

p_4 = 1 if memory utilization goals met

p_4 = 2 if memory utilization goals exceeded

p_5 = 0 if storage goals not met

p_5 = 1 if storage goals met

p_5 = 2 if storage goals exceeded

p_6 = 0 if transaction processing rates not met under low loading conditions

p_6 = 1 if transaction processing rates met under low loading conditions

p_6 = 2 if transaction processing rates exceeded under low loading conditions

p_7 = 0 if transaction processing rates not met under normal loading conditions

p_7 = 1 if transaction processing rates met under normal loading conditions

p_7 = 2 if transaction processing rates exceeded under normal loading conditions

p_8 = 0 if transaction processing rates not met under peak loading conditions

p_8 = 1 if transaction processing rates met under peak loading conditions

p_8 = 2 if transaction processing rates exceeded under peak loading conditions

Again, weighting factors can be assigned to reflect the criticality of various performance requirements in relation to the requirement to maintain the system in a known safe state.

10.3.1.1.2 Complexity Metrics

Complexity metrics measure various aspects of the inter- and intra-module complexity of the software and data as designed and/or implemented. Factors evaluated include the number of decision points, unique logic paths, entries, exits, and data structures referenced or updated, as well as module coupling and cohesion.

Cyclomatic or Static Complexity

The cyclomatic or static complexity metric is used to determine the structural complexity of a module or intramodule complexity, such that [1,2]:

$$
\begin{aligned}
SC &= \text{cyclomatic or static complexity} \\
&= E - N + 1 \\
&\simeq RG \\
&\simeq SN + 1
\end{aligned}
$$

where

N = number of nodes or sequential groups of statements

E = number of edges or flows between nodes

SN = number of splitting nodes or nodes with more than one edge emanating from it

RG = number of regions or areas bounded by edges with no edges crossing

The nodes, edges, splitting nodes, and regions are counted by creating a control graph of the module, preferably by using an automated tool. Each module has an entry and an exit node. The unique control flows between them, which are depicted graphically, depend on the logic constructs used in the module: if/then/else, do while, repeat until, do case, and so forth. As the standard notes, 10 is considered the maximum ideal for static complexity. Modules with an extremely high complexity measure are good candidates for redesign. The graph produced by this metric can also be used to determine the minimum number of unit tests required to exercise each unique path at least once.

The standard indicates that this metric can be used during the design, implementation, and operations and maintenance phases. It can also be used during the testing phase as part of error analysis. The standard gives the cyclomatic complexity metric an experience code of 3, indicating that it has received an extensive level of operational validation by industry.

As mentioned in Chapter 2, complexity is an issue for mission critical systems because it raises concerns about verification strategies and maintainability. Hence, intramodule complexity should be kept as low as practical in mission critical systems; particularly in the safety-critical and safety-related software partitions. The use of an automated tool to produce the graphs is recommended since it is likely to be less error prone than a human. The automated tool will also help uncover unintended paths through the software.

Data or Information Flow Complexity

The data or information flow complexity metric measures intermodule complexity, such that [1, 2]:

$$
\begin{aligned}
IFC &= \text{information flow complexity} \\
&= (\textit{fan-in} \times \textit{fan-out})^2 \\
WIFC &= \text{weighted information flow complexity} \\
&= IFC \times length
\end{aligned}
$$

where

$$
\begin{aligned}
\textit{fan-in} &= lfi + \textit{data-in} \\
\textit{fan-out} &= lfo + \textit{data-out} \\
lfi &= \text{local flows into a procedure} \\
\textit{data-in} &= \text{number of data structures from which the procedure retrieves data} \\
lfo &= \text{local flows from a procedure} \\
\textit{data-out} &= \text{number of data structures that the procedure updates} \\
length &= KSLOD, KSLOC, \text{ or } FP^3
\end{aligned}
$$

The standard indicates that the information flow complexity metric can be applied during the design, implementation, testing, and operations and maintenance phases. In fact, it should be applied repetitively during each of these phases to monitor targeted reductions in complexity. The goal is to achieve an intermodule complexity that is as low as reasonable; because, in general there is a strong correlation between intermodule complexity and fault rate. Excessive intermodule complexity indicates a lack of functional clarity and potential system stress points; such modules should be redesigned. The standard gives this metric an experience code of 1, indicating that it has received a limited level of operational validity by industry.

The information flow complexity metric can easily be adapted for use with mission critical systems, as shown in Figure 10.4. IFC and $WIFC$ are calculated for the safety-critical, safety-related, and nonsafety-related software, as well as for the entire system, throughout the lifecycle. This will give an accurate picture of: 1) the complexity of the software components of highest risk to mission success and the entire system; 2) trends in increasing or decreasing complexity over time; and 3) a comparison of actual complexity to the established goals.

---

[3] These terms are defined in Chapter 2.

Information Flow Complexity Report

Phase/Date:_____

Software		Phase				
Component	Goal	Reqts	Des.	Impl.	Test	O&M
1. safety-critical						
IFC						
WIFC						
2. safety-related						
IFC						
WIFC						
3. nonsafety-related						
IFC						
WIFC						
4. total system						
IFC						
WIFC						

Figure 10.4: Use of information flow complexity metric for mission critical systems.

Design Structure Complexity

The design structure metric measures the complexity of the detailed design of a software system by examining several attributes [1,2]:

$$DSM = \text{design structure metric}$$

$$= \sum_{i=1}^{6} W_i D_i$$

where

$$D_1 = 0 \text{ if top-down design}$$
$$= 1 \text{ if not top-down design}$$
$$D_2 = \text{module dependence}$$
$$= P_2/P_1$$
$$D_3 = \text{module dependence on prior processing}$$
$$= P_3/P_1$$
$$D_4 = \text{database size}$$
$$= P_5/P_4$$
$$D_5 = \text{database compartmentalization}$$

$$= P_6/P_4$$
$$D_6 = \text{module single entrance single exit}$$
$$= P_7/P_1$$

and

P_1	=	total number of modules in program
P_2	=	number of modules dependent on the input or output
P_3	=	number of modules dependent on prior processing states
P_4	=	number of database elements
P_5	=	number of nonunique database elements
P_6	=	number of database segments
P_7	=	number of modules not single entrance single exit

D_1 assumes a top-down design is desired; if not the desired methodology should be substituted in the definition. W_i is the weighting factor assigned to each derivative D_i based on the priority of that attribute, such that $0 < W_i < 1$. Additional derivatives can be defined and evaluated consistent with the needs of a particular project or development methodology.

DSM will vary such that $0 < DSM < 1$. The lower the value for DSM, the less complex the software. The derivative attributes help pinpoint the cause of complexity. The DSM value should be calculated several times during the design phase to monitor complexity reduction and/or stability.

The standard indicates that this metric can be used during the design and operations and maintenance phases. The standard gives this metric an experience code of 1, indicating that it has received a limited level of operational validity by industry.

The major advantages of this metric are: 1) its flexibility to incorporate new derivative attributes; and 2) that it can be applied at the system and subsystem level. For mission critical systems, examples of new attributes that could be defined are:

$D7$	=	0 if block recovery is implemented
	=	1 if block recovery is not implemented
$D8$	=	0 if diversity is implemented
	=	1 if diversity is not implemented
$D9$	=	0 if independence is implemented
	=	1 if independence is not implemented
$D10$	=	0 if information hiding is implemented
	=	1 if information hiding is not implemented
$D11$	=	0 if partitioning is implemented
	=	1 if partitioning is not implemented

These new attributes would be assigned high weights and DSM would then be defined as:

$$DSM = \sum_{i=1}^{11} W_i D_i$$

The DSM value would then be calculated for the safety-critical, safety-related, and nonsafety-related subsystems, as well as for the entire system.

Generalized Static Complexity

Generalized static complexity, which measures architectural complexity, is a variation of the static complexity metric. The goal is to apply the metric early in the development lifecycle to evaluate design tradeoffs and to facilitate later maintainability. Generalized static complexity also factors in resource allocation, such that [1, 2]:

$$
\begin{aligned}
GSC &= \text{generalized static complexity} \\
&= \sum_{i=1}^{E}(C_i + \sum_{k=1}^{K}(d_k \times r_{ki}))
\end{aligned}
$$

where

$$
\begin{aligned}
K &= \text{number of resources, indexed by } k = 1, \ldots, K \\
E &= \text{number of edges, indexed by } i = 1, \ldots, E \\
N &= \text{number of nodes, indexed by } j = 1, \ldots, N \\
C_i &= \text{complexity for program invocation and return along each edge } E_i \\
&\quad \text{ as determined by the user} \\
r_{ki} &= \text{1 if } k\text{th resource is required for } i\text{th edge, otherwise 0} \\
d_k &= \text{complexity for allocation of resource } k \text{ as determined by the user}
\end{aligned}
$$

The standard recommends 20 as the ideal maximum number of edges for a subsystem. Again, high complexity values highlight modules and/or subsystems that are good candidates for redesign. The standard indicates that the generalized static complexity metric can be used during the requirements, design, implementation, and operations and maintenance phases. For the metric to be utilized during the requirements or design phases, a formal specification language, such as VDM, Z, or PDL would have to be used. The standard gives the metric an experience code of 1, indicating that it has received a limited level of operational validity by industry.

Both the static and the generalized static complexity metrics can easily be adapted for use in mission critical systems, as shown in Figure 10.5. The SC and GSC values are calculated for the safety-critical, safety-related, and nonsafety-related software throughout the lifecycle.

Static and Generalized Static Complexity Report

Phase/Date:_____

Software	Goal SC GSC	Reqts SC GSC	Phase Des. SC GSC	Impl. SC GSC	O&M SC GSC
1. safety-critical					
module 1					
module 2					
module x					
subsystem					
2. safety-related					
module 1					
module 2					
module x					
subsystem					
3. nonsafety-related					
module 1					
module 2					
module x					
subsystem					

Figure 10.5: Use of static and generalized static complexity metric in mission critical systems.

Number of Entries and Exits per Module

The number of entries and exits per module metric measures the number of entry and exit points per module, such that [1, 2]:

$$
\begin{aligned}
M_i &= \text{entry and exit points for module } i \\
&= e_i + x_i
\end{aligned}
$$

where

$$
\begin{aligned}
e_i &= \text{number of entry points for module } i \\
x_i &= \text{number of exit points for module } i
\end{aligned}
$$

This metric indicates the modularity or structuredness of the software architecture. Each module will have one entry point and one or more exit points depending on the number of calls to other modules and error handling functions. The standard recommends a maximum of five exit points per module. Automated tools, such as those listed in Annex B, are available to assist in this analysis. The standard indicates that this metric can be used during the design, implementation, and operations and maintenance phases. The standard gives this metric an experience code of 1, indicating that it has received a limited level of operational validity by industry.

This metric can be successfully applied to mission critical systems to identify modules which are good candidates for redesign—those with a high number of entry and exit points. Particular attention should be paid to the number of entry and exit points in the safety-critical and safety-related modules. The number of paths in and out of a module complicates validation and verification activities in a nonlinear fashion.

Software Science Metrics

Halstead developed a set of software science metrics in the mid 1970s which measured various program complexity attributes and estimated resource requirements. During the 1970s and early 1980s these metrics received a lot of attention. Since then, the reviews have not been as enthusiastic [18]. However, it is worth discussing Halstead's work because in many ways it ushered in the current software metrics movement; several current metrics evolved from this pioneering work.

Halstead defined nine software science metrics [1, 2]:

$$
\begin{aligned}
l &= \text{program vocabulary} \\
&= n_1 + n_2 \\
L &= \text{observed program length} \\
&= N_1 + N_2 \\
\hat{L} &= \text{estimated program length} \\
&= n_1(\log_2 n_1) + n_2(\log_2 n_2)
\end{aligned}
$$

$$
\begin{aligned}
V &= \text{program volume} \\
&= L(\log_2 l) \\
D &= \text{program difficulty} \\
&= (n_1/2)/(N_2/n_2) \\
L_1 &= \text{program level} \\
&= 1/D \\
E &= \text{effort required} \\
&= V/L_1 \\
B &= \text{estimated number of errors} \\
&= V/3000 \\
&\simeq E^{2/3}/3000
\end{aligned}
$$

where

$$
\begin{aligned}
n_1 &= \text{number of distinct operators in a program} \\
n_2 &= \text{number of distinct operands in a program} \\
N_1 &= \text{total number of occurrences of the operators in a program} \\
N_2 &= \text{total number of occurrences of the operands in a program} \\
S &= \text{Stroud number, usually assigned 18 elementary mental} \\
&\quad \text{discriminations per second.}
\end{aligned}
$$

Note that n_1 and n_2 represent the basic structures of object code. The standard indicates that this set of metrics can be used during the implementation and operations and maintenance phases. Commercial tools are available to automate this process. The standard gives this metric an experience code of 3, indicating that it has received an extensive level of operational validity by industry.

10.3.1.1.3 Error, Fault, and Failure Metrics

Error, fault, and failure metrics measure the extent of errors, faults, and failures in the system artifacts throughout the lifecycle phases. Factors evaluated include the number of errors found during each lifecycle phase and the type, severity, and source of the error.

Cumulative Failure Profile

The cumulative failure profile metric provides a graphical depiction of the cumulative number of unique failures found during the lifecycle phases, such that [1, 2]:

$$
f_i = \text{total number of failures found during lifecycle phase } i
$$

This metric is flexible. The unit for which the number of failures is counted can be the entire system, by subsystem, and/or by module. The interval against which the failures are counted can be complete phases and/or subphases.

The standard indicates that this metric can be applied during all eight lifecycle phases. However, this is somewhat inconsistent with the definition provided for failure: 'termination of the ability of a functional unit to perform its required function.' Failures as thus defined would not manifest themselves until the implementation phase. If errors were counted in the earlier phases, this metric could be used in all phases. The standard gives this metric an experience code of 1, indicating that it has received a limited level of operational validity in industry.

Two variations of this metric enhance its usefulness for mission critical systems, as shown in Figure 10.6. First, the number of cumulative failures are counted by severity[4] level: negligible, marginal, critical, and catastrophic. Second, the number of cumulative failures are counted by the type of software (safety critical, safety related, nonsafety related, and the total system) in which the failure was found.

Defect Density

The defect density metric calculates the ratio of defects per lines of code or lines of design, such that [1,2]:

$$DD = \text{defect density}$$
$$= \frac{\sum_{i=1}^{I} D_i}{KSLOC \ (\text{or } KSLOD)}$$

where

D_i = number of unique defects found during the ith inspection process of a lifecycle phase

I = total number of inspections (or lifecycle phases) to date

$KSLOD$ = during the design phase, the number of source lines of design statements in thousands

$KSLOC$ = during the implementation phase and beyond, the number of executable source code statements plus data declarations

The standard indicates that this metric can be applied during all eight lifecycle phases. Given the definitions of $KSLOD$ and $KSLOC$, it is difficult to see how this metric could be applied to the concept or requirements phases since no 'design statements' will exist at that time unless $KSLOD$ is expanded to include formal specifications, such as VDM and Z. If the definition of $KSLOD$ is limited to PDL and other pseudocode, the use of this

---

[4]The IEC standards discussed in Chapters 6, 7, and 8 define these severity levels.

Cumulative Failure Profile Report

Phase / Date: _____

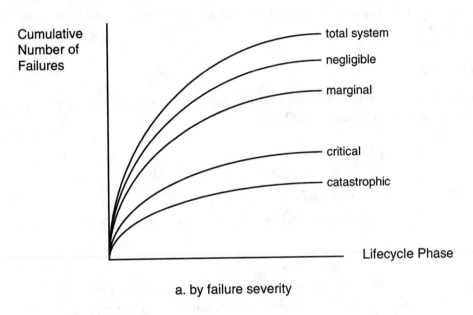

a. by failure severity

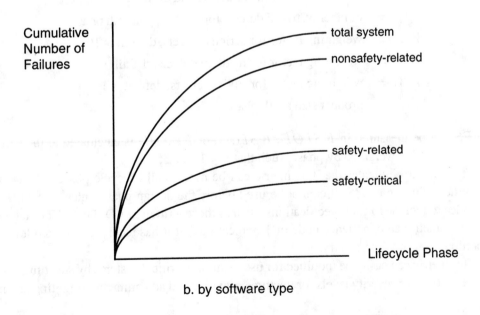

b. by software type

Figure 10.6: Use of cumulative failure profile metric in mission critical systems.

metric begins at the design phase. The standard gives this metric an experience code of 3, indicating that it has received an extensive level of operational validity by industry.

As shown in Figure 10.7, two variations can be made to this metric to enhance its usefulness for mission critical systems. First, function points can be substituted for $KSLOC$ to minimize the ambiguities encountered with LOC, as noted in Chapter 2. Second, the calculation can be expanded to measure the ratio of the severity of the faults found to the type of software.

Defect Indices

The defect indices metric calculates a relative index of software correctness throughout the different lifecycle phases, such that [1,2]:

$$
\begin{aligned}
DI &= \text{defect index} \\
&= \sum (i \times PI_i)/PS \\
&= (PI_1 + 2PI_2 + \ldots, iP_i + \ldots)/PS \\
PI_i &= (W1 \times (S_i/D_i)) + (W2 \times (M_i/D_i)) + (W3 \times (T_i/D_i))
\end{aligned}
$$

where

$$
\begin{aligned}
D_i &= \text{total number of defects detected during the } i\text{th phase} \\
S_i &= \text{number of serious defects found during the } i\text{th phase} \\
M_i &= \text{number of medium defects found during the } i\text{th phase} \\
T_i &= \text{number of trivial defects found during the } i\text{th phase} \\
W1 &= \text{weighting factor for serious defects, default is 10} \\
W2 &= \text{weighting factor for medium defects, default is 3} \\
W3 &= \text{weighting factor for trivial defects, default is 1} \\
PS &= \text{product size at } i\text{th phase}
\end{aligned}
$$

PS can be measured in $KSLOD$, $KSLOC$, or FP. PI_i is calculated at the end of each phase and is weighted by phase, such that $i = 1, \ldots, 8$.

The standard indicates that this metric can be used in all lifecycle phases. However, given the definition of PS, it cannot be used before the design phase unless $KSLOD$ is expanded to include formal specifications, such as those written in VDM or Z. The standard gives this metric an experience code of 1, indicating that it has received a limited level of operational validity by industry.

This metric can easily be modified for use in mission critical systems by substituting the four IEC standard severity levels for the three provided and adjusting the weighting factors:

$$
\begin{aligned}
DI &= \text{defect index} \\
&= \sum (i \times PI_i)/PS
\end{aligned}
$$

Defect Density Report

Phase/Date:_____

Software Type/ Fault Severity	Goal	Phase					
		Reqts KSLOD	Des. KSLOD	Impl. FP[a]	Test FP	I&C FP	O&M FP
1. Safety-critical							
negligible							
marginal							
critical							
catastrophic							
total							
2. Safety-related							
negligible							
marginal							
critical							
catastrophic							
total							
3. Nonsafety-related							
negligible							
marginal							
critical							
catastrophic							
total							
4. Total System							
negligible							
marginal							
critical							
catastrophic							
total							

[a]KSLOC or FP can be used, as long as KSLOC is accurately and consistently defined.

Figure 10.7: Use of defect density metric for mission critical systems.

$$= (PI_1 + 2PI_2 + \ldots, iP_i + \ldots)/PS$$
$$PI_i = (W1 \times (CAT_i/D_i)) + (W2 \times (CR_i/D_i)) + (W3 \times (MAR_i/D_i)) + (W4 \times (NEG_i/D_i))$$

where

$$
\begin{aligned}
D_i &= \text{total number of defects detected during the } i\text{th phase} \\
CAT_i &= \text{number of catastrophic defects found during the } i\text{th phase} \\
CR_i &= \text{number of critical defects found during the } i\text{th phase} \\
MAR_i &= \text{number of marginal defects found during the } i\text{th phase} \\
NEG_i &= \text{number of negligible defects found during the } i\text{th phase} \\
W1 &= \text{weighting factor for catastrophic defects, default is 10} \\
W2 &= \text{weighting factor for critical defects, default is 8} \\
W3 &= \text{weighting factor for marginal defects, default is 3} \\
W3 &= \text{weighting factor for negligible defects, default is 1} \\
PS &= \text{product size at } i\text{th phase}
\end{aligned}
$$

Fault Density

The fault density metric calculates the ratio of faults per lines of code, such that [1, 2]:

$$F_d = \text{fault density}$$
$$= F/KSLOC$$

where

$$
\begin{aligned}
F &= \text{number of unique faults found} \\
KSLOC &= \text{thousand lines of executable source code plus data declarations}
\end{aligned}
$$

The standard indicates that this metric can be applied during all eight lifecycle phases. However, it is difficult to imagine how it could be applied to the concept or requirements phases since no 'lines of executable source code or data declarations' will exist at that time. If the definition of $KSLOC$ were modified to include formal specifications, such as VDM or Z, then the metric could be applied to all lifecycle phases. The ongoing results obtained from applying this metric during each of the final five lifecycle phases should be analyzed and compared for trends in increasing or decreasing fault density. The standard gives this metric an experience code of 2, indicating that it has received a moderate level of operational validity by industry.

Two variations can be made to this metric to enhance its usefulness for mission critical systems. First, an equivalent calculation could be performed by substituting function points (FP) for $KSLOC$, to minimize the problems countered with LOC as noted in Chapter 2.

Second, if the severity of the faults were distinguished, the calculation could be expanded to measure fault density by severity, such that:

$$
\begin{aligned}
F_{dsi} &= \text{fault density of } i\text{th severity level} \\
&= F_{si}/KSLOC \text{ (or } FP) \\
F_{s1} &= \text{number of negligible faults} \\
F_{s2} &= \text{number of marginal faults} \\
F_{s3} &= \text{number of critical faults} \\
F_{s4} &= \text{number of catastrophic faults}
\end{aligned}
$$

Likewise, the fault density could be calculated by the type of $KSLOC$ or FP: safety critical, safety related, and nonsafety related. As shown in Figure 10.8, this approach gives a more accurate and complete picture of the fault density for a mission critical system.

10.3.1.1.4 Reliability Growth and Projection Metrics

Reliability growth and projection metrics measure or estimate various aspects of operational readiness or stability of software artifacts throughout the lifecycle phases by examining the number of errors found to date, primarily by testing, and the time it took to find them. These metrics are the most well-known category of software reliability metrics because much has been written about them [22, 26] and new models are continually being developed.

Reliability Growth Function

The reliability growth function metric estimates when a desired failure rate or fault density will be achieved, such that [1, 2]:

$$
\begin{aligned}
R(k) &= \text{reliability growth function} \\
&= R(u) - A/K \\
\lim_{K \to \infty} R(k) &= R(u)
\end{aligned}
$$

where

$$
\begin{aligned}
NR_k &= \text{total number of test cases during the } k\text{th stage} \\
NS &= \text{total number of stages} \\
nc_k &= \text{total number of successful test cases during the } k\text{th stage} \\
A &= \text{growth parameter of the model}
\end{aligned}
$$

$R(u)$ and A are estimated by:

$$
\sum_{k=1}^{NS} (nc_k/NR_k - R(u) + A/k) = 0
$$

Fault Density Report

Phase/Date:_____

Software Type/ Fault Severity	Goal	Phase Reqts KSLOD	Des. KSLOD	Impl. FP[a]	Test FP	I&C FP	O&M FP
1. Safety-critical							
negligible							
marginal							
critical							
catastrophic							
total							
2. Safety-related							
negligible							
marginal							
critical							
catastrophic							
total							
3. Nonsafety-related							
negligible							
marginal							
critical							
catastrophic							
total							
4. Total System							
negligible							
marginal							
critical							
catastrophic							
total							

[a]KSLOC or FP can be used, as long as KSLOC is accurately and consistently defined.

Figure 10.8: Use of fault density metric for mission critical systems.

$$\sum_{k=1}^{NS}(nc_k/NR_k - R(u) + A/k)1/k = 0$$

The fault reinsertion rate (r) is estimated by:

$$\sum_{k=1}^{NS}(nc_k/NR_k - R(u) + A/(k(1-r)))1/(k(1-r)) = 0$$

As the standard notes, this metric requires a high degree of test coverage and consistency in testing from one stage to the next. The standard indicates that the reliability growth function metric can be used during the testing, installation and checkout, and operations and maintenance phases. The standard gives this metric an experience code of 2, indicating that it has received a moderate level of operational validity by industry.

To adapt this metric for use with mission critical systems, $R(k)$ should be calculated for safety-critical, safety-related, and nonsafety-related software, as well as for the whole system, as shown in Figure 10.9. In this example, testing has been divided into subphases.

Reliability Growth Report

Phase/Date:_____

Type of Software	Goal	Mod.	Int.	Phase Testing Syst.	Stress	I&C	O&M
1. Safety-critical							
2. Safety-related							
3. Nonsafety-related							
4. Total System							

Figure 10.9: Use of reliability growth function metric for mission critical systems.

Run Reliability

The run reliability metric, based on the standard definition for system reliability, calculates the probability that k randomly selected runs will produce correct results, such that [1,2]:

$$
\begin{aligned}
R_k \;&=\; \text{run reliability} \\
&=\; P_r^k \\
P_r \;&=\; \text{probability of a successful run} \\
&=\; nc/NR
\end{aligned}
$$

where

NR = number of runs in a given test sample

nc = number of correct runs in a given test sample

K = number of runs specified

S = sample space of possible unique input patterns and states which produce unique output patterns and states

P = probability measure over the sample space

P_i = probability that the ith run is selected from the sample space

As the standard notes, care needs to be taken in assigning a probability distribution. The easiest case is to assume a uniform probability distribution; however, it may not accurately reflect field operations. The standard indicates that this metric can be used during the test, installation and checkout, and operations and maintenance phases. The standard gives this metric an experience code of 2, indicating that it has received a moderate level of operational validity by industry.

This metric can easily be adapted for use with mission critical systems, as shown in Figure 10.10. The sample space is determined for the safety-critical, safety-related, nonsafety-related, and total system software and the run reliability is calculated accordingly.

Run Reliability Prediction Report

Phase/Date:_____

Type of Software	Goal	Test	I&C	O&M	Actual Observed
1. Safety-critical	.99				
2. Safety-related	.99				
3. Non-safety related	.95				
4. Total System	.97				

Figure 10.10: Use of run reliability metric in mission critical systems.

The information gained by identifying the unique input patterns and states and output patterns and states of the software partitions can be used in developing test cases. Then actual observed run reliability can be compared with predicted run reliability.

Software Maturity Index

The software maturity index metric evaluates the effect of changes from one baseline to the next to determine the stability and readiness of the software. The standard provides two different ways to calculate the software maturity index [1, 2]:

$$(1) \quad SMI \; = \; \text{software maturity index}$$

$$= \; \frac{M_t - (F_a + F_c + F_{del})}{M_t}$$

$$(2) \quad SMI \; = \; \frac{M_t - F_c}{M_t}$$

where

M_t = number of software functions or modules in current baseline

F_c = number of software functions or modules in current baseline that include internal changes from the previous baseline

F_a = number of software functions or modules in current baseline that have been added to previous baseline

F_{del} = number of software functions or modules not in current baseline that have been deleted from previous baseline

The standard indicates that this metric can be used in the concept, requirements, design, installation and checkout, and operations and maintenance phases. For this metric to be used in the concept or requirements phases the specifications would have to be written in a manner such that intended functions and subfunctions could be counted, such as in a formal specification. During the implementation and test phases many changes, additions, and deletions are often made. This metric could also provide a good indicator of stability (or lack thereof) during these phases. The standard gives this metric an experience code of 1, indicating that it has received a limited level of operational validity within industry.

The software maturity index can easily be adapted for use in mission critical systems by calculating this metric for each type of software, as shown in Figure 10.11.

Software Purity Level

The software purity level metric estimates the relative fault-freeness of software at a specified time or phase, such that [1, 2]:

$$PL \; = \; \text{purity level}$$

$$= \; \frac{\hat{Z}(t_o) - \hat{Z}(t_f)}{\hat{Z}(t_o)}$$

where

t_i = observed execution time between failures

t_f = length of time in current phase when fth failure detected

Software Maturity Index Report

Baseline/Date:_____

Type of Software	Phase								
	Goal	Con.	Reqts	Des.	Impl.	Test	I&C	O&M
1. Safety-critical modules/functions changes additions deletions								
SMI	.99							
2. Safety-related modules/functions changes additions deletions								
SMI	.98							
3. Nonsafety-related modules/functions changes additions deletions								
SMI	.95							
4. Total System modules/functions changes additions deletions								
SMI	.97							

Figure 10.11: Use of software maturity index metric for mission critical systems.

$$t_o \quad = \quad \text{start of the specified phase}$$

$$f \quad = \quad \text{total number of failures in a given time interval}$$

$$\hat{Z}(t) \quad = \quad \text{estimated hazard or failure rate at time } t$$

The standard indicates that this metric can be used during the test, installation and checkout, and operations and maintenance phases. The standard gives the software purity level metric an experience code of 1, indicating that it has received a limited level of operational validity by industry. As the standard notes, this metric is limited to projects where a significant number of test cases and results can be observed. Likewise, the results obtained from this metric will vary depending on what model is used to determine the estimated hazard or failure rate.

If this metric is used for mission critical systems, the software purity level should be calculated for the safety-critical (PL_{sc}), safety-related (PL_{sr}), and nonsafety-related (PL_{nsr}) software, as well for the entire system (PL).

System Performance Reliability

The system performance reliability metric assesses system performance reliability in terms of the probability that specific performance requirements will be met. A variety of performance attributes are calculated [1,2]:

$$t \quad = \quad \text{average arrival rate of jobs}$$

$$ \quad = \quad A/T$$

$$x \quad = \quad \text{average throughput rate}$$

$$ \quad = \quad J/T$$

$$u \quad = \quad \text{average utilization}$$

$$ \quad = \quad SB/T$$

$$as \quad = \quad \text{average service time}$$

$$ \quad = \quad SB/J$$

$$WT \quad = \quad \text{waiting time distribution}$$

$$ \quad = \quad f(t, u, as, VR)$$

$$SE \quad = \quad \text{server efficiency per job}$$

$$ \quad = \quad A/(as + WT)$$

$$SPR \quad = \quad \text{total response time for each job over } k \text{ servers}$$

$$ \quad = \quad \sum_{i=1}^{K}(VR \times S)_i + \sum_{i=1}^{K}(VR \times W)_i$$

$$AQ \quad = \quad \text{average queue length}$$

$$ \quad = \quad W \times t$$

where

$$Q = \text{queue length distribution}$$

$$RT = \text{response time distribution}$$

$$ST = \text{service time distribution}$$

$$A = \text{number of functional job arrivals during time period } T$$

$$SB = \text{total amount of time server is busy}$$

$$J = \text{number of jobs completed during } T$$

$$VR = \text{number of requests per functional job for each server during time period } T$$

$$T = \text{time period over which measurements are made}$$

The standard indicates that this metric can be used in all lifecycle phases. However, it is hard to imagine any meaningful results being obtained during the concept or requirements phases. The standard gives this metric an experience code of 2, indicating that it has received a moderate level of operational validity by industry.

This metric is useful for assessing system resource utilization. Scenarios should be developed to evaluate system performance reliability during low, normal, and peak loading and the resultant impact on safety-critical and safety-related functions.

10.3.1.2   Process Metrics

Process metrics provide an assessment of the maturity and effectiveness of the process(es) used to develop a software system. The goal of collecting and analyzing process metrics is a repeatable, continually improving process which yields consistent results. There are two subcategories of process metrics that directly or indirectly relate to software safety and reliability: process/subprocess effectiveness metrics and management control metrics (see Table 10.2).

10.3.1.2.1   Process/Subprocess Effectiveness Metrics

Process/subprocess metrics measure the thoroughness of the development lifecycle activities.

Functional Test Coverage

The functional test coverage metric expresses the ratio between the number of functions tested and the total number of functions in a system, such that [1, 2]:

$$FTC = \text{functional test coverage}$$
$$= FE/FT$$

Attribute Measured	Metric	Applicable Lifecycle Phase(s)[a]	Source Definition
1. process/ subprocess effectiveness	a. functional test coverage	T IC OM	IEEE Std. 982.1,2
	b. test coverage	T IC OM	IEEE Std. 982.1,2
	c. review, audit, and inspection results	R D I T IC OM	new
	d. use of static and dynamic analysis tech.	R D I T IC OM	new
	e. use of standards	R D I T IC OM	new
2. management control	a. error distribution	R D I T IC OM	IEEE Std. 982.1,2
	b. fault days	R D I T IC OM	IEEE Std. 982.1,2
	c. staff-hours per defect detected	R D I T IC OM	IEEE Std. 982.1,2

[a]Lifecycle phases are defined as: R-requirements analysis, D-design, I-implementation, T-test, IC-installation and checkout, and OM-operations and maintenance. These may vary depending on the development methodology chosen.

Table 10.2: Process metrics [12].

where

FE = number of software functional requirements for which all test cases have been satisfactorily completed

FT = total number of software functional requirements

The standard indicates that this metric can be applied during the test, installation and checkout, and operations and maintenance phases. In fact, it should be applied repetitively during each of these phases to monitor improvements in functional test coverage for each build, version, release, and so forth. Ideally, the functional test coverage value should increase from phase to phase. The standard gives this metric an experience code of 2, indicating that it has received a moderate level of operational validity by industry.

This metric can easily be adapted for use with mission critical systems, as shown in Figure 10.12, by calculating the functional test coverage metric for the safety-critical, safety-related, and nonsafety-related functional requirements. This will insure that the safety functions receive an appropriate level of testing.

Test Coverage

The test coverage metric, a variation of the functional test coverage metric just discussed, is defined as [1, 2]:

Functional Test Coverage Report

Release/Phase/Date:_____

Type of Reqt.	Number of Reqts.	Goal	Mod.	Int.	Phase Testing Sys.	Stress	I&C	O&M
1. Safety-critical		.99						
2. Safety-related		.98						
3. Nonsafety-related		.95						
4. Total System		.97						

Figure 10.12: Use of functional test coverage metric for mission critical systems.

$$TC \quad = \quad \text{percent test coverage}$$
$$= \quad (IC/RC) \times (PT/TP) \times 100$$

where

$IC \quad = \quad$ implemented capabilities

$RC \quad = \quad$ required capabilities in system or subsystem

$PT \quad = \quad$ primitives tested

$TP \quad = \quad$ total number of primitives in system or subsystem

In this metric the primitive count includes both functional primitives, the number of unique branches or paths, and data primitives, the number of unique data equivalence classes. When evaluating test thoroughness, the number of unique paths to be exercised and the number of unique types of data with which they will have to interact need to be evaluated. This metric evaluates the robustness of the system under normal conditions, abnormal conditions, and during exception handling, which is particularly important to mission critical systems.

The test coverage metric can be used during the test, installation and checkout, and operations and maintenance phases. In fact it should be used repetitively during each of these phases to monitor improvements in test coverage. This metric is particularly useful during the operations and maintenance phase to verify the thoroughness of regression testing. The standard gives this metric an experience code of 2, indicating that it has received a moderate level of operational validity by industry.

This metric can easily be adapted for use with mission critical systems, as shown in Figure 10.13, by calculating the test coverage metric for the safety-critical, safety-related, and nonsafety-related primitives. This will insure that the safety functions receive an appropriate degree of testing.

This book proposes three new metrics to measure process effectiveness. First, the results of reviews, audits, and inspections are evaluated. Next the effective use of multiple

Test Coverage Report

Release/Phase/Date:_____

Type of Primitive	Number of Primitives	Goal	Mod.	Int.	Phase Testing Sys.	Stress	I&C	O&M
1. Safety-critical		.99						
2. Safety-related		.98						
3. Nonsafety-related		.95						
4. Total System		.97						

Figure 10.13: Use of test coverage metric for mission critical systems.

complementary static and dynamic analysis techniques, as discussed in Chapter 2, is evaluated. Following this, the effective use of national, international, and/or corporate standards is evaluated.

Review Results

The review results metric measures the effectiveness and thoroughness of the reviews conducted during the lifecycle phases and the results obtained from them. Using IEEE Std. 1028-1997 as a guide, it measures:

- the number and type of reviews held;

- whether the reviews passed, passed with corrective action required, or failed; and

- the number and severity of the corrective action items.

The type of reviews is distinguished by management reviews, technical reviews, software inspections, software walkthroughs, software audits, and whether they were in-process or final reviews. (See Figure 10.14.) If few or no corrective action items are found, particularly during in-process reviews, this may imply that the reviews were not very thorough. On the other hand, if a number of reviews failed or have a large number of corrective action items, this may indicate the need for process improvement.

Static and Dynamic Analysis

The static and dynamic analysis metric, based on Figure 2.9, measures the effective use of complementary techniques. The key is to use a combination of complementary techniques from each quadrant in Figure 2.9, for example, (cause consequence analysis, truth tables, formal specifications, testability analysis) + (Fagan inspection, formal scenario analysis) + (boundary value analysis, fault injection) + (traditional testing); not redundant techniques

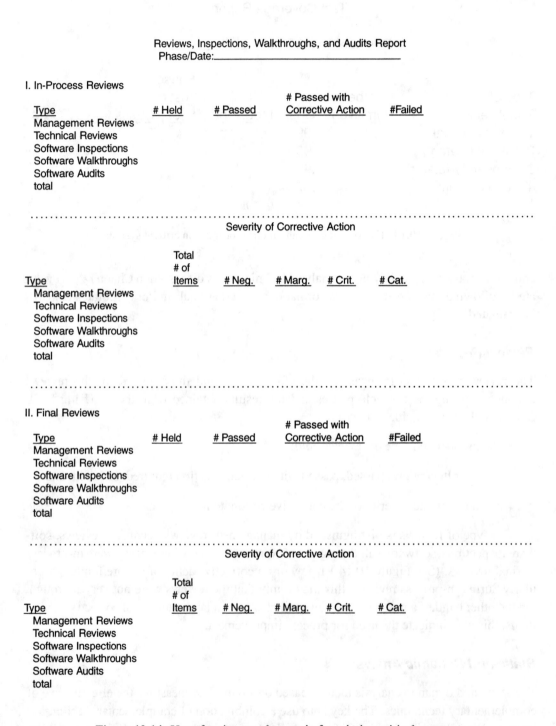

Reviews, Inspections, Walkthroughs, and Audits Report
Phase/Date:_____

I. In-Process Reviews

Type	# Held	# Passed	# Passed with Corrective Action	#Failed
Management Reviews				
Technical Reviews				
Software Inspections				
Software Walkthroughs				
Software Audits				
total				

Severity of Corrective Action

Type	Total # of Items	# Neg.	# Marg.	# Crit.	# Cat.
Management Reviews					
Technical Reviews					
Software Inspections					
Software Walkthroughs					
Software Audits					
total					

II. Final Reviews

Type	# Held	# Passed	# Passed with Corrective Action	#Failed
Management Reviews				
Technical Reviews				
Software Inspections				
Software Walkthroughs				
Software Audits				
total				

Severity of Corrective Action

Type	Total # of Items	# Neg.	# Marg.	# Crit.	# Cat.
Management Reviews					
Technical Reviews					
Software Inspections					
Software Walkthroughs					
Software Audits					
total					

Figure 10.14: Use of review results metric for mission critical systems.

(cause consequence analysis, SFMEA, SFTA) [12]. By using multiple static and dynamic, logical and functional techniques, a larger number and different types of errors will be uncovered and they will be uncovered earlier [9, 13–15, 19, 20, 29]. See Figure 10.15.

Use of Standards

The use of standards metric measures the effective use national, international, and corporate standards. In the contractual and regulatory environments, the standards to be followed are often mandated. In that case this metric should be used to measure adherence to mandated standards. In other environments, the appropriate use of standards needs to be evaluated on a case by case basis. Some questions to be evaluated include:

- Has a software engineering/lifecycle process standard been specified, such as IEC 12207?

- Have software quality management standards been specified, such as ISO 9001 and 9000-3?

- Has a software safety standard been specified, such as IEC 61508 Part 3?

- Has a software reliability standard been specified, such as SAE JA 1002?

- Is the project staff knowledgeable about and experienced in using the specified standards?

- Is the project staff complying with the specified standards?

- Given the project size, complexity, criticality, and duration, has an appropriate and compatible set of standards been specified?

10.3.1.2.2 Management Control Metrics

Management control metrics evaluate various aspects of the efficiency by which personnel resources are applied to the prevention, detection, and removal of errors.

Error Distribution

The error distribution metric, a variation of the fault days metric, monitors the phase in which errors were introduced, the type and severity of the errors. Error types include: logic errors, interface errors, integration errors, human computer interaction (HCI) errors, requirements translation errors, and so forth. The number of errors found is measured against the phase, severity, and type. The standard notes that this metric can be used during all lifecycle phases except concept. The standard gives this metric an experience code of 1, indicating that it has received a limited level of operational validity by industry.

This metric is a useful project management tool because it provides an ongoing picture of a system's error history throughout the lifecycle and highlights processes that need

Static and Dynamic Analysis Metric Report
Phase/Date:_____

I. Static Analysis Techniques Used
A. Functional

	Phase							
	R	D	I	T	IC	OM	Redundant	Complementary

cleanroom analysis
code inspections (Fagan)
formal scenario analysis
HAZOP analysis
B. Logical
cause consequence analysis
common cause failure
control flow analysis
critical path analysis
data flow analysis
decision/truth tables
emulation
formal specifications/
   methods/proofs
change impact analysis
Petri nets
simulation
sneak circuit analysis
software FMEA
software FTA
testability analysis

. . . .

II. Dynamic Analysis Techniques Used
A. Functional

	Phase							
	R	D	I	T	IC	OM	Redundant	Complementary

module testing
subsystem testing
interface testing
system integration testing
stress testing
usability testing
regression testing
alpha testing
beta testing
B. Logical
boundary value analysis
branch or path testing
equivalence classes
failure assertion
fault injection
structural testing
trajectory or statistical
   based testing

Figure 10.15: Use of static and dynamic analysis metric for mission critical systems.

improvement. This metric can easily be adapted for use with mission critical systems, as shown in Figure 10.16, by depicting the number of errors as a function of severity and software type.

Fault Days

The fault days metric evaluates the number of days between the time an error is introduced into a system and when the fault is detected and removed, such that [1,2]:

$$
\begin{aligned}
FD &= \text{fault days for total system} \\
&= \sum_{i=1}^{I} FD_i
\end{aligned}
$$

where

$$
\begin{aligned}
FD_i &= \text{fault days for } i\text{th fault} \\
&= f_{out} - f_{in} \\
f_{in} &= \text{date error was introduced into the system} \\
f_{det} &= \text{date fault was detected} \\
f_{out} &= \text{date fault was removed from the system} \\
ph_{in} &= \text{phase error was introduced into the system} \\
ph_{det} &= \text{phase fault was detected} \\
ph_{out} &= \text{phase fault was removed from the system} \\
I &= \text{total number of faults found to date}
\end{aligned}
$$

If the exact date the error was introduced is not known, it is assumed to have occurred during the middle of the corresponding phase. As the standard notes, this metric can be used during all lifecycle phases. Using the definitions provided at the beginning of the standard, an anomaly found during the requirements phase would be considered an error. Anomalies found in later phases would be considered faults.

In addition to the values specified in the standard, others can be calculated from the primitives collected to provide indicators of the effectiveness of the lifecycle activities, in particular the verification activities:

$$
\begin{aligned}
FD_{find} &= \text{days to find an error} \\
&= \sum_{i=1}^{I} FD_{findi} \\
FD_{findi} &= \text{days to find } i\text{th error} \\
&= f_{deti} - f_{ini} \\
FD_{fix} &= \text{days to fix faults}
\end{aligned}
$$

Error Distribution Report

Phase/Date:_____

1. Safety-Critical Software

Error Severity

Error Type	# Neg.	# Mar.	# Crit.	# Cat.
a. logic				
b. interface				
c. integration				
d. HCI				
e. requirements				
f. other:				

2. Safety-Related Software

Error Severity

Error Type	# Neg.	# Mar.	# Crit.	# Cat.
a. logic				
b. interface				
c. integration				
d. HCI				
e. requirements				
f. other:				

3. Nonsafety-Related Software

Error Severity

Error Type	# Neg.	# Mar.	# Crit.	# Cat.
a. logic				
b. interface				
c. integration				
d. HCI				
e. requirements				
f. other:				

4. Total System Software

Error Severity

Error Type	# Neg.	# Mar.	# Crit.	# Cat.
a. logic				
b. interface				
c. integration				
d. HCI				
e. requirements				
f. other:				

Figure 10.16: Use of error distribution metric for mission critical systems.

$$= \sum_{i=1}^{I} FD_{fixi}$$

$$FD_{fixi} = \text{days to fix } i\text{th error}$$

$$= f_{outi} - f_{deti}$$

and

$$\text{average days to find an error} = FD_{find}/I$$

$$\text{average days to fix an error} = FD_{fix}/I$$

$$\text{average error duration} = (FD_{find} + FD_{fix})/I$$

The fault days metric can easily be adapted for use with mission critical systems, as shown in Figure 10.17, by calculating the number of: errors introduced, faults detected, and faults removed by severity level. This will give an accurate picture of the number and severity of the errors/faults in the system to date, as well as the effectiveness of ongoing verification activities.

Staff-Hours per Major Defect Detected

The staff-hours per major defect detected metric measures the efficiency of the inspection process, such that [1, 2]:

$$SH = \text{staff-hours per major defect detected}$$

$$= \frac{\sum_{i=1}^{I}(T_1 + T_2)_i}{\sum_{i=1}^{I} S_i}$$

where

$$T_1 = \text{preparation time expended by the inspection team for the } i\text{th inspection}$$

$$T_2 = \text{time expended by the inspection team to conduct the } i\text{th inspection}$$

$$S_i = \text{number of nontrivial defects detected during the } i\text{th inspection}$$

$$I = \text{total number of inspections conducted to date}$$

This definition assumes that all defects found are classified as either trivial or nontrivial. Depending on the lifecycle phase, development methodology, and automated tools used, the artifact inspected will vary. Hence, this metric can be used during all lifecycle phases. The standard gives this metric an experience code of 2, indicating that it has received a moderate level of operational validity by industry.

The standard provides some guidance on how to interpret the values calculated for SH. It recommends that SH should fall consistently between 3 and 5 for new software. If SH is much less than 3, the product may have a high defect density. If SH is much greater than 5, most likely the inspection process is not being implemented properly. The

Fault Days Report

Phase/Date:_____

I. Average Fault Days

Error/Fault Severity	# of Errors	Days to Detect	Days to Fix	Error Duration Days
a. negligible				
b. marginal				
c. critical				
d. catastrophic				
e. total				

. . . .

II. Number of Errors/Faults Processed per Phase

Error/Fault Severity	Reqts I D R[a]	Des. I D R	Impl. I D R	Phase Test I D R	I&C I D R	O&M I D R	Total to Date I D R
a. negligible							
b. marginal							
c. critical							
d. catastrophic							
e. total							

---

[a]I is the number of errors introduced, D is the number of errors detected, and R is the number of errors removed.

Figure 10.17: Use of fault days metric for mission critical systems.

standard recommends investigating either occurrence because the anticipated benefit from conducting an inspection (increased reliability) will not be achieved. This metric assumes consistency during the preparation and conduct of inspections, data collection, and among the experience level of the inspection teams.

This metric can easily be adapted for use with mission critical systems by redefining S_i such that:

$$
\begin{aligned}
S_{cati} &= \text{number of catastrophic defects detected during the } i\text{th inspection} \\
S_{criti} &= \text{number of critical defects detected during the } i\text{th inspection} \\
S_{mari} &= \text{number of marginal defects detected during the } i\text{th inspection} \\
S_{negi} &= \text{number of negligible defects detected during the } i\text{th inspection}
\end{aligned}
$$

SH is then calculated for S_{cat}, S_{crit}, S_{mar}, and S_{neg} as shown in Figure 10.18. This will ensure that the inspection process is equally effective for all error severity levels.

Staff-Hours per Defect Detected Report

Phase/Date:_____

Error Severity	(SH) Goal	Reqts	Des.	Impl.	Test	I&C	O&M	Total to Date
1. negligible number hours (SH)	3–5							
2. marginal number hours (SH)	3–5							
3. critical number hours (SH)	3–5							
4. catastrophic number hours (SH)	3–5							
5. total system number hours (SH)	3–5							

Figure 10.18: Use of staff-hours per defect detected metric for mission critical systems.

10.3.1.3   People/Resource Metrics

People/resource metrics measure the appropriateness and adequacy of the resources applied to a software project. These are the newest category of metrics to be developed and the definitions have not yet been standardized. Many people/resource metrics relate to project risk management. The goal of people/resource metrics is the timely delivery of usable products. The four subcategories of people/resource metrics are: competency, schedule reality, development environment, and human computer interaction (HCI) issues (see Table 10.3). Several of these metrics result in a qualitative assessment which can be translated into a two-tier (yes/no), three-tier (not met, met, exceeded), or five-tier quantitative measurement.

Competency

Competency metrics evaluate the skills, qualifications, and limitations of the professional staff. Specific attributes evaluated include the amount of relevant formal education, experience, and certification. Competency requirements are often mandated in the contractual and regulatory environments. Many initiatives related to competency are underway. ISO 9001 requires personnel to possess demonstrated professional competence through the appropriate formal education, experience, licensing, and certification to perform assigned tasks. The American Society for Quality (ASQ) began its first examination process for certifying software quality engineers (CSQE) in October 1996. The IEEE standard taxonomy for software engineering standards [4] refers to competency as professional issues and lists the associated ethics, certification, licensing, and curriculum attributes. The U.K. and Canada are exploring the idea of requiring individuals involved in the development and assessment of safety-critical systems to be professionally certified. A model has been developed to identify the specific attributes, knowledge, and competence needed [10, 17, 24, 31].

Schedule Reality

Schedule reality metrics measure the appropriateness of: 1) the professional staff's skill mixture and availability; and 2) the mixture and availability of non–people resources. The goal is to have the right combination and quantity of resources, including people, available during the appropriate development lifecycle phases.

Development Environment

Development environment metrics measure the capabilities and limitations of the hardware, software, and communications resources used during the development lifecycle. Appropriate choices need to be made concerning the development and operational environments, because they will ultimately affect the safety and reliability of the system. These choices are particularly important when the development environment differs from the operational environment. Choices to be evaluated include: operating system(s), compiler(s), platform(s), automated tool usage, and known system constraints [20, 23, 33].

Attribute Measured	Metric	Applicable Lifecycle Phase(s)[a]	Source Definition
1. competency	a. relevant education	R D I T IC OM	new
	b. relevant experience	R D I T IC OM	new
	c. relevant certification	R D I T IC OM	new
2. schedule reality	a. skill mix & availability	R D I T IC OM	new
	b. equipment mix & availability	R D I T IC OM	new
3. development environment	a. hardware platform	R D I T IC OM	new
	b. OS(s) and utilities	R D I T OM	new
	c. compiler(s)	D I T IC OM	new
	d. automated tool usage	R D I T	new
	e. relation to operational environment	D I T IC	new
	f. known system constraints	R D I T IC OM	new
4. HCI issues	a. domain knowledge	R D I T IC OM	new
	b. HAZOP	R D I T	new
	c. formal scenario analysis	R D I T	new
	d. operational profiles	R D I T IC	new
	e. end-user training	IC OM	new
	f. instructions for use	T IC OM	new

[a]Lifecycle phases are defined as: R-requirements analysis, D-design, I-implementation, T-test, IC-installation and checkout, and OM-operations and maintenance. These may vary depending on the development methodology chosen.

Table 10.3: People/Resource metrics [12].

There are many issues to evaluate in the selection of an operating system. At a minimum the following questions should be asked. Is the operating system: real time, multiuser, single-user, multitasking or single-tasking? Was the operating system developed and certified to a national or international standard? Is the observed reliability of the operating system acceptable? What effect will the use of one operating system in the development environment and another in the operational environment have on the resultant safety and reliability? Has the operating system been optimized for the target hardware platform? How stable is the operating system in terms of the frequency of new releases and the availability of long-term support? Is the development team proficient with this particular operating system?

Many of the same issues should be evaluated in the selection of a compiler. In addition, it should be determined if the compiler was: 1) developed and certified according to a national or international standard; and 2) optimized for the target operating system and given application, such as scientific calculations, manipulating text or images, or data communications. Wichmann [33] has identified some safety issues raised in the selection of a computer language.

The appropriateness of the hardware platform should also be evaluated. The platform needs to accommodate all known logistical constraints (physical size, weight, memory, interfaces, and so forth) as well as environmental tolerances. The functional characteristics of the platform (accuracy, speed, precision) must also be evaluated.

HCI

HCI metrics measure the thoroughness to which HCI issues which affect safety and reliability have been addressed. The first concern is how well the domain knowledge has been captured; the absence of which could lead to serious errors of omission [13,23,28]. Next, an evaluation is made as to whether or not a HAZOP study and/or formal scenario analysis has been conducted, leading to the development of operational profiles. Lastly, the thoroughness of end-user training and the currency, accuracy, completeness, and understandability of instructions for use are evaluated.

10.3.2   Interaction with System Safety and Other Standards

The standard indicates that it shall be used in conjunction with ANSI/IEEE 610.12-1990, IEEE Standard Glossary of Software Engineering Terminology, and AFOTEC Pamphlet 800-2, Software Maintainability – Evaluation Guide, Vol. 3, March 1987. This implies that these two standards are incorporated by reference and form part of this standard. No other normative references are provided.

10.3.3 Roles, Responsibilities, and Qualifications of Project Members

Since this standard is a dictionary of metrics, the roles, responsibilities, and qualifications of project members are not discussed other than the competence required to apply individual metrics, such as an understanding of probability and statistics.

10.3.4 Data Items Produced

No specific data items or documents are produced through adherence to this standard other than the results obtained from the calculations. This book illustrates how to adapt the metrics for use in mission critical systems and provides sample report formats.

10.3.5 Compliance Assessment

The standard does not address the issue of compliance assessment, other than to state that successful application of the metrics is dependent on using them for their intended use and in the specified environment(s).

10.3.6 Scaling

The standard does not address the issue of scaling the metrics to correspond to the size and complexity of a particular project. On occasion, the standard mentions that successful use of a specific metric requires a large number of test cases or similar criteria.

10.4 Strengths

IEEE Stds. 982.1 and 982.2 represent a good first step to collect, document, and standardize in one place the majority of the metrics that relate directly or indirectly to software safety and reliability. The definitions of the metrics are for the most part succinct. The primitives collected can be used to calculate multiple metrics. Many of the metrics can be adapted for use with mission critical systems as demonstrated in this chapter. The standard categorizes the metrics as product or process metrics and identifies the lifecycle phase(s) in which to use them. The sheer number and variety of metrics defined in IEEE Stds. 982.1 and 982.2 reinforces the standard's contention that multiple complementary metrics should be used throughout the software lifecycle. The assignment of an experience code informs the reader of the extent to which each metric has been successfully moved from theory to practice.

10.5   Areas for Improvement

The following areas for improvement are presented for consideration when IEEE Stds. 982.1 and 982.2 undergo their next update/revision cycle. In addition, standardized definitions for the new metrics proposed by this book should be considered during the revision/update process.

The standard presents the metric definitions in a random order; this chapter compensates for that deficiency by organizing the metrics in categories and subcategories. The approach used in the standard to categorize the metrics needs to be refined. For example, the table assigns many metrics to multiple categories. Likewise, some of the lifecycle phase assignments are not practical, as shown in this chapter. Also, as noted in the discussion, some of the definitions use the terms error, fault, and failure in conflict with the definitions provided at the beginning of the standard. The experience codes reflect the status quo as of 1989; they need to be updated. The standard encourages the use of multiple complementary metrics throughout the software lifecycle. However, it provides no guidance on how to accomplish this; Section 10.8 of this chapter addresses this deficiency.

All of the metrics defined in IEEE 982.1 and 982.2 are quantitative, many of them are time related. No metrics are defined which support qualitative assessments; some should be added. All of the metrics defined are product or process metrics; no people/resource metrics are defined to complete the P^3R equation. This book addresses that deficiency through the discussion in Section 10.3.1.3.

10.6   Relationship to Other Approaches

Because this standard is a dictionary of software reliability metrics, it does not correspond to any other standard discussed in this book or available elsewhere. There is no equivalent ISO or IEC standard. Lyu [22] discusses several software reliability metrics, similar to those discussed in Section 10.3.1.1.4, however until recently these definitions had not been standardized by any national or international standards body. BS 5760 Part 8 is a first step in that direction.[5]

10.7   Results Observed to Date

The assigned experience codes are based on published results relating to the use of individual metrics which were available at the time the standard was approved. An effort was begun in mid 1999 to update IEEE Std. 982.1 and IEEE Std. 982.2.

---

[5]BS5760 Part 8: Guide to the Assessment of Reliability of Systems Containing Software, British Standards Institution (BSI), October 1998.

10.8 Summary

This chapter presents 44 metrics and 18 sample report formats, which are organized in three main categories and ten subcategories. The value of the metrics and sample reports discussed in this chapter is that they can be used to satisfy the requirement in other standards, such as IEC 61508 Part 3, to demonstrate a specific software reliability and/or integrity level. The number and type of metrics used will vary depending on the criticality, complexity, and duration of a project and contractual or regulatory requirements. For example, one project may only use 8–10 metrics, while another may require 20+ metrics to perform an adequate assessment. Likewise, the metrics used may vary by lifecycle phase.

Software safety and reliability metrics should be collected, integrated, and analyzed throughout the development lifecycle so that corrective and preventive action can be taken in a timely and cost effective manner. It is too late to wait until the testing phase to collect and assess software safety and reliability information, particularly for mission critical systems. It is inadequate and can be misleading to only use the results obtained from testing to make a software safety or reliability assessment. To remedy this situation a holistic model which captures, integrates, and analyzes product, process, and people/resource (P^3R) metrics, as recommended by Littlewood [21], is needed.

The purpose of a holistic model is to assess software safety and reliability by examining a multitude of varied aspects about a system and its development. A holistic model provides a more complete profile of safety and reliability by synthesizing multiple data points. This is a major paradigm shift from traditional software reliability models which focus on single data points gathered during testing. Instead, product, process, and people/resource (P^3R) metrics are collected, integrated, and analyzed throughout the development lifecycle.

The key is to use multiple complementary metrics, such as (requirements traceability + design integrity + performance measures), not single or redundant metrics (completeness + requirements compliance + requirements traceability) [12,21]. Individual metrics should be chosen from each category and subcategory, as appropriate, which measure different aspects of the Product, Process, and People/Resource (P^3R) maturity and capability. Goals should be established for each metric, each category of metrics, for specific phases, and overall. Evaluation criteria should be established to determine the acceptability of the actual results obtained from each metric and how they compare to the goal. This process is then repeated for each type of metric and the three categories collectively (see Table 10.4). From this more complete, ongoing, and holistic view, an informed assessment can be made about safety and reliability.

Integrated Product, Process, and People/Resource Metrics Report[a]
Phase/Date:_____

Type of Metric	Metric Category	Results Goal	Actual	Evaluation
Product[b]	1. completeness & consistency	c. 99% d. 5 e. 10		
	2. complexity	a. 10 c. .75		
	3. error, fault, & failure	b. .01%		
SUBTOTAL				
Process[c]	1. process/ subprocess effectiveness	a. 87% c. 3		
	2. management control	c. 3		
SUBTOTAL				
People/Resource[d]	1. competency	a. 3 b. 3 c. 3		
	2. schedule reality	a. 3 b. 3		
	3. development environment	a. 3 b. 3 c. 3 d. 3 e. 3		
	4. HCI issues	a. 3 b. 3 c. 3 d. 3 e. 3 f. 3		
SUBTOTAL				
TOTAL VIEW				
Current Phase				
To Date				

[a]Goals and actual results will vary from project to project. These values represent a summary or "roll-up" of the individual metric reports discussed earlier.

[b]Depending on project need, goals could be established for: 1) each software partition (safety-critical, safety-related, nonsafety-related) and the system; 2) each error severity category (negligible, marginal, critical, catastrophic); and 3) each lifecycle phase.

[c]For item 1c, this value indicates that the goals set for individual values on the Reviews, Inspections, Walkthroughs, and Audits Report were met or exceeded in all cases.

[d]A "3" for each of these metrics indicates that the minimum requirement was exceeded.

Table 10.4: Integrated product, process, and people metrics [12].

10.9   Discussion Problems

1. Which product metrics defined in Table 10.1 could be considered redundant or overlapping? Why?

2. What is the difference between the fault density and defect density metrics?

3. Assume that you are responsible for assessing a system which performs safety-critical functions. This system includes custom code, reused code, and commercial off-the-shelf (COTS) code. The functionality of this system is not overly complex; however, some of the requirements are a bit ambiguous. The final product will be an embedded real-time system with no user interface, other than at system initialization. What product and process metrics would you use during the requirements analysis and design phases to assess this system?

4. Explain the different types of information reported from the fault days and staff-hours per defect detected metrics.

5. Explain how use of the static analysis metric complements planning an appropriate strategy for dynamic analysis.

6. Develop a methodology to correlate the review results metric and the error distribution metric as part of a built-in cross-check analysis.

7. Explain the correlation between the competency subcategory of metrics and the skill mix and availability metric.

8. What factors need to be analyzed when comparing the development and operational environments? How does this relate to the known system constraints metric?

9. Explain the difference between the HAZOP, formal scenario analysis, and operational profiles metrics.

10. Develop an Integrated Product, Process, and People/Resource (P^3R) Report for the system described in question 3. Note changes that would occur in the report as the system progressed through the different lifecycle phases.

Additional Resources

Primary Works Cited

[1]   ANSI/IEEE Std. 982.1-1989, IEEE Standard Dictionary of Measures to Produce Reliable Software.

[2]   ANSI/IEEE Std. 982.2-1989, IEEE Guide for the Use of IEEE Standard Dictionary of Measures to Produce Reliable Software.

Related Safety, System, and Software Engineering Standards.

[3] ANSI/IEEE 610.12-1990, IEEE Standard Glossary of Software Engineering Terminology.

[4] ANSI/IEEE Std. 1002-1992. IEEE Standard Taxonomy for Software Engineering Standards.

[5] ANSI/IEEE Std. 1061-1998. IEEE Standard for a Software Quality Metrics Methodology.

[6] IEC 61508-7: Functional safety of electrical/electronic/programmable electronic safety-related systems – Part 7: Overview of Techniques and Measures, August 1998 (draft).

[7] AFOTEC Pamphlet 800-2, Software Maintainability – Evaluation Guide, Vol. 3, March 1987.

Selected Bibliography

[8] Bieda, John. "Software Reliability: A Practitioner's Model," *Reliability Review*, June 1996, Vol. 16, No. 2, pp. 18–28.

[9] Dale, C. "Report of the 44th Club Meeting—How Much Does Quality Cost? Northern Telecom Experience (Dave Homan)," *Software Reliability and Metrics Club Newsletter*, March 1995, p. 7.

[10] Falla, M. "Safety-Critical Software Professionals in the British Computer Society Industry Career Structure," *Safety-Critical Systems*, Chapman & Hall, 1993, pp. 181–192.

[11] Fenton, N.E. *Software Metrics: A Rigorous Approach*, Chapman and Hall, 1993.

[12] Herrmann, D. "Sample Implementation of the Littlewood Holistic Model for Assessing Software Quality, Safety, and Reliability," *Proceedings of the Annual Reliability and Maintainability Symposium (RAMS '98)*, IEEE, Anaheim, CA, January 19–22, 1998,

[13] Herrmann, D. "Software Safety and Reliability in the Regulatory Environment," *Safety and Reliability for Medical Device Software*, Health Industries Manufacturers Association (HIMA) Report No. 95-8, 1995, tab 8.

[14] Herrmann, D. "A Preview of IEC Safety Requirements for Programmable Electronic Medical Systems," *Medical Device and Diagnostic Industry*, June 1995, pp. 106–110.

[15] Herrmann, D. and Zier, D. "Using IEC 601-1-4 to Satisfy the Requirements of the FDA Software Guidance," *Medical Device & Diagnostic Industry*, December 1995, pp. 104–107.

[16] Hsia, Pei. "Testing the Therac-25: A Formal Scenario Approach," *Safety and Reliability for Medical Device Software*, Health Industries Manufacturers Association (HIMA) Report No. 95-8, 1995, tab 6.

[17] Jackson, D. "Target Qualities of Safety Professionals," *Safety-Critical Systems*, Chapman & Hall, 1993, pp. 139–152.

[18] Kan, S.H. *Metrics and Models in Software Quality Engineering*, Addison-Wesley, 1995.

[19] Lawrence, J.D., Persons, W.L., and Preckshot, G.G. "Evaluating Software for Safety Systems in Nuclear Power Plants," *Proceedings of the Ninth Annual Conference on Computer Assurance*, 1994, pp. 197–207.

[20] Leveson, N.G. *Safeware: System Safety and Computers*, Addison-Wesley, 1995.

[21] Littlewood, B. "The Need for Evidence from Disparate Sources to Evaluate Software Safety," *Directions in Safety-Critical Systems*, Springer-Verlag, 1993, pp. 217–231.

[22] Lyu, Michael R. (ed.), *Handbook of Software Reliability Engineering*, IEEE Computer Society Press and McGraw-Hill, 1996.

[23] McDermid, J.A. "Issues in the Development of Safety-Critical Systems," *Safety-Critical Systems*, Chapman & Hall, 1993, pp. 16–42.

[24] McGettrick, A. "The IEE Draft Policy on Educational Requirements for Safety-Critical Systems Engineers," *Safety-Critical Systems*, Chapman & Hall, 1993, pp. 160–166.

[25] Melton, A. (ed.) *Software Measurement*, International Thomson Computer Press, 1996.

[26] Musa, J. *Software Reliability Engineering*, McGraw-Hill, 1999.

[27] Rees, R.A. "Detectability of Software Failure," *Reliability Review*, Vol. 14, No. 4, December 1994, pp. 10–30.

[28] Rugg, G. "Why Don't Customers Tell You Everything You Need to Know? or: Why Don't Software Engineers Build What You Want?," *Safety Systems*, Vol. 5, No. 1, September 1995, pp. 3–4.

[29] Salisbury, N. "What is the Value of Independence?," *Safety Systems*, Vol. 4, No. 2, January 1995, pp. 7–8.

[30] Software Productivity Consortium, *The Software Measurement Guidebook*, International Thomson Computer Press, 1996.

[31] Thomas, J. "An Industry View of Training Requirements for Safety-Critical Systems Professionals," *Safety-Critical Systems*, Chapman & Hall, 1993, pp. 173–180.

[32] van der Muelen, M.J.P. *Definitions for Hardware/Software Reliability Engineers*, Simtech b.v., 1995.

[33] Wichmann, B.A. "Producing Critical Systems—the Ada 9X Solution," *Technology and Assessment of Safety Critical Systems*, Springer-Verlag, 1994.

Chapter 11

IEEE Std. 1228-1994, Standard for Software Safety Plans

11.1   Background

The Software Engineering Standards Committee (SESC) of the Institute of Electrical and Electronics Engineers, Inc. (IEEE) has oversight authority for the generation, approval, and promulgation of software engineering standards. Individual standards are developed by Technical Committees (TCs) and Working Groups (WGs) composed of volunteer representatives. Balloting is by individuals, not organizations or countries; members of the SESC Balloting Pool must be members of the IEEE Computer Society. IEEE Standards "represent a consensus of the broad expertise on the subject within the Institute [1]" as well as those who participate in the TCs, WGs, and balloting pool. The first IEEE software engineering standard was issued in 1980; since then more than 40 new standards have been developed. All IEEE software engineering standards are subject to a five-year review, reaffirm, update, or withdrawal cycle. After approval by the balloting pool and SESC, most IEEE software engineering standards are submitted to the American National Standards Institute (ANSI) for balloting and adoption as an American National Standard.

11.2   Purpose and Scope

In the early 1990s the IEEE SESC formed the Software Safety Plans Working Group. The group's charter was to develop a standard which specified "the minimum acceptable requirements for the content of a software safety plan ... which is used for the development, procurement, maintenance, and retirement of safety-critical software [1]." The result was IEEE Std. 1228 which was approved in March 1994.

IEEE 1228 restricts itself to software safety issues. However, it is expected that the software safety plan will be developed "within the context of the system safety program [1]." The standard states that it was specifically written for "those who are responsible for defining, planning, implementing, or supporting software safety plans [1]." The goal of the software safety plan is "to address the processes and activities intended to improve the safety of safety-critical software [1]." The standard defines the scope of safety-critical software as "software products whose failure could cause loss of life, serious harm, or have widespread negative social impact [1]." This standard does not distinguish between safety-critical and safety-related software; in addition, it uses the term 'accident' in the way that IEC standards use the term 'hazard.'

11.3   Description

To accomplish any endeavor a plan is needed to explain the activities to be undertaken, the resources needed to accomplish them, the sequence of events, and the evaluation criteria to determine if the plan has been fulfilled. The same is true for software safety; that is, a plan is needed to explain how software safety is going to be achieved and assessed on a given project.

11.3.1   Recommended and Required Practices

IEEE Std. 1228 defines a specific outline, both content and format, for a software safety plan (see Figure 11.1). This outline is comprehensive; it addresses product, process, and people/resource issues and covers the entire software development lifecycle from the concept phase through retirement. The outline also requires sections for process certification and plan approval, two topics that are often overlooked.

The topics covered by the plan fall into three categories: 1) managing software safety program activities; 2) performing software safety program activities; and 3) documenting software safety program activities.

11.3.1.1   Managing Software Safety Program Activities

If software safety is going to be achieved and assessed effectively on a project, certain management activities must be planned. The first step is to define the purpose and scope of the software safety plan and the software safety program; this should include a discussion of the software safety goals and objectives for the specific project, how these goals are going to be achieved and assessed, and a definition of acceptable risk for the project [23]. Information about the purpose and scope of the software safety plan and program is documented in section 1 of the plan.

The second step is to define project nomenclature and normative references. Project acronyms or abbreviations and their meanings should be listed. Standards which will be used on the project, such as documentation standards and design standards, should be cited, with the caveat that the latest version of each standard cited should be used. IEEE Std. 1228 requires that terminology used in the plan be consistent with IEEE 610.12-1990. An exception is permitted if a new definition "results in a significant improvement in clarity for all users of the plan [1]." Information about project nomenclature and normative references is documented in section 2 of the software safety plan.

The third step is to define project management functions, which will cover a variety of product, process, and people/resource issues faced by any software safety project. Organizational structure(s) and relationship(s) should be explained, in particular assigned activities

1.	PURPOSE
2.	DEFINITIONS, ACRONYMS, and ABBREVIATIONS and REFERENCES
3.	SOFTWARE SAFETY MANAGEMENT
3.1	Organization and Responsibilities
3.2	Resources
3.3	Staff Qualification and Training
3.4	Software Lifecycle
3.5	Documentation Requirements
3.6	Software Safety Program Records
3.7	Software Configuration Management Activities
3.8	Software Quality Management Activities
3.9	Software Validation and Verification Activities
3.10	Tool Support and Approval
3.11	Previously Developed or Purchased Software
3.12	Subcontract Management
3.13	Process Certification
4.	SOFTWARE SAFETY ANALYSIS
4.1	Software Safety Analysis Preparation
4.2	Software Safety Requirements Analysis
4.3	Software Safety Design Analysis
4.4	Software Safety Code Analysis
4.5	Software Safety Test Analysis
4.6	Software Safety Change Analysis
5.	POST DEVELOPMENT
5.1	Training
5.2	Deployment
5.2.1	Installation
5.2.2	Start-up and Transition
5.2.3	Operations Support
5.3	Monitoring
5.4	Maintenance
5.5	Retirement and Notification
6.	PLAN APPROVAL

Figure 11.1: IEEE Std. 1228 software safety plan outline [1].

and inherent responsibilities and authority [23]. Interaction between the system safety program and the software safety program must be described [23]. IEEE Std. 1228 expects that one person will have overall responsibility, oversight, approval, and enforcement authority to implement the software safety plan. That person should be identified by name in the plan. Likewise, the standard expects that the software safety program will have an appropriate degree of independence, similar to the Software Engineering Institute (SEI) Capability Maturity Model (CMM) Level 2 requirement for an independent Quality Management organization and reporting structure. This independence must be depicted in the software safety plan. The last organizational concern is the channels of communication within and among groups. The standard requires that a clear and open means of communicating safety concerns exist between the project staff and software safety program. Information about project management functions is documented in section 3.1 of the software safety plan.

The fourth step is to identify the resources required to implement the software safety plan and when they are needed; specific equipment, tools, funds, and personnel needs should be described. Along with this the minimum skill level, experience, and qualifications of personnel who will be involved in the analysis, design, implementation, validation, and verification of safety-critical software are identified [23]; that is, specific qualifications should be identified for each role or staff position, including Quality Management and Configuration Management. Information about resource requirements is documented in sections 3.2 and 3.3 of the software safety plan.

The fifth step is to explain subcontract management procedures. Most safety-critical projects today involve one or more prime contractors, subcontractors, vendors, and consultants. All of their activities need to be coordinated and consistent if the project is to succeed and safety goals and objectives are to be met [23]. How this is going to be accomplished, for example through staff meetings, design reviews, specifying standards in subcontracts, and so forth should be documented in section 3.12 of the software safety plan.

The sixth step is to define and certify lifecycle processes. Well-defined lifecycle processes, such as those promoted by IEEE Std. 1074 [15], ISO 9001 [16], ISO 9000-3 [17], and the SEI CMM [19] have been demonstrated to improve the quality of a software product. A study by Keene [22] proposes a correlation between CMM levels, the prediction of software reliability levels, and the achievement of safety integrity levels. Because of this the software safety plan should explain how lifecycle processes are going to be developed and approved and adherence to them monitored. If an organization has existing processes and/or a software engineering process group (SEPG), reference can be made to that fact. Process certification information should be documented in section 3.13 of the software safety plan.

The seventh step is to approve and release the software safety plan. Once the software safety plan has been written and coordinated with all stakeholders, it should undergo a formal approval, release, and maintenance process. This process will verify that the plan is accurate, complete, and realistic and will meet stated safety goals and objectives. This process will also ensure that the software safety plan is properly coordinated with the system safety plan and that all involved parties understand and are in agreement with it. After the plan is approved, it should be formally issued. Then the plan should go into a formal maintenance process to record any approved changes and to keep it current. The formal process(es) for approval, release, and maintenance of the software safety plan should be documented in section 6 of the plan.

11.3.1.2   Performing Software Safety Program Activities

If software safety is going to be achieved and assessed effectively on a project, certain activities must be performed. These activities include activities associated with the development of the product or system and the necessary prior preparation.

The first activity is to select a particular software development lifecycle model and methodology. This selection should be made and justified based on the size, complexity, duration, risk, and criticality of a project. The selected lifecycle methodology should be appropriate for the target system and compatible with the system engineering norms established for the project. The description must explain how activities of the software safety program will or will not be integrated with the development lifecycle and why; in other words will there be a separate software safety lifecycle and why was this determined (or not determined) to be beneficial. Information about the software development lifecycle and methodology should be documented in section 3.4 of the software safety plan.

Software safety analyses are conducted throughout the development lifecycle. The second activity is to plan what types of analyses will be conducted and when and how they will be conducted [23]. During the early lifecycle phases the emphasis will be on static analysis techniques. In later phases, a combination of static and dynamic analysis techniques will be used. It is important to select a complementary set of static and dynamic analysis techniques; more and different types of errors will be found by doing so and they will be found earlier when it is more cost effective to fix them [20, 23]. The types of analysis techniques should be selected based on the size, complexity, duration, risk, and criticality of the product or system. Another factor to consider when planning for software safety analyses, is whether or not the staff are knowledgeable and experienced in conducting the selected analytical techniques; if not plans should be made to acquire the specialized training. Activities related to planning and preparing for software safety analysis should be documented in section 4.1 of the software safety plan.

The third activity is to conduct the software safety requirements analysis. This analysis will indicate whether system safety requirements have been accurately allocated to software, that they have been refined adequately, and that there is traceability between system and software requirements [23]. This analysis will indicate whether or not the software safety requirements have the quality attributes of: accuracy, completeness, correctness, consistency, understandability, traceability, and testability [9]; in other words, objective acceptance criteria have been defined which demonstrate if each requirement has been met. Furthermore, the software safety requirements analysis will identify which software is and is not safety critical and requires partitioning, if necessary. Information about activities related to conducting the software safety requirements analysis is documented in section 4.2 of the software safety plan. The results of the software safety requirements analysis are documented in the software safety program records.

The fourth activity is to conduct the software safety design analysis. The software safety design analysis evaluates all aspects of the design to determine if the safety requirements have been incorporated accurately and effectively. The design analysis documents progress toward meeting stated system and software safety goals and objectives [23]. Logic, data, and interfaces are analyzed for both safety-critical and nonsafety-critical functions. The design is evaluated to determine if known system constraints, such as response times and memory utilization, have been taken into account adequately, particularly in regard to safety-critical functions. Preliminary timing and sizing estimates are prepared. An assessment is made whether or not the estimates are compatible with stated safety goals and objectives and system level requirements. Preliminary reliability estimates are similarly prepared and evaluated at this time. Information about activities related to conducting the software safety design analysis is documented in section 4.3 of the software safety plan. Results of the software safety design analysis are documented in the software safety program records.

The fifth activity is to conduct the software safety code analysis. This analysis evaluates the same issues that were evaluated during the design analysis: logic, data, interfaces, timing, and so forth. However, in this activity the emphasis is on the correct implementation of safety requirements. The programming style is also evaluated. Complexity is a concern because overly complex code complicates validation and verification efforts and maintainability. Complexity metrics, like those described in Chapter 10, can be used to aid in this analysis. Information about activities related to conducting the software safety code analysis is documented in section 4.4 of the software safety plan. Results of the software safety code analysis are documented in the software safety program records.

The sixth activity is to conduct the software safety test analysis. The software safety test analysis evaluates the results obtained during the test phase from using dynamic analysis techniques, such as module testing, system integration testing, stress testing, regression testing, usability testing, and beta testing. These results are analyzed and interpreted to determine if required acceptance criteria were met or not. The effect of meeting or not meeting acceptance criteria on the achievement of safety goals and objectives should be explained [23]. Any rework needed should be discussed. Metrics collected about the number, type, and severity of errors found and so forth should be presented with the analysis. Part of the analysis should be devoted to demonstrating that both the functional and structural test coverage was adequate for the criticality of the system. Any differences in testing conducted for safety-critical and nonsafety-critical software should be noted. Information about activities relating to conducting the software safety test analysis should be documented in section 4.5 of the software safety plan. Results obtained from conducting the test analysis should be documented in the software safety program records.

The seventh activity is to conduct the software safety validation and verification analysis. This analysis differs from the software safety test analysis discussed above. It captures the results of static analysis techniques and dynamic analysis techniques, other than testing, that are performed throughout the development lifecycle, beginning with the verification of requirements. Results from static and dynamic analyses are integrated, analyzed, and interpreted. In the beginning lifecycle phases, this information will provide an early indicator of whether or not the project is on track for meeting stated software safety goals and objectives [23]. Trends will become apparent from these activities [23]; for example one part of the requirements, design, or software having more errors than others. Metrics, such as those discussed in Chapter 10, should be collected and analyzed to highlight where and why errors are being introduced, the type and severity of errors found, and the interval between when an error was introduced, detected, and removed. This information should be presented as part of the analysis and used to prioritize future validation and verification activities. The analysis of validation and verification activities should highlight any differences observed in the results for safety-critical and nonsafety-critical software. A primary concern is that new hazards not be introduced during subsequent lifecycle phases or as risk control measures are implemented. Information about conducting activities related to the software safety validation and verification analysis should be documented in section 3.9 of the software safety plan. Results obtained from conducting this analysis should be documented in the software safety program records.

The eighth activity is to conduct the software safety change analysis. Software safety change analysis evaluates the impact of proposed changes on the system in general and on safety-critical functions in particular [23]. Changes are often proposed throughout the software lifecycle; some examples include requirements changes or clarification, changes in the user interface design, and changes in the target platform. IEEE Std. 1228 requires that formal change control procedures, such as those described in ANSI/IEEE Std. 828 [4], ANSI/IEEE Std. 1042 [12], ISO 9001 [16], and ISO 9000-3 [17], be in place on any project with safety-critical software. In this environment the configuration control board (CCB) focuses on the impact of proposed changes on overall safety and reliability. See Arnold [18] for a discussion of the latest techniques on how to conduct a thorough change impact analysis; too often a change impact analysis is too narrowly focused, which can have severe consequences in the safety-critical world. Information about conducting activities related to the software safety change analysis should be documented in section 4.6 of the software safety plan. Results obtained from performing the software safety change analysis should be documented in the software safety program records.

Today there is a greater emphasis than in the past on the use of off-the-shelf software, both in terms of automated software engineering tools and preexisting software components. This emphasis is derived from the fact that more tools and components are readily available and from the desire for greater economies of scale. Preexisting software components may take the form of commercial products, reused software that was developed for another project, and components from an object-oriented library. A process should be defined which explains, for all of the scenarios described above, how a determination will be made about the appropriateness and integrity of each proposed off-the-shelf software product and its intended use on the project. There are many concerns about the use of commercial software in safety-critical projects, as discussed in Chapter 2. In summary, few if any commercial products including software engineering tools are designed, built, validated, or verified to the same rigorous standards as safety-critical software. This fact must be given adequate consideration when evaluating the use of off-the-shelf software in a safety-critical project. Information about the activities related to approving or disapproving the use of off-the-shelf software and automated software engineering tools should be documented in sections 3.10 and 3.11 of the software safety plan. Any anomalies noted and suspected or confirmed safety problems associated with the use of off-the-shelf software should be documented in the software safety program records, along with their current status or resolution.

In addition to validation and verification activities, configuration management and quality management activities are ongoing throughout the software lifecycle. IEEE Std. 1228 is concerned with how these activities are performed on a project that has safety-critical or safety-related software. IEEE Stds. 730 [3] and 1028 [11] provide guidance on how to conduct these activities. The software safety plan should define the role and responsibilities of software quality management (SQM) on the project and the activities that will be conducted by the SQM staff to ensure that the safety goals and objectives are met. Specifically, the role of SQM in the preparation, approval, and effective implementation of the software safety plan should be described, as well as the SQM role in the software change control and approval process. The number, types, and scheduling of product and process reviews, audits, and inspections should be explained; any differences in these practices for safety-critical and nonsafety-critical software should be noted. The process for collecting, analyzing, and reporting the results of reviews, audits, and inspections should be explained in detail, including the use of metrics. Information about conducting SQM activities and the SQM role on the project should be documented in section 3.8 of the software safety plan. Results obtained from performing SQM activities should be documented in the software safety program records.

Likewise, the software safety plan should define the role and responsibilities of the software configuration management (SCM) on the project and the activities that will be conducted by the SCM staff. IEEE Std. 1228 expects that on a safety-critical project the SCM staff will be involved in version control, status reporting, and controlling access to all data items produced. This includes: lifecycle documentation, source code, object code, reused and off-the-shelf code, test cases and data, automated software engineering tools, and other products that comprise the development environment. The software safety plan should define the role and responsibilities of the SCM staff in regard to the change control, verification, and approval process for safety-critical software. SCM staff will create the builds used during testing and maintain baselines, along with a change history log. IEEE Stds. 828 [4] and 1042 [12] provide guidance in this area. Information about what activities are to be conducted by SCM and how and when they are to be conducted should be documented in section 3.7 of the software safety plan.

Software safety activities continue after the development lifecycle and through the transition to the operational environment. Planning and preparation for these activities should begin during the development lifecycle. The first post-development activity involves training. The operations and maintenance staff need to be trained in the correct operational procedures for the new system, particularly the procedures that relate to safety-critical functions [23]. They should also be made aware of any residual risk associated with the system [23]. If the end users differ from the operations staff, they should also be trained. This training should be comprehensive, not cursory, and allow plenty of time for the students to ask questions and become familiar with the new system. Activities related to planning and conducting post-development training should be documented in section 5.1 of the software safety plan. Lists of who attended and successfully completed training courses should be kept as part of the software safety program records.

The second post-development activity is to deploy the new system. Again planning and preparation for this activity should begin during the development lifecycle. Deployment activities will vary depending on the nature and intended use of the system. For example, the system may contain embedded software, it may perform real-time process control functions, or it may perform safety-critical diagnostic functions. In general, deployment will involve the installation, start up and transition, and cutover to standard operations. How and when these activities are to be conducted should be documented in section 5.2 of the software safety plan. Particular attention should be paid to the procedures for how to maintain the system in a known safe state at all times.

After a new system is deployed, monitoring will begin to ensure that it is performing accurately, safely, and reliably. This may involve a period of parallel operation of the old and new systems. The output or results obtained from each system when responding to identical stimuli is compared; any anomalies are noted and analyzed to determine their impact. Most safety-critical systems are monitored continuously; if a system operates in demand-mode it may only be monitored periodically. Again, the emphasis is on monitoring safety-critical functions and the ability to keep the system in a known safe state at all times. How and when monitoring activities are to be conducted should be documented in section 5.3 of the software safety plan.

Most all systems transition to a maintenance phase shortly after deployment. Maintenance activities may either be preventive, corrective, or adaptive in nature. The software safety plan should specify the process for how these activities are going to be controlled and approved, working with the SQM and SCM staffs, so that they do not negatively impact the operational safety of the system [23]. This process should specify how engineering change requests (ECRs) and system problem reports (SPRs) will be generated, evaluated, assigned, approved, and verified. The process should also specify how lifecycle artifacts and a change history log will be kept current during the maintenance phase. Information about maintenance activities should be documented in section 5.4 of the software safety plan.

The final phase of any system lifecycle is retirement or decommissioning. IEEE Std. 1228 requires that activities be undertaken to plan the retirement of a system. This should include planning for the replacement of the system, if appropriate; performing a safety impact analysis of retiring and/or replacing the current system; and ensuring that all affected parties receive adequate notification of the intended system retirement and an opportunity to provide input to this decision. Information related to the retirement of a safety-critical system should be documented in section 5.5 of the software safety plan.

11.3.1.3 Documenting Software Safety Activities

If software safety is going to be achieved and assessed effectively on a project, certain documentation activities must be planned. IEEE Std. 1228 stipulates that requirements for the content and format of lifecycle and project documentation be specified and adhered to. The standard gives the project the option of creating separate documentation for safety-critical software or developing a single set of documentation for safety-critical and non-safety-critical software. The plan should state which option was selected.

The minimum lifecycle documentation requirements for safety-critical software, defined by IEEE Std. 1228, are listed in Figure 11.2. Readers are referenced to the appropriate standards in the Additional Resources section at the end of this chapter for further guidance on the content and format of this documentation. Many of these items explain how software safety tasks and activities will be accomplished. Software project management documentation explains how the software safety program will be implemented within the context of the project and chosen development lifecycle. SCM documentation explains how configuration management activities and procedures will be used to capture and control safety-critical software and documentation; specific roles and responsibilities are identified. SQM documentation explains what SQM activities and procedures will be used to ensure that safety goals and objectives are met.

- Software Project Management
- Software Configuration Management
- Software Quality Management
- Software Safety Requirements
- Software Safety Design
- Software Development Methodology, Standards, Practices, Metrics, and Conventions
- Test Documentation
- Software Validation and Verification Procedures and Methods
- User Documentation

Figure 11.2: IEEE Std. 1228 minimum lifecycle documentation requirements for safety-critical software [1].

Software safety requirements documentation specifies requirements for the software to prevent and/or mitigate known or potential system hazards. These requirements are derived from the system safety specification, allocated to software, and must be consistent with safety goals and objectives stated in section 1 of the software safety plan.

The specified software development methodology, standards, practices, and/or conventions required to achieve project software safety goals and objectives are also documented. This includes a description of what standards and practices are to be followed, how they are to be implemented, during what lifecycle phases they are to be implemented, and the responsibilities and roles for implementing them and verifying that they have (or have not) been implemented correctly as planned. It must be demonstrated that the selected standards and practices are compatible and consistent with the selected software lifecycle, documented in section 3.4 of the software safety plan.

Test plans, procedures, and cases are required to be documented, in particular an explanation of how they evaluate safety-critical software. A test analysis report which documents, analyzes, and interprets testing results is required. This report should document how safety-critical software functions were tested at the software and system levels and how the test results demonstrated that stated software safety goals and objectives were or will be met [23].

The same process is followed for documenting validation and verification activities, procedures, and results. Validation and verification activities are ongoing throughout the development lifecycle and should include static and dynamic analysis techniques; hence the need to capture this information separately. Again, an analysis of the observed results is needed to demonstrate that stated software safety goals and objectives were or will be met [23].

The final category is user documentation, which in this case includes operations, installation, maintenance, and end-user manuals. All four categories should highlight correct procedures and sequences of events for safety-critical functions; in particular during error handling and abnormal operations. Procedures should be identified for putting the system into a known safe state, in the event of a failure, either through a graceful shutdown (fail-safe) or a transition to degraded-mode operations (fail-operational), as appropriate.

In addition to lifecycle documentation, IEEE Std. 1228 requires that software safety program records be kept. These records are similar to the risk management summary required by IEC 601-1-4 (see Chapter 7, Data Items Produced). Collectively, the software safety program records capture the evidence needed to demonstrate that stated software safety goals and objectives have or have not been met and that the residual risk is compatible with that which has been defined as acceptable for a project [23]. As shown in Figure 11.3, these records document the results of various activities and analyses, as discussed in Section 11.3.1.2. Suspected or confirmed safety problems which arise throughout the system lifecycle are documented in the software safety program records, along with the current status and/or resolution of each issue. These anomalies may be tied to the results of reviews, audits and inspections, testing, and/or SPRs generated in the field. The date an anomaly was observed should be recorded, along with an assessment of its severity. The software safety program records should also contain a chronological file of all safety certifications attempted and received, whether for an individual component, subsystem, or the entire system. The software safety program records are the primary records independent, third-party, and/or regulatory certification bodies will review before making a determination.

- Software Safety Requirements Analysis Results
- Software Safety Design Analysis Results
- Software Safety Code Analysis Results
- Software Safety Test Analysis Results
- Validation and Verification Results
- Software Safety Change Analysis Results
- Suspected or Confirmed Safety Problems
- Audit, Review, and Inspection Results
- Safety Training Records
- Safety Certification Records

Figure 11.3: Software safety program records [1].

11.3.2 Interaction with System Safety and Other Standards

IEEE Std. 1228 includes 14 standards as normative references (see Related Safety, System, and Software Engineering Standards at the end of this chapter). The standard stipulates that these 14 standards shall be used in conjunction with itself to perform the activities described in Section 11.3.1. In all cases, the latest version of any standard should be used.

11.3.3 Roles, Responsibilities, and Qualifications of Project Members

IEEE Std. 1228 requires that the organizational relationships of those responsible for creating, implementing, and enforcing the software safety plan be defined. While the standard requires that the qualifications of people responsible for implementing the plan be specified, no competency requirements are stated for the people who write the plan.

11.3.4 Data Items Produced

The only data item produced by adherence to this standard is the software safety plan. Implementation of the software safety plan produced by this standard will generate many other data items as shown in Figures 11.2 and 11.3.

11.3.5 Compliance Assessment

This standard defines the informational content and format of a software safety plan. To comply with the standard, each topic and subtopic must be addressed. If a topic is not applicable, that should be stated in the plan and an explanation of why it is not applicable should be provided. References can be made to appropriate sections in the system safety plan or other documents, rather than duplicating information. This will ensure that the most current information and version is used. Again, it is understood that the level of detail for each of these topics will be proportional to the size, complexity, duration, risk, and criticality of a project, as well as contractual and/or regulatory requirements.

11.3.6 Scaling

This standard identifies the minimum set of requirements for a Software Safety Plan. Accordingly, the only scaling permitted is to add additional or more specific requirements to the informational content and/or level of detail supplied.

11.4 Strengths

IEEE Std. 1228 has many strong points. For example, it is the first national or international consensus standard to define requirements for a software safety plan. A major benefit of IEEE Std. 1228 is that it can be used to satisfy the requirements of other standards, such as IEC 61508 Part 3 and IEC 601-1-4, for a software safety plan. The standard is very comprehensive and specifies an outline for the content and format of a software safety plan that covers managing, performing, and documenting the activities which comprise a software safety program. The standard relies on an extensive set of analyses, conducted throughout the lifecycle, to accomplish the safety goals and objectives stated in the plan. The standard covers the entire lifecycle from concept through retirement and views the software safety program as a component of the overall system safety program.

11.5 Areas for Improvement

IEEE Std. 1228 could be improved in a few areas which would broaden its general applicability and usability. The first area concerns terminology. This standard relies on IEEE 610.12-1990 for general software engineering terms and adds a few safety definitions itself. IEC has developed a large set of safety standards for electronic systems. Since IEEE Std. 1228 is the only IEEE standard to address software safety issues, it would be more appropriate to use IEC safety terminology. Secondly, IEEE Std. 1228 should distinguish between safety-critical and safety-related software to be consistent with other standards and common regulatory practices. Thirdly, the standard should move to only levying requirements for informational content and not levying requirements for format. Again, this would make IEEE Std. 1228 consistent and compatible with IEC standards. It would also be beneficial since IEEE Std. 1228 can be used to satisfy the requirements of several IEC standards for a software safety plan. (This suggestion is consistent with the IEEE 1998 Master Plan for Software Engineering Standards [21] to emphasize content and not format.) Fourthly, the standard only addresses hardcopy software safety plans. Many companies are moving toward keeping project documentation online to make sure all stakeholders have access to the documentation and more importantly access to the most current version. IEEE Std. 1228 should be updated to accommodate electronic documentation systems.

11.6   Results Observed to Date

No systematic study has been documented that evaluates the results of using this standard.

11.7   Summary

IEEE 1228 is a standard for developing software safety plans. It specifies both the informational content and format for such a plan. The outline is comprehensive; it addresses product, process, and people/resource issues and covers the entire software development lifecycle from the concept phase through retirement. The activities described by the software safety plan fall into three categories: 1) managing software safety activities; 2) performing software safety activities; and 3) documenting software safety activities. These are the activities that comprise any software safety program. IEEE Std. 1228 considers the software safety program to be part of and therefore consistent with the overall system safety program. Software safety plans developed in accordance with this standard can be used to satisfy the requirement of other standards for such a plan.

11.8   Discussion Problems

1. How do the Software Safety Program Records differ from the lifecycle documentation?

2. How are sections 4.6, software safety change analysis, and 5.4, maintenance, of the software safety plan different?

3. Who has the authority to modify the software safety plan? To enforce compliance with the plan?

4. Which sections of the software safety plan are optional? Which can be tailored?

5. Is this standard applicable to a project that only has safety-related software?

6. What additional SCM activities, beyond those associated with a traditional development lifecycle, are required to be explained in the software safety plan?

7. What additional SQM activities, beyond those associated with a traditional development lifecycle, are required to be explained in the software safety plan?

8. Describe a strategy for maintaining consistency and traceability between the system safety plan and the software safety plan.

9. Why is a separate software safety plan needed?

10. Where in the software safety plan are the software safety goals and objectives stated? The acceptable risk for a given project?

Additional Resources

Primary Work Cited

[1] IEEE Std. 1228-1994, IEEE Standard for Software Safety Plans.

Related Safety, System, and Software Engineering Standards

[2] ANSI/IEEE Std. 610.12-1990, IEEE Standard Glossary for Software Engineering Terminology.

[3] ANSI/IEEE Std. 730-1998, IEEE Standard for Software Quality Assurance Plans.

[4] ANSI/IEEE Std. 828-1998, IEEE Standard for Software Configuration Management Plans.

[5] ANSI/IEEE Std. 829-1998, IEEE Standard for Software Test Documentation.

[6] ANSI/IEEE Std. 830-1998, IEEE Recommended Practice for Software Requirements Specifications.

[7] ANSI/IEEE Std. 982.1-1989, IEEE Standard Dictionary of Measures to Produce Reliable Software.

[8] ANSI/IEEE Std. 1008-1993, IEEE Standard for Software Unit Testing.

[9] ANSI/IEEE Std. 1012-1998, IEEE Standard for Software Verification and Validation Plans.

[10] ANSI/IEEE Std. 1016-1998, Recommended Practice for Software Design Descriptions.

[11] ANSI/IEEE Std. 1028-1997, IEEE Standard for Software Reviews and Audits.

[12] ANSI/IEEE Std. 1042-1993, IEEE Guide to Software Configuration Management.

[13] ANSI/IEEE Std. 1058-1998, IEEE Standard for Software Project Management Plans.

[14] ANSI/IEEE Std. 1063-1993, IEEE Standard for Software User Documentation.

[15] IEEE Std. 1074-1997, IEEE Standard for Developing Lifecycle Processes.

[16] ISO 9001:1994, Quality Systems – Model for Quality Assurance in Design, Development, Production, Installation and Servicing.

[17] ISO 9000-3:1991, Quality Management and Quality Assurance Standards – Part 3: Guidelines for the Application of ISO 9001 to the Development, Supply and Maintenance of Software.

Selected Bibliography

[18] Arnold, R. and Bohner, S. *Software Change Impact Analysis*, IEEE Computer Society Press, 1996.

[19] Carnegie Mellon University Software Engineering Institute. *The Capability Maturity Model: Guidelines for Improving the Software Process*, Addison-Wesley, 1994.

[20] Herrmann, D. "Sample Implementation of the Littlewood Holistic Model for Assessing Software Safety and Reliability," *Proceedings of the International Symposium for Product Quality and Integrity (RAMS)*, IEEE, Anaheim, CA, January 19–22, 1998, pp. 138–148.

[21] *IEEE Master Plan for Software Engineering Standards*, 1998.

[22] Keene, S. "Modelling Software Reliability and Maintainability Characteristics," *Reliability Review*, ASQ, Part I, Vol. 17, No. 2, June 1997, pp. 5–28 and Part II, Vol. 17, No. 3, September 1997, pp. 13–22.

[23] Leveson, N. *Safeware: System Safety and Computers*, Addison-Wesley, 1995.

[24] McKinlay, A. "Software System Safety," *Proceedings of the 10th International System Safety Conference*, July 1991, p. 5.4-1-1 through p. 5.4-1-7.

Part IV

Observations and Conclusions

The 19 standards discussed in Parts II and III represent the current software safety and reliability thinking and best practices worldwide. As these standards illustrate, software safety and reliability issues and concerns cut across industrial sectors and technologies. Fifteen of the standards were issued within the last five years; three of these replaced earlier versions, while twelve were formally issued for the first time. This is not surprising since software safety and reliability engineering are relatively new engineering disciplines. Chapter 12 determines what general observations and conclusions can be drawn about the approaches taken by these standards.

Chapter 12

Software Safety and Reliability Techniques, Approaches, and Standards: Observations and Conclusions

Part I introduced the concept of software safety and reliability, the techniques used to achieve and assess it. Part II examined industry-specific software safety and reliability standards; while Part III explored software safety and reliability standards that can be used across multiple industrial sectors. Ten major recurring themes emerged from the standards throughout this process. The discussion that follows briefly reviews each of these themes and presents some concluding thoughts. (See Table 12.1.) As noted, the literature reinforces several of these themes [32, 47, 60].

12.1 Software safety is a component of system safety.

The majority of the standards discussed in this book view software safety as a component of system safety [1, 2, 5, 8, 9, 11–14]. This concept is also widely accepted in the literature [32, 47, 60]. Most include a normative reference to a system safety standard. The standards make clear that software safety, like chemical, electrical, mechanical, materials, radiation, and operational safety, contributes to system safety. In the same manner, data safety contributes to software safety [60]. There is agreement that a system component is not safe in and of itself, nor should it be analyzed in isolation [47, 60]. Likewise, a system is not safe in and of itself; rather a system is safe if all of its components and their interactions are safe.

Software, similar to other system components, has its own safety attributes, properties, and characteristics [47]. Some attributes are common across components, for example: predictable performance under normal and abnormal conditions, minimizing the likelihood of unplanned events, and controlling the consequences of unplanned events. Other attributes such as the ability to protect memory addresses or monitor the status of other system components, for example, hardware, in addition to itself, are unique to software.

1. Software safety is a component of system safety [1, 2, 5, 8, 9, 11–14, 32, 47, 60].

2. Software reliability is a component of system reliability [1–3, 5, 7, 9, 11, 29, 38, 42, 49, 52].

3. High integrity, high consequence, mission critical systems need to be both safe and reliable [38, 60].

4. A "good" software engineering process is insufficient by itself to produce safe and reliable software [1–3, 5, 8, 9, 12–14, 32, 47, 50, 60].

5. To achieve software safety and reliability, certain planning, design, analysis, and verification activities must take place [1–3, 5, 6, 8, 9, 11, 13, 14, 38, 47, 50, 60].

6. The achievement of software safety and reliability should be measured throughout the lifecycle by a combination of product, process, and people/resource metrics, both quantitative and qualitative [18, 38, 47, 48, 50, 51, 60].

7. Software safety and software reliability are engineering specialties which require specialized knowledge, skills, and experience [1–3, 5, 8, 9, 12–14, 17, 18, 47, 50, 60].

8. Some safety and reliability concerns are the same across industrial sectors and technologies, while some are unique.

9. Everyday examples should not be overlooked when classifying systems as safety critical or safety related [47, 50, 62].

10. A layered approach to standards is the most effective way to achieve both software and system safety and reliability [60].

Table 12.1: Major software safety and reliability themes.

Software safety design engineering employs techniques that are common to other system components and techniques that are unique to software [47]. Defense in depth is a technique that is widely used at the system and component levels [1, 5, 9, 11–14]. Partitioning, diversity, information hiding, defensive programming, and block recovery are examples of safety design techniques that are unique to software [1, 2, 5, 9, 11–14, 32, 47, 60]. Redundancy is commonly used in the hardware domain. However, it is of little value in the software domain because defects are simply replicated [47].

Software safety analysis and verification techniques include those which are used at the system and component levels, and those which are unique to software [47, 60]. FTA, FMECA, HAZOP studies, and sneak circuit analysis are examples of techniques that are widely used to analyze and verify the safety of components and systems [1, 2, 5, 9, 11–14, 32, 47, 55, 60]. Boundary value analysis, Formal Methods, equivalence class partitioning, and data flow analysis are examples of techniques that are primarily used to analyze and verify software safety [1, 2, 5, 9, 11–14, 32, 47, 55, 60].

The optimum approach is to employ a complementary set of safety design, analysis, and verification techniques at the system and component levels [32, 40, 47, 60]. This will provide feedback about all components so that the system architecture and design can be optimized for safety.

12.2   Software reliability is a component of system reliability.

The majority of the standards in this book agree that software reliability is a component of system reliability [1–3, 5, 7, 9, 11, 29, 38, 42, 49, 52]. All system components, like software, contribute to system reliability. Similarly, the reliability of data (for example, transmitted across communications interfaces, transferred between modules, and used in transactions) and the ability to protect it from corruption and tampering affects software reliability [60].

In general, the reliability of components is measured or predicted.[1] The measurements or predictions are combined to develop a reliability measurement or estimate for individual subsystems. A system reliability measurement or estimate represents a composite of component and subsystem measurements or predictions. Reliability measurements or predictions must factor in: 1) whether a component or subsystem executes serially, independently, or in parallel with other components and/or subsystems; and 2) whether a subsystem and/or system operates in demand mode, continuous mode, or standby mode [2, 5, 9, 11, 12, 29, 42, 49].

Software, like other components has attributes, properties, and characteristics which contribute to system reliability; some of these are the same as other components, some are unique. Reliable software produces accurate and consistent results that are repeatable

---

[1]Normal practice is to predict the reliability of a product before it is released. Then reliability is measured after a product is in the field. High integrity, safety-critical systems cannot afford to wait for reliability measurements from the field because of the consequences involved.

under low, normal, and peak loading conditions in the intended operational environment. As N. Storey [60] states, a comprehensive approach to fault management, which includes fault avoidance, fault removal, fault detection, and fault tolerance, is needed to achieve software reliability. Diversity, block recovery, voting logic, defense in depth, defensive programming, and error detection/correction are examples of software fault management design techniques promoted by the standards [1, 2, 5, 9, 11–14].

FMECA and reliability block diagrams are commonly used to analyze system and component level reliability. The development of operational profiles for software facilitates the assignment of values to nodes in an FMECA [49]. The optimum approach is to employ complementary system and software reliability design, analysis, and verification techniques. This will provide feedback about system components so that the architecture and design can be optimized for reliability.

As the standards note, there are several fundamental differences between software reliability and the reliability of other system components. First, software failures are systematic, in other words, the result of an error of omission or an error of commission during the development lifecycle [9, 50, 60]. In contrast, failures of other system components are random, in other words, the result of physical wear out over time and variability introduced during the manufacturing process [38, 47]. Second, software reliability is dependent on the logic path that is executed, not time [29, 51]. This gives rise to the concept of latent defects—defects that were present in the software from inception, but not discovered until a particular logic path is executed. (The most well-known example of a latent defect is the Y2K problem.) In contrast, the reliability of other system components is time dependent.

Different types of models are needed to measure software reliability due to these unique characteristics [38, 47, 48]. There are currently three major categories of software reliability models: quantitative time-related models, quantitative nontime-related models, and qualitative models. The definitions of quantitative reliability models were not standardized until recently; BS5760 Part 8 [22, 52] is a first step in that direction. Much has been written about quantitative software reliability models in other books [49]. Rather than repeat that information, this book has exposed the reader to the newer and less well-known qualitative models.

The earliest software reliability models fell into the first two categories. They were derived from hardware reliability models and in simplest terms measured the number of errors found/predicted to be remaining and how long it took/will take to find them. These traditional software reliability models have several limitations when applied to high integrity safety-critical software [38, 51]: 1) they do not distinguish between the severity of the consequences of the errors—negligible, marginal, critical, or catastrophic; 2) they do not distinguish between types of errors—functional, performance, safety, reliability, or security; 3) they do not take into account errors found by static analysis techniques or prior to testing; 4) they are not applicable to high integrity safety-critical systems because the results are not accurate beyond 10^{-3} or 10^{-4} at best [48]; and 5) the testing phase is too late to find out that a system will not achieve its reliability requirements. As Storey [60] and others have noted, these models measure the effectiveness of finding and removing defects.

The third and newest category, qualitative models, assesses software reliability from a comprehensive set of product, process, and people/resource metrics which are collected and analyzed throughout the lifecycle. K. Kapur [42] defines qualitative reliability as:

> Those reliability disciplines which have an unknown degree, but improving effect on product reliability.

He recommends a four-step approach to qualitative reliability [42]:

1. identify failure modes,

2. isolate failure causes,

3. predict failure effects, and

4. determine potential corrective actions.

As mentioned in Chapter 2, Littlewood, at the Centre for Software Reliability (CSR), has done some pioneering work in this area through the development of a holistic model [48]. Two research projects are underway at the CSR to expand this concept, IM-PRESS and DISCS [51, 53]:

- IMPRESS aims to combine disparate evidence about dependability using Bayesian Belief Nets (BBNs) in order to support stronger claims about reliability predictions.

- DISCS is studying design diversity as both a means to achieve high levels of dependability and as a way of making claims about a system's fitness for purpose.

As M. Neil and N. Fenton [53] point out, BBNs can:

> ...accommodate both subjective judgements (elicited from domain experts) and probabilities based on objective data [and] combine diverse types of evidence from both product and process to provide improved predictions of product reliability/quality.

M. Bouissou, F. Martin, and A. Ourghanlian have undertaken a similar project, SERENE, to develop a methodology and tool to combine dependability information from diverse sources into a logical whole based on BBNs. From their experience they conclude that [29]:

> Assessment of safety-critical systems including software cannot rely on conventional techniques, based on statistics and dependability models. In such systems, the predominant faults are usually design faults, which are very hard to predict. Therefore the assessment can only be qualitative, and is performed by experts, who take into account various evidence sources.

A system reliability engineer is faced with the challenge of integrating reliability measurements from different models and types components. For example, hardware reliability measurements are based on clock time, while quantitative time-related software reliability predictions are based on CPU or execution time [7]. At present there is little guidance on how to accurately integrate dissimilar reliability measurements to determine system reliability. This is an area for further research and standardization.

An ongoing debate in industry, academia, and the international standards community concerns whether or not software reliability can be measured quantitatively. It would be useful to reframe the debate in terms of how to use all three categories of models, in conjunction with each other, since they measure different aspects of software reliability. The development of a comprehensive and convincing software reliability case requires that information from diverse sources be collected, integrated, and analyzed [38]. And as M. Falla [32] observes:

> To concentrate wholly on either qualitative or quantitative data alone, is to discard information.

This will require a new software reliability paradigm and a broader definition; one which corresponds to the reality of software.

One possible approach is to view software reliability, like software safety, as a continuum rather than a single discrete measurement. Reliability integrity levels (RILs) could be defined similar to safety integrity levels (SILs):[2]

RIL 0   =   not reliability related
RIL 1   =   low reliability
RIL 2   =   medium reliability
RIL 3   =   high reliability
RIL 4   =   ultra-high reliability

Definitions could be developed for the RILs which support and integrate qualitative and quantitative assessments for components, like software, and systems following the strategy promoted by IEC 61508 Part 3 for SILs. This is an area for further research and standardization.

---

[2]Note that SILs are limited to the likelihood of safety-critical or safety-related systems or functions performing correctly under stated conditions within a stated period of time. SILs do not apply to all software functions or whether these functions will produce accurate and consistent results repeatedly under low, normal, and peak loading conditions.

12.3 High integrity, high consequence, mission critical systems need to be both safe and reliable.

As the standards and the literature make clear, safety and reliability are different attributes of a system [38, 47, 60]. Software safety is concerned with features and procedures which: 1) ensure that a system performs predictably under normal and abnormal conditions; 2) minimize the likelihood of an unplanned event occurring; and 3) control and contain the consequences of an unplanned event; thereby preventing accidental injury, death, and/or damage to the environment. In contrast, software reliability is concerned with the ability to produce accurate and consistent results repeatedly under low, normal, and peak loading conditions in the intended operational environment. A system could require different reliability and safety integrity levels, for example, RIL 4 and SIL 2 or vice versa. However, it is hard to imagine certifying or deploying a high integrity system that is safe but not reliable or reliable but not safe. As a result high integrity, high consequence, mission critical systems need to be both safe and reliable.

As the standards demonstrate, software safety and reliability engineering are concurrent engineering activities which build upon basic "good" software engineering practices [1–3, 5, 8, 9, 11–14]. They involve additional design, analysis, measurement, and verification activities that occur concurrently with the software development activities. These activities may be incorporated into the software development lifecycle, system safety lifecycle, or system reliability lifecycle. Because safety and reliability cannot be tested or measured into a product after it is built, it is important that software safety and reliability activities begin during the concept phase and continue throughout the lifecycle [47].

Communication and coordination between software safety engineers, software reliability engineers, and developers is essential [8, 47]. Communication and coordination between software safety and reliability engineers and system safety and reliability engineers is equally essential [8, 47]. Information and the results of analyses should be exchanged and discussed. Some analysis techniques like FTA and FMECA are used by both safety and reliability engineers; however the results are interpreted from different perspectives.

High integrity, mission critical systems are the ideal environment to implement integrated product teams. This will ensure that safety and reliability issues are analyzed comprehensively from multiple vantage points. In the ideal world the architecture and design of a system will be optimized for safety and reliability. In reality, given time, cost, and other constraints, certain tradeoffs are usually made between safety and reliability. Open communication and coordination between safety and reliability engineers will allow informed tradeoff decisions to be made [47].

Lastly, because high integrity mission critical systems need to be both safe and reliable, software safety cases and software reliability cases should be developed in parallel [38]. This will promote a more rigorous assessment of safety and reliability and (hopefully) facilitate regulatory approval.

12.4   A "good" software engineering process is insufficient by itself to produce safe and reliable software.

All of the standards make the statement that a "good" software engineering process is insufficient by itself to produce safe and reliable software [1–3,5,8,9,12–14]. To make this point they include a general purpose software engineering standard as a normative reference, then focus on the additional specialized software safety and reliability activities to be performed. The literature makes this observation as well [32,47,50,60].

Basic "good" software engineering practices do not address safety or reliability issues. These practices are geared toward commercial grade software that executes in an office environment. The emphasis is on correct functionality, not safety and reliability. A limited amount of error handling is provided, but it relates to functionality not hazard prevention. Performance requirements are considered in some cases, but not all. Safety, reliability, and security requirements are not defined or implemented. There is no provision for conducting hazard analyses or risk assessments. The criticality of software modules is not determined. Must work and must not work functions are not identified. There is no concept of designing a system to fail safe or fail operational to prevent hazardous consequences; instead, it is assumed that the end user will simply reboot their system if it crashes.

Software safety and reliability engineering builds upon basic "good" software engineering practices. Additional design, analysis, measurement, and verification activities are performed throughout the lifecycle [47,60]. Metrics are collected which analyze defects by type, source, severity, and frequency to monitor progress toward meeting safety and reliability goals and identify the need for redesign and/or reallocation of safety and reliability requirements among system components [9,13]. In addition, software safety and reliability engineering places greater emphasis on static analysis techniques.

A notable difference is the attitudes towards the use of COTS. Competitive pressures are driving commercial software vendors to increased levels of software reuse. High integrity, mission critical software suppliers are taking a more cautious approach, given the difficulty of thoroughly verifying and validating COTS products. More comprehensive guidance is needed in this area. As L. Kaufman, R. Gretlein, and R. Hayne [43] point out:

> While reuse can be a cost effective practice, it can also pose reliability problems... In reuse, it is quite possible that certain software defects that are unobserved in one operational environment will manifest themselves in another.

Another difference concerns the use of neural networks, fuzzy logic, and heuristics. These techniques are gradually being incorporated into commercial products. However, as Falla [32] observes:

> All of these techniques present problems for safety-related systems as it is not yet known how to determine the safety of this type of system.

Figure 12.1 illustrates these differences in a hypothetical comparison. The SEI SW-CMM and ISO 9001 with ISO 9000-3 are two of the most well-known approaches to basic "good" software engineering practices. SW-CMM consists of five graded maturity levels; each representing more rigorous software engineering processes. The overall goal is defect prevention. This is accomplished, in theory, through repeatable software engineering processes that produce a product of predictable quality. Most sources agree that ISO 9001 with ISO 9000-3 roughly equates to an SW-CMM level 2.5.

SILs are used to determine analysis, design, and verification activities and independence requirements in the high integrity, mission critical environment. ISO 9001 and ISO 9000-3 are frequently cited as normative references by software safety and reliability standards to ensure that basic "good" software engineering practices are followed. As shown in the figure, ISO 9001 with ISO 9000-3 equates to SIL 0. Software safety and reliability engineering activities build upon this foundation. Keep in mind that this is only a hypothetical comparison; the SEI SW-CMM does not specifically address software safety and reliability.

12.5   To achieve software safety and reliability, certain planning, design, analysis, and verification activities must take place.

Safety and reliability cannot be tested or measured into a software product after it is built; rather certain planning, design, analysis, and verification activities must take place [47, 50, 60]. The testing phase is too late to find out that a system does not meet its safety and reliability requirements; it is also extremely costly to correct safety and reliability deficiencies that late in the project schedule.

The development of a software safety plan and a software reliability plan should be the starting point of any project [1–3, 5, 6, 8, 9, 11, 13, 14, 38, 47, 60]. IEEE Std. 1228 (Chapter 11) discusses how to develop a software safety plan, while SAE JA 1002 (Chapter 3) discusses how to develop a software reliability plan. These plans should describe how the safety and reliability requirements allocated to software will be achieved, how the SIL will be determined for software components, and the safety and reliability design, analysis, measurement, and verification activities that will be performed during each lifecycle phase. Organizational roles and responsibilities, resource requirements and when they are needed, and schedules should be defined. It is important for these plans to be in place before any software development activities begin.

The majority of the standards discussed in this book recommend (or require) varying, by SIL, the design, analysis, and verification activities that are conducted, the rigor with which they are conducted, and the amount of detail needed to prove that they were conducted correctly [1, 2, 5, 9, 11, 12, 14, 17]. Early drafts of IEC 61508 established this precedent, which was then reflected in the final version and the derivative standards. For example, more emphasis is placed on static analysis techniques and independence requirements at higher

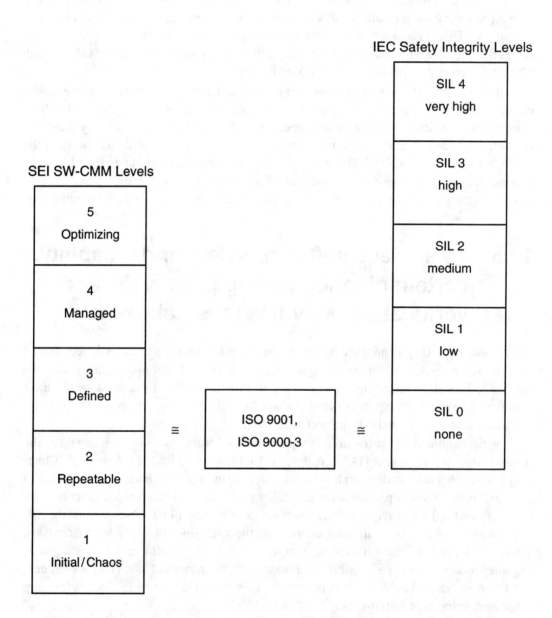

Figure 12.1: Hypothetical relationship between common process measurements and SILs.

SILs. Software safety and reliability cases collect, organize, and analyze information that proves that software safety and reliability requirements are consistent with system safety and reliability requirements and that these requirements have been achieved [38]. They, in effect, close the loop with the software safety and reliability plans: they demonstrate that these plans were executed and the results obtained from doing so.

The optimum approach is to use a complementary set of design, analysis, and verification techniques throughout the lifecycle. More and different types of defects will be uncovered through the use of complementary techniques [40,47]. This will help determine whether or not a project is on track for achieving and/or maintaining its safety and reliability requirements.

Current design, analysis, and verification techniques are listed in Table 12.2. The table indicates whether these techniques are used primarily for safety or reliability analyses, techniques that are complementary or redundant, and their intended use. Formal studies are underway to evaluate the effectiveness of some of these techniques [32] and undoubtedly new techniques will be developed in the future. As Falla [32] points out, software safety and reliability engineering techniques can be used effectively in other domains as well, such as computer security and information assurance:

> Many of the results ... are equally applicable to ... business-critical systems where the hazards to be avoided include the loss of ability to deliver a critical service or the catastrophic loss of valuable data. There are also parallels with system security where the undesired event is successful hostile action against the system (e.g. theft or corruption of data).

N. Leveson [47] has made this observation as well.

Engineering Activity	Type	Complementary/ Redundant	Intended Use/Results
I. Safety & Reliability Design			
- accounting for all possible logic states	S	C1	Prevent system from entering unknown or undefined and thus potentially unsafe states.
- block recovery	B	C1	Recover from an error and transition to a known safe state.
- defensive programming, defense in depth	B	C1	Prevent single points of failure and common mode failures.
- diversity	B	C1	Prevent common cause errors, particularly in safety-critical and safety-related software.
- error detection/correction, fail safe, fail operational	B	C1	Transition to a known safe state; e.g. fault containment.
- Formal Specifications, Animated Specifications	S	C1	Ensure correctness, consistency, and completeness of requirements and design.
- information hiding, encapsulation	S	C1	Prevent: 1) corruption of safety-critical and/or safety-related software and data; and 2) introduction of errors during maintenance and enhancements.
- partitioning	S	C1	Prevent corruption of safety-related or safety-critical software and data by nonsafety-related software and/or data.
- structured methodologies	B	C1	Facilitate safety and reliability verification, validation, maintenance, and enhancement activities.
- use of design and coding standards	B	C1	Facilitate safety and reliability verification, validation, maintenance, and enhancement activities.
II. Safety & Reliability Analysis			
- cause consequence analysis	S	R2	Identify the consequences and severity of potential failures.
- change impact analysis	B	C2	Prevent safety and reliability errors from being introduced during maintenance or enhancements.
- common cause failure analysis	B	R1	Identify potential for multiple failures to originate from the same design fault(s).
- develop software reliability case	R	C2	Collect, organize, and analyze information that proves that software reliability requirements are consistent with system reliability requirements and that they have been achieved [38].
- develop software safety case	S	C2	Collect, organize, and analyze information that proves that software safety requirements are consistent with system safety requirements and that they have been achieved [38].

Engineering Activity	Type	Complementary/ Redundant	Intended Use/Results
- event tree analysis	B	R2	Prevent defects through analyses of sequences of operator and system events which could lead to failures and/or unsafe states.
- FMECA	B	C2, R2	Prevent hazards through analysis of failure modes, their causes, severity, and likelihood.
- Formal Proofs	S	C2	Demonstrate through formal mathematical proofs that that the requirements, design, and implementation are correct, complete, and consistent.
- formal scenario analysis	B	C2	Develop operational profiles, capture domain knowledge, and must work/must not work functions; identify HCI safety and reliability issues.
- FTA	S	C2, R1	Prevent hazards by identifying the root cause of an undesired system event.
- hazard analysis	S	C2	Identify potential hazards associated with using a system so that appropriate mitigation features can be designed in to prevent them.
- HAZOP studies	S	C2	Capture domain knowledge about operational environment, parameters, modes, etc. so that this information can be incorporated into the requirements and design.
- highlighting requirements likely to change	B	C2	Enhance system maintainability; in particular in regard to safety and reliability.
- Petri nets	S	C2	Identify potential race and deadlock conditions.
- reliability block diagrams	R	C2	Support initial reliability estimates and design optimization efforts.
- response time, memory constraint analysis	B	C2	Ensure that the software will perform correctly under low, normal, and peak loading conditions within specified memory, response time, and other constraints [47].
- sneak circuit analysis	S	C2	Identify unexpected paths through a program that could initiate undesired functions, inhibit functions, or cause incorrect timing and sequencing.
III. Safety & Reliability Verification			
- boundary value analysis	B	C3	Verify that the software performs correctly at the limits and boundaries of all input parameters.

Engineering Activity	Type	Complementary/ Redundant		Intended Use/Results
- clean room	B	C3	R4	Prevent defects through an evaluation of the completeness, consistency, and correctness of requirements, design, and implementation [20,21,47].
- design reviews	B	C3		Verify, with all stakeholders, that design is correct, consistent, and complete.
- equivalence class partitioning	B	C3		Determine from the specification and design, the minimum set of test data that will adequately test each input domain.
- evaluate acceptability of residual risk	S	C3		Verify that the specified SIL has been met, that residual risk has been reduced to ALARP, and that residual risk is acceptable within known operational constraints.
- evaluate effectiveness of risk control measures	S	C3		Verify the integrity of risk control and mitigation measures. Make recommendations to optimize safety and reliability design features and procedures.
- failure assertion	B		R3	Verify that system detects and responds correctly to erroneous data, conditions, and states.
- fault injection	B	C3	R3	Verify that system detects and responds correctly to erroneous data, conditions, and states.
- formal code inspections	B		R4	Prevent defects in lifecycle artifacts by analyzing control flow, data flow, completeness, internal consistency, consistency with predecessor artifacts, correctness, understandability, unambiguousness, verifiability, and compliance with project standards [20,21,47].
- functional testing	R	C3		Verify that functional requirements are correct and that they have been implemented correctly.
- interface testing	B	C3		Verify that interface requirements are correct and that they have been implemented correctly.
- peer reviews	B	C3		Verify with all members of the development team that requirements, design, and implementation are correct, consistent, and complete [20,21,47].
- performance testing	B	C3		Verify that performance requirements are correct and that they have been implemented correctly.
- probabilistic testing	B	C3		Verify design integrity against operational profiles.

Engineering Activity	Type	Complementary/ Redundant	Intended Use/Results
- regression testing	B	C3	Verify that changes have been implemented correctly and that they do not adversely affect system performance, safety, and reliability.
- requirements traceability	B	C3	Verify that all functional, performance, safety, reliability, and security requirements have been implemented correctly.
- review software reliability case	R	C3	Determine if the claims made about the software's reliability are justified by the supporting arguments and evidence [38].
- review software safety case	S	C3	Determine if the claims made about the software's safety are justified by the supporting arguments and evidence [38].
- root cause analysis	B	C3	Determine root cause of defects discovered during verification activities, including why they were not detected earlier.
- stress testing	B	C3	Verify that system responds correctly under peak loading conditions. Determine system saturation/overload point.
- testability analysis	B	C3	Verify that design integrity supports analysis of the controllability and observability of internal nodes.
- usability testing	B	C3	Verify that HCI design is understandable and usable by end users and that it does not contribute to induced or invited errors.

Key: S - primarily supports software safety engineering analysis
  R - primarily supports software reliability engineering analysis
  B - supports both software safety and reliability engineering analyses
  Cx - groups of complementary techniques
  Rx - groups of redundant techniques

Table 12.2: Menu of software safety and reliability engineering design, analysis, and verification techniques.

12.6 The achievement of software safety and reliability should be measured throughout the lifecycle by a combination of product, process, and people/resource metrics, both quantitative and qualitative.

The majority of the standards discussed in this book and the literature agree that the achievement of software safety and reliability should be measured throughout the lifecycle by a combination of product, process, and people/resource metrics, both quantitative and qualitative [18,47]. Leveson [47] points out the limitations of quantitative measures and the need for qualitative measures. N. Fenton [33] has proposed that requirements in standards be categorized as product, process and resource requirements. This would clarify the nature of a requirement in a standard during development and compliance assessment activities and facilitate the use of metrics.

Software safety and reliability engineering activities are ongoing throughout the software lifecycle [47,50,60]; hence, measuring progress toward meeting safety and reliability requirements should be an ongoing activity. These measurements provide insights into the effectiveness of the strategy for achieving safety and reliability and the success of mitigation efforts. Because the measurements begin early in the lifecycle, they identify the need for redesign and/or reallocation of safety and reliability requirements when it is schedule and cost effective to do so [38,50]. Another use of these measurements is to provide evidence needed in software safety and reliability cases [38].

Specific types of software safety and reliability measurements should be scheduled to coincide with key decision points and milestones. Objective criteria should be established for each measurement, including how the results will be evaluated and interpreted and the need for an independent review. The acceptability (or non-acceptability) of the results should be discussed with all stakeholders before proceeding to the next phase. In addition, software safety and reliability measurements should be compatible and coordinated with system safety and reliability measurements. There will not be a one-to-one correspondence, but a mechanism is needed to demonstrate software's contribution to achieving system safety and reliability goals.

A comprehensive safety and reliability assessment requires that a combination of product, process and people/resource metrics be collected and analyzed [38,47,48,50,60]. Different metrics and different categories of metrics measure different aspects of a system and the processes and resources used to develop it [18]: Product metrics provide an assessment of the maturity of a product and an indicator of its operational effectiveness, especially in regard to safety and reliability. Process metrics provide an assessment of the maturity and effectiveness of the processes used to develop software. People/resource metrics measure the appropriateness and adequacy of resources applied to a software project. It is critical to have the correct type, quality, and quantity of resources on a project and to have them at the appropriate time. Many projects get off track because they have the wrong skill mix, such as coders trying to do requirements analysis.

The Littlewood holistic model, discussed in Chapter 2, is one of the first to integrate all three categories of metrics and qualitative and quantitative measurements. This model represents a paradigm shift from relying on a single measurement to relying on the cumulative weight of multiple disparate measurements.

Table 12.3 presents an integrated worksheet for assessing software safety and reliability through a combination of product, process, and people/resource metrics, consistent with the Littlewood model. For each category and subcategory, complementary metrics are chosen (from those discussed in Chapter 10) that are appropriate for a given project. The table indicates whether metrics are complementary or redundant, quantitative and/or qualitative, and potential links to system safety and reliability measurements.

A 100-point allocation is distributed among the metric categories and subcategories according to the project's priorities. The allocation may vary by lifecycle phase. Objective criteria are established to determine if the actual measurements were acceptable, exceeded expectations, or were unacceptable. The points assigned to each metric are prorated accordingly. Total actual points are tallied for each metric category and overall. Various percentages can then be calculated to measure current results compared to the goal, previous measurements, and so forth.

Project/Subsystem: _____

Lifecycle Phase/Milestone: _____   As of date: _____   Required SIL: _____

Metric Category/ Subcategory [18][3]	Complementary/ Redundant	Qualitative/ Quantitative[4]	Links to System Safety & Reliability Measurements	Max. Rating	Actual Rating
Product Metrics					
1. completeness and consistency:		both	Measurements can be applied to the completeness and consistency of system requirements.	8	
- completeness	C				
- requirements compliance	C				
- requirements traceability	C				
- design integrity	C				
- performance measures	C				
2. complexity:		quantitative		9	
- cyclomatic	C, R2				
- information flow	C, R1				
- design structure	R1				
- generalized static	R2				
- number of entries and exits per module	R2				
3. error, fault, and failure:		quantitative		15	
- cumulative failure profile	C				
- defect density	C, R1				
- defect indices	C				
- fault density	R1				

---

[3]Complementary metrics are chosen that are appropriate for a project from those discussed in Chapter 10.
[4]Some measurements include both quantitative and qualitative components.

Metric Category/ Subcategory [18]	Complementary/ Redundant	Qualitative/ Quantitative	Links to System Safety & Reliability Measurements	Max. Rating	Actual Rating
4. reliability growth and projection:		quantitative	Some measurements can be integrated with system-level reliability estimation.	8	
- reliability growth	C				
- run reliability	C, R1				
- software maturity index	C				
- software purity level	R1				
- system performance reliability	C				
subtotal				40	
II. Process Metrics					
1. process/subprocess effectiveness:		both		15	
- functional test coverage	C, R1				
- test coverage	R1				
- review, audit, and inspection results	C				
- use of static and dynamic analysis techniques	C				
- use of standards	C				
2. management control:		quantitative		15	
- error distribution	C				
- fault days	C				
- staff-hours per defect detected	C				
subtotal				30	

Metric Category/ Subcategory [18]	Complementary/ Redundant	Qualitative/ Quantitative	Links to System Safety & Reliability Measurements	Max. Rating	Actual Rating
III. People/Resource Metrics					
1. competency: - relevant education - relevant experience - relevant certification	C C C	qualitative	Equivalent competency requirements can be defined for all engineering disciplines.	7.5	
2. schedule reality: - skill mix and availability - equipment mix and availability	C C	qualitative	An assessment can be made of the reality of the entire system development schedule by assigning values to each component.	7.5	
3. development environment: - hardware platform - OS(s) and utilities - compilers - automated tool usage - relation to operational environment - known system constraints	C C C C C C	qualitative	An assessment can be made of the appropriateness of the development environment for each system component.	7.5	

Metric Category/ Subcategory [18]	Complementary/ Redundant	Qualitative/ Quantitative	Links to System Safety & Reliability Measurements	Max. Rating	Actual Rating
4. HCI issues:		qualitative	An assessment can be made of HCI issues at the system level.	7.5	
- domain knowledge	C				
- HAZOP studies	C				
- formal scenario analysis	C				
- operational profiles	C				
- end-user training	C				
- instructions for use	C				
subtotal				30	
Grand Total				100	

Key: C - complementary metrics
    R - redundant metrics

Table 12.3: Sample integrated worksheet for assessing software safety and reliability.

459

12.7 Software safety and software reliability are engineering specialties which require specialized knowledge, skills, and experience.

As discussed earlier, software safety and reliability engineering involves performing additional specialized activities beyond basic "good" software engineering practices. Consequently the software safety and reliability knowledge and skill set is also specialized [47, 50, 60].

The majority of standards discussed in this book acknowledge this by levying competency and/or professional certification requirements for staff involved in the development and assessment of safety-critical, safety-related, and high reliability software [1–3, 5, 8, 9, 12–14, 17, 18]. Specific education, training, and experience requirements are defined, such as knowledge of and experience using FTA, FMECA, and HAZOP studies; and skill in knowing how to implement defensive programming and evaluate residual risk. Several countries are also beginning to require professional software safety and reliability certification. As a step in that direction, ASQ recently expanded its Certified Reliability Engineer (CRE) exam to include software reliability.

This underscores the need for universities to start offering software safety and software reliability courses as a standard part of the Computer Science curriculum. Given the rapidly expanding role of software in safety-critical, high reliability applications, safety and reliability engineers without any software engineering experience and software engineers without any safety or reliability engineering experience are often asked to perform functions for which they do not have the necessary training [47]. This is an unhealthy situation, literally. Staff lacking the appropriate software safety and reliability engineering background are unable to determine: 1) if a product is safe or reliable; and 2) if the processes used to develop and assess it are appropriate and sufficient. This situation is akin to asking a general practitioner to perform neurosurgery in the medical sector. It also highlights the importance of people/resource metrics.

Software engineering professional ethics are directly related to professional competency and certification [60]. A joint ACM/IEEE Computer Society task force recently developed a Software Engineering Code of Ethics and Professional Practice [25]. Because of the potential for hazardous consequences, software safety and reliability engineers must present accurate and complete assessments under all circumstances. They must have the ability to present "bad news to the boss," stand by their assessments and recommendations, and inform management of the consequences of not following their recommendations. A corollary to professional ethics is legal liability. As Falla [32] notes, when safety-critical or safety-related systems are concerned:

> Legal liability can fall on the manufacturer, supplier, distributors, or certifier of products.

The joint ACM/IEEE Computer Society Task Force is also defining a standardized software engineering body of knowledge (SWEBOK). The objectives of this project are to [26]:

- characterize the contents of the SWEBOK;

- provide a topical access to the SWEBOK;

- promote a consistent view of software engineering worldwide;

- clarify the place of, and set the boundary of, software engineering with respect to other disciplines such as computer science, computer engineering, and mathematics; and

- provide a foundation for curriculum development and for individual certification and licensing.

The SWEBOK currently consists of 10 components [26]:

- software configuration management,

- software construction,

- software design,

- software engineering infrastructure,

- software engineering management,

- software engineering process,

- software evolution and maintenance,

- software quality analysis,

- software requirements analysis, and

- software testing.

The preliminary formal comment and review of the SWEBOK took place during the summer of 1999. After the SWEBOK is approved, it is envisioned that an additional body of knowledge will be defined for software engineering specialties, such as software safety/reliability/security/dependability. Current information about the status of the SWEBOK can be obtained from the Web site:

www.swebok.org

It is preferable that software safety and reliability engineers have an independent reporting channel, so they are not subjected to undue pressure from managers whose primary concern is schedule and budget. This approach is similar to the requirement for independent reporting channels for quality management organizations in ISO 9001 and the SEI SW-CMM.

12.8   Some safety and reliability concerns are the same across industrial sectors and technologies, while some are unique.

As is evident from the standards, a generic set of safety and reliability concerns are common across industrial sectors and technologies. In general, software safety is concerned with features and procedures which: 1) ensure that a system performs predictably under normal and abnormal conditions; 2) minimize the likelihood of an unplanned event occurring; and 3) control the consequences of an unplanned event; thereby preventing accidental injury, death, and/or damage to the environment. In general, software reliability is concerned with accurate and consistent results that are repeatable under low, normal, and peak loading in the intended operational environment. The goal is predictable performance under all conditions; that is, no unknown or unsafe states are encountered.

A comprehensive fault management approach is pursued to achieve this goal: fault avoidance, fault removal, fault detection, fault tolerance, and formal proofs of correctness [60]. Of course, potential faults have to be identified before they can be avoided or tolerated. This is usually accomplished by FTA. The standards specify a variety of specialized design, analysis, and verification activities to prevent the introduction of faults and to tolerate those that escaped detection, in particular those with safety and reliability ramifications. High integrity, mission critical systems are also designed with the ability to fail safe, fail operational, and/or attempt recovery. The standards emphasize the need for adequate system warnings, alerts, and training for end users and maintenance staff, especially about residual risk [1, 2, 5, 9, 11–14].

Parallel to this are the unique safety and reliability concerns of specific industrial sectors and technologies. These unique concerns have prompted industry and technology specific implementations of IEC 61508 Part 3, such as EN 50128, the MISRA™ Guidelines, and the IEE SEMSPLC Guidelines. Some of the unique concerns are summarized below.

Two concerns in the railway industry are: maintaining a minimum safe distance between trains, known as "headway," and having current information about which tracks are in use or are scheduled for use. This requires continuous monitoring of train speeds and locations and projecting arrival times. Sophisticated algorithms are used to transmit information to and from trains, conductors, and signalling control centers. Unlike automobiles or airplanes, trains do not have the option of changing lanes or altitude to avoid collisions.

Three concerns in the automotive industry are: the concept of controllability, risk hysteresis, and shared bus communications/controller area networks (CANs). The MISRA™ Guidelines define controllability as "the ability of vehicle occupants to control the situation following a failure." Automotive manufacturers can design in features to enhance controllability. However, there are many factors over which they have no control: road conditions; weather conditions; actions of drivers, passengers, or pedestrians; and the state in which a vehicle is maintained. Risk hysteresis is also a concern; that is, the addition of safety features to automobiles often leads to riskier behavior on the part of drivers. Size and weight considerations lead automotive designs to make extensive use of shared bus communications and CANs. This raises concerns about the accurate timing, sequencing, and reception of transmitted information [60].

Failure to prevent disease progression is a concern in the medical industry. If a device fails to operate at all or is minimally operational, as in the case of underdosing, the therapy is ineffective and the disease it was supposed to treat progresses unabated. The reverse situation is overdosing, where the amount of medicine, radiation, oxygen, and so forth exceeds that prescribed and injures the patient. Medical treatments rely on the accurate delivery of specific dosages when and where prescribed. This factor must be considered during the hazard analysis.

All industrial sectors rely on instruments providing accurate information to decision makers/decision making processes. This is particularly true in the petrochemical industry, process control industry,[5] and aerospace industry. Pilots rely on accurate readings from instruments measuring air speed, air temperature, altitude, and so forth. Air traffic controllers rely on the accuracy of information transmitted to and from airplanes and ground radar to schedule takeoffs and landings. This information must not only be accurate but timely.

In the defense industry, the consequences of failing to complete a mission must be considered when performing a hazard analysis. Defense equipment generally operates under hostile conditions with the intent of achieving a specific objective or mission. Failure to accomplish that mission may also have hazardous consequences. This may lead to some latitude in assessing the acceptability of residual risk which is not present in other industries.

PLCs and ASICs present two challenges: the use of nonprocedural languages which are difficult to understand and analyze, and the need to safely and reliably interface with existing plant equipment, most of which is not digital.

In all of these situations it is essential to thoroughly capture domain knowledge, particularly information about the operational environment, modes, states, parameters, and must work and must not work functions. Many industry unique safety and reliability requirements and/or constraints will be identified this way. As Leveson and Reese [46, 47] and CE-1001-STD Rev. 1 (Chapter 6) point out, once these requirements have been captured they must be: 1) reviewable and verifiable by domain experts; and 2) understandable by developers.

---

[5]J. Harauz [36] reports that work has begun on an IEC standard, IEC 61511, for the process industries that will be an industry specific implementation of IEC 61508.

12.9 Everyday examples should not be overlooked when classifying systems as safety critical or safety related.

It is common to only view highly visible systems, such as nuclear power plants, medical equipment, defense equipment, and aircraft, as safety critical or safety related. In reality, many more mundane everyday software applications are also safety critical or safety related [47, 50, 62]. (Specific standards for these applications have not been developed to date; however the standards discussed in Part III are applicable.) A few examples of systems often overlooked include: software controlled microwave ovens, gas burners, elevators, escalators, and 911 systems.

Another category which is often overlooked is systems which generate information from which safety-related decisions are made; examples are drawings for utility companies, navigational maps for shipping and aerospace, designs for bridges or roads, and medical informatics. As J. Tilloston [62] reminds us:

> ...we should not forget the less glamorous and less spectacular areas of system safety... These are the areas of safety-related management information systems (mostly mainframe and PC-based conventional business systems at SILs 1–2). The risks here are less obvious and it is possible to overlook them. Even though the percentage risk on each system is much smaller, because of the large number of systems involved, the overall risks can be higher.

The functions a system performs and the uses of the information it generates should be considered when classifying a system as safety critical, safety related, or nonsafety related [47, 62].

The failure of 911 systems in major metropolitan areas has made the news several times recently. The failure of a 911 call to go through, regardless of whether it is for the police, fire department, or medical assistance, prevents the mitigating action from taking place. In the incidents reported, both the primary and secondary switches failed for a period of several hours. This is not surprising since most telecommunications systems are designed around the concept of redundancy. As mentioned earlier, redundancy does not improve software reliability; it simply replicates defects [47]. This strategy should be revised for safety-related telecommunications systems so that diverse software is implemented.

12.10   A layered approach to standards is the most effective way to achieve both software and system safety and reliability.

The taxonomy of standards that are used to develop a system should correspond to the realities of the system that will be built and how it will be assessed. As mentioned earlier, software safety is a component of system safety while software reliability is a component of system reliability [38,42,47,60]. Software safety and reliability are concurrent engineering activities that build upon basic "good" software engineering practices. The standards employed on a project should reflect these facts.

An integrated modular or layered approach to standards, as shown in Figure 12.2, is the optimum approach. An integrated standards framework promotes an integrated engineering effort [60]. Safety and reliability issues are dealt with effectively at the component and system levels. Each engineering discipline understands their responsibilities. Coordination of engineering activities, communication, and the exchange of information between engineering groups is simplified. Another advantage is that individual standards can be updated to incorporate new techniques, methodologies, and/or technology as needed without having to reissue the entire framework. In contrast, trying to implement overlapping and conflicting stovepipe standards is very difficult, error prone, and costly.

The majority of the standards discussed in this book follow a layered approach and are part of an integrated standards framework. This is accomplished by including other applicable standards as normative references. In general, the first layer references basic "good" software engineering standards. Software safety and reliability standards in layer two build upon the requirements and practices of the first layer. System safety and reliability standards in layer three build upon the requirements and practices of the second layer. The second and third layer refer to technique specific standards, such as DEF STAN 00-58 which explains how to conduct HAZOP studies.

International consensus standards have several advantages over "homegrown" standards. First, due to the process by which they are developed, international consensus standards represent the experience, insights, and lessons learned from multiple projects, companies, and countries [60]. Second, the use of international consensus standards allows all stakeholders to know what has and has not been done during the development and assessment of a product. Third, international consensus standards drive the global economy and regulatory environment, promoting mutual recognition of compliance assessment activities. The worldwide recognition and acceptance of ISO 9000 is but one example. As J. Harauz [36] points out:

The rise in the use of commercial international standards is being driven by worldwide progress in trade liberalization, interpenetration of sectors, worldwide communication systems, needs for global standards of emerging technologies, and needs of developing countries.

Table 12.4 characterizes the software safety and reliability standards discussed in this book.

As a final thought, I would like to conclude with a quote from R. Shaw [58]:

Unless it be thought that the problems of handling software safety have now been solved ... it is worth noting that much has still to be achieved.

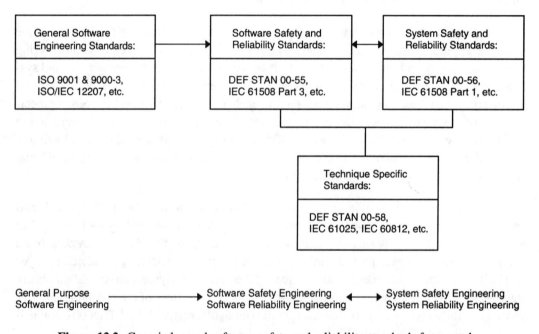

Figure 12.2: Generic layered software safety and reliability standards framework.

Standard[6]	Software Safety Standard	Integrates with System Safety Standard	Software Relibility Standard	Integrates with System Reliability Standard	Integrates with Basic Software Engineering Standard	Integrates with System Engineering	Compliance Assessment Critera Defined	Supports Qualitative and Quantitative Assessments
GROUND TRANSPORTATION INDUSTRY								
3.1 EN 50128:1997	x	x	x	x	x		x	x
3.2 MISRA™ Guidelines	x	x	x	x	x		x	x
3.3 SAE JA 1002			x	x	x			x
AEROSPACE INDUSTRY								
4.1 RTCA/DO-178B	x							x
4.2 ESA ECSS-Q-80A	x	x	x	x	x	x	x	x
4.3 NASA-STD-8719.13A NASA GB 1740.13	x							x
4.4 AIAA R-013			x					
DEFENSE INDUSTRY								
5.1 MIL-STD-882D	x	x	x	x	x		x	x
5.2 DEF STAN 00-55	x	x	x	x	x		x	x
5.3 NATO COTS Guidelines								
NUCLEAR POWER INDUSTRY								
6.1 IEC 60880	x	x	x		x			x
6.2 CE-1001-STD Rev 1	x	x	x	x	x	x	x	x
BIOMEDICAL INDUSTRY								
7. IEC 601-1-4	x	x			x		x	x
NON–INDUSTRY SPECIFIC STANDARDS								
8.1 IEC 61508-3:1998	x	x					x	x
8.2 IEC 300-3-9:1995			x	x			x	x
8.3 ISO/IEC 15026:1998			x	x			x	
9. IEE SEMSPLC Guidelines	x	x						x
10. IEEE Std. 982.1,982.2			x		x			
11. IEEE Std. 1228-1994	x				x			

[6]If a standard is part of an integrated standards framework, the responses apply to the entire framework.

Standard[7]	Requires Software Safety/Reliability Competency, Professional Certification	Requires Software Safety Plan	Requires Software Safety Case	Requires Software Reliability Plan	Requires Software Reliability Case	Requires Design Features by SIL[8]	Requires Analysis and Verification Activities by SIL[9]	Requires Independence
GROUND TRANSPORTATION INDUSTRY								
3.1 EN 50128:1997	x	x				x	x	x
3.2 MISRA™Guidelines	x	x				x	x	x
3.3 SAE JA 1002	x			x	x			x
AEROSPACE INDUSTRY								
4.1 RTCA/DO-178B						x	x	x
4.2 ESA ECSS-Q-80A	x	x	x	x		x	x	x
4.3 NASA-STD-8719.13A NASA GB 1740.13		x						x
4.4 AIAA R-013								
DEFENSE INDUSTRY								
5.1 MIL-STD-882D	x	x						x
5.2 DEF STAN 00-55	x	x	x	x	x	x	x	x
5.3 NATO COTS Guidelines								
NUCLEAR POWER INDUSTRY								
6.1 IEC 60880						x	x	x
6.2 CE-1001-STD Rev 1	x					x	x	x
BIOMEDICAL INDUSTRY								
7. IEC 601-1-4	x	x	x			x	x	x
NON–INDUSTRY SPECIFIC STANDARDS								
8.1 IEC 61508-3:1998	x	x	x			x	x	x
8.2 IEC 300-3-9:1995								
8.3 ISO/IEC 15026:1998								
9. IEE SEMSPLC Guidelines	x	x	x					
10. IEEE Std. 982.1,982.2	x					x	x	x
11. IEEE Std. 1228-1994		x						

Key: x - criteria applies
        P - partial applicability

Table 12.4: Characterization of software safety and reliability standards.

---

[7] If a standard is part of an integrated standards framework, the responses apply to the entire framework.
[8] See Tables 3.1 and 8.4 for the assignment of design features, analysis, and verification activities by SIL.
[9] See Tables 3.1 and 8.4 for the assignment of design features, analysis, and verification activities by SIL.

12.11   Discussion Problems

1. Most of the standards discussed in this book vary the design, analysis, and verification activities according to what parameter? Explain the rationale behind this.

2. Discuss the relationship between concurrent engineering and integrated product teams.

3. How does data affect software safety? How does data affect software reliability?

4. What is the optimum approach to measuring software safety and reliability? Why is this so?

5. What role do standards serve within software safety and reliability engineering?

6. What information does a qualitative software reliability model capture that a quantitative model does not and vice versa?

7. What happens when software safety and/or system safety are analyzed in isolation?

8. Give an example of a safety-critical system that need not be reliable. Give an example of an ultra-high reliability system that need not be safe.

9. When do software safety and reliability engineering activities begin? When are they over?

10. List the safety-critical and safety-related systems you have interacted with so far today.

11. Give examples of activities performed by software safety and reliability engineers that are not performed by a software engineer developing commercial grade software.

12. Why is professional ethics a major component of certifying safety, reliability, and quality engineers?

13. Given that each industrial sector and technology has some unique software safety and reliability concerns, what is the best method for capturing these concerns?

Additional Resources

Primary Works Cited

[1]   EN 50128:1997, Railway Applications: Software for Railway Control and Protection Systems, the European Committee for Electrotechnical Standardization (CENELEC).

[2]   Development Guidelines for Vehicle Based Software, The Motor Industry Software Reliability Association (MISRA™), November 1994.

[3]   JA 1002, Software Reliability Program Standard, Society of Automotive Engineers (SAE), 1998.

[4]   RTCA/DO-178B: Software Considerations in Airborne Systems and Equipment Certification, December 1992.

[5]   Space Product Assurance: Software Product Assurance, European Space Agency, ECSS-Q-80A, 19 April 1996.

[6]   NASA-STD-8719.13A: Software Safety, NASA Technical Standard, September 15, 1997 and NASA GB-1740.13.96: Guidebook for Safety-Critical Software – Analysis and Development, NASA Glenn Research Center, Office of Safety and Mission Assurance, 1996.

[7]   ANSI/AIAA R-013-1992, Recommended Practice: Software Reliability.

[8]   MIL-STD-882D: Mishap Risk Management (System Safety), U.S. Department of Defense (DoD) Standard Practice, (draft) 20 October 1998.

[9]   DEF STAN 00-55: Requirements for Safety Related Software in Defense Equipment, Part 1: Requirements and Part 2: Guidance, UK Ministry of Defence (MoD), 1 August 1997.

[10] Commercial off-the-Shelf (COTS) Software Acquisition Guidelines and COTS Policy Issues, Communications and Information Systems Agency, NATO, 10 January 1996, 1st revision.

[11] IEC 60880:1986-09, Software for Computers in Safety Systems of Nuclear Power Stations.

[12] CE-1001-STD Rev. 1, Standard for Software Engineering of Safety Critical Software, CANDU Computer Systems Engineering Centre for Excellence, January 1995.

[13] IEC 601-1-4(1996-06), Medical Electrical Equipment – Part 1: General Requirements for Safety – 4. Collateral Standard: Programmable Electrical Medical Systems.

[14] IEC 61508-3:1998, Functional safety of electrical/electronic/programmable electronic safety-related systems – Part 3: Software requirements.

[15] IEC 300-3-9:1995-12, Dependability Management – Part 3: Application Guide – Section 9: Risk Analysis of Technological Systems.

[16] ISO/IEC 15026:1998-04-29, Information Technology – System and Software Integrity Levels.

[17] SEMSPLC Guidelines, Safety-Related Application Software for Programmable Logic Controllers, IEE Technical Guidelines 8:1996.

[18] ANSI/IEEE Std. 982.1-1989 and 982.2-1989, Measures to Produce Reliable Software.

[19] IEEE Std. 1228-1994, Standard for Software Safety Plans.

[20] ANSI/IEEE Std. 1012-1998. IEEE Standard for Software Verification and Validation Plans.

[21] ANSI/IEEE Std. 1059-1994. IEEE Guide for Software Verification and Validation Plans.

[22] BS5760 Part 8: Guide to the Assessment of Reliability of Systems Containing Software, British Standards Institution (BSI), October 1998.

[23] IEC 60812:1985 - Analysis Techniques for System Reliability—Procedure for Failure Modes Effects Analysis (FMEA).

[24] IEC 61025:1990 – Fault Tree Analysis (FTA).

Selected Bibliography

[25] ACM/IEEE Computer Society Joint Task Force, *Software Engineering Code of Ethics and Professional Practice*, version 5.0, October 1998.

[26] ACM/IEEE Computer Society Joint Task Force, *Standardized Software Engineering Body of Knowledge (SWEBOK)*, draft 0.5, June 1999.

[27] Barrell, T. and Darlison, T. "The Safety of PES in the Offshore Industry," *Safety and Reliability of Software Based Systems*, Springer-Verlag, 1995, pp. 201–216.

[28] Bieda, J. "Software Reliability: A Practitioner's Model," *Reliability Review*, Vol. 16, No. 2, June 1996, pp. 18–28.

[29] Bouissou, M., Martin, F., and Ourghanlian, A. "Assessment of a Safety-Critical System Including Software: A Bayesian Belief Network for Evidence Sources," *Proceedings of the Annual Reliability and Maintainability Symposium (RAMS'99)*, IEEE, 1999, pp. 142–150.

[30] Broy, M. and Jahnichen, S. *KORSO: Methods, Languages, and Tools for the Construction of Correct Software*, Springer-Verlag, 1995.

[31] Devine, C., Fenton, N. and Page, S. "Deficiencies in Existing Software Engineering Standards as Exposed by 'SMARTIE'," *Safety-Critical Systems*, Chapman & Hall, 1993, pp. 255–272.

[32] Falla, M. (ed.) "Advances in Safety Critical Systems: Results and Achievements from the DTI/EPSRC R&D Programme in Safety Critical Systems," June 1997, available from: www.comp.lancs.ac.uk/computing/resources/scs/index.html.

[33] Fenton, N. "How to Improve Safety Critical Systems Standards," *Safer Systems*, Springer-Verlag, 1997, pp. 96–110.

[34] Forder, J., Higgins, C., McDermid, J. and Storrs, G., "SAM—A Tool to Support the Construction, Review and Evolution of Safety Arguments," *Directions in Safety-Critical Systems*, Springer-Verlag, 1993, pp. 195–216.

[35] Hamlet, D. and Voas, J. "Faults on its Sleeve: Amplifying Software Reliability Testing," *Proceedings of the International Symposium on Software Testing and Analysis*, ACM Press, June 1993, pp. 89–98.

[36] Harauz, J. "International Trends in Software Engineering and Quality System Standards: Ontario Hydro's Perspective, Part 1," *Software Quality Professional*, March 1999, pp. 51–58.

[37] Hatton, L. *Safer C: Developing Software for High Integrity and Safety-Critical Systems*, McGraw-Hill International, Ltd., 1995.

[38] Herrmann, D. and Peercy, D. "Software Reliability Cases: The Bridge Between Hardware Reliability, Software Reliability, System Reliability and System Safety," *Proceedings of the Annual Reliability and Maintainability Symposium (RAMS'99)*, IEEE, 1999, pp. 396–402.

[39] Herrmann, D. "A Methodology for Evaluating, Comparing, and Selecting Software Safety and Reliability Standards," *Proceedings of the 10th Annual Conference on Computer Assurance (COMPASS)*, IEEE, June 1995, pp. 223–232.

[40] Herrmann, D. "A Preview of IEC Safety Requirements for Programmable Electronic Medical Systems," *Medical Device and Diagnostic Industry*, June 1995, pp. 106–110.

[41] Jones, C. *Patterns of Software Systems Failure and Success*, International Thomson Computer Press, 1996.

[42] Kapur, K. "Reliability as an Integrated Part of the Total System Safety Program," *Tutorial Notes, 16th International System Safety Society Conference*, Seattle, WA, September 14–19, 1998.

[43] Kaufman, L., Gretlein, R. and Hayne, R. "A Quantitative Assessment of the Application of Software Reliability to Reusable Code," *Proceedings of the Annual Reliability and Maintainability Symposium (RAMS'99)*, IEEE, 1999, pp. 165–170.

[44] Kelly, T. "Software Safety—by Prescription or Argument?" *Safety Systems*, Vol. 7, No. 2, January 1998, pp. 6–7.

[45] Lawson, H. "Infrastructure Risk Reduction," *Communications of the ACM*, Vol. 40, No. 6, June 1998, p. 120.

[46] Leveson, N. and Reese, J. "SpecTRM: A Toolset to Support the Safeware Methodology," *Proceedings of the 16th International System Safety Conference*, 1998, pp. 256–262.

[47] Leveson, N. *Safeware: System Safety and Computers*, Addison-Wesley, 1995.

[48] Littlewood, B. "The Need for Evidence from Disparate Sources to Evaluate Software Safety," *Directions in Safety-Critical Systems*, Springer-Verlag, 1993, pp. 217–231.

[49] Lyu, M. *Handbook of Software Reliability Engineering*, IEEE Computer Society Press, 1998.

[50] McDermid, J.A. "Issues in the Development of Safety-Critical Systems," *Safety-Critical Systems*, Chapman & Hall, 1993, pp. 16–42.

[51] "Measuring and Predicting Software Reliability and Safety, Information Technology Update from Engineering and Physical Sciences Research Council (EPSRC)," *IMPACT*, No. 22, March 1999, p. 5.

[52] Mellor, P. "Closing the Loop on Software Dependability Standards: BS5760 Part 8," *Safety Systems*, Vol. 8, No. 2, January 1999, pp. 8–10.

[53] Neil, M. and Fenton, N. "Applying Bayesian Belief Networks to Critical Systems Assessment," *Safety Systems*, Vol. 8, No. 3, May 1999, pp. 10–13.

[54] Picciolo, G. "Software Based Systems Dependability Requirements in the Process Industries," *Safety and Reliability of Software Based Systems*, Springer-Verlag, 1995, pp. 276–287.

[55] Raheja, D. *Assurance Technologies: Principles and Practices*, McGraw-Hill, 1991, Chapter 9, pp. 261–312.

[56] Sandom, D. and Macredic, R. "Software Hazards and Safety-Critical Information Systems," *Safety Systems*, Vol. 7, No. 3, May 1998, pp. 11–12.

[57] Seidwitz, E. and Stark, M. *Reliable Object-Oriented Software*, SIGS, 1996.

[58] Shaw, R. "Safety Cases—How Did We Get Here," *Safety and Reliability of Software Based Systems*, Springer-Verlag, 1995, pp. 43–95.

[59] Sparkman, D. "Standards and Practices for Reliable Safety-related Software Systems," *Proceedings of the Third IEEE International Symposium on Software Reliability Engineering*, October 1993, pp. 318–328.

[60] Storey, N. *Safety-Critical Computer Systems*, Addison-Wesley, 1996.

[61] Thomas, M. "Safety Cases for Software Based Systems," *Safety and Reliability of Software Based Systems*, Springer-Verlag, 1995, pp. 328–337.

[62] Tilloston, J. "In the Foothills of System Safety," *Safety Systems*, Vol. 7, No. 1, September 1997, pp. 11–13.

[63] Wichmann, B. "Objective Test Criteria: Some Proposals for Bespoke Software," National Physics Laboratory, U.K., NPL Report CISE 16/98, March 1998.

[64] Wright, C.L. and Zawilski, E. "Existing and Emerging Standards for Software Safety," *Proceedings of IEEE Software Engineering Standards Application Workshop*, San Francisco, 1991.

Annex A

Organizations Involved in Software Safety and Reliability Standards

Current contact information is provided below for the organizations involved in the development and promulgation of the standards discussed in this book. The majority of standards are copyright protected and are offered for sale for a nominal fee. Most standards organizations follow a 3–5 year review/update cycle; so, be sure to request the latest version of a standard when ordering.

1. Association for the Advancement of Medical Instrumentation (AAMI)
    3330 Washington Blvd., Suite 400
    Arlington, VA 22201-4598
    USA
    (t) +1.703.525.4890   (f) +1.703.276.0793

2. American Institute of Aeronautics and Astronautics (AIAA)
    1801 Alexander Bell Drive
    Reston, VA 20191
    USA
    (t) +1.703.264.7500   (f) +1.703.264.7551

3. American National Standards Institute (ANSI)

Any standard recognized as an American National Standard is for sale from ANSI. This includes AIAA, AAMI, IEEE, SAE, and other standards which have received ANSI recognition. ANSI is also the focal point for obtaining IEC and ISO standards in the U.S.

    ANSI
    Customer Service
    11 West 42nd Street
    New York, NY 10036
    USA
    (t) +1.212.642.4900   (f) +1.212.302.1286
    (w) www.ansi.org

4.   European Committee for Electrotechnical Standardization (CENELEC)
Central Secretariat
rue de Stassart 35
1050 Brussels
BELGIUM
(w) www.cenelec.be

5.   European Space Agency (ESA)
Publications Division
ESTEC, P.O. Box 299
2200 AG Noordwijk
The NETHERLANDS
(w) www.estec.esa.nl

6.   Health Industries Manufacturers Association (HIMA)
1200 G. Street NW, Suite 400
Washington, DC 20005-3814
USA
(t) +1.202.783.8700   (f) +1.202.783.8750

7.   International Electrotechnical Committee (IEC)

Standards published by the International Electrotechnical Commission (IEC) are available for purchase from the American National Standards Institute (ANSI) in the United States or the equivalent national standards body in other countries, such as: CEF, BSI, VDE, SCC, and so forth. Additionally, these standards may be purchased directly from the IEC.

International Electrotechnical Commission (IEC)
Customer Services Centre
3, Rue de Varembe
P.O. Box 131
1211 Geneva 20
SWITZERLAND
(t) 41.22.919.02.11   (f) 41.22.919.03.00
(w) www.iec.ch

Standards Association of Australia
International Services
No. 1 The Crescent
2140 Homebush N.S.W.
AUSTRALIA
(t) 61.2.746.4700   (f) 61.2.746.8450

British Standards Institution (BSI)
BSI Sales Department
389 Chiswick High Road
London W4 4AL
UK
(t) 44.181.996.7000   (f) 44.181.996.7001
(e) info@bsi.org.uk   (w) www.bsi.org.uk
    orders@bsi.org.uk

Standards Council of Canada (SCC)
Customer Service
45 O'Connor Street, Suite 1200
Ottawa, Ontario K1P 6N7
CANADA
(t) +1.613.238.3222   (f) +1.613.995.4564

Comite Electrotechnique Francais
UTE - Immeuble LAVOISIER
F-92052 Paris La Defense Cedex
FRANCE
(t) 331.46.91.1212   (f) 331.47.89.4775

VDE - VERLAG Gmbh
Sales Department
Bismarckstrasse 33
D-10625
Berlin
GERMANY
(t) 49.30.34.80.01.16   (f) 49.30.34.17.093

Standards New Zealand
10th Floor - Standards House
155 The Terrace
6001 Wellington
NEW ZEALAND
(t) 64.4.498.5991   (f) 64.4.498.5994

PSB Building
1 Science Park Drive
SC-118211
SINGAPORE
(t) 65.772.9686   (f) 65.776.1280

8.   Institution of Electrical Engineers (IEE)
       P.O. Box 96
       Stevenage
       Herts SG1 2SD
       UK
       (t) 01438.313311   (f) 01438.742792

9.   Institute for Electrical and Electronics Engineers (IEEE)
       IEEE Standards Activities
       445 Hoes Lane
       P.O. Box 1331
       Piscataway, NJ 08855-1331
       USA
       (t) +1.908.562.3811   (f) +1.908.562.1571
       (w) http://standards.ieee.org

10.   Indiana Medical Device Manufacturers Council, Inc. (IMDMC)
       1908 E. 64th Street, South Drive
       Indianapolis, IN 46220-2186
       USA
       (t) +1.317.257.8558   (f) +1.317.259.4191

11.   International Society for Measurement and Control (ISA)
       67 Alexander Drive
       P.O. Box 12277
       Research Triangle Park, NC 27709
       USA
       (t) +1.919.549.8411   (f) +1.919.549.8288
       (e) info@isa.org

12.   Motor Industry Research Association (MIRA)
       Automotive Electronics Department
       Watling Street
       Nuneaton, Warwickshire CV10 0TU
       UK
       (t) 01203.355430   (f) 01203.350322
       (w) www.misra.org.uk

13.	National Aeronautics and Space Administration (NASA) Headquarters
Director, Safety and Risk Management Division
Office of the Associate Administrator for Safety and Mission Assurance
Washington, DC 20546-0001
USA
(w) www.ivv.nasa.gov or www.gsfc.nasa.gov

14.	National Council for Clinical Laboratory Systems (NCCLS)
940 West Valley Road, Suite 1400
Wayne, PA 19087-1898
USA
(t) +1.610.688.0100	(f) +1.610.688.0700

15.	Nuclear Regulatory Commission (NRC)
Office of Nuclear Regulatory Research
Division of Systems Technology
Washington, DC 20555-0001
USA

16.	Engineering Standards
Nuclear Operations Services and Support
Ontario Power Generation, Inc. MS: H10 F5
700 University
Toronto, Ontario
CANADA M5G 1X6
(t) +1.416.592.7235	(f) +1.416.592.8176 or 8802

17.	Requirements and Technical Concepts for Aviation, Inc. (RTCA)
1140 Connecticut Avenue NW, Suite 1020
Washington, DC 20036-4001
USA
(t) +1.202.833.9339	(f) +1.202.833.9434

18.	Society of Automotive Engineers (SAE)
400 Commonwealth Drive
Warrendale, PA 15096-0001
USA
(t) +1.412.776.4841	(w) www.sae.org

19.   U.K. Ministry of Defence (MoD)
        Directorate of Standardisation
        Kentigern House
        65 Brown Street
        Glasgow G2 8EX
        UK
        (t) 0141.224.2531   (f) 0141.224.2503
        (w) www.mod.uk

20.   U.S. Department of Defense (DoD)
        DODSSP
        Building 4/Section D
        700 Robbins Avenue
        Philadelphia, PA 19111-5094
        USA
        (t)+1. 215.697.2667 or 2179   (f) +1.215.697.1462
        (w) www.dodssp.daps.mil

Annex B

Commercial Products Available to Assist in Performing Software Safety and Reliability Analyses

The following is a sample listing of commercial products, available at the time of publication, which can assist in automating part of the software safety and/or reliability assessment process. The tools are listed alphabetically by name. No attempt is made to recommend one tool over the other or to discuss cost information; rather the intent is to make readers aware that these tools are available. All tools listed in this annex are PC-based. Inclusion in this list does not imply endorsement of a product by the author or publisher. Likewise, the lack of a product being included in this list does not imply nonendorsement.

Appendix A of *The Handbook of Software Reliability Engineering*, edited by Michael Lyu, lists the characteristics of seven quantitative software reliability estimation and prediction tools. These tools were developed as research projects by industrial, government, or academic labs between 1988–1994. Since they are not commercial products that are marketed, maintained, and supported in the usual way a standard commercial product is, they are not included here.

1. **tool name:** a.l.d. Total Solution™

    tool type: reliability prediction, risk analysis support
    This toolset supports failure reporting, analysis and corrective action system (FRACAS), field reliability estimation, MIL-STD 1629A FMECA and testability analysis, process and design FMEA, and decision lifecycle cost-effectiveness analysis.

    vendor: Advanced Automation Corp. (AAC)
    P.O. Box 4644
    Rome, NY 13442-4644
    USA
    (t) +1.315.336.2071 or +1.800.292.4519
    (e) callald@trendline.co.il

2. **tool name:** Asent™

   tool type: Reliability and maintainability analysis support.
   This tool provides reliability, maintainability, and testability analysis in a multi-user environment.

   vendor: Raytheon Systems Company
   13532 N. Central Expressway, M/S 67
   Dallas, TX 75243
   USA
   (t) +1.972.344.2277
   (f) +1.972.344.2288

3. **tool name:** BRAVO™

   tool type: fault tree and event tree analyses
   This tool performs fault tree and event tree analyses to obtain reliability, availability, and maintainability (RAM)/risk analysis results for complex engineered systems.

   vendor: JBF Associates, Inc.
   1000 Technology Drive
   Knoxville, TN 37932
   USA
   (t) +1.423.966.5232
   (f) +1.423.966.5287

4. **tool name:** C++VS™

   tool type: validation support
   The C++ Validation Suite (VS)™ provides automated validation support for C++ code. It analyzes exception handling, template testing, name spaces, and conformance to industry standards and supports over 50,000 test cases.

   vendor: Perennial Validation, Inc.
   4699 Old Ironsides Drive, Suite 210
   Santa Clara, CA 95054
   USA
   (t) +1.408.748.2900
   (f) +1.408.748.2909
   (e) info@peren.com

5. **tool name:** CAFTA™

   tool type: risk analysis support
   This tool supports the generation and analysis of fault trees and cut sets and the calculation of uncertainty distributions for system failure probabilities.

   vendor: SAIC
   4920 El Camino Real
   Los Altos, CA 94022
   USA
   (t) +1.650.960.3322
   (f) +1.650.960.5965
   (e) software_support@cpqm.saic.com

6. **tool name:** Care™

   tool type: Reliability, availability, maintainability, & supportability analysis support
   This integrated tool suite provides reliability, availability, maintainability, and supportability analyses in a multiuser environment using a single database. The types of analyses supported include: reliability block diagrams, FMECA, FTA, MTBF, MTTR, Markov modelling, and lifecycle costing.

   vendor: BQR Reliability Engineering, Ltd.
   7 Bialik Street
   P.O.B. 208
   Rishon Lezion 75101
   Israel
   (t) 972.3.966.3569
   (f) 972.3.969.8459
   (e) info@bqr.com
   (w) www.bqr.com

7. **tool name:** Decide™

   tool type: risk management support
   This tool helps decision makers use risk criteria to select the best alternative or define improvements to alternatives for issues ranging from the simplest to the most complex.

   vendor: JBF Associates, Inc.
   1000 Technology Drive
   Knoxville, TN 37932
   USA
   (t) +1.423.966.5232
   (f) +1.423.966.5287

8. **tool name:** ETA™

   tool type: risk analysis support
   This tool develops event trees and reports for accident sequence analysis.

   vendor: SAIC
   4920 El Camino Real
   Los Altos, CA 94022
   USA
   (t) +1.650.960.3322
   (f) +1.650.960.5965
   (e) software_support@cpqm.saic.com

9. **tool name:** HAZOPtimizer™, FaultrEASE™

   tool type: risk analysis support
   HAZOPtimizer™uses a flexible column format to simplify documentation for HAZOPs and other risk and hazard identification methods. FaultrEASE™creates fault trees using prune, clone, and graft commands on whole branches. The tree reformats instantly after each edit.

   vendor: Arthur D. Little, Inc.
   Acorn Park
   Cambridge, MA 02140
   USA
   (t) +1.617.498.5476
   (f) +1.617.498.7161

10. **tool name:** HazTrac™

    tool type: risk analysis support
    This tool supports hazard analyses (PHA, SHA, SSHA, and FMEA), maintains a hazard tracking database, and complies with MIL-STD-882D.

    vendor: Hoes Engineering
    1801 Hanover Drive, Suite D
    Davis, CA 95616
    USA
    (t) +1.530.756.3999
    (f) +1.530.756.3970

11. **tool name:** Insure++^{TM}

    tool type: design analysis
    This tool uses mutation testing technology to analyze code paths for run-time bugs, memory leaks, API errors, algorithm errors, and execution errors. The precise location of the error is provided along with a complete diagnosis of the error.

    vendor: ParaSoft Corp.
    (w) www.parasoft.com
    (e) info@parasoft.com

12. **tool name:** KB3^{TM}

    tool type: reliability modelling
    This tool provides a knowledge-based workbench that assists in building reliability models, examines classes of components, their behavior, and failure modes. Functional analysis, FMECA, and FTA can be performed on different operational scenarios.

    vendor: EDF (Electricite de France), DER/ESF
    1 Avenue du General de Gaulle, BP 408
    92141 Clamart Cedex
    France
    (t) 01.47.65.43.21
    (e) assistance.kb3@edfgdf.fr
    (w) www.edf.fr/der/esf/kb3/kb3.en.htm

13. **tool name:** LOGISCOPE^{TM}, ObjectGEODE^{TM}, ObjectPartner^{TM}

    tool type: design analysis
    This toolset, designed for mission critical systems, supports the design, analysis, simulation, and test of real-time and distributed applications.

    vendor: Verilog
    3010 LBJ Freeway, Suite 900
    Dallas, TX 75234
    USA
    (t) +1.800.424.3095
    (e) info@verilogusa.com

14. **tool name:** MEADEP™

    tool type: Reliability and availability prediction

    This tool provides analysis of hierarchical hardware and software models to support system reliability and availability predictions, parametric analysis, and tradeoff studies. Analysis of degraded-mode operations and recovery scenarios is included. Reliability block diagrams, Markov modelling, and MTBF calculations are in accordance with MIL HDBK 781.

    vendor: SoHar Inc.

    8421 Wilshire Blvd., Suite 201

    Beverly Hills, CA 90211-3204

    USA

    (t) +1.323.653.4717

    (f) +1.323.653.3624

    (w) www.sohar.com/meadep

15. **tool name:** Reusable Library of Fault Tolerant Technique Executives

    tool type: Reusable Code and Objects, Software Components

    The Object-Oriented Library of Fault-Tolerant Technique Executives provides user applications with object-oriented, plug- and-play fault tolerant capabilities. Clients use the library to build fault tolerant, object-oriented applications by taking the following actions:

- Choose an available technique, such as N-Copy, Programming, or Retry Blocks and check out the technique executive's class declarations and object code from the library.
- Check out relevant high-level accessories for the technique, including classes for Decision Mechanisms, Acceptance Tests, or Data Re-expression Algorithms.
- Write application-specific, lower-level subclasses for the technique (if needed).
- Make the application code reference the classes selected from the library.
- Link user code with the library-provided object code.
- Invoke executive objects and let them orchestrate the chosen fault tolerance technique.

    vendor: Quality Research Associates, Inc.

    2875 Williams Farm Drive

    Dacula, GA 30019-1568

    USA

    (t) +1.770.513.3959

    (f) +1.770.513.3129

    (e) lpullum@qrainc.com

16. **tool name:** PC-lint™

    tool type: design analysis
    This tool analyzes C/C++ code for access violations; inconsistencies in assignments, conditionals, variables, member values, argument constraints, and pointers; uninitialized variables, inherited nonvirtual destructors, strong type mismatches, ill-formed macros, and inadvertent name-hiding.

    vendor: Gimpel Software
    3207 Hogarth Lane
    Collegeville, PA 19426
    USA
    (t) +1.610.584.4261
    (f) +1.610.585.4266
    (w) www.gimpel.com
    (e) sales@gimpel.com

17. **tool name:** PHA Leader™

    tool type: process reliability analysis
    This tool facilitates the preparation, documentation, and follow-up tasks associated with any process reliability analysis, using techniques such as HAZOP analysis, what-if/checklist analysis, or FMECA.

    vendor: JBF Associates, Inc.
    1000 Technology Drive
    Knoxville, TN 37932
    USA
    (t) +1.423.966.5232
    (f) +1.423.966.5287

18. **tool name:** PSI Software™

    tool type: reliability prediction, risk analysis support
    The PSI toolset performs system reliability analysis according to MIL-STD-756 and MIL-HDBK-338, maintainability prediction according to MIL-HDBK-472, and FMECA according to MIL- STD-1629A.

    vendor: Powertronic Systems, Inc.
    13700 Chef Menteur Highway
    New Orleans, LA 70129
    USA
    (t) +1.504.254.0383
    (f) +1.504.254.0393

19. **tool name:** QRA Roots™

    tool type: failure analysis support
    This tool stores, evaluates, and retrieves failure data, such as failure/repair rates and probabilities, and human error probabilities.

    vendor: JBF Associates, Inc.
    1000 Technology Drive
    Knoxville, TN 37932
    USA
    (t) +1.423.966.5232
    (f) +1.423.966.5287

20. **tool name:** RADWAY!™

    tool type: lifecycle management
    RADWAY!™provides a toolset which integrates lifecycle management functions (planning, requirements, design, implementation, testing, and so forth) and reporting based on IEEE software engineering standards.

    vendor: InfoTech, Inc.
    10800 Farley, Suite 320
    Corporate Woods Building 75
    Overland Park, KS 66210
    USA
    (t) +1.800.723.5880
    (f) +1.913.663.3476
    (e) radway_sales@radway.com

21. **tool name:** RAPTOR (Rapid Availability Prototyping for Testing Operational Readiness)

    tool type: reliability estimation
    This tool generates reliability block diagrams and system reliability models. Parallel and serial relationships are accommodated. Failure rates and sparing strategies for individual blocks are used to calculate system reliability. Individual blocks can represent software components.

    vendor: HQ AFOTEC/SAL
    8500 Gibson Blvd. SE
    Kirtland AFB, NM 87117-5555
    USA
    (t) +1.505.846.8010
    (e) murphyk@afotec.af.mil

22. **tool name:** RBDA™

> **tool type:** reliability estimation
> This tool performs availability analysis using reliability block diagrams.

> **vendor:** SAIC
> 4920 El Camino Real
> Los Altos, CA 94022
> USA
> (t) +1.650.960.3322
> (f) +1.650.960.5965
> (e) software_support@cpqm.saic.com

23. **tool name:** REHMS-D™, Reliable Human-Machine System Developer

> **tool type:** risk management support
> This tool helps decision makers identify performance shaping factors to enhance the design process for reliable human task performance.

> **vendor:** KPL Systems
> 703 Cannon Road
> Silver Spring, MD 20904
> USA
> (t) +1.301.625.9457
> (e) kplsys@prodigy.net
> (w) http://pages.prodigy.com/TWBT41B/kplsystem

24. **tool name:** Relex™

> **tool type:** reliability prediction
> Relex™ performs system-level reliability predictions based on MIL-HDBK-217, highlights areas needing reliability improvement, calculates system MTBF, and creates process and design FMEAs.

> **vendor:** Relex Software Corp.
> 540 Pellis Road
> Greensburg, PA 15601
> USA
> (t) +1.724.836.8800
> (f) +1.724.836.8844
> (e) info@relexsoftware.com

25. **tool name:** Reliability Engineering Software Tools™

    tool type: reliability prediction, risk analysis support
    This toolset performs reliability prediction according to MIL-HDBK-217, calculates MTTR, generates reliability block diagrams and calculates reliability using Markovian analysis, and generates FMEAs and FTAs. Sixteen tools are included.

    vendor: Item Software, Inc.
    2190 Towne Centre Place, Suite 314
    Anaheim, CA 92806
    USA
    (t) +1.714.935-2900
    (f) +1.714.935-2911
    (e) itemusa@itemsoft.com or sales@itemsoft.uk.com

26. **tool name:** RELYS™

    tool type: software reliability estimation
    The basic version of the RELYS™ Toolbox includes a cost estimation module MAITCO, quantitative reliability prediction module, quantitative reliability estimation module, and a problem reporting/tracking tool.

    vendor: Philotech
    Systementwicklung und Software GmbH
    Seemullerstrasse 8
    D-81549 Munchen
    GERMANY
    (t) 0.89.68.30.78
    (f) 0.89.68.30.79

27. **tool name:** RMPlanner™

    tool type: risk management support
    This tool provides a comprehensive framework for coordination and communication for a risk management program. It assists in preparing a Risk Management Plan and includes features such as offsite consequence analysis.

    vendor: JBF Associates, Inc.
    1000 Technology Drive
    Knoxville, TN 37932
    USA
    (t) +1.423.966.5232
    (f) +1.423.966.5287

28. **tool name:** SADT™(System Dependability Assessment Tool)

    tool type: reliability prediction

    This tool determines system dependability from reliability block diagrams, fault trees, Markov models, mission reliability analysis, and sensitivity analysis. It includes software and human reliability parameters, to allow assessment of the system level effects of software failures and/or incorrect actions by human operators.

    vendor: AST Engineering Services, Inc.
    12200 E. Briarwood Avenue, Suite 260
    Englewood, CO 80112
    USA
    (t) +1.303.790.4242 x130
    (f) +1.303.790.4242
    (e) info@advsystech.com

29. **tool name:** Safety Analysis Software™

    tool type: risk analysis support

    This toolset performs change analysis, cause consequence analysis, fault tree analysis, MORT analysis, operational readiness analysis, and statistical analysis, and generates safety checklists.

    vendor: Conger & Elsea, Inc.
    6365 E. Alabama Road, MS 13
    Woodstock, GA
    USA
    (t) +1.800.875.8709

30. **tool name:** SAM 2000

    tool type: safety analysis support

    SAM 2000 is an integrated toolset which supports the development, documentation, communication, and analysis of safety cases through the use of the Goal Structuring Notation (GSN). The SAM 2000 toolset includes a:

    - model editor to describe the system
    - risk calculator to build risk classification tables, calculate risk classifications, and target likelihoods
    - hazard log editor
    - preliminary hazard identification template
    - HAZOP editor
    - functional failure analysis editor
    - FMEA editor

- FTA editor
- event tree analysis editor
- reliablity block diagram editor

vendor: York Software Engineering, Ltd.
Glanford House, Bellwin Drive
Flixborough, Scunthorpe
North Lincolnshire, DN15 8SN UK (t) +44.0.1724.877520
(f) +44.0.1724.846256
(e) sam@yse-ltd.co.uk
(w) www.yse-ltd.co.uk

Index

abnormal conditions, 14, 16, 92, 131, 132, 240, 264, 328, 352, 355, 356, 398, 439, 445, 462

abnormal conditions and events (ACEs), 259

ACM

Code of Professional Ethics, 460

joint ACM/IEEE Computer Society task force, 460, 461

software engineering body of knowledge (SWEBOK), 461

Ada, 39, 49, 143, 200, 255

AIAA, 125, 158–160

ALARP, 280–281

applied to biomedical industry, 281

concept, 96, 280

risk regions, 96, 280–282, 294

tolerable level of risk, 284

American National Standards Institute

ANSI, 10, 40, 119, 275, 318, 419

arithmetic errors, 106

floating point conversion, 106, 131, 154

artificial intelligence, 90

ASICs, 217, 463

ASQ, 7, 42, 408, 460

automated tools, 10, 37, 51, 117, 129, 200, 202, 336, 366, 382, 383, 405, 425, 426, 481–492

CASE tools, 36, 38, 206, 245, 318

ISO/IEC 14102:1995, 39, 67

qualification of, 131, 245

safety and reliability concerns, 35, 38, 39, 131

standards for selection of CASE tools, 39

usage, 35, 36, 94, 103, 117, 131, 376, 408, 409

Bayesian Belief Networks

BBNs, 443

measuring software dependability, 443

block recovery, 33–34, 117, 152, 173, 185, 206, 212, 354, 441, 442

backward, 33, 374

forward, 33, 374

n-block, 33, 34, 374

boundary value analysis, 109, 263, 322, 399, 441

British Standards Institution

BS5760 Part 8, 412, 442

BSI, 10, 412

CANDU Computer Systems Engineering Centre for Excellence

CE-1001-STD Rev. 1, 229, 246–267, 463

CASE statements, 32

accounting for all logic states, 30

otherwise clause, 30, 32, 209, 237

cause consequence analysis, 93, 208, 335, 399, 401

CENELEC

EN 50128, 83–100, 119, 120, 462

EN 60601-1-4, 300

European Committee for Electrotechnical Standardisation, 9, 62, 83, 275, 300

change control, 149, 186, 199, 241, 255, 287, 295, 331, 425

change impact analysis, 89, 94, 156, 241, 255, 322, 328, 331, 349, 425